THE
MIDDLE EAST IN THE
TWENTIETH CENTURY

THE
MIDDLE EAST IN THE
TWENTIETH
CENTURY

Martin Sicker

PRAEGER

Westport, Connecticut
London

Library of Congress Cataloging-in-Publication Data

Sicker, Martin.
  The Middle East in the twentieth century / Martin Sicker.
    p. cm.
  Includes bibliographical references and index.
  ISBN 0-275-96893-6 (alk. paper)
    1. Middle East—History—20th century.   I. Title.
  DS62.8.S54   2001
  956.04—dc21   00-064943

British Library Cataloguing in Publication Data is available.

Library of Congress Catalog Card Number: 00-064943
ISBN: 0-275-96893-6

First published in 2001

Praeger Publishers, 88 Post Road West, Westport, CT 06881
An imprint of Greenwood Publishing Group, Inc.
www.praeger.com

Printed in the United States of America

The paper used in this book complies with the
Permanent Paper Standard issued by the National
Information Standards Organization (Z39.48–1984).

10 9 8 7 6 5 4 3 2

Contents

Introduction   1

1.   Britain and the Arabs, 1914–20   5

2.   Britain, France, and the Zionists, 1914–20   23

3.   The Palestine Quagmire, 1920–39   41

4.   The Emergence of Transjordan, 1920–28   59

5.   France, Syria, and the Emergence of Lebanon, 1920–36   67

6.   Britain and Iraq, 1918–39   77

7.   Transition in the Arabian Peninsula, 1910–36   89

8.   The British Protectorate in Egypt, 1914–38   101

9.   Turmoil in Transcaucasia, 1917–21   113

10. Developments in Iran, 1914–37   125

11. The World War II Period, 1939–45   139

12. The Geopolitics of Oil, 1914–47   153

13. Prelude to the Arab-Israeli Conflict, 1945–48   169

14. The First Arab-Israeli War and Its Aftermath, 1948–52   181

15. The Suez Crisis, 1951–57   191

16. The Nasserist Era, 1952–67   203

17.   Inter-Arab Rivalry and the 1967 War   217

18.   The Torturous Road to Camp David, 1967–79   229

19.   Crisis and Conflict in Lebanon, 1970–85   247

20.   Conflict in the Persian Gulf Region, 1973–99   259

21.   At Century's End   271

Selected Bibliography   275

Index   285

Introduction

To understand the geopolitical history of the Middle East in the twentieth century, I would suggest that it is best to approach the subject simultaneously from two distinct but interrelated perspectives, the global and the regional, the latter being circumscribed by the former. Viewed in this manner, the turbulent history of the region during the period under consideration may be seen to fall into three relatively distinct phases. The imperialist phase, which began in the nineteenth century and lasted until the end of World War II, was followed by the Cold War between the Soviet Union and the West that continued to the beginning of the last decade of the century. The last phase, which began with the demise of the Soviet Union and is one that challenges many long held perceptions and is therefore poorly comprehended, is the one taking shape before our eyes. In each of these relatively distinct stages, developments within the region were and continue to be shaped and constrained by extra-regional forces. I emphasize relatively distinct because the history of the Middle East is essentially seamless. The stages described here overlap and in some instances unfold simultaneously.

The history of the region from the beginning of the century to World War I has been discussed, to a considerable extent, in an earlier volume, *The Islamic World in Decline: From the Treaty of Karlowitz to the Disintegration of the Ottoman Empire*. Because of space limitations, some of the significant events of the first two decades of the century, particularly as they concern the history of Turkey and the Ottoman Empire, will not be reprised in this work. However, events of that period that were not discussed in the previous work, such as those taking place in Palestine, Arabia, and Transcaucasia during the war, will be treated at length in the present book in the context of the restructuring of the Middle East by the victorious Western powers.

Under normal circumstances, in the wake of the disintegration of the Ottoman Empire at the end of World War I, the Middle East would have been carved up among the victors, each governing the lands allocated to them as colonies, protectorates, or spheres of influence. However, in this case, the intrusion of an idealistic American president, Woodrow Wilson, prevented this from happening.

Wilson insisted that the principle of self-determination of peoples should be the basis for the disposition of the lands of the former Ottoman Empire instead of a partition among ambitious colonial powers. Under the twelfth of his "Fourteen Points," he spelled out his view of the Turkish peace settlement. The Turkish provinces should be constituted as a new sovereign Turkish state; the inhabitants of non-Turkish provinces should be granted self-determination. This approach would nullify the various bilateral agreements for dividing the spoils, such as the Sykes-Picot agreement between Britain and France, which were consummated during the course of the war. Wilson thus introduced a new and unprecedented element into international political affairs that would effectively deny the victors the spoils of their victory, an idea that did not sit well with the imperial-minded leaders of the victorious allies. Field Marshall Jan Smuts, the future leader of South Africa, jumped into the breech between Wilson and his European colleagues and proposed a solution that could bridge their differences. He suggested the novel idea of establishing mandates over the former enemy territories. Under this scheme, there would be no annexation of these lands. However, the victorious powers would be made internationally responsible for the nurturing and development of these backward ethnically-based states, under the supervision of the League of Nations.

Britain quickly adopted Smuts's proposal because it was in a position to determine which mandates it would receive to meet its strategic interests. It needed Palestine to facilitate the defense of the Suez Canal and, as a secondary consideration, to make good on its well-publicized pledge to the Jews, under the Balfour Declaration, to give them a homeland there. It needed Iraq to provide security for the traditional overland route to India through Iran and Afghanistan and to protect the oil supplies coming from southern Iran and the new oilfields discovered in Mosul and Kirkuk. As far as Britain was concerned, the rest of the non-Turkish territories, with the possible exception of Maronite Lebanon, could be given to the Arabs. The French, however, who were also willing to go along with the Smuts proposal, wanted a bigger slice of the pie and set their sights on Syria, which would put them in a position to prevent British domination of the entire region.

Russia, which signed a separate peace with Germany before the war ended, was momentarily immobilized as it struggled to reconstitute itself as the Soviet Union. However, it was not long before it too began to pursue its strategic interests along lines similar to the other imperialist powers, no longer by outright conquest but through the establishment of paper republics nominally tied to it by treaty but actually through a variety of powerful control mechanisms. Moreover, as the new Soviet Union's Marxist-Leninist political program became anathema to the Western powers, Russia found itself increasingly geopolitically and geostrategically isolated. It was not long before the old tsarist dream of access to the Mediterranean Sea and the Indian Ocean through the Middle East became the reality of Soviet strategic policy.

Because of these considerations, the reawakening and in some instances the emergence of indigenous national aspirations, within the territories that came under either the League of Nations mandate system or the Soviet embrace, produced a variety of newly constituted political entities. All of these strove for independence and sovereignty but not all were successful. However, the terms, "independence" and "sovereignty," took on connotations quite different from their traditional meanings.

Independence in the Middle East came to mean local autonomy and sovereignty came to mean merely the ability to sit with the major powers in international forums such as the League of Nations and later the United Nations. Thus, Iraq entered the League of Nations in 1932 as a sovereign independent state, despite the fact that it was in effect still under British military control. Similarly, the Ukraine and Byelorussia were both later admitted to the United Nations as sovereign states notwithstanding the fact that at the time both were part of the Soviet Union, and could hardly be considered independent and sovereign by any stretch of the imagination.

The regional history of the Middle East in the twentieth century, more than ever before, has unfolded within the context of global politics. The sovereignty and independence of the states of the region have been constrained to varying degrees by the wishes, needs, interests, and ambitions of major powers, none of which are part of the region itself. An extreme example of this is the case of Iraq in the last decade of the century, an independent sovereign state with geopolitical ambitions of its own. When it attempted to pursue those ambitions militarily it quickly found itself under attack by the United States, which cobbled together an international alliance under the umbrella of the United Nations to give a fig leaf of legitimacy to the pursuit of its own national interests in the region. The point here is not the despotic character of the Iraqi regime and its dictator. The fact is that the question of whether Iraq has a historically justifiable claim to the territory of Kuwait is really quite irrelevant. Even if the claim is historically valid, the reality is that it was not in the interest of the United States and its allies to permit Iraq to occupy and annex Kuwait. It is quite conceivable that in the future a similar Iraqi move might be found acceptable. After all, the present states of Iraq and Kuwait are both artificial British constructs. Indeed, the Mosul region of northern Mesopotamia was attached to the new political entity of Iraq after World War I, which was previously only a geographical expression, at British insistence because of the oil deposits it contained. By so doing, Britain simply discounted the desire of the predominantly Kurdish population for independence, not because it was invalid but because that desire was not viewed as compatible with British interests in the region. Indeed, throughout the century, the major powers, especially the United States and Britain, have gone out of their way to prevent the emergence of an independent Kurdistan for geopolitical reasons of their own, none of which have anything to do with the appropriateness or legitimacy of Kurdish national ambitions.

However, as already suggested, these geopolitical considerations have varied over time, being very different in the period between the world wars than in the period of intense East-West rivalry that followed. The geopolitical environment within which the history of the Middle East is unfolding in the present post–Cold War era is radically different from what preceded it. These changing geopolitical realities constitute the framework for this examination of the Middle East in the twentieth century, and the organizing principle for the selection of materials from the truly vast amount of information about the history of the region that is available.

In examining the several geopolitical stages in the history of the region, it will be necessary to devote a substantial portion of this work to an examination of the imperialist phase because it was during that period that the present state structure of the Middle East came into being. The remaining chapters will examine the role that the states of the region played in the East-West confrontation and how their policies and actions were constrained by the global powers. The book will conclude with a brief discussion of the change in the global geopolitical structure that began in the final decade of the century and its impact on the region.

1

Britain and the Arabs, 1914–20

For more than a century, Britain's principal foreign policy concern outside the European continent was the security of its empire in India. To protect its interests there the British had gone to great lengths to block Russian imperial expansion into Afghanistan and Turkestan. They had gone to war to prevent the collapse of the Ottoman Empire in the mid-nineteenth century because of the need to maintain the existing regional balance of power. Britain thus emerged as the traditional ally of the sultans against the tsars.

As events unfolded in 1914, it was with some dismay that the British witnessed the emergence of a Turkish-German relationship that seemed likely to result in an alliance against Britain in the war that loomed on the horizon. Of particular strategic concern to Britain were the implications of such an alliance for the security of the Suez Canal. Since the construction of the waterway, it had become the preeminent route of access to India, and its security was a matter of the highest priority. A potentially hostile Ottoman state close by posed what British military planners considered an unacceptable threat. Moreover, the Germans had recently completed construction of the Berlin to Baghdad Railway, and German access through Ottoman territory to the Persian Gulf could pose a potential threat to Britain's sea lines of communication to the East. Finally, there was also the matter of the Hejaz Railway.

Although the Hejaz Railway did have some military significance in that it could be used to bring reinforcements into the Arabian Peninsula, it was not that aspect of it that was of primary concern to Whitehall. The British were far more interested in and worried about its religious significance. The sultan's Hejaz Railway was exceptionally popular throughout the Muslim world, including India, because it dramatically reduced the physical burdens of the obligatory pilgrimage to Mecca. Sultan Abd al-Hamid, who had built the line that could bring the pilgrims as far as Medina, was also the caliph of Islam. As such, he was actively engaged in promoting pan-Islamic sentiment as a way of buttressing the ties that were barely holding the Ottoman Empire together. The possibility that Britain could find itself at war with the sultan presented it with a serious dilemma. Ruling over more than 70 million Muslims in India and another 16 million in the Nile River basin, Britain had become responsible for the world's largest Muslim population. There was thus a reasonable fear that promotion of Muslim unrest, particularly if exacerbated by the Ottoman sultan-caliph, could be used to wreak havoc on British imperial interests in Africa and Asia.

The British were highly vulnerable in this regard. They knew it, and so did the Germans. Once Britain openly declared itself against a Germany allied with the leading figure in the Muslim world, it was widely expected that the British Empire in the East would soon undergo convulsions leading to its dissolution. This perception was clearly reflected in a letter from the chief of the Imperial German General Staff, Count von Moltke, to his Foreign Ministry. Von Moltke declared that the initiation of "insurrection in India, Egypt and the Caucasus . . . is of utmost importance. Thanks to the Pact with Turkey, the Foreign Ministry will be able to realize these ideas and to arouse the fanaticism of Islam."[1]

Part of the plan, as outlined by the German Foreign Ministry, was to turn Anglo-Egyptian army units against the British by advising them that the sultan-caliph would soon declare war on England. The missions to be assigned to the Egyptian troops were to wipe out the British officer corps, make the Suez Canal inoperative, and to sabotage communications, railways, and port installations in Port Said, Suez, and Alexandria. The signal that would trigger the actions by the Egyptian troops was to be a frontal attack on the canal by 20,000–30,000 Turkish troops, supported by some 70,000 Bedouins. The latter were to be under the leadership of the sherif of Mecca, Hussein, whose cooperation in such an assault on the British in Egypt was expected by the Sublime Porte in Istanbul.

Hussein, however, quickly recognized the relatively significant role that the Hejaz could play in a British-Ottoman conflict in the Middle East. Hejaz's location along the East Bank of the critical line of communications to the east that passed through the Suez Canal and the Red Sea would give whoever was able to take advantage of its position a significant strategic asset. Hussein decided that he would not automatically align himself with the sultan as he was expected to do, and, indeed, as he was committed to do by the very terms of his appointment as sherif. But, precisely because he was the official guardian of the holy cities of Islam, Hussein saw himself as being in a position to negotiate for his allegiance with both the Germans and the British. However, he was by nature a cautious man and wished to sound out the British without further straining his already tenuous relations with the military regime in Istanbul.

Accordingly, one of Hussein's sons, Abdullah, arrived in Cairo en route to Istanbul in February 1914 and paid a courtesy call on General Kitchener, the resident British agent. Abdullah described the sorry state of relations between the Turks and the Arabs, who were growing increasingly restive under Ottoman rule. He suggested to Kitchener that if the Turkish military regime attempted to depose his father, the outbreak of a revolt in the Hejaz was highly probable. In such an event, Kitchener reported to London, Abdullah hoped that "the British Government would not allow reinforcements to be sent by sea for the purpose of preventing the Arabs from exercising the rights which they have enjoyed from time immemorial in their own country round the holy places."[2] Kitchener was noncommittal in his response, but instructed Ronald Storrs to continue to explore the matter with Abdullah.

Abdullah met with Storrs in April 1914, following instructions from Hussein to explore the possibility of an agreement with Britain, "in order to maintain the status quo in the Arabian peninsula and to do away with the danger of wanton Turkish aggression."[3] Once again the meeting was inconclusive, with the British showing little interest in establishing a direct relationship with Hussein, who was at the time an Ottoman vassal. British interest in such a relationship developed rapidly once the Ottoman-German alliance became a reality.

When war broke out in Europe in August 1914, Kitchener became the British secretary of state for war. He instructed Storrs on September 24 to determine from Abdullah whether, "should present armed German influence at Constantinople coerce Sultan against his will and Sublime Porte to acts of aggression and war against Great Britain, he and his father and Arabs of Hejaz would be with us or against us."[4] What Kitchener was really asking was whether the sherif of Mecca would in fact support non-Muslim Britain against Muslim Turkey.

Abdullah pressed Hussein to give the British an affirmative response. His younger brother Feisal, on the other hand, urged his father to remain loyal to the Turks and thereby earn their gratitude. Hussein appreciated that aligning with the British involved serious risks for him. He would be branded a traitor to the Islamic cause, which was being led by the Ottoman caliph-sultan, and efforts to unseat him might therefore find some support within his own Arab constituency. Hussein decided to stall for time. He instructed Abdullah to respond to Kitchener with a message stating in effect that, although he was favorably inclined to a relationship with Britain, his position as an Islamic leader made it difficult for him to abandon a posture of neutrality. For him to do so would require certain assurances from Britain. Those assurances were spelled out in a message from Abdullah that reached Cairo on October 30. "The people of the Hejaz will accept and be well satisfied with more close union with Great Britain . . . so long as she protects the rights of our country and the rights of the person of His Highness our present Emir and Lord . . . and so long as it supports us against any foreign aggression, and in particular against the Ottomans, especially if they wish to set up anyone else as Emir."[5]

Although a prospective Arab uprising against the Turks might prove beneficial as a means of tying down some Ottoman forces in Arabia, it was never considered a significant factor in British war planning. Of far greater interest to the British was the possibility of using the religious prestige of the sherif of Mecca to offset and discredit an Ottoman call for a Holy War that might arouse the Muslim masses of India and the Nile basin.[6] It was with this consideration in mind that Kitchener sent a message to Abdullah on October 31 informing him of Turkey's entry into the war as an ally of Germany. The message also contained the offer of explicit British guarantees of Hussein's position as sherif and the defense of Hejaz. In addition, in a blatant appeal to Hussein's personal ambitions, Kitchener hinted that Britain would lend its support to Hussein's future candidacy for the caliphate, the highest religious position attainable in the Muslim world. As Kitchener put it, "It may be that an Arab of true race will assume the Khalifate at Mecca or Medina, and so good may come by the help of God out of all the evil that is now occurring." Finally, he stated, "If the Arab nation assists England in this war . . . England will . . . give Arabs every assistance against external foreign aggression."[7]

In addition to transmitting Kitchener's message to Abdullah, Storrs, acting without authorization, implied a British commitment of support to the general liberation of the Arabs from Turkish rule, if they allied themselves with England. He suggested that "the cause of the Arabs, which is the cause of freedom, has become the cause also of Great Britain."[8] This tendency on the part of British officials to employ rhetorical flourishes in their communications with the Arabs rather than more precise diplomatic language caused many unnecessary and highly troublesome misperceptions regarding British intentions in the region. In fact, it caused problems within the British government itself. The India Office conceded that the logical outcome of Arab political control over the Muslim holy cities would be the appointment of an Arab as caliph. However, they disagreed that such a course of events would serve Britain's interests. According to one India Office official, "What we want is not a United Arabia: but a weak and disunited Arabia, split up into little principalities so far as possible under our suzerainty—but incapable of co-ordinated action against us, forming a buffer against the Powers in the West."[9]

Abdullah received Kitchener's message, with Storrs' amplifications, on November 16. It was exactly what he had hoped for. It not only guaranteed the security of both the Hejaz and the Hashemites, it also implied the possibility of British support for the general liberation of the Arabs of the Middle

East from Ottoman rule, under the Hashemite banner. Hussein instructed Abdullah to send a response back to Cairo affirming his surreptitious support of Britain. However, he continued to hedge about committing himself to any overt action in such regard until he was truly prepared to face the possible consequences of an open break with the sultan. He therefore sent Feisal to Istanbul to determine whether there was any real likelihood of receiving tangible compensation from the Porte for his continued loyalty to the Ottoman regime. In the meanwhile, Hussein continued to make the most of his evidently favorable posture of neutrality and entered into duplicitous cooperation with German efforts to undermine the British position in the Middle East.

According to German Foreign Ministry documents, the Germans made contact with both Hussein in Hejaz and his arch rival Ibn Saud in Nejd, seeking to enlist their support against the British. A center for regional revolutionary activity was established in Damascus and was linked to the German consulates in both Medina and Jeddah. The German understanding with Hussein provided that, in return for regular subsidy payments, the sherif would facilitate the dissemination of German anti-British propaganda in the territories under his control, in addition to other unspecified activities. The last payments listed in the German records were made in June 1915—six months after Hussein received Kitchener's message.[10] As a result, there appears to have been a brief period of overlap when both the Germans and the British were compensating Hussein for his services against each other.

As the British anticipated, once Turkey entered the war, the sultan promptly tried to capitalize on his role as caliph to rouse the Muslims as a body against the Entente Powers. He quickly issued the call for a holy war. The *Shaikh al-Islam*, the highest religious functionary in the Ottoman Empire, issued a formal pronouncement declaring it to be the sacred personal duty of every Muslim to rise against Britain, France, and Russia, which he castigated not as enemies of the sultan but of Islam. Abd al-Hamid then issued a proclamation to the Ottoman armed forces on November 11, charging them with the mission of liberating all Muslims from subservience to the governments of the Entente. Lastly, a manifesto signed by the *Shaikh al-Islam* and 28 other religious dignitaries was issued on November 23, calling on all Muslims to participate in the defense of Islam and the holy places. Following these formal steps there followed a massive barrage of propaganda for support of the war effort that was calculated to appeal to the masses. Itinerant preachers, teachers, and agitators visited virtually every nook and cranny of the Muslim world carrying the sultan's message. For geopolitical reasons, particular emphasis was placed on agitating against the entente powers among the Arabs, who were best positioned geographically to interfere with military activities, especially those of Britain, in much of the Middle East.

Kitchener's message of October 31, 1914 reached Hussein at about the same time as Abd al-Hamid's call for him to participate in the holy war. Hussein stalled the Ottomans by arguing that, although he prayed for the success of the *jihad*, it was impracticable for him to participate in it actively at that time. The British were in control of the Red Sea and were therefore positioned to blockade the Hejazi ports. This would cut off all imports, including food, and if the supply of food ran out there was a strong possibility of a revolt against the sherif, which would further weaken the Ottoman position in Arabia and work to the advantage of the British. Accordingly, until the supply lines to the Hejaz could be assured of adequate protection, Hussein could not run the risk of a British blockade, nor was it in the Porte's interest that he do so. Although this argument seemed contrived, the Porte had no practical choice other than to accept it, at least for the moment, and began to plot Hussein's removal and replacement by a more accommodating sherif. Hussein properly concluded that his personal future within the Ottoman imperial framework was becoming increasingly dubious.

At the end of January 1915, an emissary from the Arab nationalist leaders of Syria and Iraq arrived in Mecca with an invitation for Hussein to assume the leadership of a revolt intended to achieve Arab independence from the Turks. Feisal went to Damascus in March to determine how serious the Arab nationalists were and whether they were capable of carrying out the planned revolt. He discovered that the main factor inhibiting the outbreak of an Arab nationalist revolt was the fear of British, French, Italian, and Russian ambitions in the Middle East. It made little sense to the nationalists to throw off the Muslim Turkish yoke in order to be swallowed up by the Christian Europeans. Feisal personally shared their misgivings, which was the basic reason for his disagreement with Abdullah over whether to join forces with the British.

Feisal returned to Damascus in May 1915 to find that the leaders of the Arab nationalist societies had drawn up a protocol which specified the terms they demanded as a condition for undertaking a revolt against the Turks in support of the entente. The protocol essentially called for British recognition of the independence of the Arab territories lying between the Mediterranean and the Persian frontier, and from Anatolia to the Indian Ocean. Moreover, they insisted that only if the entente powers undertook a specific commitment that would result in the emergence of a sovereign Arab state, would it be worth the risks of a revolt against the Turks who were certain to attempt to suppress it with great brutality.

Feisal returned to Mecca on June 20 and briefed Hussein exhaustively regarding his discussions in Damascus. Hussein subsequently decided to make an offer of Arab allegiance to the British based on the terms of the Damascus protocol, in addition to a requirement for a definite commitment of support from Britain to his candidacy for the caliphate, originally hinted at in Kitchener's message of October 31, 1914. Hussein nonetheless seems to have remained ambivalent about the offer he was making. His unsigned and undated letter to Sir Henry McMahon, the British High Commissioner in Egypt, was enclosed in a personal letter from Abdullah to Storrs, dated July 14, 1915.

McMahon was taken aback by the audacity of the Arab nationalist demands in the Damascus protocol. He had previously advised Foreign Secretary Edward Grey that, with regard to his negotiations with the Arabs, the term "independent Sovereign State has been interpreted in a generic sense because the idea of an Arabian unity under one ruler, recognized as supreme by other Arab chiefs, is as yet inconceivable to the Arab mind."[11] Ronald Storrs, who stayed on as oriental secretary after Kitchener's departure, commented that upon seeing Hussein's note, "We could not conceal from ourselves (and with difficulty from him) that his pretensions bordered upon the tragi-comic."[12]

It was clear that the full independence of the vast region, as demanded in the Damascus protocol, was grossly inconsistent with the prevailing Anglo-French ideas about the future of Syria and Iraq. Moreover, there was substantial doubt that an Arab uprising, when considered in the light of the overall war effort, would be of sufficient import to justify such far-reaching political commitments on the part of Britain. Accordingly, McMahon's response of August 30 included a mere reaffirmation of British support for the liberation of the Arabs from Turkish rule, and a more positive commitment concerning Hussein and the caliphate. With regard to the territorial demands, McMahon argued "negotiations would appear to be premature and a waste of time on details at this stage, with the War in progress and the Turks in effective occupation of the greater part of those regions."[13] He noted further that, at the time, the Arabs were in fact assisting the Turks and Germans, rather than demonstrating their opposition to them.

As anticipated, the evasive British reply did not satisfy Hussein. He wrote to McMahon again on September 9 demanding clarification of Britain's position on the question of the independence of the Arab territories. "The fact is that the proposed frontiers and boundaries represent not the suggestions of one individual whose claim might well await the conclusion of the War, but the demands of our people who believe that those frontiers form the minimum necessary to the establishment of the new order for which they are striving. This they are determined to obtain."

It took more than a month for the British to formulate a reply. The message that McMahon finally transmitted to Hussein regarding the nature and extent of the British commitment to Arab territorial ambitions has ever since been a subject of intense controversy. In essence, McMahon's letter to Hussein of October 24, 1915 accepted the proposed Arab frontiers in the Damascus protocol, with some significant exceptions. McMahon stated: "The districts of Mersin and Alexandretta, and portions of Syria lying to the west of the districts of Damascus, Homs, Hama and Aleppo, cannot be said to be purely Arab, and must on that account be excepted from the proposed delimitation."

Hussein believed he had won a major political victory. In his response to McMahon of November 5, he conceded the British point regarding Mersin and Adana. However, with regard to the "vilayets of Aleppo and Beirut and their western maritime coasts," he insisted that "these are purely Arab provinces in which the Moslem is indistinguishable from the Christian, for they are both the descendants of one forefather." Significantly absent from this correspondence was any mention of the Jews of Palestine, a factor that Hussein would be forced to take cognizance of later. From the British perspective, Palestine could readily be considered as falling within their expressed reservation regarding the areas that "cannot be said to be purely Arab, and must on that account be excepted from the proposed delimitation." What Hussein obviously did not realize was that at the same time that the British were negotiating for his support, they were doing likewise with the Jews. The latter also had territorial interests and aspirations in the region, and were busily engaged in building settlements within the Vilayet of Beirut, which included the Sanjaks of Beirut, Acre, and Balqa, that is, the northern half of Palestine.

The government of India remained adamantly opposed to supporting an Arab revolt in Mesopotamia, which it continued to view as inimical to Britain's interests. Sir Arthur Hirtzel perhaps best articulated its position in an internal India Office memorandum.

A strong Arab State might be more dangerous to Christendom than a strong Ottoman State, & Lord Kitchener's policy of destroying one Islamic State merely for the purpose of creating another, has always seemed to me disastrous, from the point of view no less of expediency than of civilisation. The justification of the policy of H.M.G. lies mainly in the fact that the Arabs have shown themselves incapable of creating or maintaining such a State; &, inasmuch as it will be to the joint interests of France, Russia & ourselves to prevent them from doing so in fact—while enabling them to present a suitable facade to the world—the policy is probably also sufficiently free from practical danger. The danger of it, to my mind, lies in its disingenuousness.[14]

Interestingly, one of the main supporters of the agreement with Hussein, Sir Reginald Wingate, who replaced McMahon as high commissioner in Egypt, saw Britain as being in an essentially "no lose" position. He suggested to Gilbert Clayton in a private note written in November 1915: "What harm can our acceptance of his proposals do? If the embryonic Arab state comes to nothing, all our promises vanish and we are absolved from them—if the Arab state becomes a reality, we have quite sufficient safe-guards to control it and although eventually it might act towards its 'Allied' creators as Bulgaria has acted towards Russia—I think it is within our power to erect such barriers as would effectively prevent its becoming a menace, which the Indian Government appears to fear."[15]

Secretary of State for India Austin Chamberlain acknowledged that the government was compelled to abide by the unwarranted and unprecedented commitment that McMahon had made on his own initiative. Nonetheless, he harbored great doubts about Hussein's credibility as a leader. He noted that "my information is that the Grand Shareef is a nonentity without power to carry out his proposals." Accordingly, he insisted in his memorandum of November 8, 1915 to the Foreign Office that McMahon's commitments be clarified. "The next step should be to make clear to them that promises made by McMahon are dependent on immediate action by them in sense of their offers and will not be binding on us unless they do their part at once."[16]

McMahon's third note to Hussein on December 17 reflected the intense pressure he was under as a consequence of the commitments he had made. Echoing Chamberlain's adamant position, he now demanded that Hussein begin to make good on his promises. He wrote: "It is most essential that you spare no effort to attach all the Arab peoples to our united cause and urge them to afford no assistance to our enemies. It is on the success of these efforts and on the more active measures which the Arabs may thereafter take in support of our cause, when the time for action comes, that the permanence and strength of our agreement must depend."[17] He then pointed out that there were also French interests involved in the vilayets of Beirut and Aleppo, and that Britain was not in a position to negotiate those interests with Hussein on behalf of France.

Detailed British negotiations with the French regarding the disposition of Ottoman territories in the Middle East, that were to culminate in the Sykes-Picot agreement of 1916, began in December 1915. Although Hussein was not officially informed about the negotiations, he was informally kept aware of the Anglo-French discussions by Muhammad al-Faruqi, who served as an intermediary between Mecca and Cairo. Detecting the clear change of tone in McMahon's latest communication, Hussein saw no value in attempting to force the British into further concessions on Syria. However, he made it clear in his reply to McMahon of January 1, 1916 that he reserved the right to reaffirm his claim to the Beirut region after the war was concluded. McMahon, in his final note of January 30, acknowledged Hussein's reservation and expressed his appreciation of the emir's readiness to defer pressing those demands that would clearly have a negative effect on Anglo-French relations while the war was in progress.

Some further insight into what the McMahon-Hussein correspondence meant to the British at the time may be garnered from the comment made by Clayton, who was director of military intelligence in Cairo, on March 11, 1916. It was not McMahon's intention, he asserted, to promote "the establishment of a powerful Arab Kingdom. . . . All we want is to keep the friend-ship and, if possible, the active assistance of the various Arab chiefs . . . while at the same time, working towards maintenance of the *status quo ante bellum*, and merely eliminating Turkish domination from Arabia." On April 17, 1916, Clayton reaffirmed that, "to set up a great Arab State . . . was never my idea. . . . The conditions throughout Arabia, Syria and Mesopota-mia did not allow of such a scheme being practical, even if anyone were so foolish as to attempt it. . . . The object we have to aim at is, I consider, to work to preserve all the various elements in the Arab territories very much in the same position as they were before the war, but minus the Turks. In this way we shall have an open field to work in."[18] It is evident that the Hussein-McMahon correspondence, which one British diplomat later characterized as "a monument of ambiguity," meant significantly different things to the different parties involved.[19] Arnold J. Toynbee, a member of the staff of the Arab Bureau at the time, pointed out the deficiencies of the correspondence as a basis for Anglo-Arab relations:

Our commitments to King Hussein are not embodied in any agreement or treaty or even acknowledged by both parties. In this way they differ from those to Russia, France, Italy and certain independent Arab rulers such as the Idrisi and Bin Saud. They can only be analysed by summarizing the history of our dealings with the King during the War, under different heads. And the position is complicated by the King's habit of ignoring or refusing to take note of conditions laid down by us to which he objects and then carrying on as if the particular question had been settled between us according to his own desires.[20]

While these negotiations with Britain were going on, Hussein was si-multaneously carrying on negotiations with the Turks in an effort to obtain a commitment of support from them for continued Hashemite rule in the Hejaz. Feisal, who was anxious to find a way to reach an accommodation with the Turks, was dispatched to Istanbul in September 1915 to offer as-surances of his father's continuing loyalty to the sultan. The Porte, how-ever, was not sufficiently forthcoming with regard to the assurances sought by Hussein. Feisal left the Ottoman capital empty-handed, with lit-tle choice but to help prepare the now seemingly inevitable Arab revolt. He returned to Damascus in early January 1916 for the purpose of fomenting a revolt by the Arab divisions in the Turkish army that would occur once au-thorization was received from Hussein.

When McMahon's final note arrived in Mecca, Hussein nonetheless de-cided to try once more to obtain a guarantee of his position from the Turks. He demanded immediate assurances from the Porte in February 1916 re-garding the hereditary claims of the Hashemites to the Hejaz. Once again, the desired assurances were not forthcoming. Instead, Djemal Pasha, one of the ruling triumvirate of the Committee of Union and Progress, and the de facto dictator of Syria and Palestine, advised him that a Turkish force of some 3,500 troops was soon going to march through the Hejaz en route to Yemen. Hussein suspected an ulterior motive for the troop movement and became determined to prevent any bolstering of the Turkish garrison in Arabia, especially at a time when he was conspiring to lead a revolt against the sultan. He had his loyal Bedouin troops surround Medina and thereby prevent the Turkish garrison there from receiving additional supplies and reinforcements. Feisal, who was still in Damascus at the time, was bewildered by Hussein's seemingly impulsive step. Confronted by Djemal with regard to his father's actions, Feisal sought to convince him that he and the Hashemites were not traitors to the sultan. According to Djemal, he protested: "How could we be traitors, members of a family descended from the Prophet, a family whose greatest honor it is to be the most devoted and loyal followers of the Khalif."[21]

At about the same time, the Turkish authorities in Syria began a roundup of Arab notables suspected of involvement in the independence movement. On May 6, 21 of them were summarily executed in Damascus and Beirut for "treasonable participation in activities of which the aims were to separate Syria, Palestine and Iraq from the Ottoman Sultanate and to constitute them into an independent State."[22] At this point it became quite clear to Hussein that it was no longer realistic to expect to reach an acceptable mutual accommodation with the Turks, and he decided to trigger the revolt. But first he had to get Feisal out of Turkish hands.

Within a few days, Feisal received a secretly delivered message to return to Mecca as soon as possible. He managed to convince Djemal that, as a demonstration of his loyalty to the Porte, Hussein had raised an expeditionary force of Bedouin warriors that was to be placed at the disposal of the Turkish Army. It was now necessary for Feisal to return to the Hejaz in order to lead this Bedouin force back to Damascus to join Djemal's Fourth Turkish Army. According to Djemal, Feisal went so far as to swear "by the glorious soul of the Prophet to return at an early date at the head of his warriors," to help "fight the infidels to the death."[23] Djemal apparently was convinced by this story and allowed Feisal to leave Damascus on May 16. Needless to say, it was the last that Djemal ever saw of him. Once Feisal was safely back in the Hejaz, Hussein gave the signal to begin the Arab revolt a few weeks later, in June 1916.

The insurrection registered a number of initial successes in the Hejaz, where Hussein's influence was strongest. By the end of the summer of 1916, the relatively small Turkish military presence along the Arabian Red Sea coast had virtually been eliminated. This was potentially significant for the war effort in that it precluded the use of the Hejazi coast for the refueling of German submarines preying on traffic transiting the Suez Canal. However, the revolt soon seemed to run out of steam. Within a few weeks, the British sponsors of the Hussein connection were not only embarrassed by the fact that nothing of any particular significance was happening on the

Arab front, they were actually concerned that the whole enterprise might prove counterproductive, as predicted by its opponents in the India Office. Aside from the coast, the Turks held fast to their positions in the Hejaz, including Medina and the important rail terminal there.

Before the revolt started, the British were led to believe that Hussein could rally a force of a quarter million Arabs to his banner. It was soon evident, however, that the most he could actually muster as a reliable force was between 3,000–4,000 tribesmen. By July 9, McMahon was pleading with London for military assistance to cut off the Turks and "prevent early collapse of Sherif's movement."[24]

The revolt not only failed to inspire a general Arab uprising against the Turks in Mesopotamia and Palestine, where the Arabs remained passive throughout the war, it also produced little reaction in Syria, the center of Arab nationalism, before Hussein's forces entered Palestine the following year. The Hashemites even failed to gain the allegiance of more than a few tribal leaders in the Arabian Peninsula. In fact, the tribes near Medina, in Hussein's own backyard, remained loyal to the sultan throughout the war. Moreover, it was only after British officers took over the planning and effective direction of the Arab war effort that the Arab troops raised by Hussein and Feisal became a credible force capable of harassing the Turkish lines of communication.

Notwithstanding the sorry state of the Arab revolt, having been led by his advisers to believe that what he was about to do reflected his mutual understanding with the British, Hussein declared himself king of the Arabs on October 30, 1916. Shocked by Hussein's audacity, and anticipating another barrage of criticism for this latest act of folly, McMahon promptly wrote to the Foreign Office absolving himself from any complicity in Hussein's act.

Whatever references the Sherif may make to terms and expressions used in previous, and what would appear to be imaginary, communications, the records of our correspondence will, I am sure, prove not only that we have abstained from saying anything that implies the future existence of any supreme ruler in Arabia, but also that geographical terms that in English may have been loosely expressed by such words as Country, Kingdom, Empire etc., have in the Arabic version been expressed by the interchange of such words as "mamlakah," "doulah," and "hukumah" none of which necessarily imply the existence of a king. Also in certain passages the term Arab Government has been expressed in the plural.[25]

Britain and France both objected strenuously to Hussein's presumption to speak for all the Arabs and decided to acknowledge him only as the king of Hejaz. From Hussein's perspective, however, this challenge to his status was both unreasonable and inconsistent with what he understood to be Britain's far reaching commitments to him. They had explicitly encouraged him to view himself as the future caliph of Islam. Since the sultan currently held the position of caliph, it was only appropriate that the sultan of the Turks should be replaced in that exalted position by the king of the Arabs. In Hussein's view, becoming caliph therefore logically meant first becoming king of the Arabs.

Hussein evidently was primarily motivated by an ambition to build a dynastic Hashemite empire to replace the soon to be defunct Ottoman Empire. Arab nationalism was a secondary if not lower order consideration. Indeed, whatever fervor might be generated by Hussein's support of an ill-defined notion of Arab nationalism would be yoked to the Hashemite banner, and employed as an instrument for realizing Hussein's dreams of empire.

T.E. Lawrence, who would later glorify the Arab revolt for reasons unrelated to any concern with the legitimacy of Hashemite goals and ambitions, had few if any illusions about the strength and character of Arab nationalism during the period in which it emerged. He also had no illusions regarding Hussein's ability to forge a coherent Arab national state. In a November 1916 report, he wrote to Cairo: "Their idea of nationality is the independence of tribes and parishes and their idea of national union is episodic, combined resistance to an intruder. Constructive politics, an organized state, and an extensive empire are not only beyond their capacity, but anathema to their instincts. . . . Unless we, or our Allies, make an efficient Arab empire, there will never be more than a discordant mosaic of provisional administrations."[26]

From the British perspective, Hussein's self-proclaimed importance was hardly commensurate with his actual strength and contribution to the defeat of the Turks. The latter had recovered from their initial shock at the Arab revolt in the fall of 1916 and became determined to retake Mecca and replace Hussein with someone more reliable. By December 1916, the Turks went on an offensive and seemed likely to recapture Rabegh in their drive towards Medina. The effect of the Turkish drive was soon felt among Hussein's forces, which began to disintegrate as a result of the extensive desertions that were taking place. Hussein, however, preferred to place the blame for his difficulties on the British, suggesting that the problem was inadequate British support of the Arab war effort. At one point, Feisal went so far as to threaten to enter into peace negotiations with the Turks unless increased material support was forthcoming.[27] Because the British had already supplied Hussein's army with more than 50,000 rifles and appropriate quantities of ammunition, they assumed that what Hussein was really after was an increase in his cash subsidy.

During the early part of 1917, Feisal concentrated on building up his forces and broadening his power base among the Bedouin tribes of northern Hejaz and Transjordan. His core army of some 600 men was estimated to have been augmented by 20,000 to 25,000 ill disciplined Bedouin irregulars. One of the more significant Bedouin additions to his alliance was

Auda Abu Tayeh, chief of the Tawayha branch of the Huwaitat tribal confederation.

Auda proposed an audacious surprise attack on the strategically important Turkish-held port of Aqaba, an attack he successfully carried out during the first week of July 1917. The new British commander, General Edmund Allenby, was impressed by the unanticipated success of the attack on Aqaba and decided to make greater tactical use of Hussein's forces to create diversions that would keep the Turkish forces off balance as his own troops marched northward through Palestine. Large quantities of additional war supplies soon began flowing to the Arab forces through the recently captured Red Sea port. However, it was discovered in August 1917 that Auda had been in contact with the Turks, who were trying to negotiate a deal with him that would lead to his defection. When confronted by Lawrence with evidence of his perfidy, Auda responded by threatening to hand Aqaba back to the Turks unless he received a larger share of the booty.[28]

Because the Turks were putting up very stiff resistance to the British advance through Palestine, and Allenby needed whatever help the Arabs might provide, it was decided to accede to Auda's demands; the subsidy to Hussein was enlarged once more. At the same time, it appears that Hussein harbored some resentment about the role assigned to his forces by the British, which placed them in an ancillary, but still precarious position. The capture of Aqaba meant in effect that the Hejaz was secure, despite the continued presence of the Turkish garrison in Medina. This had always been Hussein's primary concern. It is unclear that he was really committed to endangering his slim army to defeat the Turks in Palestine and Syria. As noted by Richard Aldington, in his definitive debunking of the myth of the Arab revolt created and popularized by T.E. Lawrence, Feisal's forces preferred to remain in the "desert areas close to the British army, from which small raids could be made with comparative immunity. Beyond those areas, where there was real danger to be found and real damage to be done, the Arabs did nothing but talk and conspire."[29]

With the defeat of the Turks in Sinai, British forces were positioned for an offensive through Palestine into Syria. However, the Turkish determination to block the British advance in Palestine was greater than Allenby had anticipated. As a result, the British offensive ground to a halt by April 1917 at Gaza, where it remained bogged down for a year. As the British and Arab forces pushed further northward in the spring of 1918, Turkish resistance became more dogged. In the face of the increasing Turkish determination to hold the line, the accompanying Arab offensive slowed and then dissipated. When Allenby took advantage of an opportunity created through a diversionary action to cross the Jordan River and seize Amman, a critical situation developed. The British forces holding the city did so with the expectation that there would be a simultaneous Arab offensive in the Jordan valley designed to relieve the Turkish pressure on Allenby's overextended lines of communication. However, when Feisal's forces attacked Ma'an, they were repulsed with heavy losses. Subsequent attempts to cut the Turkish lines of communication also failed to provide the necessary relief. For three months the British unsuccessfully urged the Arabs to mount a new offensive. As a consequence of their failure to do so, Allenby's forces were compelled to abandon Amman.

That same summer, Feisal once again toyed with the idea of abandoning the British in exchange for a Turkish evacuation of Amman, which would then be turned over to Hussein. It appears that he was prepared to settle for an enlargement of the Hashemite kingdom of Hejaz to include Transjordan. When Lawrence learned that Feisal was in contact with a representative of Djemal Pasha, he sent Hussein a clear warning not to betray Britain. Hussein vigorously denied the accusation of double dealing, and Feisal terminated his negotiations. Hussein's forces played virtually no further role in the Middle East fighting until near the very end of the war in the region. Then, facing almost no opposition as the Turkish front collapsed, Feisal resumed his advance through Transjordan towards Damascus, which fell on October 1, 1918.

As the war in the Middle East moved toward a conclusion, the British began to focus increasingly on the agreements concerning the division of the spoils worked out earlier with the French (to be discussed later). In particular, as stated pointedly in the British Cabinet by Lord Milner, they wanted "to diddle the French out of Syria."[30] The only practicable way of doing this was to establish an acceptably plausible Arab claim to the country. Accordingly, the British had begun preparing the basis for such a claim in the spring of 1918. At that time, a group of seven Arab notables living in Cairo decided to request clarification from the British government regarding its policies for region in the post-war period. The official government response, which subsequently became known as the Declaration to the Seven, was given on June 16. In that response, the British government, in specific reference to "territories liberated from Turkish rule by the *action of the Arabs themselves*," committed itself to "recognize the complete and sovereign independence of the Arabs inhabiting those territories, and support them in their struggle for freedom."[31]

On the basis of this commitment, the British, most notably Lawrence working in conjunction with Feisal, conspired to arrange for the *Arab liberation* of Syria. The procedure that was followed is described by the historian, Muhammed Kurd Ali: "Wherever the British Army captured a town or reduced a fortress which was to be given to the Arabs it would halt until the Arabs could enter, and the capture would be credited to them."[32]

Matters became somewhat more complicated with regard to the conquest of Damascus. Allenby, as the commander-in-chief of the allied armies, had ordered the British as well as French and Australian forces driving the Turks from Damascus to stop their advance outside the city. In this way, Feisal would be allowed to enter the city first with his Arab forces and establish a provisional government. The plan was predicated on the assumption that the Turkish forces in the city were completely cut off from any retreat, and would therefore have no alternative but to surrender to Feisal. However, this fundamental assumption turned out to be false. The Australian commander, Brigadier Wilson, discovered that he could not complete the envelopment of the Turkish forces without entering the city first. That he did, out of military necessity, and the Turkish commander surrendered the city to him rather than to Feisal, who had not yet entered Damascus.[33] Allenby confirmed this when he told the delegates to the Paris Peace Conference: "Shortly after the capture of Damascus, Feisal had been allowed to occupy and administer the city."[34]

In any case, the stage seemed to be set for the fulfillment of the commitments implied, if not explicit, in the McMahon-Hussein correspondence. After all, at the time of the signing of the armistice of Mudros on October 30, 1918, the British were unquestionably the dominant power in the Middle East. There were about 200,000 British troops in the region, while the French forces amounted to a mere 6,000. Under the circumstances, Lloyd George concluded that it was time to rectify some of the provisions of the Sykes-Picot agreement of 1916 that gave the French a bigger slice of the Ottoman pie than he thought warranted. The time seemed ripe because French Premier Georges Clemenceau was more concerned about getting British support for his demands for French control of the Rhine and the Saar River basins than he was about territorial acquisitions in Asia. Clemenceau knew that the British were reluctant to alter the basic balance of power in western Europe and that to get them to change their mind would entail the payment of a steep political price.

Clemenceau came to London in November 1918 to find out what price the British would demand as compensation for the support of French claims in Europe. As Lloyd George recalled: "When Clemenceau came to London after the War, I drove with him to the French Embassy through cheering crowds. After we reached the Embassy he asked me what it was I specifically wanted from the French. I instantly replied that I wanted Mosul attached to Irak, and Palestine from Dan to Beersheba under British control. Without any hesitation he agreed."[35] In this manner, Britain rearranged the bases for the mandatory regimes that would later be endorsed by the League of Nations to suit its national interests.

The British army was in effective control of Syria, Palestine, and Iraq. However, the growing nationalist agitation in Syria, an area in which Britain had little direct interest, served as a distraction from their concentration on areas of far greater concern and a source of continuing friction with the French. It was therefore decided in the mutual interests of both powers to come to an arrangement made for administering the former Ottoman territories. An agreement to this effect was concluded between France and Britain on September 15, 1919. The Lebanon and the coastal area of Syria as far north as Cilicia were handed over to the French. The Syrian interior, including the cities of Damascus, Hama, Homs, and Aleppo, were placed under the rule of Emir Feisal of the Hejaz who was authorized by the arrangement to establish an indigenous civil regime in the territory. Palestine and Iraq remained entirely under British domination, the French having conceded their claims to Mosul in exchange for a share of its oil deposits and a free hand in Syria. The boundaries of the territories that were to be included under the British and French mandates were decided between the two powers and delineated and confirmed in the Anglo-French Convention of December 23, 1920.

NOTES

1. Jon Kimche, *The Second Arab Awakening*, p. 32.
2. Elie Kedourie, *In the Anglo-Arab Labyrinth*, p. 5.
3. Ibid., p. 7.
4. Ibid., p. 15.
5. Ibid., p. 17.
6. A.L. Tibawi, *Anglo-Arab Relations and the Question of Palestine 1914–1921*, p. 51.
7. Kedourie, *In the Anglo-Arab Labyrinth*, p. 18.
8. Ibid., p. 19.
9. Briton Cooper Busch, *Britain, India, and the Arabs, 1914–1921*, p. 62.
10. Kimche, *The Second Arab Awakening*, p. 34.
11. Isaiah Friedman, *The Question of Palestine, 1914–1918*, p. 67.
12. Ronald Storrs, *Orientations*, p. 161.
13. George Antonius, *The Arab Awakening*, p. 416. The complete Hussein-McMahon correspondence is included in the appendices to Antonius' book.
14. Busch, *Britain, India, and the Arabs*, p. 92.
15. Kedourie, "Cairo and Khartoum on the Arab Question."
16. Friedman, *The Question of Palestine*, p. 73
17. Ibid., pp. 73–74. Friedman takes issue with Antonius' translation which he considers as "faulty and distorts the meaning of McMahon's intention" (p. 352, n.38).
18. Ibid., p. 68.
19. Reader Bullard, *Britain and the Middle East*, p. 69.
20. Friedman, *The Question of Palestine*, pp. 95–96.
21. Howard M. Sachar, *The Emergence of the Middle East: 1914–1924*, p. 130.
22. Antonius, *The Arab Awakening*, p. 190.
23. Sachar, *The Emergence of the Middle East*, p. 130.
24. Friedman, *The Question of Palestine*, p. 78.
25. Kedourie, *In the Anglo-Arab Labyrinth*, p. 147.
26. T.E. Lawrence, *Secret Dispatches from Arabia*, p. 39.
27. Lawrence, *Seven Pillars of Wisdom*, p. 571.
28. B.H. Liddell Hart, *"T.E. Lawrence"—In Arabia and After*, p. 201.

29. Richard Aldington, *Lawrence of Arabia, A Biographical Enquiry*, p. 210.
30. David Lloyd George, *The Truth About the Peace Treaties*, p. 1047.
31. Antonius, *The Arab Awakening*, pp. 433–434.
32. Kedourie, *England and the Middle East*, p. 21.
33. Kedourie, *Chatham House Version*, p. 51.
34. David Lloyd George, *Memoirs of the Peace Conference*, vol. 2, p. 691.
35. Ibid., p. 1038.

2

Britain, France, and the Zionists, 1914–20

The newly founded Zionist (Jewish nationalist) movement, the goal of which was the restoration of the Jews to their ancient homeland, declared at its inaugural meeting in 1897: "The object of Zionism is the establishment for the Jewish people of a home in Palestine secured by public law."[1] One of the reasons for this awkward formulation was the need to avoid antagonizing the sultan, who had already made clear his unwillingness to permit the establishment of any autonomous political entity in any of the lands of the Ottoman Empire. The Jews were in no position at the time to achieve any of their nationalist aims in Palestine, such as the building of settlements and communal infrastructure, without at least the benign neglect of the Ottoman authorities. It was therefore considered prudent to cast the Zionist goal in terms of a homeland rather than an independent state. It was assumed that the Porte would find this formulation less objectionable.

At the Tenth Zionist Congress in August 1911, with the Ottoman government having become even more sensitive to the emergence and growth of indigenous nationalist movements within the shrinking imperial borders, it was deemed necessary to attempt to appease the Porte even further. Zionist aims were therefore recast in a manner that appeared to disavow any desire for Jewish political independence in Palestine. The President of the Zionist Organization declared: "The aim of Zionism is the erection for the Jewish people of a publicly recognized, legally secure home in Palestine. Not a Jewish state, but a home in the ancient land of our forefathers, where we can live a Jewish life without oppression and persecution. What we demand is that the Jewish immigrant to Palestine be given the opportunity of naturalizing as a citizen without limitation, and that he can live unhindered in accordance with Jewish customs."[2]

That this new formulation did not really deceive anyone regarding ultimate Zionist intentions became disturbingly evident in Palestine immediately after the outbreak of World War I. The Zionist Organization, whose
members were to be found in all the belligerent countries on both sides, had
of necessity adopted a public position of complete neutrality. Notwithstanding the official Zionist policy, Djemal Pasha, the Turkish supreme
commander in Syria and Palestine, issued special instructions for "combat-
ting the activity of the seditious movement which is attempting, under the
name of Zionism, to erect a Jewish Government in the Palestinian portion
of the Ottoman Empire."[3] Djemal's perception of the political implications
of Zionist colonization was buttressed by that of Baha-ad-din Bey, the former Commissioner for Jewish Affairs in Palestine at the Porte, who was
now governor of Jaffa. In a detailed report, he gave the following description of the character of Zionist colonization:

The attempt of the Jews to separate themselves from the rest of the inhabitants; their
retention of foreign nationality; their submission of litigation to Jewish courts . . .
their own symbols of statehood, in particular the blue and white flag . . . their purchase of land in an attempt to possess themselves of the country; their disrespect of
Turkish authority and of the Turkish language in schools which inculcate Jewish
nationalist and anti-Turkish sentiment; and the autonomy of the Jewish colonies,
with their own law courts and defense services.[4]

There was in fact a good deal of truth in this characterization of Zionist
activity in Palestine. The Zionists clearly intended to build autonomous
Jewish structures in Palestine that would provide the basis for an ultimately independent Jewish state. They placed little value on Turkish institutions or authority, which were afflicted by the universally deplored
corruption for which the Porte had become infamous. And, in fact, most of
the Jews who had settled in Palestine before the outbreak of the war had not
applied for Ottoman citizenship. It was beyond question that they had
greater assurance of physical security by retaining the nationality of their
countries of origin. They thus preferred to rely on the intervention in their
behalf by the European consulates that wielded considerable authority under the Capitulations system.

The onset of the war placed the Zionists and most particularly the Zionist settlers in Palestine in a quandary, since there were large numbers of
Jews residing in the countries of the opposing sides. This argued for the
neutrality adopted by the Zionist Organization. However, such a stance on
the part of the Jewish community in Palestine would be seen as treasonous
by the Turkish authorities. An example of what was to be expected took
place toward the end of 1914, when the expulsion of all Jewish foreign nationals was ordered. The order created a storm of protest and precipitated
the political intervention of the German government, Turkey's ally. The order was eventually rescinded, but not in time to avoid the expulsion of

some 6,000 Russian Jews. This led to a major naturalization campaign in the country to avert the destruction of the community.

Notwithstanding Djemal's strong antipathy to Jewish as well as Arab nationalism, during the early war period Zionist emissaries continued to approach both the Ottoman and German governments. They attempted to convince them of the benefits they could derive from their support of Zionist aspirations, which were always portrayed in minimalist terms. However, none of this was to any avail and, as the Turkish repression in Palestine increased, there was a notable shift of Zionist interest towards the Entente Powers.

By early 1915, some 10,000 Jews from Palestine had been given asylum in Egypt by the British authorities. It was there that a movement to recruit a Jewish legion to fight the Turks in Palestine was inaugurated. Although the British indicated some interest in the idea, they preferred to limit it to a Jewish transportation unit to be assigned elsewhere for service. When it became clear that the unit was not going to serve in Palestine, some of the original proponents of the idea withdrew from the effort and continued to agitate for the formation of a Jewish Legion that would fight to liberate Palestine from the Turks. Nonetheless, the other Jewish leaders accepted the British proposal and by April 1915 some 500 volunteers were accepted into the Zion Mule Corps, which was to serve with distinction during the Gallipoli campaign.

That same winter the British became engaged in a series of complex negotiations with France regarding the post-war disposition of the territories of the Ottoman Empire that they had already decided to dismantle. With the French loss of the Suez Canal to the British after 1875, Syria had become a primary element of their imperialist program for expansion in East Asia. Syria could serve as the Mediterranean terminal for an overland route to the Indian Ocean, to replace the Canal. Consequently, France sought relentlessly to gain control over the ports of Syria and Palestine that could serve as rail terminals for a line linking the two bodies of water. In addition, France sought to maintain its naval supremacy in the Mediterranean. Toward this end, it had established a chain of naval bases along the North African littoral and was now anxious to have an equivalent position at the Mediterranean's eastern end. Between 1910 and 1913, France repeatedly tried to convince the Turkish government to award it concessions for the construction of modern ports at Jaffa, Haifa, and Tripoli. They already had a predominant position in Beirut. With the rise of the Arab nationalist movement after the outbreak of the war, French control of the ports was seen also as a potentially crucial factor in the future of Franco-Arab relations. Those ports provided ready access to the Hejaz Railway for the very large numbers of Muslim pilgrims on their way to and from Mecca and Medina.

The secret negotiations between McMahon and Hussein, discussed in the preceding chapter, and most especially McMahon's commitment to support Arab nationalist aims in Syria, made it imperative that Britain reach an understanding with France as soon as possible. Not to do so would leave Britain open to charges of perfidy and might negatively affect the cohesion of the Entente at a time when it was engaged in a hard-fought war in Europe.

The French were aware that the British officials in Cairo were having discussions with representatives of the Arabs about the future of Syria, which in their view extended from Cilicia to the Egyptian border and which constituted the immediate focus of their primary ambitions in the Ottoman Middle East. Accordingly, negotiations conducted by Mark Sykes and George Picot, representing Britain and France respectively, began in November 1915 and concluded in March 1916. They produced a draft agreement that set forth a series of proposed post-war territorial arrangements in the Middle East that were predicated on the disintegration of the Ottoman Empire.

However, while the British Foreign Office was quite pleased with the results of the negotiations, the War Office was notably less sanguine about it. William R. Hall, head of intelligence at the Admiralty, had a number of reservations about the draft. Among other things, he was concerned about the way it dealt with Palestine and the Jews. In essence, the Sykes-Picot agreement called for the tripartite partition of Palestine into French, British, and internationally administered zones that would also accommodate Arab nationalist demands to some extent. The agreement seemed to be predicated on the assumption that the Jewish interest in Palestine was primarily sentimental and would be satisfied by the proposed internationalization of Jerusalem and its environs, while the rest of the country was left to the Arabs under European supervision. Hall, by contrast, had a much better sense of the character of Zionist aspirations in Palestine. He argued that "the Jews have a strong material, and a very strong political, interest in the future of the country." He anticipated significant Jewish opposition "throughout the world, to any scheme recognizing Arab independence and foreshadowing Arab predominance in the southern Near East."[5]

Although the specifics of the Sykes-Picot negotiations were highly confidential, it was not long before some intimations of what was going on became known in British Zionist circles. There was mounting suspicion that Foreign Secretary Edward Grey was contemplating a joint declaration by Britain, France, and Russia that would suggest a possible three-power condominium in Palestine. This generated strongly critical commentaries in the publication of the British Palestine Committee that evoked complaints from Sykes to Chaim Weizmann, who had become the principal Zionist leader in England. Sykes suggested that the articles, which were widely circulated, were adversely affecting the conduct of his negotiations. Presumably, they seemed to imply that Sykes was deliberately leaking the information to the Zionists.

Israel Sieff, who was responsible for the publication, wrote to Weizmann on February 4, 1916 in response to Sykes' repeated complaints about the critical commentaries appearing in *Palestine.* "I cannot too strongly insist upon the danger of allowing Sir Mark to believe that we Zionists can agree to a condominium . . . if we do not combat this idea from the outset." Again on February 19, Sieff wrote: "There is no doubt in my mind that Sir M. has come to an agreement with the Arabs and his interest in Jewish political aspirations in Palestine is only secondary. . . . I am sure that you will concede that to us Jews, Palestine without the whole of the Hauran and the Hejaz Railway, means not only a cramped and restricted Palestine without any hope of extension, but also a Palestine continually threatened by a strong Arab group which will make our position East of the Jordan precarious for all time." Sieff then went on to plead with Weizmann not to allow the future of the Jewish state be stifled before it is even born, nor to amputate important parts of it for the sake of an agreement with the Arabs. While Sykes' negotiations on behalf of the Zionists were appreciated, "it would be very dangerous for us to give way" on the matter of the possession of the Hauran and the Hejaz Railway.[6]

The Sykes-Picot agreement divided the Near East into three major zones of control and influence. The so-called Blue Zone, which included Cilicia and the coastal area from Alexandretta south as far as Acre, encompassing Lebanon, the northern Galilee and the Hula region, was to be assigned to France. In addition, a French protectorate was to be established in the interior of Syria north of the Yarmuk River and the Mosul region of upper Mesopotamia. The Red Zone, which included central and lower Mesopotamia (Iraq), was allocated to Britain. A British protectorate was also to be established over the region between the Red Sea and Iraq, south of the Yarmuk, which included the Negev and southern Transjordan. The two protectorates together were to constitute a vaguely conceived single Arab state. The Brown Zone, which included the area of central Palestine from Acre south to Gaza and east to the Sea of Galilee, the Jordan River and the Dead Sea, was to be a condominium of France, Britain, and Russia. The Brown Zone, which was in essence the region surrounding Jerusalem, Nazareth, and Bethlehem, was a compromise designed to accommodate Russian interest in the holy places of importance to the Orthodox Church.

Parts of the agreement were in apparent conflict with the vague commitments made to the Arabs through the Hussein-McMahon correspondence, as well as with the commitments that were soon to be made to the Zionists. Nonetheless, all the documentation involved was considered to be sufficiently vague to allow it to be construed in any manner that would best serve British interests once the fighting ended. And, in fact, by the time the ink was dry on the agreement, a series of events had taken place that made it no longer palatable to the British, especially with regard to Palestine.

Almost immediately after the Sykes-Picot agreement was concluded, the Russians decided that they would be willing to see the Brown Zone transferred to the French Blue Zone in exchange for territorial concessions in Turkish Armenia. They attached two stipulations. One was that the Orthodox holy places should be internationalized and granted unimpeded access to the sea. The second was that France should obtain Britain's consent to the change. The British, however, were opposed to the idea and became concerned about Franco-Russian collusion in Palestine that might be detrimental to Britain's interests. This led Lord Crewe, acting on behalf of British Foreign Secretary Edward Grey, to seek ways of strengthening Britain's hand in Palestine. One way was through the support of Zionist settlement there. The argument was made that if the British took the lead in sponsoring Jewish settlement in Palestine, the settlers themselves would insist on the retention of British political influence there and would have the support in this of the Jews of the world, including those of the other Entente countries.

Crewe decided to pursue this approach, and on March 11, 1916 sent a message to the allied governments, through the British ambassadors in Paris and St. Petersburg. It spoke of the benefits to be realized in terms of Jewish support for the war effort from the United States, if the allied governments would endorse an arrangement supportive of Jewish colonization in Palestine. The cable also stated: "We consider, however, that the scheme might be made far more attractive to the majority of Jews if it held out to them the prospect that when in course of time the Jewish colonists in Palestine grow strong enough to cope with the Arab population they may be allowed to take the management of the internal affairs of Palestine (with the exception of Jerusalem and the Holy Places) into their own hands." It then noted, reflecting the wave of criticism the Foreign Office had received from the Zionists in England, "that some influential Zionist opinion would be opposed to an international protectorate." Surprisingly, the Russian minister Sazanov responded that the Russian government viewed the "proposed settlement of Jews in Palestine with sympathy, but that the Holy Places must be excluded from any such scheme."[7] The French, on the other hand, responded rather negatively, as the Foreign Office had expected.

Another consideration was the dramatic change in the British perception of the strategic importance of Palestine as the war progressed. The primary British strategic concern in the region was the protection of the Suez Canal and the waterways leading to India. Before the war, it was generally assumed that a substantial desert region such as Sinai was equivalent to a fortified frontier. Since the Egyptian-Turkish boundary was set across the eastern end of the Sinai, the latter served as a natural barrier of sufficient depth to provide adequate protection against a land assault on the Suez Canal. However, in 1915, a substantial and well-equipped Turkish force crossed the desert and penetrated as far as the east bank of the canal. A year later, a British force crossed the Sinai from Egypt, laying a railroad and pipeline as it advanced

By 1916, it seemed self-evident that advances in military technology had increased mobility to the point where the Sinai desert itself could no longer be considered as an adequate defensive barrier. It therefore became important to assure that Palestine itself was in friendly hands in order to ensure the security of the canal. The Sykes-Picot agreement, however, assigned Syria to France; and France had made it clear that it considered Syria to include central Palestine, notwithstanding its designation as the international Brown Zone. Moreover, the agreement explicitly required that all pre-war concessions in Palestine granted by the Turks were to be recognized as valid and were to continue in effect after the war. This meant that the French railway concessions there would be developed further, thereby interfering with Britain's own plans for the future of the region.

Another factor of some importance affecting British perceptions of the Middle East during this period was their rather unrealistic estimate of the extent to which the Jews of Turkey were able to influence Ottoman policy. They also poorly conceived the assumed ramifications of this influence on the attitude of Jews elsewhere towards support of the war aims of the Entente Powers, especially in the United States. The British perception was based to some degree on the pre-war view (August 22, 1910) of the British embassy in Istanbul, which asserted that the ruling Committee of Union and Progress represented "a Judaeo-Turkish dual alliance, the Turks supplying a splendid military material and the Jews the brain, enterprise, money . . . and a strong press influence in Europe. . . . The Jews, in order to maintain their position of influence in Young Turkey circles, have to play up to, if not encourage, Turkish 'nationalistic' tendencies, and the two elements make a distinctive strong combination."[8]

With the outbreak of the war and the alignment of Turkey with Germany, the Foreign Office began to discuss whether there were any practicable ways of severing the Turkish-Jewish alliance in order to weaken Turkey's ability to continue to prosecute the war. A good example of this internal debate is the minute prepared by Hugh O'Beirne on February 28, 1916. "It has been suggested to me that if we could offer the Jews an arrangement as to Palestine which would strongly appeal to them we might conceivably be able to strike a bargain with them as to withdrawing their support from the Young Turk Government which would then automatically collapse."[9]

Notwithstanding the ongoing discussion of the question in British government circles, nothing of any significance happened until after the Lloyd George government took power in December 1916. By contrast with the predecessor Asquith administration, which was traditionally Europe-oriented, Lloyd George was an "Easterner," that is to say he was strongly focused on the needs of the empire in Africa and Asia. It quickly became clear that none of the arrangements for the region between Syria and Egypt that had previously been worked out were any longer considered acceptable. In particular, the British government was now adamantly opposed to the internationalization of any part of Palestine. This policy change had the complete support of the Zionist Organization, which had long agitated against the truncation of Palestine. Moreover, because a formal treaty solemnized neither the Sykes-Picot agreement nor McMahon's promises to Hussein, Lloyd George's government did not feel irrevocably bound by them.

In April 1917, an inter-departmental sub-committee on territorial desiderata was established under the chairmanship of Lord Curzon. The basic assumption under which the committee operated was that there would be no decisive victory in the war. Instead, it was expected to end in an armistice followed by a negotiated settlement favorable to the Entente. It was therefore considered essential to take the steps necessary with respect to both Germany and Turkey to ensure that neither belligerent would be in a position in the foreseeable future to reopen hostilities with Britain. The group recommended adoption of the principle that British policy must seek "to eliminate all bases, actual or potential, which might be used by Germany to threaten the sea communications of the British Empire, or which might constitute a direct military or political menace to any of its constituent parts."[10]

General Jan Smuts of South Africa, who was a leading member of the committee, took a special interest in Palestine and argued that the security of communications between Egypt and the East could only be assured if the country, along with Mesopotamia, came under British control. The committee accepted Smuts' arguments and included the following in its recommendations to the Cabinet:

The acquisition by Germany—through her control of Turkey—of political and military control in Palestine and Mesopotamia would imperil communication between the United Kingdom, on the one hand, and the East and Australasia, on the other, through the Suez Canal, and would directly threaten the security of Egypt and India. It is of great importance that both Palestine and Mesopotamia should be under British control. To ensure this it is desirable that His Majesty's Government should secure such modification of the Agreement with France of May 1916 as would give Great Britain definite and exclusive control over Palestine and would take the frontier of the British sphere of control to the river Leontes and North of the Hauran. Turkish rule should never be restored in Palestine or Mesopotamia.[11]

Even before receiving the committee's recommendation, Lloyd George had already raised the question of Palestine coming under British control at the Inter-Allied Conference at St. Jean de Maurienne in April 1917. However, the other Entente members received it rather coolly. Indeed, the conference had concluded that both French and Italian forces should participate in the Palestine campaign, a decision that was greeted in the Italian press as a prelude to the establishment of an international regime over the holy places as called for in the Sykes-Picot agreement. The requirements of British policy were now clear. It remained to find a way to undo the specific constraints of the Sykes-Picot agreement with regard to Palestine.

Thus it came about at the beginning of 1917 that Sir Mark Sykes, co-author of the Sykes-Picot agreement, began secret exploratory meetings with the Zionist leaders in Britain to determine whether the latter might be helpful in effectively nullifying the agreement that bore his name. There is a general presumption that the contacts were kept secret not so much to keep the French from finding out about them as to keep the British Foreign Office itself in the dark. This was necessary from Sykes' standpoint in order to avoid interference from the regular Foreign Office bureaucrats who were expected to oppose on principle any tampering with the international agreement. Sensitive to their concerns, Sykes was determined to find a way to avoid a direct confrontation with France over Palestine that might necessitate an overt British repudiation of the agreement.

On February 7, 1917, Sykes met with a number of prominent Zionist leaders who were as yet unaware of the details of the agreement with the French. Disingenuously, he told them that "no pledge had been given by the British government to France with regard to Palestine and the question has been kept open," in the negotiations regarding the post-war settlement in the Near East.[12] He suggested that the French, who really had no standing to make any claims on Palestine, were likely to be the most troublesome opponents of Zionist aspirations. He indicated that he had already convinced even the Russian foreign minister, S.D. Sazanov, to support Zionist colonization. The French, however, would constitute the principal stumbling block to complete agreement on the matter among the Entente powers. It would therefore be in the Zionist interest, he argued, to help Britain find a way to get the French to back down from their claims, which would result in the attachment of Palestine to Lebanon and Syria. In effect, Sykes' scheme was that the Zionists should spearhead the demand that Palestine come under British control in exchange for a commitment that the Zionists would be accorded a privileged position to pursue their goals there under British sponsorship.

One means of achieving these goals would be through the establishment of a Zionist Chartered Company having limited autonomy that would organize and oversee the colonization and settlement program. Bearing in mind the agreed southern limits of the Blue Zone assigned to the French, Sykes proposed that the Chartered Company limit its colonization activity to a region whose northern boundary would be a line drawn from Acre to the east of the Jordan. The southern limit, which would abut British controlled territory north of the Sinai, could be negotiated later with the British government. Also bearing in mind French and Russian sensibilities with regard to the holy sites of Christendom, he proposed that the area along the railroad between Jerusalem and Jaffa be internationalized.

The Zionist leaders took strong exception to these proposals, which appeared to disregard the realities of existing Zionist settlement in Palestine. They noted that the northern limit of settlement proposed by Sykes would exclude the already existing Jewish colonies in the Upper Galilee, and would place them under French jurisdiction. Furthermore, the proposed international zone would have excluded Jerusalem and the existing Jewish settlements near Jaffa from the Jewish homeland. Such a severely delimited zone of settlement was not what the Zionists had in mind, nor was it one that they were prepared to accept. Sykes, bearing in mind the limits to how far he might dare push the French, suggested in response that, notwithstanding the Zionists' concerns and reservations, such arrangements might be required to accommodate the French who were showing little interest in the Zionist enterprise.[13]

On April 8 Sykes wrote to the foreign secretary, Lord Balfour, apprising him of the plan to use the Zionists as an instrument for keeping the French out of Palestine. He noted that at the moment it might be "dangerous to moot the idea of a British Palestine, but if the French agree to recognize Jewish Nationalism and all that it carries with it as a Palestinian political factor, I think it will prove a step in the right direction, and will tend to pave the way to Great Britain being appointed patron of Palestine."[14]

Reflecting their concerns over Sykes' apparent readiness to negotiate away their interests, the Zionist leadership mounted a concerted campaign in France, Italy, Russia, the United States and, perhaps most especially, in Britain to gain public recognition and approbation of Zionist aspirations. This campaign soon began to have positive results, most importantly in France. In the meantime, the overthrow of the tsar and the Russian monarchy in March 1917 occasioned a renewed urgency to British efforts to draw the Zionists closer. There was a strong concern that without the tsar Russia's contribution to the war effort might come to an end, resulting in the collapse of the eastern front. It was considered imperative that everything possible be done to keep the new provisional government of Russia committed to continuing its participation in the war, and the Zionists were seen as an instrument that might help in achieving that goal. The British appear to have been convinced that the Jews of Western Europe and the United States could have significant influence on their co-religionists in Russia, many of whom were in the forefront of the socialist forces that seemed to be consolidating their power there. This had the effect of opening many doors in London, presenting new opportunities for the Zionist leaders to promote their cause.

The Zionist leadership had been aware for more than a year of the existence of a secret Anglo-French agreement on Palestine. However, it was not until the middle of April 1917 that Chaim Weizmann first became formally aware of the existence of the Sykes-Picot agreement and its provisions. He met with Lord Robert Cecil at the Foreign Office on April 25 and expressed his concern that

this arrangement embodies all the faults of an Anglo-French and an international settlement and is, moreover, aggravated by the fact that Palestine is cut up in two halves and the Jewish colonizing effort, which had been going on before the war for more than thirty years, is thus annihilated. By the separation of Galilee from Judea, Palestine has been deprived of a very valuable part of the country. . . . The Zionists will particularly suffer because around the Lake of Tiberias the country is dotted with Jewish colonies. . . . We would always consider it an unjust partition and it would certainly constitute a Jewish *irredenta*.[15]

Throughout 1917, the Zionist Organization, through its publication *Palestine*, kept up a barrage of critical commentary on the question of the boundaries of Palestine. Laying aside maximalist religious claims to Palestine in its biblical dimensions, the secular leadership of the Jewish national movement based their claims on geopolitical and security grounds. Security for the Jewish national homeland would require control over the desert areas to the south and east from which repeated nomadic invasions of Palestine had taken place in the past. In the north, similar considerations would require control of the Bekaa valley between the Lebanon and Mount Herman, the historic gateway into the country from Syria. Furthermore, northern Palestine had repeatedly been severed from the center and south by armies sweeping into the Jezreel valley from the Hauran region and the Yarmuk valley. It was therefore essential that these territories be included within the homeland to maintain its integrity. From the standpoint of economic viability, the country would have to develop both its industrial and agricultural bases to make it capable of absorbing the immigration necessary to meeting the Zionist aims. Because the country was almost completely lacking in coal or petroleum, and had very little water resources, it was essential that the falls of the Litani and Yarmuk rivers be included within its boundaries to assure a constant supply of adequate hydroelectric power. In addition, the only remaining timber stands in the region were in the Gilead, in Trans-Jordan. Finally, because the only remaining large continuous stretches of arable land were to be found in the Negev and Trans-Jordan, these territories were deemed essential to Palestine's economic viability as well. The British Government was thus well aware that the Zionists in London had done their homework, and that the arbitrary lines drawn on the Sykes-Picot map would be fought against vigorously and relentlessly by the proponents of the Zionist cause.

By late spring, the Zionists in London began to press their demands for a formal public commitment from the British government. On June 13, Weizmann wrote to Sir Ronald Graham, a senior official at the Foreign Office, that "it appears desirable from every point of view that the British Government should give expression to its sympathy and support of the Zionist claims on Palestine. In fact, it need only confirm the view which eminent and representative members of the Government have many times expressed to us, and which have formed the basis of our negotiations throughout the long period of almost three years."[16]

The Foreign Office evidently agreed and, at Balfour's suggestion, the Zionists were invited to submit a draft statement for consideration. After a great deal of internal debate among the Zionist leadership and many drafts, it was decided to sacrifice comprehensiveness to a focus on fundamental principles. Accordingly, a draft declaration was submitted to Balfour on July 18 for the approval of the War Cabinet, and ultimately for promulgation by the British government. The declaration reduced the broad range of Zionist concerns to two major points:

His Majesty's Government accepts the principle that Palestine should be reconstituted as the National Home of the Jewish People.

His Majesty's Government will use its best endeavors to secure the achievement of this object and will discuss the necessary methods and means with the Zionist Organization.[17]

The draft declaration came before the War Cabinet for consideration on September 3. The British leaders were now confronted by a seemingly intractable dilemma. On the one hand, they continued to see the value of an alliance with the Zionists in terms of their aims for a British Palestine. On the other hand, what the Zionists were asking of them implied long-term commitments that they might not be able or even wish to fulfill, given the prevailing understandings among the Entente Powers regarding the post-war settlement. Unable to reach a firm decision on the matter, the question of the draft declaration was simply allowed to lapse from the cabinet's agenda. Furthermore, and probably of far greater importance than the cabinet's concern about the Allies, there was the staunch opposition to the Zionist declaration by the ardently anti-Zionist Jewish member of the War Cabinet, Sir Edwin Montagu.

In the meantime, at the Foreign Office, Graham was becoming increasingly concerned over the delay in getting the cabinet to take action and its possible negative consequences. He wrote: "The result of this delay is that the Zionist leaders are rendered uncertain, if not dissatisfied, and that their propaganda on behalf of the Allies has practically ceased. . . . We are anxious to induce M. Sokolow to proceed to Russia as soon as possible with a view to impressing the British case upon the Jews and to arousing Jewish enthusiasm for the expulsion of the Turks from Palestine . . . but he will not go until this question of an assurance is settled nor will Dr Weizmann take any more active steps."[18]

That same day, Graham also prepared a minute for the record that further stressed the potential seriousness of continued procrastination by the cabinet:

This further delay will have a deplorable result and may jeopardize the whole Jewish situation. . . . We might at any moment be confronted by a German move on the Zionist question and it must be remembered that Zionism was originally if not a German at any rate an Austrian idea. The French have already given an assurance of sympathy to the Zionists on the same lines as is now proposed for His Majesty's Government, though in rather more definite terms. The Italian Government and the Vatican have expressed their sympathy and we know that President Wilson is sympathetic and is prepared to make a declaration at the proper moment. . . . The moment this assurance is granted, the Zionist Jews are prepared to start an active pro-Allied propaganda throughout the world. . . . I earnestly trust that unless there is a very good reason to the contrary the assurance from His Majesty's Government should be given at once.[19]

Graham's concerns were further reflected in Balfour's statement to the War Cabinet on October 4, in which he cautioned that continued delay on the question would play into Germany's hands. Under Balfour's pressure, Montagu's parochial objections were ultimately overridden. When Herbert Samuel, another Jewish member, was solicited for his views on the draft declaration, he responded that the policy embodied therein "seems to me to be right. If the Turks are left ostensibly in control of Palestine, the country is likely to fall in course of time under German influence. If Germany or any other Continental Power is dominant there, Egypt would be exposed to constant menace. The best safeguard would be the establishment of a large Jewish population, preferably under British protection."[20]

The question of the boundaries within which the Jewish national home was to be construed was also an item of some discussion. Lord Curzon had submitted a memorandum on the issue to the cabinet in which he suggested that the proposed declaration should apply to a region of approximately 10,000 square miles, "including 4,000 square miles to the east of the Jordan."[21] After some further careful redrafting at the Foreign Office, the declaration was approved by the War Cabinet on October 31, and transmitted in the form of a letter to Lord Rothschild on November 2. It stated:

His Majesty's Government view with favour the establishment in Palestine of a national home for the Jewish people, and will use their best endeavors to facilitate the achievement of this object, it being clearly understood that nothing shall be done which may prejudice the civil and religious rights of existing non-Jewish communities in Palestine, or the rights and political status enjoyed by Jews in any other country.[22]

Notwithstanding the purposeful ambiguity of phrases such as "a national home" and "use their best endeavors," the declaration was received almost universally as the initial step towards the creation of a Jewish state in Palestine. As far as most realistic observers were concerned, the "national home" of the Balfour Declaration was the same as the "home" of the Zionist Basle Resolution of 1897. "Home" was a euphemism for a future state. That this was clearly understood at the time is demonstrated by Lloyd George's description of the intentions of the War Cabinet in approving the Declaration. "It was not their idea that a Jewish State should be set up immediately by the Peace Treaty without reference to the wishes of the majority of the inhabitants. On the other hand, it was contemplated that when the time arrived for according representative institutions in Palestine, if the Jews had meanwhile responded to the opportunity afforded them by the idea of a National Home and had become a definite majority of the inhabitants, then Palestine would thus become a Jewish Commonwealth."[23] The key word here is "immediately." There was no question in their minds that the declaration contemplated an eventual Jewish state.

At the time of the Balfour Declaration, as Graham had warned, the German government was doing whatever it could to bring the Zionist movement to its support in the hope that this might help undermine the Allied war effort. In conjunction with Turkey, it was even developing a plan for a chartered company for Zionists that would have local autonomy and a right of immigration into Palestine.[24] There is thus a certain irony in the fact that the much dreaded German declaration of support for Zionist aspirations was finally issued on January 5, 1918, two months too late to have any impact. The German Under-Secretary of State, Freiherr Axel von dem Bussche-Haddenhausen, stated: "With regard to the aspirations of Jewry, especially of the Zionists, towards Palestine, we welcome the recent statement of Talaat Pasha, the Grand Vizier, as well as the intentions of the Ottoman Government, made in accordance with its traditional friendship towards the Jews in general, to promote a flourishing Jewish settlement in Palestine, in particular by means of unrestricted immigration and settlement within the absorptive capacity of the country; local self-government in accordance with the country's laws, and the free development of their civilization."[25]

The intense British concern over what the Germans might do with regard to the Zionists pointedly suggests that the pronouncement of British support for Zionism, as reflected in the Balfour Declaration, fundamentally had very little to do with the effectiveness of Zionist propaganda in Britain or the pro-Zionist sympathies of certain British officials. It was essentially nothing more than a wartime measure taken by the British government exclusively for the furtherance of tangible British national and imperial objectives. The primary aim was not to give the Jews the basis for a state in Palestine any more than the McMahon correspondence was intended to lay the basis for a pan-Arab state stretching from the Arabian Sea to the Turkish border. Indeed, they were both steps taken to help make the victory over Germany and Turkey more definitive and to assure that Britain's strategic interests in the Near East would be well served.

By the time the War Cabinet finally decided to take action on the question, it was already clear that the Zionists were probably no longer needed to help reverse the provisions of the Sykes-Picot agreement that dealt with Palestine. Because of Britain's overwhelming commitment of forces to the region, it was generally expected, even by the French, that London would have the final say regarding the disposition of Turkish territories in the Near East. There were, however, other compelling reasons for the continued courtship of the Zionists. The Russian Revolution seemed to be heading in the direction of a separate peace with Germany and Britain wanted to do whatever it could to prevent or delay the collapse of the eastern front. Furthermore, it was believed that the Zionists could be helpful in overcoming the reluctance of many in the United States who were not enthusiastic about American involvement in a European war. Thus, from the perspective of British policymakers, both Weizmann and the Zionists and Hussein and the Arab nationalists provided fortuitous opportunities to advance British aims at very little cost.

An agreement was also reached between the Zionist Organization and the British Government to establish a Zionist Commission, under Weizmann's leadership, that would go to Palestine to begin to lay the foundations for the forthcoming Jewish national home. On March 2, 1918 Balfour informed the chief political officer in Palestine, General Gilbert Clayton, about the functions and status of the Zionist Commission that was on its way to the country. He told Clayton that the commission was being sent by the government "in order to assist you in carrying into effect such measures as can be taken, consistent with your operations, to give concrete form to this Declaration."[26]

Clayton reported to Balfour some six weeks later his views about the Zionist Commission's aims and the problems faced by the British administration in Palestine in promoting them. On April 18, he wrote that it was inevitable that the British officials "should experience some difficulties in consequence of the fact that up to date our policy has been directed towards securing Arab sympathy in view of our Arab commitments. It is not easy therefore to switch over to Zionism all at once in the face of a considerable degree of Arab distrust and suspicion." Moreover, he suggested, "in the interest of Zionism itself, it is very necessary to proceed with caution." He noted that he had explained this to Weizmann so that the latter might better appreciate why the Military Administration found it necessary "to turn down, or delay, some of the schemes put forward by the Commission. . . . Arab opinion both in Palestine and elsewhere is in no condition to support an overdose of Zionism just now." Clayton concluded his report with an urgent request that the government should allow the local officials to deal with the Zionist Commission according to their best judgment and not to force them "into precipitate action which might well wreck our whole policy, both Arab and Zionist."[27] This report reflected Clayton's considered judgment that Zionist aims were in direct conflict with Arab aims and that they were essentially irreconcilable. However, his views were not necessarily reflective of all the British experts in the region.

Two days after Clayton issued his report to Balfour, Major Kinnahan Cornwallis, Director of the Arab Bureau in Cairo, sent a confidential report to his superior on the state of Arab opinion regarding the Zionist Commission. He flatly contradicted Clayton's assertion that the Military Administration in Palestine was fully informed on the Zionist program and the commitments of the British government in such regard. He noted that, since the arrival of the Commission, "the Palestinians tend more and more to divorce themselves from Syria and most of the criticisms are now coming from Syrians, who having no direct interest in the matter, seek to disguise the fact by an exaggerated expression of concern."[28] Captain Ormsby-Gore, Liaison Officer with the Commission, sent a similar but more positive assessment to the head of the Cabinet secretariat on April 19, 1919.

It was thus clear that there was a sharp divergence of view among the British experts regarding the impact of and reaction to the Zionist enterprise. It was the perspective of Clayton, however, whether well founded or not, that dominated the attitude of the British administration in Palestine, and later in London as well. Symptomatic of this perspective was the fact that the British administration did not permit the formal publication of the Balfour Declaration in Palestine until after the San Remo Conference in 1920. In view of this, the highly problematic relations between the Zionists and the British that characterized the next three decades are not at all surprising.

NOTES

1. Israel Zangwill, "Nordau," *The Jewish Standard*, January 28, 1944.
2. Nevill Barbour, *Nisi Dominus*, p. 52.
3. Adolph Boehm, *Die Zionistische Bewegung*, p. 293.
4. Nathan M. Gelber, *Hatzharat Balfur veToldoteha*, p. 190.
5. Isaiah Friedman, *The Question of Palestine, 1914–1918*, p. 111.
6. Jon Kimche, *The Unromantics*, pp. 26–28.
7. Friedman, *The Question of Palestine*, pp. 53–59.
8. Ibid., p. 54.
9. Ibid., p. 53.
10. Jon Kimche, *The Second Arab Awakening*, p. 54.
11. Ibid., p. 55.
12. H.F. Frischwasser-Ra'anan, *The Frontiers of a Nation*, p. 77.
13. Ibid., p. 78.
14. Kimche, *The Second Arab Awakening*, p. 60.

15. Frischwasser-Ra'anan, *The Frontiers of a Nation*, p. 83.
16. Leonard Stein, *The Balfour Declaration*, p. 462.
17. Ibid., p. 470.
18. Kimche, *The Second Arab Awakening*, p. 63.
19. Ibid.
20. Stein, *The Balfour Declaration*, p. 528.
21. David Lloyd George, *The Truth About the Peace Treaties*, p. 1126.
22. Kimche, *The Second Arab Awakening*, p. 64.
23. Lloyd George, *Memoirs of the Peace Conference*, Vol. II, p. 737.
24. Palestine Royal Commission, *Report*, 1937, p. 23.
25. Friedman, *Germany, Turkey and Zionism 1897–1918*, pp. 382–383.
26. Kimche, *The Unromantics*, p. 52.
27. Ibid., pp. 53–54.
28. Ibid., pp. 55–56.

3

The Palestine
Quagmire, 1920–39

From the outset, the British military administration in Palestine proceeded methodically to undermine the Jewish position in the country. Apologists for Britain's regime in Palestine tend to promote the specious argument that if the British authorities were occasionally at fault in their administration of affairs there it was because of their commitment to fair play and impartiality. The responsibility of the British officials was to carry out the policy of their government, and that policy clearly intended that they discriminate between Jew and Arab in order to facilitate the development of a Jewish national homeland in Palestine. The British cabinet was well aware of the fact, both at the time that they approved the Balfour Declaration and when they later had it included in the Mandate, that the vast majority of the residents of Palestine were Arabs. They surely understood that the Declaration clearly intended that the Jews be given preferential treatment over the other inhabitants of the country.

The simple truth seems to be that General Allenby and the senior officers at British military headquarters in Cairo thought the decision of the cabinet was wrong and they were determined not to assist in its implementation. While the war was still on, the military justified its opposition on the basis that the discontent among the Arabs that was likely to result from the government's pro-Zionist policy would be exploited by the Turks in a way that could impede the war effort. After the war, the same deviation from the government's policy would be justified on the basis of other plausible arguments, not the least of which was the disarming appeal to the British sense of fair play. In essence, this was not the first time nor would it be the last that bureaucrats, both military and civilian, would undertake to ignore or deliberately sabotage a governmental policy with which they disagreed, and

ultimately succeed in creating facts that caused the policy to be formally re-
voked or modified. In the case at hand, the government itself was later to
adopt the "fairness" argument for reneging on its 1917 policy when it no
longer served its interests to be perceived as pro-Zionist. However, this
was not to happen for some time, or at least not while Lord Balfour was still
foreign secretary.

Balfour personally was well aware that the policy of the Declaration contradicted the idea of self-determination for the Arabs of Palestine, but he
was not troubled by this fact. Indeed, the concept of self-determination was
by no means considered by Britain, or by Woodrow Wilson who elevated
the idea to a principle, then or at any time after, to apply universally and in-
discriminately. Balfour was quite explicit about his view that the idea of
self-determination did not apply to the people of Palestine. He wrote to
Lloyd George on February 19, 1919: "Our justification for our policy is that
we regard Palestine as being absolutely exceptional; that we consider the
question of the Jews outside Palestine as one of world importance, and that
we conceive the Jews to have an historic claim to a home in their ancient
land."[1] In August, Balfour addressed this issue again in a "Memorandum
respecting Syria, Palestine, and Mesopotamia," where he dealt with the
problems of reconciling British policy with the principle of self-determination enshrined at American insistence in the League of Nations Covenant.
He acknowledged that there was a fundamental contradiction, but insisted
nonetheless: "The four powers are committed to Zionism. And Zionism, be
it right or wrong, good or bad, is rooted in agelong traditions, in present
needs, in future hopes, of far greater import than the desires and prejudices
of the 700,000 Arabs who now inhabit that ancient land."[2]

Suffice it to note that this restatement of policy by Balfour was made after the war was over, but that the anti-Zionist policy of the military administration remained unaffected. London did nothing to make its own agents
conform to its official policy. It was becoming increasingly apparent that
Britain's Palestine policy was being directed not from the Foreign Office in
London but from General Allenby's headquarters in Cairo, and the latter
had no intention of supporting implementation of any of the policies that
would achieve the stated goals of the Balfour Declaration. The rationale
used to underpin the military's position in this regard was its ostensibly
primary obligation to preserve the status quo in Palestine. Allenby and his
subordinates interpreted this as authorizing them to ignore the policies of
their government if they concluded that such policies conflicted with the
maintenance of the status quo.

As the 1920 Muslim holiday of *Nebi Musa* approached, which coincided
with Easter and Passover, there were persistent rumors of an impending
large-scale pogrom that would be directed against the Jews of Jerusalem. It
was suspected that the incident was being staged at this time in anticipation of the San Remo Conference of the Allied powers that was to take place

several weeks later. It was widely anticipated that the Balfour Declaration would come up for consideration as the Allies reached final decisions on the dismemberment of the Ottoman Empire. Some Arab leaders believed that if serious disturbances directed against the Jews were to take place, the conferees might think twice before giving international sanction to a Jewish homeland in Palestine in the face of obviously strong local Arab opposition.

On April 4, as anticipated, the fervor of the Arab celebrants was whipped up by inflammatory speeches and anti-Jewish rioting broke out. Notices appeared all over Jerusalem that read: "The Government is with us, Allenby is with us, kill the Jews; there is no punishment for killing Jews."[3] Large numbers of Arabs gathered at the Dome of the Rock mosque in the Old City to begin the traditional procession to the nearby hill that Muslims believe to be the burial site of Moses. As the procession began, an Arab mob suddenly rushed into the Jewish quarter and a good deal of mayhem and pillage took place. The British took no action to stop the rioting, and British troops prevented anyone from entering or leaving the Old City.

Sir Herbert Samuel, who was appointed the first civil high commissioner under the Palestine Mandate awarded to Britain by the League of Nations, arrived in Palestine to take up his post on July 1, 1920, and within days demonstrated his intention of governing with evenhandedness toward both Arabs and Jews. One of his first acts was to declare an amnesty for all those who had been imprisoned in connection with the Nebi Musa riots in Jerusalem. In doing so, as might have been anticipated, he pleased the Arabs and offended many Jews who resented the fact that he had effectively drawn a moral equivalence between the Arab perpetrators and the Jewish defenders.

Following the Nebi Musa riots in Jerusalem in April 1920, the mayor of the city, Musa Kazim al-Husseini, was dismissed from his post and was replaced by Ragheb Nashishibi. The Husseinis and Nashishibis were the two most prominent clans in Palestine and had long dominated local politics. In March 1921 Kamal al-Husseini, the mufti of Jerusalem, died. The high commissioner, in what was intended as a clear display of his sensitivity to the nuances of Arab interests, decided that it was important to appoint another member of the Husseini clan to the position in order to maintain the local political balance between them and the Nashishibis. The procedure for appointing a mufti, however, had long been specified in the Ottoman law that was still operative in Mandatory Palestine. A Muslim electoral college was to recommend three competent and qualified candidates, one of which would be selected for the position by the Sheikh al-Islam, the spiritual head of the Muslims of the Ottoman Empire. Since the Ottoman regime was now defunct, the British high commissioner assumed the authority to make the appointment.

The Husseinis chose to promote the candidacy of Haj Amin al-Husseini, who less than a year earlier had received a pardon from the high commissioner for his role in inciting the riots in Jerusalem. Haj Amin had already been rejected as a candidate by the electoral college because he was not deemed qualified to serve as a Muslim religious leader and jurist (as a student at al-Azhar University in Cairo he had failed his qualifying examination). Nonetheless, his name was added to the list of nominees at the insistence of some British officials. In the electoral college poll, Haj Amin (the only Husseini candidate) received only enough votes to rank fourth on the roster, which meant that his candidacy would be discarded since the college would only recommend the top three names, all of which were Nashishibis.

At this point Samuel intervened in the electoral process to ensure the outcome he desired. As noted by Norman Bentwich, legal secretary of the civil administration at the time, "it is true that Amin was not among the first three elected candidates from whom, according to the Turkish regulation, the High Commissioner, as Governor, had to choose. Some manipulation was required to bring him into the list."[4] Samuel somehow induced Sheikh Husam ad-Din, the Nashishibi candidate with the most votes, to decline consideration, thereby bringing Haj Amin into the range of consideration. He was then awarded the position of mufti, which traditionally had life tenure.

As long as Feisal appeared to be in control of Syria, the Arab leaders in Palestine sought to bring the country under his regime. However, once the French dislodged Feisal from Damascus in the summer of 1920, the Arab leaders turned inward and began to seek recognition by Britain of their demand for Arab self-determination in Palestine. On December 13, 1920, the Third Palestine Arab Congress (the first two were meetings of the Syrian National Congress) convened in Haifa. Among the resolutions passed at the meeting was a call for British recognition of the Arab right to self-determination and the establishment of a national government responsible to a council elected by those Arabic-speaking persons who were resident in Palestine at the start of the war in 1914. The congress proclaimed its unequivocal rejection of the Balfour Declaration, and demanded revocation of those concessions already granted to the Jews in implementation of the provisions of the document.

At the end of March 1921, the Arab Executive Committee presented a petition to Colonial Secretary Winston Churchill demanding British repudiation of the Balfour Declaration and a cessation of Jewish immigration. Churchill's response was that he would not make concessions under pressure and that Britain could not and did not wish to renege on its commitments to the Jews. The Arab reaction came a month later. On May 1, 1921 an outbreak of anti-Jewish violence took place in Jaffa that followed closely the pattern of the Nebi Musa riots of the previous year. Despite this, the situation in the country remained relatively peaceful though tense throughout the remainder of Samuel's tenure as high commissioner, which was characterized by a persistent catering to Arab sensibilities at the expense of the Jewish community. This had the unintended result of both enraging the Jews and emboldening the Arabs to make increasing demands as the price of domestic peace.

Field Marshal Lord Plumer, who succeeded Herbert Samuel as high commissioner in August 1925, although a military man, apparently inherited none of the biases displayed so visibly by his colleagues in the earlier military administration of the country. He was fully committed to carrying out the policies of the British government, as they were understood in London rather than in Cairo. He gave economic development his highest priority, and was disinclined to allow himself to become ensnared in the complex internal politics of the country. Frederick H. Kisch head of the political department of the Zionist Executive in Palestine, wrote in his diary after his first official meeting with the new high commissioner: "I conclude that Plumer's attitude to our submissions will be 'Is the request justified under the policy of H.M. Government?—If so, I must grant it, and carry it through.' The last High Commissioner's first reaction was: 'What will the Arabs say to this?'"[5] Plumer's "no nonsense" approach to dealing with the Arabs made it clear to them that he could not be pressured into unwarranted concessions like his immediate predecessor. It was also understood that he was prepared to use military force to deal with any contingency that arose.

Under Plumer's administration, the security situation in the country appeared to have improved significantly and, under pressure from London to reduce overseas expenditures, Plumer agreed to decrease the number of British troops stationed in Palestine with the understanding that, in case of emergency, reinforcements would be sent from Egypt. The Palestine Gendarmerie was disbanded and the British garrison was reduced to a squadron of armored cars. However, with the appointment of Sir John Chancellor, who took over as Plumer's successor in December 1928, the security situation in the country deteriorated rather significantly, at least as far as the Jewish community was concerned.

The Seventh Arab Congress had met in June 1928 and had finally established a united front that included the Nashishibi and Husseini factions, thereby giving greater weight to the Arab nationalist movement's demand for self-determination and conversion of the Palestine Mandate to Arab self-government. Before long, there were clear indications that another outbreak of Arab violence against the Jews would follow to force the British to make further concessions toward that goal.

A series of anti-Jewish attacks soon took place starting with a pogrom in Jerusalem on August 23, 1929, triggered in part by a propaganda campaign launched during the preceding week that claimed that the Jews were planning to attack and raze the mosques on the Temple Mount. The collusion of British officials with the Arab rioters was blatant. In numerous incidents the Arab attackers fled when the British forces arrived on the scene or were driven off by those Jews who had arms with which to defend themselves. In each instance, however, the British proceeded to disarm the Jews rendering them defenseless against further attack.

The pogroms in Jerusalem on August 23rd and Hebron on the 24th were followed by an attack on the Jews of Safed on the 29th and by assaults on Jewish settlements throughout the country. In total, 133 Jews were killed and 339 were wounded, most of them defenseless Orthodox anti-Zionists. One hundred sixteen Arabs are also known to have been killed and 232 wounded, due almost entirely to action by the police. The high Arab death toll at the hands of the British authorities indicates that British complicity in the riots was sporadic and not well coordinated. It also suggests that while the British had no intention of helping the establishment of a Jewish state in Palestine, they also had no intention of turning the country over to the Arabs. Their actual policy appears to have been one of divide and rule.

Once again, as in the cases of the riots of 1920 and 1921, in response to outcries in England and other Western countries the British government announced the appointment of a commission to investigate the causes of the violence. It was widely expected that the Labour Party, that had recently formed a coalition government, would see to it that the commission would be more objective than the heavily criticized Haycraft Commission of 1921. Some of the leading members of the party such as Josiah Wedgwood and Prime Minister Ramsey MacDonald had been consistent supporters of the Balfour Declaration and the idea of a Jewish national home. Lord Passfield (Sidney Webb), the colonial secretary, announced the appointment of the commission to be headed by Sir Walter Shaw on September 3, 1929. He affirmed that "No inquiry is contemplated which might alter the position of this country in regard to the Mandate or the policy laid down in the Balfour Declaration of 1917 and embodied in the Mandate, of establishing in Palestine a national home for the Jews."[6]

For a brief moment it seemed as though the erosion of the Balfour Declaration that had begun with Herbert Samuel had come to an end. However, by the end of the month it was clear that the MacDonald government would not reverse the policy of its predecessor. The Shaw Commission arrived in Palestine in late October 1929 and returned to Britain at the beginning of January 1930. The commission not only whitewashed the high commissioner and the Palestine administration; it also absolved the mufti and the Arab Executive of any significant responsibility for the riots, which it concluded were spontaneous and not preplanned.

The Labour-led government discarded its earlier position with regard to its obligations under the Balfour Declaration somewhere along the line. It now adopted the idea suggested by the Shaw Commission that the mandate and the Balfour Declaration really imposed on Great Britain two separate but equal obligations to both Jews and Arabs. This notion was patently false, as was made abundantly clear by Balfour and Lloyd George on a number of occasions. Nonetheless, Prime Minister MacDonald announced on April 3, 1930 the new official policy of the British government with regard to its obligations under the Mandate. "A double undertaking is involved, to the Jewish people on the one hand, and to the non-Jewish population of Palestine on the other; and it is the firm resolve of His Majesty's Government to give effect, in equal measure, to both parts of the Declaration and to do equal justice to all sections of the population of Palestine."[7]

The beginning of the 1930s saw the transfer of leadership of the Palestine Arabs from the landowning Western-oriented politicians of the Muslim-Christian Associations and the Arab Congress, represented by Musa Kazim, to the Supreme Muslim Council and Haj Amin al-Husseini. There was a considerable difference between the two. Musa Kazim represented the old school of Arab nationalists in Palestine who originally saw their future within a Greater Syria, and who remained somewhat disoriented after this notion was quashed by the French. The mufti, on the other hand, was primarily interested in power and religion. He wanted to become the caliph of Islam.

The caliphate, the most prominent institution in Islam, had been held for centuries by the Ottoman sultans. It was abolished by Kemal Ataturk in 1924 and was promptly arrogated by King Hussein of Hejaz, who as a Hashemite claimed lineal descent from the daughter of the Prophet. He held the position for only a very brief period because he was overthrown by Abd al-Aziz Ibn Saud, King of Nejd, that same year. A Pan-Islamic Congress was held in Mecca in 1926 but failed to agree on a suitable candidate. The office of caliph thus remained vacant and Haj Amin began to campaign for the position. To bolster his claim, he supported steps to make Jerusalem an important Muslim center, something it had never really been. In January 1931 the body of Muhammad Ali, the former leader of the Indian Caliphate Committee, was interred in the *Haram ash-Sharif* precinct on the Temple Mount. A few months later, the former King Hussein of Hejaz was similarly buried there.

Haj Amin together with Shawkat Ali, the new leader of the Indian Caliphate Committee, called for a world Islamic Congress to be held in Jerusalem in December 1931. One of the main purposes of the religious convocation was to establish a University of al-Aqsa in Jerusalem, making it a major center of Muslim learning and giving its mufti enhanced status in the Muslim world. The move was strongly opposed by the heads of Cairo's ancient al-Azhar University, which had long been the cultural and religious center of the Arab and Muslim world. The Islamic Congress failed to achieve the mufti's purposes, primarily because the rival Palestinian clan of the Nashishibis understood what Haj Amin was after and did all they could to prevent him from obtaining it. They could not abide the notion of the Husseinis capturing the caliphate.

Nonetheless, Haj Amin succeeded in making himself the preeminent Arab leader in Palestine and in changing the intrinsic character of the Arab-Zionist confrontation. The earlier Arab leaders were vehemently anti-Zionist without holding any particularly strong feelings toward the Jews as such. The mufti changed all this. Under his leadership Arab nationalism became identical with anti-Semitism. His program for achieving the goals of Arab nationalism was simple—a Holy War against the infidel.

Under this simplistic scheme no distinction could be drawn between Jewish and British infidels, all of whom were presumed to be in league with each other against the Muslim Arabs. It was to take some time before his ideas spread throughout significant portions of the Arab population of Palestine. However, he had already shown the extremes of which he was capable. Previous Arab outbreaks, such as that of 1920, were primarily anti-Zionist in character. Those in 1929 were another matter. The pogroms of that year were distinctively anti-Jewish, drawing no distinctions between Zionists and non-Zionists. Hebron, for example, where one of the deadliest assaults took place, had an essentially anti-Zionist Jewish population.

The renewed effort initiated by the new high commissioner, Sir Arthur Wauchope, to institute a legislative council was characterized by the mufti's followers as part of an elaborate and intolerable British plot to dilute Arab control over the country in order to accommodate the Jews. The Arab Executive Committee held a rally in Jaffa on March 26, 1933 that called for a boycott of both Jewish and British goods and a policy of non-cooperation with the British administration. It also called for a general strike to take place on October 13. It then sponsored a protest march in Jerusalem, in defiance of a government ban, that was forcefully dispersed by the police. A similar event took place in Jaffa on October 27, where the police also had to use their guns to restore order. This was followed by outbreaks in Haifa and Nablus and by new disturbances in Jerusalem on October 28 and 29. To Wauchope's surprise, the outbreak of Arab violence in October 1933 was directed not at the Jews but exclusively at the British. The logic of the mufti's decision in favor of this approach was remarkably simplistic. In his view, without British support the Zionists would be powerless to stand in the way of Arab rule in Palestine. Consequently the path to the defeat of Zionism led to a prior confrontation with its British backers.

The riots in Haifa, Jaffa, Jerusalem, and Nablus resulted in the death of 26 Arabs and one Englishman, with 178 Arabs and 56 British suffering injuries. One of the Arabs who was injured was the venerable Musa Kazim, who died several months later, in March 1934, leaving a fractionated Arab community that the mufti was easily able to dominate. The leaders of the outbreaks were offered suspended sentences in exchange for a commitment to stay out of politics for a period of three years. The mufti, who conveniently left the country to collect funds for his university project before the demonstrations actually began, was exonerated of any blame, although one of his aides, Sheikh Muzaffar, went to jail rather than accede to the terms insisted on by the British for suspension of his sentence.

On April 2, 1936 the Arabs were invited to send a delegation to London to discuss the matter of a legislative council. The invitation was accepted but the Arab leadership was still divided over the question of whether to accept the British offer of a home rule constitution. Some of the Arab leaders had come to the realization that acceptance of the British offer would give them effective control of the country even if the Jews should elect to participate in the new political process. However, this would also mean an acknowledgment of the validity of the Balfour Declaration and the Palestine Mandate, something that was difficult for the ardent nationalists among them to accept now after categorically rejecting the establishment of a legislative council for that very reason for more than a decade.

While the Arabs deliberated about what to do, a series of debates took place in Parliament that clearly indicated that the mood of the House of Commons was running against the government's proposals. There were many who held that their effective implementation would require a longer period of British tutelage than that provided for in the proposal to insure that a genuinely democratic legislative system would be established. To forestall any domestic political embarrassment over a possible failure by the government to carry the day on the issue, the government effectively dropped the constitutional scheme for Palestine on April 8, 1936. It announced that it was delaying action on the proposal pending further discussions with the proposed participants. Within days, there was a new and major outbreak of Arab violence.

In the early spring of 1936, British domination of the eastern Mediterranean region came under serious challenge for the first time since 1918. The Italian-Ethiopian War was drawing to a close with a troublesome loss of prestige for Britain, which adamantly opposed but was unable to prevent Italian adventurism in Africa. To make things worse, Italian agents were busy spreading anti-British propaganda throughout the region. A real threat of a war between Italy and Britain seemed to be emerging. During April, negotiations were being concluded for the Anglo-Egyptian treaty (signed August 21) and the Anglo-Iraqi treaty (ratified June 30), agreements that moved these Arab countries towards independence. These developments, along with the highly divisive issue of the legislative council that the high commissioner had reintroduced, contributed to a state of tension in Palestine. Many Arab leaders came to believe that the hour was at hand to force Britain to make some major concessions to Arab nationalism and the demand for Arab self-determination in Palestine.

On April 20 an Arab National Committee was set up at Nablus to advocate and organize a general strike that would force the British authorities to accede to the Arab demands for self-rule that had been presented to the high commissioner the previous November. Within days similar committees sprang up throughout the country and the general strike began on April 22 with an almost complete cessation of Arab business activity and labor. Three days later, a new organization composed of Palestinian Arab notables, the Arab Higher Committee, under the leadership of the mufti, Haj Amin al-Husseini, was established to assume leadership of the strike and subsequent negotiations with the British authorities.

The Arab Higher Committee submitted its demands to the high commissioner in a letter that called for the prohibition of Jewish immigration, the prohibition of the transfer of Arab lands to Jews, and the establishment of a national government responsible to a representative council. In the absence of a conciliatory gesture from the Palestine administration, it resolved to continue the general strike until the British government changed its current policy, beginning with an immediate cessation of all Jewish immigration. At this point, sensitive to criticism of its stewardship of the mandate by the League of Nations, the British government was unwilling to make such a concession under obvious Arab pressure. A general congress of local Arab committees convened in Jerusalem on May 8. It unanimously adopted a resolution calling not only for a continuation of the strike, but also for civil disobedience in the form of a refusal to pay taxes after May 15, unless the government prohibited any further Jewish immigration.

The security situation took a sharp turn for the worse on May 16 with the shooting of several Jews as they left a Jerusalem cinema. The high commissioner imposed a curfew and collective fines on the Arab community, but was reluctant to make use of the reinforcements that had arrived earlier in the month to quell the nascent rebellion. On May 23, some 60 Arab agitators were taken into custody and placed in concentration camps, as were some of the prominent leaders of the strike. On June 19, to facilitate police operations, the British ordered the destruction of 237 houses in Jaffa. Then, on June 30, 137 Arab government officials, including all the senior members of the administration and the judiciary, presented a memorandum to the high commissioner that blamed the disturbances on the government's breach of faith in carrying out the promises made to the Arabs by the British authorities. Several weeks later some 1,200 junior level Arab officials signed a similar memorandum. The following month a similar but more extreme and abusive letter was presented by the judges of the Muslim courts, which operated under the jurisdiction of the mufti's Supreme Muslim Council. It warned the British authorities of the dire consequences of a failure to change their policies.

However, despite the official British position condemning the strike, the evidence of complicity on the part of the Palestine government bureaucracy was unmistakable. Three American senators, Austin, Copeland, and Hastings, who visited Palestine in 1936, took the British administration to task. Senator Copeland stated bluntly, "there are really two strikes going on in Palestine. One is conducted by Arab terrorists, who throw bombs and snipe at passersby in the streets and highways. The other is conducted silently by the Mandatory Government of Palestine against the proper administration of justice. The prolongation of the terror in the Holy Land is due ... to a manifest sympathy for the vandals and assassins displayed by many officers who are sworn to uphold the law ... creating a condition which could not but shock any American observer."[8]

During the summer of 1936 the armed revolt became more serious. Within a few weeks of its onset, the general strike achieved its intended effect of drawing the attention of the neighboring Arab states to the Palestinian Arab cause. Various committees for the defense of Palestine were set up in Amman, Baghdad, Beirut, and Damascus. The guerrilla bands operating in the countryside were soon augmented and supplied with additional arms and trained leaders from Syria and Iraq. One of the more prominent of the latter was Fawzi ad-Din al-Qawkaji, a Syrian who had once been a military advisor to King Ibn Saud and was more recently an officer in the Iraqi army who resigned his commission to participate in the Palestine disorders. He appointed himself generalissimo of the rebel forces.

At the same time, the British attempted to make use of the good offices of the Arab rulers in British-dominated territories in resolving the mounting crisis. On June 16 and again on August 4, Emir Abdullah of Transjordan met with members of the Arab Higher Committee in Amman and tried unsuccessfully to get them to end the strike and to accept the offer of a royal commission to study their grievances. A similar intervention was then attempted by Nuri as-Said, foreign minister of Iraq, acting on behalf of King Ghazi. He assured the Arabs of Palestine that "the Palestine Government would not only announce stoppage of Jewish entry into Palestine but would also declare an amnesty for individual Arabs participating in the outbreaks, as *quid pro quo* concessions for Arab cessation of the strike."[9] When this turned out to be untrue the Arabs were more frustrated than ever.

British passivity with regard to Arab mischief making finally came to an end in September 1936. The seriousness of the disturbances and their possible repercussions in other Arab countries forced the British cabinet to devote its attention to the problem on September 2. Two days later the War Office announced plans for a further bolstering of the Palestine garrison. This was followed on September 7 with a Colonial Office statement of policy that reaffirmed the determination of the government to uphold the mandate and to carry out its coequal obligations to both Arabs and Jews.

The Arabs now found themselves in a difficult position. The strike had already gone on for about six months and the enthusiasm of Arab businessmen for its continuation was waning. Although the strike had never been total, the Arab community had endured enormous financial losses and was near economic exhaustion. There was particular concern among growers over the possibility of forfeiting the coming citrus season. Wauchope informed the Arab Higher Committee on September 12 that the British, whose forces in Palestine had now grown to 20,000, were prepared to take serious military steps to suppress the disturbances. Confronted by this challenge the Arab leaders decided to retreat. They found a face-saving device in the joint appeal of King Ibn Saud, King Ghazi, and Emir Abdullah, which stated: "We have been deeply pained by the present state of affairs in Palestine. For this reason we have agreed with our Brothers the Kings and the Emir to call upon you to resolve for peace in order to save further shedding of blood. In doing this, we rely on the good intentions of our friend Great Britain, who has declared that she will do justice. You must be confident that we will continue our efforts to assist you."[10]

Simultaneously with the publication of this appeal on October 11, the Arab Higher Committee announced that it was acceding to the wishes of the Arab potentates and calling an end to the general strike and the accompanying disorders, to take effect on the following day. The British, presumably as part of the deal, allowed al-Qawkaji to slip across the Jordan and made no move to disarm the guerrilla bands that remained in the hills. The latter viewed the end of the strike as a respite that provided an opportunity for some rest and the leisure to recruit additional volunteers before renewing the armed struggle. As one writer observed: "By putting an end to the strike the Arabs had relinquished their non-violent, and retained their violent, weapons."[11] The protracted violence had produced 1,351 casualties, including 187 Muslims, 10 Christian Arabs, 80 Jews, and 28 British dead.

The Peel Commission, which was formed to investigate the causes of the unrest, issued a report on July 7, 1937 that made it clear that, notwithstanding the government's commitment to the policy of equal obligation in carrying out the mandate, "the primary purpose of the Mandate, as expressed in its preamble and its articles, is to promote the establishment of the Jewish National Home." However, it went on to argue, the mandate did not "contemplate, however remotely, the forcible conversion of Palestine into a Jewish State against the will of the Arabs. For that would clearly violate the spirit and intention of the Mandate System. It would mean that national self-determination had been withheld when the Arabs were a majority in Palestine and only conceded when the Jews were a majority. . . . The international recognition of the right of the Jews to return to their old homeland did not involve the recognition of the right of the Jews to govern the Arabs in it against their will."[12]

With the absence of any evidence that the Arabs were prepared to accept Jewish domination in Palestine, the commission concluded that the mandate had become unworkable and should be abrogated. The commission acknowledged that it was unrealistic to believe that both Arab and Jewish nationalist aims could be fulfilled within a common state. It also held that it was equally unrealistic to attempt to sacrifice the claims of one to the other. The only practicable solution appeared to be some arrangement that would permit and facilitate the simultaneous but separate development of the Jewish and Arab communities.

Accordingly, the commission recommended the division of Palestine and Transjordan into three entities. A sovereign Jewish state would include all of Palestine north of Beit Shean and all of the coastal area north of a point midway between Gaza and Jaffa. An Arab state would be composed of the rest of Palestine and Transjordan. A third area that would remain under a permanent British mandate would include Jerusalem, Bethlehem, Lydda, Ramle, and a corridor to the sea at Jaffa. Jaffa itself, notwithstanding the fact that it would be totally surrounded by Jewish territory, would become part of the Arab state. It further proposed that Nazareth, the Sea of Galilee and an area near the head of the Gulf of Aqaba should be permanently attached to the district of Jerusalem under a British mandate. Then, without blushing, the commission proposed that, because the new Arab state would incorporate impoverished Transjordan while losing Jewish revenues, the Jewish state should provide an annual subsidy for its operation.

Simultaneously with the publication of the commission's report, the government issued another White Paper on the subject. "In the light of experience and of the arguments adduced by the Commission they are driven to the conclusion that there is an irreconcilable conflict between the aspirations of the Arabs and Jews in Palestine, that these aspirations cannot be satisfied under the terms of the present Mandate, and that a scheme of partition on the general lines recommended by the Commission represents the best and most hopeful solution of the deadlock."[13] The White Paper went on to state that, pending the completion of a detailed partition scheme, steps would be taken to prevent Jewish land purchases that might be prejudicial to the probable terms of the scheme.

The reception given the Peel Commission proposals was rather lukewarm in Zionist circles and no warmer among the Arabs. Notwithstanding the split that began to emerge in the Arab ranks once again between the Husseinis and Nashishibis, on July 11 the Nashishibi-dominated National Defense Party rejected partition as incompatible with Arab aspirations. The Arab Higher Committee followed suit on July 23. The Iraqi government expressed its displeasure with the proposal, and issued a warning to Abdullah of Transjordan, the only Arab leader who might have expected to gain something from the partition scheme. He was cautioned that the wrath of the Arab world would come down on the head of anyone who agreed to serve as the leader of the Arab state proposed under the partition plan.

The year following the Peel Commission report was characterized by an upsurge in Arab violence in Palestine and Arab hostility outside the country. On September 27, 1937, the murder of the district commissioner of Galilee in Nazareth forced the British to take action. The Arab Higher Committee was declared illegal and the mufti was removed from his position as president of the Supreme Muslim Council. The following day arrest orders were issued for Jamal Husseini and five other members of the committee who were held morally responsible for the recent outbreak of violence. Jamal escaped to Syria. The mufti, fearing arrest as well, fled secretly to Lebanon on October 15 and set up residence in a village north of Beirut.

The Arab Higher Committee soon reconstituted itself in Damascus and continued to direct the violence in Palestine from there. More than a rebellion against the British, it became a struggle for control of the Arab community itself and the consolidation of Husseini dominance in Arab Palestine. Political opponents of the mufti were terrorized and murdered, and wealthy Arabs were subjected to extortion while others were forced to contribute to the struggle in other ways.

One unanticipated consequence of Arab violence in 1936 was the growth of the Jewish constabulary, recruited primarily from the villages, which increased in size from some 3,500 at the end of 1936 to about 5,000 a year later. The combined defensive capabilities of the legal Jewish constabulary and the illicit defense organization Haganah were sufficient to assure that no isolated Jewish villages or settlements would have to be abandoned. In fact, beginning with the outbreak of Arab attacks, new Jewish settlements were being established at the rate of about one a month. Many of these were located in areas where previous settlements did not exist or were few in number, both in anticipation of a curtailment of future land transfers and a desire to expand the areas of Jewish settlement in the event of a partition of the country.

On March 3, 1938, Sir Harold MacMichael arrived in Palestine to replace Wauchope as high commissioner. MacMichael came bearing a reputation as one highly sympathetic to the Arab cause. Although he pledged himself to the elimination of lawlessness in the country, his regime was soon characterized by precisely the opposite. Arab depredations increased significantly in both frequency and severity.

During the first six months of 1938 the Arab campaign took on the aspect of an organized guerrilla war, with bands operating from bases in the hills of Samaria and Galilee. Attacks were mounted against Jewish settlements and British military patrols. Roads and railway tracks were mined, and attempts were made to sabotage the oil pipeline from Iraq that terminated at the refineries in Haifa. Unsympathetic Arab village mayors and police were assassinated, and new recruits were forcibly enlisted in the mufti's gangs.

By the summer of 1938, it was quite obvious to the British that the idea of partition had fully run its course. The Arabs simply would not accept it even though the Jews were prepared to be far more accommodating. Colonial Secretary Malcolm MacDonald had advised Chaim Weizmann in early

July that continued pursuit of the partition scheme would destabilize the entire Arab and Muslim world. In September, John Shuckburgh, undersecretary for the colonies, spoke with Weizmann about two possible alternatives to partition; one called for a five-year limitation of Jewish immigration, while the second reintroduced the notion of establishing several Jewish-controlled cantons. In November, the Woodhead Commission, appointed in January 1938 to look into the details of implementing partition, effectively buried the partition proposal in its report, which concluded that it was simply impracticable.

The MacDonald White Paper of 1939, which was essentially a capitulation to Arab demands, reiterated the standard revisionist position of the government that the framers of the mandate "could not have intended that Palestine should be converted into a Jewish State against the will of the Arab population of the country."[14] It then finally made explicit what had long been British policy in practice: "His Majesty's Government, therefore, now declare unequivocally that it is not part of their policy that Palestine should become a Jewish State."[15] What the British government did desire to see was the emergence of an independent state "in which the two peoples in Palestine, Arabs and Jews, share authority in government in such a way that the essential interests of each are secured."[16]

Accordingly, the White Paper declared: "The objective of His Majesty's Government is the establishment within ten years of an independent Palestine State in such treaty relations with the United Kingdom as will provide satisfactorily for the commercial and strategic requirements of both countries in the future." It also assured that during the transition period "both sections of the population will have an opportunity to participate in the machinery of government, and the process will be carried on whether or not they both avail themselves of it."[17] Moreover, it all but took the position that the obligation to foster the creation of a Jewish national home, in accordance with the undertaking of the Balfour Declaration and the mandate, had been fulfilled. Palestine was now to be treated like the other mandated territories and prepared for self-government, that is, to become an Arab state. The policy statement warned, however, that British relinquishment of the mandate was dependent on the creation of conditions in the country that would allow the independent Palestine State to come into being. The absence of such conditions might necessitate a continuation of the mandate past the 10-year period estimated in the document.

Notwithstanding the extent of Britain's capitulation to Arab demands, the MacDonald White Paper was roundly condemned and rejected by the Arabs. This was probably the greatest blunder in modern Arab history. Had they accepted its terms and cooperated with the British in its implementation, the future Jewish state might have been stillborn. Instead, they refused to budge from their position of total intransigence. On May 30, the Arab Higher Committee issued a statement that declared: "The ultimate decision as to the fate of a virile people depends on its own will, not on White or Black Papers. Palestine will be independent within the Arab union and will remain Arab forever."[18]

The government's Palestine policy was also attacked in both Houses of Parliament in rather harsh terms. The Labour Party attempted to move an amendment that would have declared the White Paper to be contrary to the mandate, and received the backing of Winston Churchill and other members of the ruling party. In June 1939, the Permanent Mandates Commission met to consider the White Paper and rejected the arguments that were made by the colonial secretary in its defense. The commission reported to the League of Nations that "the policy set out in the White Paper was not in accordance with the interpretation which, in agreement with the Mandatory Power and the Council, the Commission had placed upon the Palestine Mandate."[19]

It was at last painfully obvious to most Zionist leaders that the long-standing policy of reliance on Britain's commitment to the Balfour Declaration had proven to be a failure, although few were prepared to admit as much publicly. The question before them now was how the anti-Zionist British policy could be sufficiently undermined to force London to reverse it. David Ben-Gurion became the dominant spokesman for this viewpoint. He argued, in effect, that the White Paper was the logical consequence of a policy that led the Jews to support Britain even when it was sacrificing Jewish interests to appease the more militant Arabs. It seemed obvious that the only way Britain could be forced to reverse its policy would be for the Jews to impede implementation of the White Paper to such an extent that the British would find it necessary to appease them instead of the Arabs. He declared: "The White Paper had created a vacuum which must be filled by the Jews themselves. The Jews should act as though they were the State in Palestine and should so act until there would be a Jewish State there. In those matters in which there were infringements by the Government, the Jews should act as though they were the State."[20]

NOTES

1. Jon Kimche, *The Unromantics*, pp. 72–73.
2. *Documents on British Foreign Policy, 1919–1939*, Vol. IV, p. 345.
3. Richard Meinertzhagen, *Middle East Diary 1917–1956*, p. 82.
4. Norman Bentwich, *My 77 Years*, p. 73.
5. Frederick H. Kisch, *Palestine Diary*, p. 201.
6. *The Times*, September 4, 1929.
7. Paul Hanna, *British Policy in Palestine*, p. 101.
8. William B. Ziff, *The Rape of Palestine*, p. 415.
9. *New York Evening Post*, August 28, 1936.
10. *The Times*, October 12, 1936.
11. John Marlowe, *The Seat of Pilate*, p. 141.

12. Palestine Royal Commission, *Report*, pp. 39–42.
13. Paul A. Hanna, *British Policy in Palestine*, p. 131.
14. Great Britain, *Palestine, Statement of Policy*, Cmd. 6019, 1939, p. 3.
15. Ibid., p. 4.
16. Ibid., pp. 5–6.
17. Ibid., p. 6.
18. *Palestine: A Study of Jewish, Arab, and British Policies*, vol. 2, p. 908.
19. Ibid., p. 927.
20. Ibid., p. 929.

4

The Emergence of Transjordan, 1920–28

As already indicated, with the end of the war, the various promises and commitments made by the British government, and sometimes by those acting in its name but exceeding their instructions and authority, to both Arabs and Jews created an untenable situation in Palestine. The widely recognized commitment made by Britain in the Balfour Declaration to create a Jewish national home in Palestine was subsequently incorporated into the League of Nations Mandate and thereby given international legal status. This commitment was of course completely at odds with the less explicit promises made by British officials to the sherif of Mecca that implicitly suggested that Palestine would be part of the emerging Arab national entity.

As far as the British officials entrusted with the responsibility for administering Palestine following the conclusion of hostilities were concerned, their government had placed them in an extremely awkward position. In the view of many of them, the realities on the ground in the country did not fit well with the schemes devised around conference tables in London and elsewhere. Thus, in his comments on the official inquiry into the outbreaks of Arab violence in May 1921, the high commissioner attributed the difficulties to the government's pro-Zionist policy.

That there is discontent with the Government has appeared during this inquiry, but we are persuaded that it is due partly to the Government policy with regard to a Jewish National Home in Palestine, partly to Arab misunderstandings of that policy, and partly to the manner in which that policy is interpreted and sought to be applied by some of its advocates outside the Government. It culminates in a suspicion that the Government is under Zionist influence, and is therefore led to favour a minority to the prejudice of the vast majority of the population. We have been assured, and we believe, that had there been no Jewish question, the Government would have had no political difficulty of any importance to deal with so far as its domestic affairs are concerned. We consider that any anti-British feeling on the part of the Arabs that may have arisen in the country originates in their association of the Government with the furtherance of the policy of Zionism.[1]

The implications of the high commissioner's report were quite clear. If the government wanted peace in the area, it would have to accommodate Arab concerns even if it meant reneging on its commitments to the Jews. It was not long before the British government came to the same view and, as discussed in the preceding chapter, began systematically to attempt to prevent the emergence of the Jewish National Home it was committed to foster under the Mandate for Palestine. The first major backtracking on its commitments came with the arbitrary partition of Palestine.

At the time, Palestine was generally considered to include both Cis-Jordan and Trans-Jordan and was treated as such by the League of Nations. The region of Trans-Jordan had become of significance to Britain during the war primarily because of the Hejaz railway that passed through it. With the end of the war, it reverted to a state of benign neglect by both the British and Feisal's civil regime in Damascus that was theoretically responsible for the region. At the time, the British were deeply engaged in attempting to delimit the scope of the French sphere of control in Lebanon and Syria. In the course of the negotiations, the British made a number of concessions. One of these was that the British would withdraw their forces from the coastal zone in Syria and from the Arab zone that was under Feisal's administration north of the Yarmuk River. Trans-Jordan was to remain under British control.

In the meanwhile, George Curzon had become foreign secretary and was concerned that the French would use the continuing British occupation of Trans-Jordan south of the Yarmuk as an excuse for continued French military occupation of Syria. This would undermine Feisal's position in Damascus and negate the purposes for which the British had allowed him to set up an administration there in the first place. Moreover, the British were determined to prevent the French from gaining control of the north-south railway that passed through Damascus, Hama, Homs, and Aleppo. Were this to occur, the French would have gained a significant advantage over the British in the ability to mobilize and concentrate military forces for action in the region. Accordingly, the British decided to withdraw their forces, at least temporarily, from Trans-Jordan.

The immediate consequence of the withdrawal was the reversion of the territory to a state of anarchy where the Bedouin raided and pillaged at will. The problem of security in the region was exacerbated by the growing estrangement between Feisal and his father Hussein. While the latter continued to dream of a vast Hashemite empire, Feisal had come to realize that this dream was not going to be transformed into a reality and had therefore accepted the throne of Syria for himself as an independent monarch. Although Feisal made no serious attempt to administer Trans-Jordan from Damascus, he did make an occasional gesture intended to demonstrate and justify his claim to jurisdiction over the territory. At the same time, Hussein, who claimed the territory for the kingdom of the Hejaz, made contradictory gestures there. Thus it came about that although a governor of the territory appears to have been appointed in Aqaba, no one was quite sure about to whom he was responsible because he occasionally received contradictory instructions from Mecca and Damascus. Adding to the confusion, Damascus appointed a governor of Ma'an at the same time that the governor of Aqaba was instructed by Mecca to take control of the town. It would take some time before the Hejaz-Trans-Jordan border was finally demarcated.

In the summer of 1920, after Feisal was forced out of Syria (to be discussed in the next chapter), the situation in Trans-Jordan deteriorated rapidly. It became in essence a no man's land whose 300,000 peasants and semi-nomads were ruled by local sheikhs who did as they pleased. The British were unsure of how to deal with the situation. On the one hand, they were unwilling to commit the military forces necessary to hold a territory of little consequence to them. On the other hand, the Bedouin, emboldened by the general anarchy and confusion, began to mount an increasing number of attacks on Jewish settlements west of the Jordan River. This posed a direct threat to the stability that the British were trying to institute in Palestine. Furthermore, the growing instability of Trans-Jordan, coupled with the fact that many of Feisal's followers and dissident Syrian nationalists took refuge there after his expulsion from Damascus, raised the possibility of a French intervention in order to prevent the prevailing turmoil from spilling over into Syria.

On August 7, 1920, Herbert Samuel, the recently appointed high commissioner in Palestine, cabled London requesting permission to include Trans-Jordan directly under his administration in order to institute order there. This would remove the risk of a French attempt to control the region from Damascus. London, however, was still unwilling to commit significant resources to an area it considered a backwater. Moreover, the insurrection against the British in Mesopotamia at the time made the government very wary of getting further entangled in direct rule over Arab territories. Accordingly, Lord Curzon proposed that Samuel merely send a few political officers to places like Salt and Kerak to encourage local self-government and to provide advice in that regard.

On August 21, Samuel went to Salt to address a gathering of some 600 notables who, as he later reported, indicated a desire that Britain establish an administration that would assure stability and security in the territory. Accordingly, in the summer of 1920, a few British Arabic-speaking officers together with some local Arab elders set up a number of local governments in the area of northern Trans-Jordan between Kerak and Irbid. The most important of these were the National Government of Moab in Kerak under Alec Kirkbride, and the Government of Amman a few miles further north under his younger brother Alan. Another arrangement was worked out in the Ajlun area where a treaty was negotiated with some local sheiks on September 2, 1920. A fourth such local government was set up at Salt. These governments, however, were without any real power and were incapable of exercising control over the large area entrusted to them. The raids across the Jordan continued to increase, and Trans-Jordan also became the base for raids into Syria, which infuriated the French. They demanded that Britain pacify Trans-Jordan and indicated that, unless such was done soon, France would undertake the task itself.

There was good reason at the time to believe that Hashemite ambitions lay behind a good deal of the instability in the region. Samuel sent an urgent message to the War Office on September 21 with the information that King Hussein had made an appeal to the sheiks of Kerak, Adwan, and Balka to prepare for an uprising under the leadership of one of his sons. The appeal stated in part: "This is the time to show your ardor and zeal in connection with your religion and country. Be united and assist your co-religionists to a deliverance of our country from the infidels. One of my sons is proceeding to you with funds and provisions."[2] A week later there was a complaint from the French that Hussein's sons Ali and Abdullah were planning an attack on Deraa.

Abdullah was sorely disappointed that he had been rejected by the British as leader of the Arab delegation to the Paris Peace Conference in favor of his younger brother Feisal, and was in disfavor with his father because of disagreements on the handling of problems in the Arabian Peninsula. He therefore saw the expulsion of Feisal from Syria as an opportunity to project himself onto the center stage of the Arab national movement.

In the autumn of 1920, Abdullah set out from Medina with an army of some 2,000 tribesmen, and headed toward the town of Ma'an, which was still considered Hejazi territory at the time, about 150 miles south of Amman. He arrived there on November 5 and announced his intention to march through Trans-Jordan to Damascus where he was going to attack and expel the French and restore the throne to his brother Feisal.

Abdullah proceeded slowly and cautiously, waiting to see what the British reaction would be. The British requested that Feisal, who was in London at the time for talks about his own future, intervene with Abdullah to cease any provocative actions. Notwithstanding Feisal's assurances, Samuel warned London of the problems that would arise if Abdullah proclaimed a Hashemite government over Trans-Jordan. "If such an event took place the consequences which I have repeatedly pointed out . . . must ensue. Inter-tribal disorder and recurrence of raids into Palestine together with insecurity of Palestine's chief source of food supply would threaten serious re-action here."[3]

In January 1921, Abdullah advanced on Kerak, in Moab, at the head of his army, and Kirkbride appealed to Samuel for instructions. He had a force of only 50 policemen and did not know quite what to do. Several weeks later, he received a remarkably uninformed response from Jerusalem: "It is considered most unlikely that the Emir Abdullah would advance into territory which is under British control."[4] Two days later Abdullah marched into British-controlled Moab. Unable to stop him, Kirkbride welcomed him instead. The National Government of Moab simply went out of existence. Buoyed by his success, Abdullah decided to proceed to Amman. By March 1921, Abdullah and his forces effectively occupied all of Trans-Jordan.

This audacious move by Abdullah placed the Colonial Office under Churchill, which had just taken over Middle Eastern affairs from the Foreign Office, on the horns of a dilemma. On March 1, Chaim Weizmann sent a letter to Churchill in which he expressed concern about developments in Trans-Jordan. He went on to restate and reaffirm Zionist claims to the area of Trans-Jordan west of the Hejaz Railway, an area that had always been considered by the British government as an essential part of Palestine. As an initial step in assuming responsibility for the Middle East, Churchill had organized a conference of regional political officers that began its deliberations in Cairo on March 12. However, by the time the Palestine Political and Military Committee, chaired by Churchill, met on March 17, Abdullah and his forces were already in Amman.

The British had previously reached a general consensus that, even though Trans-Jordan came under the Palestine mandate, it was inadvisable to allow Zionist settlement to cross the Jordan River because it would create a heavy and costly security burden. On the other hand, Samuel was opposed to the idea of making Trans-Jordan a separate and independent Arab entity. He argued that Abdullah could not be allowed to take control of the territory and use it as a base for military attacks against Syria. The question was how to stop him? There seemed to be only two options. Either the British army had to be sent in to evict him from Trans-Jordan, or the French had to be permitted to cross the frontier to do so. Both options were politically unacceptable. The government was unlikely to go to the expense of sending an army to fight in Trans-Jordan, and it was equally unlikely that British policy would permit a French occupation of the area.

There was, however, another alternative suggested by Churchill. He argued that it was most important that the ruler of Trans-Jordan be compatible with that of Iraq, since British strategy called for a direct overland link between Egypt and the Persian Gulf. Because Feisal had been given the throne of Iraq, it might well serve British interests to make his brother Abdullah ruler of Trans-Jordan, or to appoint a Bedouin leader approved by him. The simplest and least costly alternative would be to accept Abdullah's *fait accompli* and make the most of it. Abdullah and his army could be employed to act as an arm of the British mandate and maintain order in the territory.

Abdullah was invited to Jerusalem to meet with Churchill and his staff on May 27, 1921. The British set forth several conditions for his being recognized as ruler of Trans-Jordan. First and foremost, Abdullah was to make sure that no actions against the French in Syria would be launched from Trans-Jordan, in which he was to establish and maintain order. He was also to renounce all rights to and claims against the throne of Iraq. He would have to recognize the British mandate over Trans-Jordan as part of the Palestine mandate, and would establish a government to administer the territory on behalf of and in the name of Great Britain. The high commissioner of Palestine would send a representative to Amman to serve as the adviser to Abdullah's government. He was also told that, at some unspecified time in the future, the British government would recognize the independence of Trans-Jordan. The initial arrangement was supposed to have been for a six-month period during which Abdullah was to restore order to the territory while Samuel arranged for its governmental infrastructure.

Abdullah unconditionally accepted the British proposals. Even though he was ostensibly the king-designate of Iraq according to the proclamation of the Iraqi nationalists in Damascus in 1920, it was clear to him that he was unacceptable to the British in that capacity. They clearly preferred to see his brother Feisal on the throne in Baghdad. This would be his last opportunity to gain a throne for himself. The British much later came to understand that Abdullah never had any intention of doing something as foolhardy as attacking the French in Syria. However, had he announced that he was simply taking over Trans-Jordan the British would most likely have kicked him out. As it was, they were quite ready to give it to him as compensation for not complicating their relations with the French.

From the British perspective, the new arrangement for Trans-Jordan was not trouble-free. Before long, both the Palestine administration and the Colonial Office came to view Abdullah as both incompetent and unreliable. By June 1921, there was a virtual consensus that Abdullah should go. The question was how to get rid of him in a politically acceptable manner. In the summer of 1921, T.E. Lawrence was sent to Hejaz to negotiate an agreement with the increasingly erratic Hussein. While there he was also to smooth the way for a return of Abdullah to Hussein's court. Stopping to see Samuel on his way, Lawrence presented him with his views on Trans-Jordan, the main thrust of which was that Trans-Jordan should be united with Palestine. However, since the government was opposed to sending military forces there, such a union could only be brought about peacefully if the indigenous population of the territory agreed. It was Lawrence's judgment that Abdullah's continued misrule would accomplish that if he were left in place a while longer. British ambivalence concerning Abdullah ultimately became resignation and no actions were taken to remove him. By default, his temporary position in Trans-Jordan soon turned into a permanent arrangement.

The arbitrary British creation of an Arab Emirate of Transjordan required a previously non-existing legal framework to be constructed to allow this new entity to be recognized formally. British political officer Colonel Richard Meinertzhagen noted in his diary on June 21, 1921: "The Colonial Office and the Palestine Administration have now declared that the articles of the mandate relating to the Jewish Home are not applicable to Transjordan and that the severance of Transjordan from Palestine is in accordance with the terms of the McMahon pledge. This discovery was not made until it became necessary to appease an Arab Emir."[5] Accordingly, a provision was included in the revised final draft of the League of Nations Mandate for Palestine, which provided the *after the fact* basis for Britain's separation of Transjordan from Palestine. Article 25 stated that, "In the territories lying between the Jordan and the eastern boundary of Palestine as ultimately determined, the Mandatory shall be entitled, with the consent of the Council of the League of nations, to postpone or withhold application of such provisions of this mandate as he may consider inapplicable to the existing local conditions, and to make such provision for the administration of the territories as he may consider suitable to those conditions."

On April 25, 1923, Herbert Samuel declared in Amman, in the name of the British government, that: "Subject to the approval of the League of Nations, His Majesty's Government would recognize the existence of an independent government in Transjordan under the rule of His Highness the Amir Abdullah; provided that such government was constitutional and placed His Britannic Majesty's Government in a position to fulfill its international obligations in respect of the territory by means of an agreement to be concluded between the two Governments."[6] Although Abdullah announced the independence of Transjordan on May 25, 1923, it was still to take more than two decades before independence became a reality.

In the meanwhile, the frontiers of Transjordan were expanded by the forcible annexation of the districts of Maan and Aqaba from the Hejaz. This gave Transjordan, otherwise landlocked, a port with access to the sea. Then, in the fall of 1925, the Haddah Agreement with Nejd established a 100 kilometer-wide corridor between Nejd and Syria, giving both Iraq and Transjordan a common frontier. At the time, this was deemed highly desirable because it provided a common frontier between the two Hashemite-ruled territories. In return, Transjordan ceded to Nejd almost all of the Wadi Sirhan and the oasis of Qaf.

Britain finally signed a treaty with Abdullah on February 20, 1928 that recognized the existence of an independent government in Transjordan. However, this independence was more ephemeral than real. The treaty did not recognize Transjordan as a sovereign state. Article 2 stated: "The powers of legislation and of administration entrusted to His Britannic Majesty as Mandatory for Palestine shall be exercised in that part of the area under Mandate known as Trans-Jordan by His Highness the Emir through such constitutional government as is defined and determined in the Organic Law of Trans-Jordan and any amendment thereof made with the approval of His Britannic Majesty."[7] In addition, the emir had to agree to be advised in matters relating to foreign affairs, finance and fiscal policy, and jurisdiction over foreigners by the British Resident in Amman who was under the British High Commissioner for Palestine.

It was not long before the British began to exploit the opportunity presented by the arrangement with Transjordan for consolidating their influence in the Middle East. It was Samuel who, from his strategic position as high commissioner, served as the architect of British influence in Transjordan. In his view, it was better situated for their broader interests than Palestine. Moreover, there was no Zionist problem there to complicate matters for the British. It was a marriage of convenience. After 1922, when the British decided to channel their air routes to Iraq and India across Transjordan, the country became an important link in the imperial communications structure. Royal Air Force bases were built at Amman and Ziza, and the RAF assumed responsibility for the security of the territory. In exchange for his cooperation, Abdullah got the subsidy he needed to stay solvent.

NOTES

1. Cmd. 1540, 1921. Quoted in J. de V. Loder, *The Truth About Mesopotamia, Palestine & Syria*, p. 117.

2. Aaron S. Klieman, *Foundations of British Policy in the Arab World*, p. 74.

3. Ibid., p. 75.

4. Jon Kimche, *The Second Arab Awakening*, p. 155.

5. Richard Meinertzhagen, *Middle East Diary 1917–1956*, p. 100.

6. Benjamin Shwadran, *Jordan a State of Tension*, pp. 141–142.

7. Royal Institute of International Affairs, *Great Britain and Palestine 1915–1945*, p. 16.

5

France, Syria, and the Emergence of Lebanon, 1920–36

From the very outset, Feisal's position in Syria was rather tenuous. He had been given the opportunity to establish a regime in Damascus by the British because it was believed that his Hashemite credentials would give him the necessary credibility with the Syrian Arab nationalists to keep their demands in check. However, the nationalists were prepared to accept Feisal's authority only as long as doing so served their perceived interests. To the extent that the emir sought to placate his constituents, it inevitably placed him on a collision course with the French who were determined to expand the extent of their sphere of control in Syria inland from the narrow confines of the coastal region.

Barred by the terms of their arrangements with the French from intervening in Feisal's behalf, the British effectively abandoned him, making it necessary for him to reach his own accommodation with the French. Accordingly, Feisal went to Paris in the fall of 1919 to negotiate a treaty with Clemenceau that would regularize the relations between France and Syria. Recognizing the intense pressure Feisal was under from his nationalist constituency, Clemenceau sought to be as forthcoming in the negotiations as French interests would permit. However, he bluntly cautioned Feisal: "I advise you to settle for this treaty and sign it while I'm in power; for I assure you that it is impossible for me to be followed by any government that would be even partially satisfied with what I am willing to accept now."[1] Although Feisal personally seems to have been inclined to heed Clemenceau's advice, his advisers were sharply divided over it. Unsure of what to do, Feisal decided to delay a decision on the agreement until after he returned to Damascus and was able to get a better sense of its acceptability in the prevailing political climate.

Feisal was in almost continuous engagement in external negotiations for political as well as financial support of his regime. As a result, he had actually been in Syria for a total of only five months during the period from November 1918 to January 1920, when he returned to Damascus from Paris after a four-month absence. Because of his protracted absences, he effectively lost control of political developments in his capital. During his most recent absence, dramatic changes had taken place in the country. British troops and advisers withdrew in November 1919, as French forces occupied Lebanon. Syrian nationalists were agitating not only against the French and the British, who had handed the coastal region of the country over to the French, but also against Feisal and the Hashemites who had concurred with the arrangement. Feisal concluded that his political survival depended on aligning himself with the nationalists.

On March 6, 1920 Feisal convened a Syrian General Congress that promptly repudiated the proposed accommodation that he had just recently negotiated with Clemenceau, making an implacable enemy of France in the process. Two days later, the Congress proclaimed the independence of a United Syria that included both Lebanon and Palestine. The Congress elected Feisal as the constitutional monarch of the new Syrian state. It also arrogated a presumed responsibility for the broader region and proclaimed the independence of Iraq, designating Feisal's brother Abdullah as its king. The British foreign minister, Lord Curzon, promptly advised Feisal that Britain would not recognize him as king of Syria and that it rejected the competence of the Syrian group to speak for Palestine and Mesopotamia.

Shortly thereafter, the British and French concluded that the time had arrived to dispose of the outstanding problems in the region. The Allied Supreme Council that met in San Remo on April 19, 1920 subsequently addressed their concerns. A week later, the Supreme Council unanimously awarded the mandate for Syria to France, while Britain became the mandatory power for Palestine and Mesopotamia.

These decisions left Feisal in an extremely awkward position, as nationalist agitation in Syria continued to mount and extremist groups began harassing French troops in Lebanon, as well as attacking Maronite Christian communities along the Lebanese coast. Feisal finally crossed the point of no return when he interfered with unfettered French use of the Rayak-Aleppo railroad, which was essential for bringing reinforcements and supplies for the French troops stationed in Cilicia. This was a critical issue for the French, who were facing a formidable insurrection of the Turkish nationalist movement in Cilicia that they believed was being supported by Mustafa Kemal, who was becoming increasingly aggressive and was perceived as posing a serious threat to the French position in the region. As far as Paris was concerned, the Syrian restrictions placed on their freedom of movement constituted effective support of the Turkish insurgents. French concern was aroused further by Feisal's authorization of conscription in December 1919. They assumed, contrary to Feisal's assurances, that this buildup of Arab forces was for the purpose of ultimately challenging the French position in the coastal area.

On July 14, 1920 the French high commissioner, General Maurice Gourard, issued an ultimatum to Feisal that demanded undisputed access to the Rayak-Aleppo railway. He also demanded the punishment of those who actively opposed the French occupation of the western part of the country, and the imposition of certain other provisions that would effectively nullify Syrian independence and reduce the country to a French protectorate. Feisal, encouraged by the British to comply with the French demands, had no viable alternative to accepting the terms of the ultimatum. However, even though he responded favorably before the deadline on July 20, French forces marched into the Syrian interior, and on July 22 presented Feisal with additional demands that even further reduced Syrian autonomy and almost completely eroded his authority. Feisal hesitated to accept these new demands, and the French occupied Aleppo on July 23. The Syrian forces mobilized to block their way were handily defeated at Maysalun the following day and the back of the resistance was broken. The French then marched into Damascus and imposed their control of the city. On August 1, Feisal was expelled from Syria.

The French acted expeditiously to quash Syrian nationalist sentiment by effectively partitioning the country internally. First, it was decided to enhance the position of the Maronites of Lebanon, to whom the French had a special relationship. Thus, the high commissioner proclaimed the creation of the State of Great Lebanon in Beirut on September 1, 1920. The territory of the new Grand Liban was to include not only the old Ottoman administrative district but also the city of Beirut and the districts of Tyre, Tripoli, the Bekaa valley, and Baalbek. However, the new Grand Liban now encompassed areas that gave Maronite Lebanon a large Muslim population, providing the basis for the inter-communal conflicts that would repeatedly ravage the country in the future. Lebanon came under direct French control and was administered as a colony.

The remainder of Syria was divided into a number of autonomous regions. On August 31, 1920, a new entity was created on the coastal region north of Lebanon, a district in which there was a heavy concentration of Nuseiri or Alawis, a secret sect considered by some to be on the fringes of Islam that had been much persecuted by the Turks. It was constituted as the independent territory of the Alawi, and subsequently transformed in July 1922 into the State of the Alawi or Alaouite, as it was known in French. Here again, the French partition included a large number of non-Alawis that were never comfortable with the idea of being a minority in an Alawi-dominated state. Then, on September 12, 1921, France made the small coastal strip between Alaouite and the Turkish frontier into a separate autonomous Sanjak of Alexandretta, in view of the large Turkish-speaking population. These steps effectively cut off what remained of Syria from the coast. It also sought to capitalize on the traditional rivalry between Syria's two largest cities, Damascus and Aleppo, each of which had been the capital of an Ottoman vilayet, and formed them into separate states. Then, on March 4, 1921, a separate entity was created for the Druse in a new autonomous State of Jebel ad-Druse, which became independent on April 5, 1922.

Contrary to French expectations, the peoples of the states of Damascus and Aleppo overwhelmingly demanded union between them, and so a federation of Damascus, Aleppo, and Alaouite was set up. This arrangement lasted only a couple of years until the summer of 1924, when the new French high commissioner for Syria, General Weygand, dissolved the federation and combined Damascus and Aleppo into a single Syrian state, with Alaouite reverting to its former independence. In sum, Syria had been carved into four separate states, five if autonomous Alexandretta be included. The French then poured oil on the fires of discontent in the country by appearing to give preferment to the Maronites in Lebanon over the majority Sunnite Muslims in Syria. This impression was given reinforcement by the choice of Beirut rather than Damascus as the headquarters of the French high commissioner.

The French approach to the administration of the mandate for Syria was essentially to ignore France's mandatory responsibilities and to treat the country as a colony to be exploited for French interests. Resentment against the French grew throughout the country and erupted in a major insurrection in the summer of 1925. Somewhat surprisingly, it broke out in the territory least expected, the Jebel ad-Druse.

Under the treaty of March 4, 1921, the Druse, an amalgamation of often feuding clans, were to be governed by an indigenous elected governor who functioned under the overall authority of the French high commissioner. The first such elected governor was Salim Pasha al-Atrashi. Following his death several years later, the Druse chiefs could not agree on a suitable native replacement. As a result, the French adviser to the governor filled the position and ruled the Jebel ad-Druse as a benevolent despot. His attempts to liberate the peasants from the often oppressive domination of their feudal lords put him on a collision course with the latter, whom he tried to suppress with harsh methods that were an offense to Druse pride.

In July 1925, a revolt broke out under the leadership of Sultan Pasha al-Atrashi that rapidly spread throughout the country. Within a few weeks, the Druse managed to capture as-Suweida, the capital of the state, and to place the French garrison in the citadel under siege, as well as to wipe out a French relief column of some 3,000 men. On August 24, Sultan al-Atrashi attacked Damascus, where he was joined by a group of Syrian nationalists. Unfortunately for the rebels, a number of Syrian notables continued to hope that the French would come to their senses and carry out the mandate as intended. Without their support, the rebels were unable to take Damascus and retreated to the Jebel ad-Druse, where they established a provisional government. It called on the people to fight for "the complete independence of Syria, one and indivisible, both the coastal region and the interior, the establishment of a national government, and the free election of a Constituent Assembly to draft the constitution, the withdrawal of the foreign army of occupation, and the creation of a national army to guarantee security and apply the principles of the French Revolution and the rights of man."[2]

The insurrection, which had spread to the area around Damascus, southern Lebanon, Aleppo, Homs, and Hama, went on for some two years despite the large and well-equipped French forces committed to suppressing it. From October 18 to 20, 1925, Damascus was bombarded by aircraft and tanks, causing extensive damage. The French also reportedly employed systematic terror in their effort to quickly put an end to the rebellion, decimating and burning whole villages. To make matters worse, the French also employed Christian Armenian and Circassian auxiliaries, arousing considerable anger among the Muslims. Similarly, they armed the Christian Lebanese as a line of defense against the Druse and Muslim rebels in southern Lebanon, giving the Maronites rather than French troops the responsibility of blunting the Druse attacks in their territory. By these means, the French contrived to transform what was in essence a nationalist struggle into an inter-communal religious conflict. It was not until June 1927 that the back of the insurrection was broken. Sultan al-Atrashi and a number of followers were forced to flee first to Transjordan and then to Arabia. Following this, disturbances in other parts of the country soon petered out.

In the meanwhile, Henri de Jouvenal was sent by Paris to become the first civilian high commissioner in Syria at the end of 1925. He undertook a series of negotiations with the leaders of the insurrection in Syria, as well as with the executive committee of the Syro-Palestinian Congress in Cairo. De Jouvenal made a number of promises to reform the French administration in the country, but the Syrian nationalists would not put any credence in them. They resolutely demanded that the mandate should be replaced with a treaty with France for a limited period, and that Syria should be given full internal autonomy immediately. Moreover, they insisted that all of Syria, with the exception of the original Maronite enclave in Mount Lebanon, be re-unified, and that a general amnesty be declared.

While unwilling to make such concessions, De Jouvenal did attempt to introduce constitutional reforms. The Syrian president, Subhi Bey, resigned and French bureaucrats and military officers governed the country until De Jouvenal appointed Ahmed Nami Bey president on April 28, 1926. Public opinion, however, was so unanimous with regard to the demand for a treaty, similar to that negotiated by the British with Iraq in place of the mandate, that De Jouvenal ultimately became swayed by the argument. On June 17, he told the Permanent Mandates Commission that only such a treaty could bring peace to Syria, and negotiations soon began in Paris with representatives of the Syro-Palestinian Congress. However, at the point where the negotiations seemed on the verge of an agreement, the French government broke off the negotiations. De Jouvenal resigned and was replaced by Henri Ponsot, who arrived in Beirut in October 1926.

With the end of the insurrection in mid-1927, Ponsot became more open to a moderate accommodation with the nationalists. Martial law and press censorship were abolished in February 1928, and a general amnesty, except for the principal nationalist leaders, was proclaimed. The following month, authorization was given for the election of the National Constituent Assembly, and an election that took place in April, one in which the nationalists predominated notwithstanding the efforts of the government to influence the outcome. The Assembly opened in Damascus on June 9 and elected a nationalist leader, Hashim al-Atassi, who had served as prime minister under King Feisal in 1920, as its president. A drafting committee came up with a proposed new constitution that made no mention of the mandate, declared Syria a parliamentary republic, and asserted that all previously Ottoman Syrian territories constituted an indivisible political unit. All the partitions instituted by the French were completely ignored.

Ponsot rejected these provisions and demanded their revision, but the majority of the Assembly refused to budge. He therefore adjourned the Assembly for three months on August 11, 1928, and once again on November 5, to allow time to work out a solution to the impasse. Finally, on February 5, 1929, the Assembly was suspended indefinitely. Ponsot proposed that the draft constitution be retained as is, but that a transition clause be added to the effect that for as long as the mandate continued in force, no article in the constitution would be applied in a manner that conflicted with France's mandatory obligations. The assembly rejected the proposal and Ponsot dissolved it on May 14, 1930, the high commissioner promulgating the new constitution, as drafted by the Assembly but with the controversial transition clause included, on May 22.

Although the new constitution provided for a greater degree of autonomy than the country had experienced previously, the fact that the French remained in complete control of foreign and defense policy, as well as the security of minorities, rankled the Syrian nationalists who continued to agitate against the French. The situation remained highly volatile for a number of years and reached a boiling point in December 1935 with the death of Ibrahim Hananu, leader of the Syrian National Bloc, an organization committed to the expulsion of the French. A general strike that turned unexpectedly violent began in Damascus and soon spread to other cities.

The French regime responded by imposing martial law, but soon concluded that, given the geopolitical realities faced by France at the time, only significant concessions to the nationalists could forestall their needing to cope with a major insurrection. The fact was that France was not in a position to assign additional forces to maintain order in Syria at a time when Nazi Germany was rearming and beginning to flex its muscles along the French frontier. As a conciliatory gesture, High Commissioner D. de Martel appointed a veteran politician acceptable to the nationalists, Ata al-Ayyubi, as prime minister in February 1936. The latter soon headed a delegation to Paris to resume negotiations over a treaty.

The French government continued to insist that Jebel ad-Druse and the district of Latakia be excluded from the proposed Syrian state, so that they could continue to protect the Druse and Alawite minorities in these enclaves. France also proposed to continue to maintain a significant degree of political and military control of the country. These terms were completely unacceptable to the Syrian nationalists and the discussions seemed to be going nowhere until there was a major change in the composition of the French regime in June 1936, when an essentially anti-imperialist Popular Front government came into power. With a new foreign minister, Yves Delbos, who was sympathetic to the aspirations of the Syrian nationalists, a Franco-Syrian treaty was soon concluded and subsequently ratified by the Syrian parliament on December 27, 1936.

The agreement essentially scrapped the previous mandatory relationship but retained a not insignificant amount of French influence in foreign and military affairs. In the event of war, the Syrians were obliged to place all their facilities at France's disposal, even though they were not obligated to participate in any hostilities. The French were to be able to make use of two air bases and to maintain troops in Syria for a period of eight years after the agreement was ratified, i.e., until the end of 1944. The French troops were to be garrisoned exclusively in the Jebel ad-Druse and Latakia, areas where no Syrian troops were to be permitted.

THE EMERGENCE OF LEBANON

For their part, the Christian Lebanese made it clear that they insisted on remaining separate from Syria, and the National Lebanese League in Egypt made this demand in a memorandum sent to the League of Nations in September 1925. Moreover, they demanded that a freely elected national assembly should draft a constitution for the country, and that Lebanon should be admitted to the League of Nations as an independent and sovereign state. France, however, was not prepared to go that far at once. Instead, De Jouvenal submitted a draft constitution to the Lebanese Council in May 1926 which, with some minor revisions, was quickly adopted over the objection of all the Muslim members of the council and promulgated on May 23, laying the foundation for a new Republic of Lebanon. The constitution provided for a two-chamber legislature, the Chamber of Deputies that replaced the existing Representative Council, which in effect remained in office for the remainder of its term until 1929, and the Senate, which was nominated by the high commissioner. On May 26, the two chambers elected the first president of the Lebanese Republic, Charles Debbas, who was Greek Orthodox. In only a few days, the entire legislative and administrative apparatus of the state had been put in place. The demands of the Syrian nationalists for a plebiscite were rejected and all further discussion of unification with Syria was prohibited.

Although the new Lebanese constitution recognized Lebanon as an independent state, it made no mention of the matter of sovereignty. Moreover, Lebanese independence was also restricted by the terms of the mandate, which were incorporated into the constitution. The legislative and executive powers of the French high commissioner continued in force. The high commissioner remained entirely responsible for foreign and military affairs, and could veto any decision by the Lebanese authorities that he considered detrimental to the mandate, security and the preservation of public order, or to international obligations. The constitution was subsequently revised on October 17, 1927 to enhance the power of the executive; it combined the two legislative chambers into one, with the president of the republic appointing one-third of the members, and reduced its power.

Although the French were pleased with what they had created in Lebanon, the Lebanese were themselves less sanguine about the achievement. Perhaps the principal problem the country faced was dealing with the wide variety of religious groupings, each representing a political force that had to be accommodated if there was to be social peace. A provision of the constitution effectively entitled each religious community to be represented in the public service as well as the government. This not only made for an excessively large and cumbersome bureaucracy, it also exacerbated the problem of developing a sense of Lebanese national identity, which raised the sensitive political issue of unity with Syria, something the Muslim communities as well as some Christians advocated. Thus, in March 1926, a conference of Lebanese notables was convened in Beirut, in which all religious communities were represented. All the participants, with the notable exception of the Maronites, declared in favor of either the union of all of Lebanon with Syria, or at least the return to Syria of those territories detached from it in 1920. It was clear that Lebanese nationalism was almost exclusively a Maronite ideology. The question of the foundations of Lebanese nationalism remains an issue that has continued to plague the country to this day.

Using the Franco-Syrian treaty of 1936 as a model, a similar treaty that called for the recognition of Lebanon as an independent state within three years of ratification was concluded on November 13, 1936. The treaty of amity and alliance was to stay in effect for 25 years, and provided for foreign and military affairs to remain in French hands. Nonetheless, the treaty failed to pass muster in the French chamber of deputies, which refused to ratify it. Lebanon was perceived as an asset that the French were simply unwilling to part with. This brought about an immediate deterioration in relations between the two countries that persisted until 1941.

NOTES

1. Abu Khaldun Sati al-Husri, *The Day of Maysalun*, p. 49.
2. Hans Kohn, *Nationalism and Imperialism in the Hither East*, p. 192.

6

Britain and Iraq, 1918–39

Iraq had been under British Indian army occupation since early 1918. The British found themselves in a large neglected territory with an ethnically and religiously diverse population of some three million people, almost entirely Muslim but part Shiite and part Sunni, including about 700,000 Kurds. Despite this, the British cabinet somehow came to the remarkably uninformed conclusion that Iraq was a culturally and politically coherent region. Accordingly, London issued a guideline on March 29, 1918 that envisioned direct British rule over the vilayet of Basra, that is the littoral of the Persian Gulf, and Arab self-rule in the interior under British tutelage. A seasoned civilian high commissioner, Sir Percy Cox, was appointed to establish an Anglo-Indian administration. On April 7 he warned the British government that its guideline for Iraq would produce chaos in the country, and he simply ignored it. In the absence of any coherent policy instructions from the British government, he ran the country as he saw fit, with an iron and ruthlessly efficient hand. Cox would later write: "By the end of the war, the people of Mesopotamia had come to accept the fact of our occupation and were resigned to the prospect of a permanent British administration."[1] Upon his departure for reassignment to Tehran in May 1918, his successor, Arnold Wilson, a lieutenant colonel in the Indian army, continued to maintain tight control of the country for more than a year.

Nonetheless, the seeds of nationalist discontent began to be sown during Wilson's administration by disenchanted indigenous officials and military officers who formerly served under the Turkish regime and who now found no place for themselves in the Anglo-Indian administration that tightly controlled the territory. Some of these turned to Syria for employment and thereby constituted a link with the active nationalist movement in that country, serving as a channel for Syrian propaganda in Iraq. It not only created a popular perception that Feisal's indigenous administration had established effective control over Syria, Iraqi nationalists in Syria also began clandestinely to distribute inflammatory pamphlets such as one that appeared in Baghdad in May 1919. It proclaimed, "We want independence and we will have independence as we are not slaves. We will not have entire independence except under the shade of the Arab flag and within the Arab union. The life of the Arabs is in their Union. Demand your independence until death."[2]

The subsequent declaration of Syria's independence by the Syrian Congress on March 8, 1920 and the election of Feisal as its king inflamed the situation further. Iraqi nationalists in Syria held a simultaneous Iraqi Congress in Damascus and declared that "we in our capacity as representatives of the people declare unanimously the independence of the country of Iraq . . . and support the independence of Syria; and declare the political and economic unity of Iraq and Syria. We declared [sic] his Royal Highness the prince Abdulla as constitutional king."[3] This poured even more fuel on the flames of insurgency.

Tensions increased significantly after the announcement of the establishment of the British mandate on May 3, 1920. The nationalists rejected the authority of the League of Nations to create and distribute mandates as well as the British claim that they were assuming responsibility in Iraq in response to the League. They viewed the mandate system as merely another form of imperialism and a vehicle for colonization, and the British claims of international responsibility as disingenuous. In fact, Iraqi nationalists echoed the views of Lord Curzon, speaking as the British foreign secretary, who essentially made the same point in the House of Lords on June 25, 1920. "It is quite a mistake to suppose . . . that under the Covenant of the League, or any other instrument, the gift of the mandate rests with the League of Nations. It does not do so. It rests with the Powers who have conquered the territories, which it then falls to them to distribute, and it was in these circumstances that the mandate for Palestine and Mesopotamia was conferred upon and accepted by us, and that the mandate for Syria was conferred upon and accepted by France."[4]

At the same time that the outbreaks of violence began to escalate, the British government finally came to the conclusion that the costs of maintaining its control in Mesopotamia were excessive, and that a practical accommodation with Iraqi nationalism would pose no serious threat to British interests there. Wilson was to be relieved of his responsibilities and replaced by his predecessor, Sir Percy Cox, who was given explicit instructions to establish a new indigenous administration in the country that would defuse the resentment caused by the existing Anglo-Indian administration. On June 20, 1920, Wilson, acting under the government's instructions, issued a statement to the press indicating the change in policy direction. "H.M.'s Government having been entrusted with the Mandate for Iraq anticipate that the Mandate . . . contain provisions to facilitate the development of Iraq as a self-governing State until such time as it can stand by itself, when the Mandate will come to an end." The statement noted further that Cox would return to Baghdad in the autumn as the chief British representative to replace the military administration. "Sir Percy Cox will be authorized to call into being, as provisional bodies, a Council of State under an Arab President and a General Assembly representative of and freely elected by the populace of Iraq."[5]

The explosion of open revolt came on June 30, just at the time that the mobile Indian army units in Mesopotamia were being reduced in size and deployed over a vast area to minimize operating expenditures. At the time there was a total of some 34,000 British and Indian troops in the country that were available for active service. These were outnumbered by about three to one by the insurgents. Starting in the northwestern frontier region, small rebel forces began attacking, capturing, and massacring the troops of the isolated frontier garrisons. By August, the insurgency had spread to most of the country as some 30,000 Anglo-Indian reinforcements began to arrive to help in the pacification effort.

Cox arrived in Baghdad on October 11, 1920 and began organizing a new civil government. He established a temporary council of state under the leadership of the *naqib* (Muslim communal leader) of Baghdad, Abd al-Rahman, which was to function until a national assembly could be convened to enact an organic law for the country. In the meanwhile, domestic pressure mounted and it became a matter of some urgency for the British government to come up with a permanent solution that would dramatically reduce the costs, both human and financial, of the British presence in the Middle East.

In response to these pressures, the British concluded that it would be best that a native government be established to administer the country and that it be placed in the hands of an Arab ruler instead of a British high commissioner. A number of possible candidates for the position of constitutional monarch of the new state of Iraq, including Abdullah, who had already been given the nod by the Iraqi nationalists, and Ibn Saud, ruler of the Nejd in Arabia, were given consideration. However, Cox's clear preference was Feisal, who had just recently been evicted from Syria by the French.

Cox's predecessor, Wilson, who had a rather low opinion of Abdullah, had telegraphed the Foreign Office a compelling rationale for the choice of Feisal.

Feisal alone of all Arabian potentates has any idea of practical difficulties of running a civilised government on Arab lines. He can scarcely fail to realise that foreign assistance is vital to the continued existence of an Arab State. He realises the danger of relying on an Arab army. If we were to offer him the Amirate of Mesopotamia not only might we re-establish our position in the eyes of Arab world, but we might go far to wipe out accusation which could otherwise be made against us of bad faith both with Feisal and with people of this country, if H.M. Government eventually decides drastically to restrict its commitments in this country there would be better prospects of its being done with Feisal here than by any other possible arrangement.[6]

There were, however, two obstacles that had to be overcome before Feisal could be placed on the throne of Iraq. First, in an interview with his British friend Kinahan Cornwallis, that was instigated by Lord Curzon, Feisal refused to consider taking the position unless the British government unequivocally rejected his brother Abdullah and that he be the popular choice for it. He made it clear that his father, Sherif Hussein, was in favor of Abdullah becoming the ruler of Iraq and that he would not seek to gain another throne for himself, having lost that of Syria, at his brother's expense. Moreover, he did not wish to appear as a pawn of the British. The second problem was how the French would react to having a resentful Feisal ruling a country that bordered Syria.

The solution was to have Cox, as Cornwallis put it in his report of the meeting with Feisal, "quietly and unostentatiously to engineer the election for Feisal."[7] This would overcome Feisal's concerns, as it would demonstrate that he was the choice of the people of Iraq. It would also put the French in a position where they would have to accept the *fait accompli*, if there were no evidence that the British had rigged the affair. As the Foreign Office put it on January 9, 1921: "So far as French difficulty is concerned, procedure suggested seems calculated to place us in most favourable position possible. We could hardly be accused of promoting Feisal's candidature if his name was not even put forward until after Abdullah's claim had been considered and rejected by Iraq State."[8]

A few weeks later, on March 1, the government transferred all Middle Eastern affairs to the Colonial Office that now was under the leadership of Winston Churchill. He, in turn, almost immediately convened a meeting of all senior military and civilian officers in the region to discuss ways and means of reducing the burdens of British administration in the Middle East. The meeting was held in Cairo from March 12 to 22, 1921 and came up with a series of guidelines that set the tone for British policy in the region for decades to come. During this meeting Churchill dealt with Feisal's concerns about usurping the claim of his brother Abdullah to the Iraqi throne by finding an alternate opportunity for the latter in Trans-Jordan.

On June 14, Churchill announced that Britain favored Feisal's candidacy and would support him if he were to be elected king. The British then orchestrated Feisal's arrival in Baghdad two weeks later and arranged for his election by the Council of Ministers. Without any competing candidates, Cox having seen to it, Feisal was duly elected king on July 11. To give the election a façade of popular support, Cox asked the Ministry of the Interior to conduct a sort of referendum in which representatives of towns and communities might indicate their support for the resolution of the Council of Ministers declaring Feisal king of Iraq. It is noteworthy that the only ones that refused to play along with this charade were the Kurdish population of the Mosul district that adamantly opposed the linkage of part of the traditional territories of Kurdistan with Iraq in a unitary state. Cox formally installed Feisal as king of Iraq on August 23, 1921.

Notwithstanding the establishment of an autonomous Iraqi government, Britain still remained the mandatory power on behalf of the League of Nations. Accordingly, it was in Britain's interest to define the British-Iraqi relationship by a treaty that could be adopted by the council of the League as the official mandatory instrument. An Anglo-Iraqi treaty was signed on October 10, 1922. However, ratification of the treaty by the Iraqi constituent assembly proved to be problematic because the leaders of the new Iraqi government had in mind a rather different kind of relationship with the mandatory power than that envisioned by the British. In the Iraqi view, the treaty, which they wanted to take the place of the mandate, would have given the British an advisory role instead of the supervisory role contemplated by the mandate system. After protracted negotiations and a good deal of arm twisting by Cox, a treaty document acceptable to the British was finally ratified by the Iraqi constituent assembly on June 10, 1924, by a vote of 37 to 24 at a night session when only 69 of the 100 deputies were present. The council of the League of Nations subsequently adopted it on September 27 that same year.

The arrangement arrived at by the Anglo-Iraqi Treaty of 1922 was confusing at best, with neither side being able to express cogently the precise status of Iraq. Thus, the British high commissioner Sir Henry Dobbs reported to the Permanent Mandates Commission in 1926 that Iraq was self-governing with the assistance of a small group of advisers and inspectors. However, at the same time, he also asserted that he, as high commissioner, "had the right to advise the Government of Iraq in regard to the finances of the country and the right to insist that this advice should be accepted." Moreover, "Iraq could not claim the assistance of the British forces in the repression of disorders or invasions provoked by actions or by a policy entered upon against the advice of the British Government."[9] The reality was that, notwithstanding the trappings of independence accorded it under the Anglo-Iraqi Treaty for domestic purposes, and confirmed in the Iraqi constitution that came into force on March 21, 1925, Iraq remained a British mandatory territory for all practical purposes.

Pressure for a new treaty between Britain and Iraq arose out of the League of Nations decision in December 1925 to assign the former Turkish vilayet of Mosul to Iraq. The League grant was made on condition that Britain conclude a new treaty that would effectively prolong the mandate for 25 years, or until Iraq was admitted to membership in the League, whichever came first. Such admission would have registered international acceptance of Iraq's independence and sovereignty. Accordingly, a new treaty was signed on January 13, 1926 that extended it for the required period, but with the additional stipulation that the question of Iraq's eligibility for admission into the League be examined every four years beginning in 1928. The British government did not support Iraq's entry into the League in 1928, but soon gave strong indications that it would do so in 1932. On June 30, 1930, the British high commissioner, Sir Francis H. Humphrys, and the Iraqi prime minister, Nuri Pasha as-Said, signed a new treaty of alliance between Britain and Iraq, setting the stage for its independence and admission to the League in 1932.

The 1930 treaty annulled all previous agreements and recognized Iraq's full independence in both domestic and foreign affairs. However, the treaty also granted Britain the right to maintain two airbases in Iraq for the purpose of safeguarding the route to India for 25 years, the life of the treaty, and to maintain troops in Mosul and at Baghdad's airport for a period of five years.

Despite some anxiety about whether Britain would actually make good on its commitments, a concern caused by the half-year delay in bringing Iraq's application for membership before the Assembly of the League of Nations, Iraq was admitted as a sovereign state into the international community. On October 3, 1932, the mandate came to an end and the British high commissioner became the British ambassador.

Following independence, Anglo-Iraqi relations entered into a downward spiral, partly because of a desire by the fledgling state to flex its muscles and partly because of the unanticipated death of King Feisal in 1933. The inexperienced and irresponsible 21-year-old Ghazi succeeded him, but was unable to bring coherence to the political scene. The result was a fundamental split in the ruling oligarchy over the question of the British alliance. One faction headed by Nuri as-Said and other generals favored continued cooperation with Britain. Their opponents, led by Yasin al-Hashimi, Rashid al-Gailani, and others, constituted a larger group that were against the Anglo-Iraqi treaty, and it was this latter group that dominated the Iraqi political arena in the years immediately following the death of Faisal.

Things came to a head on October 29, 1936 when General Bekr Sidki, exasperated by the squabbling among the political factions, led a coup that overthrew the government of Yasin al-Hashimi and effectively forced the king to ask Hikmat Suleiman, an associate of Bekr Sidki, to form a new government. In fact, however, the military dictatorship of Bekr Sidki, who was assassinated on August 11, 1937, ruled the country.

Following the assassination, the government came under a moderate politician, Jamil al-Mafdai. However, the army continued to govern behind the scene and removed Jamil al-Mafdai in 1938, replacing him with Nuri as-Said, an outspoken supporter of the alliance with Britain. It is noteworthy that, although the British did not cherish the idea of working with what amounted to a military dictatorship, they did nothing to alter the internal situation in Iraq. It seems that they were actually quite pleased about the rapprochement with Turkey that took place under Bekr Sidki because it supported their own efforts to improve relations with Turkey in the likelihood of a general war in Europe.

Anti-British sentiment rose to the fore once again following the accidental death of King Ghazi on April 4, 1939, stimulated further by German and Italian propaganda. Since Ghazi's heir to the throne was his infant son Feisal II, a regency acceptable to the British was established under his maternal uncle Prince Abdul Ilah.

THE QUESTION OF MOSUL

One of the territorial issues that lingered on into the post-war period was the disposition of Mosul. The question of the status of the vilayet of Mosul in northern Iraq, which Britain seized in 1918, became a major issue between Britain and Turkey because of its strategic importance to both countries. For Britain, control of Mosul was seen as an important element in the defense of India against Russian encroachment. Mosul lies near the crossroads of three major land routes to India from Europe; the northern route from Moscow through Orenburg-Tashkent-Samarkand-Bokhara-Kabul-Peshawar; the central route from Moscow through Rostov-Baku-Teheran-Isfahan-Kerman-Quetta; and the southern route from London through Istanbul-Mosul-Baghdad-Isfahan or Kerman-Quetta. For Turkey, on the other hand, Mosul represented the point of intersection of the roads connecting all of southern Anatolia and was therefore considered essential to the security of that region.

The relatively high and impassable mountains north of Mosul permit it to serve as a natural defensive base. Turkish control of these mountains and the adjoining plains to the south, which represent the most fertile region of the country, would also give it effective strategic dominance over Iraq. Moreover, the districts of both Baghdad and Basra depend largely on waters deriving from Mosul for irrigation. From the British perspective, the mountains of Mosul provided a strategic window into Turkey, Iran, and Transcaucasia. It represented a line of defense protecting the route to India from assault from the north and would contribute greatly to Britain's control of the Persian Gulf, the mouth of the Shatt al-Arab, and the major port at Basra. In fact, the primary purpose of the Mesopotamian campaign in the war was to secure the Gulf against attack from the north, and this could only be accomplished by control of the strategic heights north of Mosul.

The negotiations over Mosul were destined for a stalemate. Turkey refused to go along with the British proposals, and it was clear that Britain had no intention whatever of returning any territory taken by its forces in Asia, especially one that contained large deposits of oil. Turkey was subsequently placed under enormous pressure when agreement on Mosul was tied to the readiness of the Allies to evacuate their forces from Istanbul, which they refused to do until the entire treaty was ratified. Britain and Turkey reached an agreement on Mosul on June 26, 1923 that provided for maintenance of the status quo in the territory, still under British occupation, which was to remain in effect while direct negotiations continued for another nine months. If these bilateral negotiations were unsuccessful, the issue was to be turned over to the council of the League of Nations for resolution. The negotiations between the two parties were inconclusive and the conference came to an end on June 5, 1924. Britain subsequently submitted the question of Mosul to the council of the League of Nations in August, which appointed a commission to report on conditions in the territory. It further stipulated that until the report was forthcoming, the status quo was to be maintained. However, a major dispute arose over what the status quo frontier was, and the League had to step in to avert the outbreak of an armed conflict over the matter. An extraordinary meeting of the council was convened in Brussels at the end of October 1924 and a provisional frontier line, the so-called Brussels line, was drawn.

Britain used all its influence to assure that the League's report on Mosul came to the conclusion that the territory south of the Brussels line should be awarded to Iraq. The League, however, also stipulated that the award to Iraq was contingent on the League mandate for Iraq remaining in force for an additional 25 years, and that Kurdish demands for autonomy be respected. The League finally resolved the status of Mosul on December 16, 1925 in favor of Britain, which was given a 25 year mandate over the territory.

Turkey effectively rejected the League's decision and entered into an alliance with the Soviet Union on December 17, 1925. The timing, however, was inopportune for Turkey, which was concerned about an attack by Italy at that time. As a result, Turkey yielded on the Mosul question and signed the Treaty of Ankara on June 5, 1926, which generally established the Brussels line as the Turko-Iraqi frontier.

THE KURDISH PROBLEM

The question of Mosul at the end of World War I also brought to the fore the problem of the Kurds, who were the dominant population of the former vilayet and neighboring areas in Turkey and Iran. The Kurds had made several attempts at establishing their independence in the nineteenth century, under the leadership of Badr Khan in 1843 and Sheikh Obaidullah in 1880. Following the Young Turk revolution in Turkey in 1908, the Kurds developed a nationalist movement in the modern sense of the term. Kurdish deputies in the Ottoman parliament were its spokesmen and nationalist clubs and newspapers began to spring up under the leadership of Sheikh Abdul Kader, a Turkish senator.

At the end of the war, a Kurdish government was established at Sulaimaniya in the northeastern part of the former vilayet under the leadership of Sheikh Mahmud Barzanji. At the outset, the Kurdish government briefly accepted a British protectorate as a political necessity in view of the Turkish position with regard to Mosul. However, for reasons that are not entirely clear, Sheikh Mahmud proclaimed Kurdish independence on May 20, 1919, and initiated a hopeless struggle against the British. He was captured on June 18 and was exiled to India. The Kurdish government was disbanded and a direct British administration, with appointed Kurdish officials, was established in its place.

A spokesman for the Kurds, Sherif Pasha, appeared at the Paris Peace Conference and made the Kurdish case for national independence before the Supreme Council. Great Britain, France, and Italy, specifically acknowledged the Kurdish claim in the Treaty of Sevres on August 10, 1920, the preamble of which recognized the autonomy or eventual independence of Kurdistan.

Unrest in the area, nurtured to some extent by Turkey, caused the British to recall Sheikh Mahmud from exile in September 1922 in the hope that he would be able to stabilize the situation. Sheikh Mahmud, however, was not satisfied with the subservient role carved out for him by the British and took matters into his own hands. In November, he proclaimed himself king of Kurdistan and tried to establish an independent state and government. In the meanwhile, it became evident that the Treaty of Sevres, which called for Kurdish independence, was not going to be ratified, and a new set of negotiations began at Lausanne. It was clear that the Turks were adamantly opposed to granting any form of autonomy to the Kurds in Turkey and that the idea of uniting the Kurds of Iraq and Turkey was a non-starter. This made the situation in Mosul more volatile than before, and the British sought to mollify the Kurds with opportunities for national development. The British and Iraqi governments issued a joint proclamation to this effect at the end of December 1922. "His Britannic Majesty's Government and the Government of the Kingdom of Iraq recognize the rights of the Kurds living within the boundaries of the Iraq to set up a Kurdish Government within these boundaries, and hope that the different Kurdish elements will, as soon as possible, arrive at an agreement between themselves as the form which they wish that Government should take, and the boundaries within which they wish it to extend."[10]

Sheikh Mahmud did not even bother to respond to this offer and began to organize an attack on the British, with Turkish support. He was subsequently driven out of Sulaimaniya in March 1923, but occupied it again for a year after the British troops withdrew. After Mosul was assigned to Iraq in 1925, Sheikh Mahmud continued to wage a guerilla war from the Persian frontier until he finally surrendered in the summer of 1927.

In contrast to Turkey, which attempted to assimilate the Kurds and thereby provoked a national insurrection in 1925, Iraq did not attempt to denationalize the Kurds. As the Iraqi premier put it to the parliament on January 21, 1926: "This country cannot survive, unless all the elements that make up the Iraqi State enjoy their rights. We shall concede their rights to the Kurds. Their officials shall be chosen from among themselves, their official language shall be their own language, and their children shall be taught in the schools in their mother tongue."[11] Nonetheless, these commitments were not really taken very seriously by subsequent Iraqi governments, particularly with regard to the use of the Kurdish language and the appointment of Kurdish officials. At the beginning of 1929, a number of Kurdish deputies put forth a scheme to create a special Kurdish administrative unit within Iraq, but their demand was rejected on the basis that it was separatist in principle.

When negotiations were underway for the Anglo-Iraqi Treaty of 1930, the Kurds became particularly alarmed that no provisions were made in the treaty safeguarding their position in Iraq or with regard to the various commitments previously made by Iraqi authorities. Under pressure from the League of Nations, Britain and Iraq drew up some safeguards and guarantees to meet the principle Kurdish concerns. However, once the text of the treaty was published, the Kurds sent repeated petitions for help to the League.

In September 1930, serious riots broke out in Sulaimaniya, and the following month Sheikh Mahmud appeared in Iraq once again, with a Kurdish force that he brought with him from Iran, and triggered a major insurrection that lasted from October 1930 to May 1931. He demanded a mandate for Kurdistan that would be administered by Britain. It took months of hard fighting by Iraqi forces, aided by the British air force, to subdue the Kurdish insurgents. Within a year, another rebellion broke out under the leadership of Sheikh Ahmed Barzanji. In March 1932, an Iraqi column was attacked and saved from annihilation only by the heavy intervention of the British air force, which not only attacked the Kurds but also dropped sorely needed supplies to the Iraqi forces. Continuing British attacks from the air ultimately forced Sheikh Ahmed to retreat across the Turkish frontier where he surrendered to the Turkish authorities.

NOTES

1. Lady Gertrude Bell, *Letters*, vol. 2, p. 219.

2. F.O. 371/4149/110528. Police report for week ending 31.5.19, para. 241.

3. Ghassan R. Atiyyah, *Iraq, 1908–1921: A Socio-Political Study*, p. 303.

4. *Parl. Debates*, H. of L., 5th S., Vol. XL (1920), p. 877 (cited by Philip W. Ireland, *Iraq: A Study in Political Development*, p. 263).

5. Sir Arnold Wilson, *Mesopotamia, 1917–1920: A Clash of Loyalties*, p. 263.

6. F.O. 371/5038/E 9252. Copy of a telegram from Civil Commissioner, Baghdad, to Foreign Office, dated July 31, 1920.

7. F.O. 371/6349/E583/100/93. Note of an interview with Feisal on January 7, 1921 by Cornwallis, dated January 8, 1921.

8. F.O. 371/6349/E557/100/93. From the Secretary of State for the Foreign Office to the High Commissioner, Mesopotamia, January 9, 1921.

9. League of Nations, *Permanent Mandates Commission*, Tenth Session (1926), p. 52.

10. *Report on Iraq Administration*, April, 1922–March, 1923, Colonial No. 4, 1924, cited by Hans Kohn, *Nationalism and Imperialism in the Hither East*, p. 226.

11. *Report submitted to the Council by the Commission Instituted by the Council Resolution of September 30, 1924.* League of Nations Document, C. 400, M. 147, 1925, vii, p. 76, cited by Hans Kohn, *Nationalism and Imperialism in the Hither East*, p. 227.

7

Transition in the Arabian Peninsula, 1910–36

British policy toward the Arabian Peninsula at the outset of the First World War was directed primarily toward obtaining allies among the indigenous rulers of the territory that would rise up against the Ottoman forces that were deployed in the area. The responsibilities for carrying out this policy were effectively divided between the Foreign Office and the India Office. The former was active in this regard in western Arabia and was particularly interested in protecting the Suez Canal and shipping in the Red Sea. The India Office, on the other hand, was primarily concerned with security of British interests in the Persian Gulf region. The efforts of the two governmental bureaucracies were not always coordinated and the commitments they made not always compatible.

The focus of British attention in the western part of the peninsula was on the vilayet of the Hejaz, which was garrisoned by some 20,000 Turkish troops. The key to achieving British aims there was Hussein ibn Ali, the sherif and emir of Mecca and effectively the indigenous ruler of the Hejaz. After extensive negotiations that included a number of promises that the British would later renege on, as well as substantial payments of hard currency, the Arab revolt against the Turks broke out in the Hejaz on June 10, 1916.

At the same time, the India Office focused its efforts on enlisting the support of Abd al-Aziz ibn Saud, the emir of Nejd in the northeast who was incrementally extending his control to the various independent tribal groupings and territories along the littoral of the Persian Gulf. Abd al-Aziz was also paid in hard currency, although at a much lower rate than his Hejazi counterpart. In his case, because he was disinclined to fight the Turks, the most the British were able to purchase was his neutrality.

Arnold J. Toynbee later described these arrangements and their utility in somewhat caustic terms. "Indeed, the officials of the India Office, had they been driven into a corner by infuriated British tax-payers, might have represented with some plausibility that in purchasing Ibn Sa'ud's benevolent neutrality at 5,000 pounds sterling a month they had made a better bargain than their colleagues at the Foreign Office who had contracted to pay 200,000 pounds a month of the tax-payer's money for Husayn's military cooperation."[1]

The fact that there was a history of bad blood between the two Arab chieftains was discounted as of little importance given British concerns with regard to prosecuting the war against the Turks in the Middle East. The hostility between Hussein and Abd al-Aziz dated back to 1910, when the former, recently appointed emir of Mecca by the Ottoman sultan, undertook an expedition on the latter's behalf to impose Ottoman influence in the inland desert region. In the course of this foray, which led them to the frontier of Nejd, Hussein's forces encountered a small Saudi force led by Abd al-Aziz's brother Saad. Saad was taken captive and a demand for his ransom was made to Abd al-Aziz. Without any negotiating leverage, Abd al-Aziz was compelled to agree to pay a ransom to Hussein and to recognize Ottoman sovereignty over his territory. Once Saad was released, however, Abd al-Aziz reneged on his agreement, claiming that it had been concluded under duress.

Although contact between the British and Abd al-Aziz began in 1911 with the arrival in Riyadh of Captain W.I. Shakespear, a representative of the Indian government, nothing of any consequence happened until 1913 because all of the British holdings in the Persian Gulf were essentially surrounded by the Turks. In February 1913, however, a Saudi force under Feisal ad-Duwish attacked the Turks in the coastal province of al-Hasa and drove them out. By April, it seized Uqair, Qatif, Kut, and Hofuf, bringing nearly a half-century of Turkish occupation to an end. This brought the Saudis to the frontiers of Kuwait and the coastal sheikdoms that were under British protection. Then, when Turkey entered the war on the side of Germany in November 1914, Nejd and its Saudi rulers took on a new strategic importance, posing a potential threat to the Gulf, Mesopotamia, and the Hejaz.

In January 1915, at the time when Hussein was negotiating with the British regarding an Arab uprising, there was an exchange of correspondence between Abdullah, son of Hussein, and Abd al-Aziz in which the latter was asked to clarify his position with regard to the Turks and the British. Since Abd al-Aziz was at the time similarly negotiating for a treaty with the British, he was reluctant to make any such clarification and urged Abdullah to show similar restraint. Abdullah's response was to lead a force into western Nejd, which Abd al-Aziz could not interpret as anything other than a hostile act similar to that of 1910, but regarding which he was not in a position to do anything. At the time, Abd al-Aziz was deeply engaged in ongoing conflicts with rebellious tribes, particularly the Ajman and others such as the Rashidi, who rejected his claims of supremacy and were being supplied with arms by the Turks.

Abd al-Aziz wanted and needed a treaty with the British as much as the British wanted to enlist him on their side against the Turks. The negotiations lasted for about a year and culminated with the signing of the Anglo-Saudi Treaty on December 26, 1915. Under the terms of the pact, signed by Abd al-Aziz and Sir Percy Cox, representing the government of India, Britain recognized Abd al-Aziz as the independent ruler and absolute chief of the tribes of Nejd, al Hasa, Qatif, and Jubail, and their territories and ports on the Persian Gulf. Britain also undertook to defend Abd al-Aziz against any foreign power, after due consultation. In return, the treaty required that any successor to Abd al-Aziz "shall not be a person antagonistic to the British Government in any respect." Abd al-Aziz also agreed not to enter into "any correspondence, agreement, or treaty, with any Foreign Nation or Power." Finally, Abd al-Aziz was precluded from ceding, selling, leasing, or granting concessions to any part of his territories to any foreign power or its subjects "without the consent of the British Government."[2]

With the desired treaty in hand, and notwithstanding his antipathy toward the Hashemites, as an accommodation to the British, in 1916 Abd al-Aziz was prepared to align himself with Hussein. However, he first wanted assurances from Hussein that his sovereignty would be respected, something that Hussein dismissed out of hand and replied to in an insulting manner. Hussein's response was quite understandable in view of the fact that he was planning to declare himself King of the Arab Lands (*Malik al-bilad al-arabiya*), something he did on November 2, 1916 at a ceremony in the Grand Mosque at Mecca. Needless to say, this act would ensure him enemies in the Arab world, perhaps the most notable of which would be Abd al-Aziz. In fact, the British were so concerned about the fallout from Hussein's announcement that, presumably under their influence, only Russia among the members of the Entente accepted his new title. On January 3, 1917, Britain, France, and Italy recognized Hussein only as king of the Hejaz.

In any case, by September 1916, when Abd al-Aziz finally defeated the Ajman with the help of British loans and arms, he made it clear to Cox that he no longer had any wish to align himself with Hussein. An agreement was eventually reached that the most useful role for Abd al-Aziz in the war against the Turks would be for him to concentrate on reducing the threat from the Rashidis, with whom he had reached an earlier accommodation. The latter were allied with the Turks and were in a position to menace the flank of the British advance in Mesopotamia from Basra to Baghdad. However, this was probably an unrealistic expectation. "As can be seen from the

British military handbook for 1916 on Arabia there was more than a hint of suspicion that Abd al-Aziz was not only not taking an active part on the Allied side but that he was turning a blind eye to the smuggling of camels and the supplies they bore to the Rashidis in Ha'il and thence to the Turks in Damascus."[3] Indeed, he appears to have been in continuing contact with Djemal Pasha in Damascus, to whom he explained his alignment with the British as a consequence of their naval stranglehold on the Persian Gulf that made it necessary for him to placate them in such a manner.

It took until September 1918 before Abd al-Aziz actually agreed to march on Ha'il and the Rashidis. The expedition, however, turned into something of a farce when his forces captured some 2,000 camels and large numbers of sheep, and then decided it was time to go home because they really didn't have any quarrel with the Rashidis. As Abd al-Aziz frankly told his British adviser, Henry St. John Philby, "Remember, we are fighting Ibn Rashid for your sake only, for we have no unsatisfied claims upon him.... The real enemy of Nejd, high and low, is the Sherif [i.e., Hussein]."[4]

By that time, however, the British had come to the conclusion that there was no longer any military need for an active Saudi role against the Turks in central Arabia. The view of the Arab Bureau, as expressed by D.G. Hogarth to Philby in Jeddah was that it better served British interests to focus its support on Hussein. "Now, ibn Saud is human after all and what will happen when he ... dies? The same old anarchy again! Whereas, if and when the Turks go, the Sherifian family alone has the religious and political prestige needed ... for building something permanent in Arabia to fit the country into the picture of the modern world. Anyway, we are committed to the Sherifian cause and we can't afford to upset things by encouraging ibn Saud's pretensions."[5] As a result, Philby had to inform Abd al-Aziz that he would not receive the 1,000 rifles and ammunition that had been promised to him. Abd al-Aziz blamed the change in British position on Hussein. "It is the Sherif who is responsible for this blow at me—he has utterly deceived the rulers of Egypt and I will attack him if, to humour him, your Government persists in treating me so ill."[6]

Abd al-Aziz was as good as his word, and a series of confrontations took place in 1918 between Hussein's and Abd al-Aziz's forces over the oasis of Khorma in the undefined borderlands east of Taif. This oasis had previously been part of Hussein's domain, but it changed sides after Abdullah foolishly insulted its ruler, Khalid ibn Luwai. Hussein's forces, under Hammad ibn Zaid, tried three times to dislodge the Saudis and were decisively defeated. In March 1919, Lord Curzon convened an interdepartmental conference in London to determine what, if anything, the British ought to do about the deteriorating security situation in the peninsula. Under the considerable influence of the Cairo-based Arab Bureau, it was concluded that in an all-out struggle between the Saudis and the Hashemites, the latter would prevail because of their superior arms and training. Philby, who had a more realistic sense of the situation argued against this position but to no avail. Curzon stated flatly, "Our policy is a Hussein policy and Hussein must receive our support as long as such support is not likely to involve us in any military adventures in the deserts of Arabia."[7]

Encouraged by the support tendered by the British, and against the advice of his prime minister, Ibrahim Hakki Pasha, Hussein launched a major expedition under the leadership of Abdullah to retake Khorma. A Hashemite force of some 5,000 men arrived on the scene in May 1919, with Abdullah announcing that his mission was not confined to Turaba alone and that he planned to celebrate the forthcoming feast of *Id al-Adha* in the heart of the Nejd. Abd al-Aziz responded to this taunt forcefully. A Saudi force soon converged on the sleeping Hashemite camp on the night of May 25 and killed everyone except a few who managed to escape including Abdullah, who got away still dressed in his night clothes.

The destruction of Abdullah's eastern army dealt a severe blow to Hussein, who was left only with the troops at Medina under command of his son Ali. The remainder of the Hashemite forces had gone to Syria with Feisal. Nonetheless, Abd al-Aziz was not yet in a position to undertake a direct attack against Hussein and the conquest of the Hejaz. For one thing, the British seemed to be too closely committed to the Hashemites, and it was not clear how they would react if Hussein were directly challenged at this point. Another concern was that the Muslim world might not yet be ready to accept ultra-conservative Wahhabi control of the holy cities. It appears that Abd al-Aziz may have been made aware of Lawrence's earlier proposal concerning what to do in the event that he should conquer the Hejaz. "If he abandons the Wahhabi creed, we will not do too badly. If he remains a Wahhabi, we will send the Moslem part of the Indian Army to recover Mecca and break the Wahhabi movement."[8]

In any case, Abd al-Aziz still had other battles to fight for control of the peninsula before attacking the Hejaz. A secret anti-Saudi alliance had been forged between the Hashemites and the Rashidis, and the ruling family of Kuwait. In 1919 and 1920, there were skirmishes along the Kuwaiti frontier in the north that were resolved only when it became clear that the British were preparing to come to Kuwait's defense. Similar clashes took place during the period of the Iraqi revolt from July to December 1920 along the newly imposed borders between Iraq and Nejd, until British deterrence proved effective in bringing them to a halt. Hussein also stirred up the Ajman to revolt against Saudi suzerainty. In the southwest, Hussein sought support against Abd al-Aziz from the semi-independent Idrisis who had ruled the coastal plain of Asir since the middle of the nineteenth century. With the departure of the Turks, the Hashemites sought to establish their control of the region. The Saudis intervened to prevent this and the Idrisis quickly acknowledged Abd al-Aziz's suzerainty. From Abd al-Aziz's perspective, Nejd was under threat from a northern arc of

Hashemite kingdoms stretching from the Hejaz to Transjordan to Syria, and when the Hashemites were evicted from Syria, to Iraq. It was essential for his security to eliminate, or at least to mitigate this threat.

By July 1921, the Saudis had defeated the last of the Rashidi rulers, Muhammad ibn Talal, and had conquered Ha'il and the Jebel Shammar, and had proclaimed the new Sultanate of Nejd and Its Dependencies, with its borders abutting the British mandates to the north. During the struggle for Shammar, some of the tribes of the area fled north to Iraq, where some found refuge among the Amarat Anizah. This created a serious problem, because the desert traditionally knows nothing of international frontiers or boundaries. Because the desert tribes often shifted position in search of new wells and pasture or in annual migrations, the issue was the loyalty of vassal tribes to their leader. Not yet attuned to the implications of international borders, which tended to restrict his suzerainty over the tribes that owed him fealty, Abd al-Aziz demanded not only the return of the Shammar tribes but also the acknowledgement by the Amarat Anizah of his suzerainty.

With new confidence after their victory in Jebel Shammar, the Saudis struck both north and south, taking the Hejazi town of Khaibar as well as the two fertile mountainous areas of Ghamid and Zahran. In July 1921, Saudi forces captured Jauf in the Wadi Sirhan, giving them access along the natural corridor formed by the wadi into the heart of Transjordan. In August, Saudi elements were raiding within fifteen miles of Amman, and along the Iraqi frontier. The raids into Iraq and Transjordan precipitated a violent British reaction. In November 1921, the Royal Air Force pursued and caught up with a band of some 1,500 raiders and annihilated them, only eight returning to Nejd. This taught Abd al-Aziz a lesson that he remembered in the years that followed.

The British concluded that it was now essential to resolve the situation on the borders of the mandated territories, especially since they were seriously considering building a strategic railway from the Persian Gulf to the Mediterranean that passed through the disputed territories. In December 1921, a conference of representatives of Nejd, Kuwait, and Iraq was convened to resolve the border issues between the three. The conference produced a series of agreements that were incorporated into the Treaty of Muhammara that was signed on May 5, 1922. Under the treaty, the Shammar tribes were recognized as belonging to Nejd, while the Muntafik, Dhafir, and Amarat tribes were assigned to Iraq. Abd al-Aziz, however, refused to ratify the treaty because he claimed that his representatives had erred in assigning certain of his tribal areas to King Feisal. He requested that the matter be reconsidered.

In response, Sir Percy Cox, now high commissioner in Iraq, convened a conference in November 1922 at the port of Uqair that was attended by Abd al-Aziz and representatives of Kuwait and Iraq. Cox, representing the might of the British Empire, made some fairly arbitrary decisions and re-drew the map of the region in dispute. He drew a line on a map of Arabia from the Persian Gulf west to Jebel Anaizan, close to the Transjordan fron-tier, effectively awarding to Iraq a large chunk of territory claimed by Nejd. To compensate Abd al-Aziz, he took some two-thirds of the territory of Ku-wait and gave it to Abd al-Aziz. Then, south and west of Kuwait, he carved out two zones that were declared to be neutral between the parties, the Ku-wait Neutral Zone and the Iraq Neutral Zone. The territories of these zones were coveted by all of the parties because of the expectation that they con-tained valuable oil deposits. Under Cox's arrangement, the parties would have a half-share of each. These new arrangements were made part of the Treaty of Muhammara.

The treaty held generally, although there continued to be some cross-border raids, the most serious of which was an attack on the Iraqi tribes in March 1924 that left 186 people dead and over 26,000 sheep and other livestock seized. Steps were subsequently taken to more clearly de-fine the Nejd-Iraqi frontier, and a treaty to this effect was concluded be-tween Abd al-Aziz and Sir Gilbert Clayton on November 1, 1925. A court was established to assess and affix blame for any future border infractions, which were primarily predatory incursions into Nejd by tribes from across the border. A serious frontier dispute between Nejd and Iraq broke out in the fall of 1927 over the Iraqi construction of two fortified police posts be-tween 75 and 90 miles north of the frontier. Nejd claimed that this violated Article 3 of the Uqair Protocol which prohibited construction of fortifica-tions near the frontier, Iraq claiming that the forts were well beyond what could reasonably be construed as being near the frontier. This dispute dragged on until February 1930, and had repercussions that seriously jeop-ardized peace in the border area.

In February 1928, tribes from Nejd attacked tribes in Iraq and Kuwait, and precipitated British intervention. British aircraft bombarded the headquar-ters of the attacking tribes some 130 miles south of the neutral zone, which generated exaggerated rumors of an impending holy war of all the Nejd tribes against Iraq, Transjordan, and Kuwait. New attempts to resolve the frontier problem were pursued by Clayton when he became high commis-sioner for Iraq in 1929. At the same time, however, the three tribes responsi-ble for the incursions into Iraq repudiated Abd al-Aziz's suzerainty. It took him until January 1930 to subdue the rebellious tribes, following which he met with King Feisal aboard a British warship in the Persian Gulf on Febru-ary 23 and concluded a treaty of friendship between Iraq and Nejd.

CONQUEST OF THE HEJAZ

The 1922 Uqair Conference had been reasonably successful in reaching a *modus vivendi*, with the cooperation of Feisal against the wishes of Hussein, on the unresolved issues between Nejd and Iraq. A comparable attempt to resolve the issues between Abd al-Aziz and the Hashemites with regard to Transjordan and the Hejaz took place at a conference held in Kuwait in December 1923. The effort foundered, however, primarily because of Hussein's intransigence. He appears to have been convinced that the British were unqualifiedly bound to support him. As a practical matter, this left the question of relations between Nejd and Hejaz to be settled on the battlefield, with the British later aligning themselves with the winner.

During this same turbulent period in the peninsula, Hussein seems to have focused all of his attention to trying to get the British to make good on their promises, real and implicit, regarding the disposition of the Arab lands of the former Ottoman Empire. For their part, the British were anxious to sign a treaty with him that would recognize their special interests in the region, particularly Palestine where a serious uprising, evidently encouraged and supported by Hussein, took place in 1920. In July 1921, T.E. Lawrence was sent to negotiate such a treaty. The British thought that with one of Hussein's sons on the throne in Iraq and another in control of Transjordan, Hussein could be brought to see that by his settling for Hejaz, the Hashemites would in effect dominate most of the Arab lands. To give him further encouragement, the British also offered him an annual subsidy of 100,000 pounds and a statement that Britain would protect the interests of Hejaz.

Hussein, however, was unyielding and continued to demand that Palestine be part of the Arab realm. Lawrence tried to reason with him, pointing out that a treaty with Britain might very well be the salvation of his kingdom. After all, he argued, without such a treaty, how would Hussein protect himself from Abd al-Aziz given that his army had been destroyed at Turaba in 1919. Hussein remained intransigent and the negotiations dragged on through 1923 without success. At this point, it seemed clear that Hussein was either terribly misinformed about developments in the region or delusional. The British agent at Jeddah wrote in April 1923: "His majesty believes that he is to be recognized forthwith as the head of a state comprising Palestine, Transjordan, Iraq and the Hejaz . . . to ensure the speedy formation of a United States of Arabia, within which each ruler is to keep his present territories and titles and to send a representative to the seat of central government (not necessarily Mecca) to represent local interests in the common Arabian Ministry of Foreign Affairs."[9]

Hussein's failure to agree to the treaty ultimately destroyed any hope he may have had of resisting the Saudi advances. His sons Abdullah, Ali, and Feisal understood this but they were unable to influence their father on this issue. He simply failed to grasp that Hejaz was no longer a significant player in the post-World War I Middle East. Lawrence's forewarnings to Hussein became realities in March 1924, when Hussein, evidently indulging in a megalomania that was quite incommensurate with his actual circumstances took a step that was the proverbial straw that broke the camel's back, and effectively sealed his fate.

As one of the steps undertaken by Kemal Ataturk in his radical modernization of Turkey, the caliphate, still held by the successor of the last sultan, was abolished on March 3, 1924. Hussein viewed this as the opportunity he had long awaited to restore the caliphate to the Arabs. The idea of a Hashemite Arab Caliphate was initially broached by the British during the negotiations over a prospective Arab revolt against the Turks, and evidently had great appeal for Hussein. However, he realized that it would be counterproductive to lay claim to the position while the Ottomans held it. Ataturk's action opened the door for him and, with the encouragement and active support of his son Abdullah, he launched a hurried campaign for recognition of his assumption of the position. Cables were sent from Amman to the *ulema* in most Muslim countries seeking their approval. Favorable responses came from Damascus and Baghdad, but the largest Muslim countries, India and Egypt, were taken aback by the proposal. Other countries did not even bother to respond. Notwithstanding the tepid response, on March 6, Hussein announced that he had assumed the caliphate.

The most critical reaction took place in India, where it was widely believed that Hussein would not have dared to do such a thing without British permission, and that the whole thing was a British plot to place their protégé atop the Muslim pyramid. Britain, always sensitive to their role as rulers of a country with the world's largest Muslim population, reacted by refusing to accord recognition to Hussein's self-appointment. To make matters worse, they withdrew the subsidy that they had continued to provide to Hussein, seriously undermining his ability to maintain any semblance of a government. This was seen on the other side of the peninsula as a sign that Britain would no longer come to Hussein's aid if he were to be threatened by his enemies within Arabia. His foolhardy self-appointment as caliph, coupled with Britain's evident turning of its back on him, gave the Saudis and their Wahhabi followers the spur to finally rid the peninsula of the Hashemites in general and Hussein in particular.

To ensure support for the forthcoming struggle, a conference of the tribes loyal to the Saudis was convened in Riyadh in June. The sheikhs and the *ulema*, still smarting from their exclusion by the Hashemites for the previous five years from participation in the annual pilgrimage to Mecca, concurred that the time had arrived to take strong action. However, having witnessed British policy reversals before, Abd al-Aziz was leery about a full-scale attack on Mecca. For one thing, he was uncertain about what the British might do. For another, he was not sure how well his desert troops would fare in a contest in the mountains of Hejaz. It was decided to mount an assault against the Hejazi summer capital at Taif first, to put great pressure on Hussein and perhaps force him into serious negotiations, as well as to see how the British reacted.

Saudi forces began the conquest of Taif on September 1, 1924 with an assault on one of the fortresses on the town's perimeter. The place went into a panic, especially after the Hashemite forces closed the gates of the town, not permitting anyone to leave. At the same time, the defending forces under Ali moved away from Taif to a more strategic position on the road to Mecca. Feeling abandoned, an agreement was worked out with the Saudis to surrender the town, and the gates were opened to them on September 5. However, upon entering Taif, some shots were directed toward the Saudi forces, triggering a massacre of some 300 residents. News of what took place in Taif caused a panic in Mecca, leading to an exodus of more than half the city's population to the walled seaport at Jeddah. Hussein then appealed to the British for help, but they refused to be drawn into the conflict and simply ignored his request for aircraft with which to bomb the Saudi forces.

The British found themselves entreated by an array of Hejazi notables pleading for them to establish a protectorate over the Hejaz, and thereby forestall the Saudis from taking the country. Another group, including the mayor and the military governor of Jeddah indicated that they would be supportive of a British mandate in the Hejaz, just as there was in both Transjordan and Iraq. However, the British rejected these suggestions out of hand. Their primary concern was that any attempt to impose non-Muslim rule over the holy cities in the Hejaz would have unacceptable repercussions in India. Any doubt about this was resolved by a cable sent on behalf of the Caliphate Committee of India to *The Times*, which stated, "we warn the British Government to desist from anything having the remotest semblance of such an attempt."[10] The British abandoned Hussein to his fate.

Under pressure from the Hejazi notables, Hussein reluctantly agreed to abdicate in favor of Ali, who became king of a tottering and bankrupt Hejaz on October 4, 1924. However, any expectations that the British would come to the aid of the new Hashemite ruler were soon to be quashed. Ali's representative in London was instructed to sign the Anglo-Hejazi Treaty that Hussein had refused to do earlier. But it was too late. He was told by the British that "the Foreign Office considers it desirable to wait a little before undertaking obligations to a *prince* who may not be in a position to give effect to his side of the agreement."[11]

Without sufficient forces to hold defenseless Mecca against the Saudis, Ali withdrew from the city in face of the Saudi advance, which reached Mecca on October 16, and established his government in Jeddah. However, he soon received a letter from Abd al-Aziz informing him that the change of regime would make no difference, and that there could not be peace in the peninsula as long as any Hashemite ruled in Hejaz. Ali's defense minister, Tahsin Pasha, ultimately convinced him that in a conventional conflict, the Hejazi army, with its superior equipment and training would prevail over the Nejdis. Ali's judgment in this regard was poor, but it seemed to be valid because the Saudi forces did not move beyond Mecca. What Ali didn't know was that the temporary halt had been ordered by Abd al-Aziz because of his fear of retaliation by the European powers if any of their subjects in Jeddah were harmed in the course of the war with the Hashemites.

The siege of Jeddah finally began on December 6, 1924 and lasted for a year, ending with Ali's surrender on December 17, 1925, Abd al-Aziz having agreed to allow the British to carry him into exile in Iraq three days later. For internal political reasons, primarily to satisfy those who strongly wished to retain the independent identity of Hejaz, Abd al-Aziz accepted the recommendation of the political leaders in Jeddah to establish a dual monarchy under which the sultan of Nejd also became the king of Hejaz. Accordingly, on January 8, 1926, Abdul Aziz ibn Saud became the king of Hejaz and sultan of Nejd and Its Dependencies. That same year a Saudi protectorate was established over Asir, by invitation of the incumbent Idrisi ruler who sought thereby to protect his territory from encroachment by Imam Yahya of Yemen. Asir and Hejaz together added about 250,000 square miles of territory to Abd al-Aziz's realm, making him the ruler of a united Arabia stretching from the Red Sea to the Persian Gulf, that he would rename the Kingdom of Saudi Arabia in 1932. However, his enormous realm was virtually completely encircled by either the sea or by political entities protected by the British, whose power Abd al-Aziz respected and would not challenge.

Saudi rule in Asir did not go uncontested, however, and a rebellion broke out in 1933. Asir's ruler, Hassan al-Idrisi fled to Yemen and carried out a number of cross-border raids, apparently with Imam Yahya's complicity. This led to a Saudi declaration of war in March 1934 and an invasion of Yemen. The Yemeni forces were defeated handily and the Imam sued for peace. Abd al-Aziz, in a treaty signed on June 23, 1934, agreed to a restoration of the status quo ante, and made no other demands for territorial concessions, a move which led to stability in the border region.

A treaty of non-aggression and brotherhood that was concluded on April 2, 1936 ostensibly resolved the outstanding differences with Iraq. Yemen joined the pact the following year.

NOTES

1. Arnold J. Toynbee, *Survey of International Affairs, 1925*, vol. 1, p. 283.
2. J.C. Hurewitz, *Diplomacy in the Near and Middle East: A Documentary Record: 1914–1956*, vol. 2, pp. 17–18.
3. Leslie McLoughlin, *Ibn Saud: Founder of a Kingdom*, p. 50.
4. Ibid., p. 60.
5. H. St. John B. Philby, *Arabian Days*, p. 157.
6. McLoughlin, *Ibn Saud*, p. 61.
7. Philby, *Arabia*, p. 268.

8. FO 608/80 to Col. A.T. Wilson, cited by Randall Baker, *King Husain and the Kingdom of Hejaz*, p. 197.

9. Randall Baker, *King Husain and the Kingdom of Hejaz*, p. 170.

10. *The Times*, October 4, 1924

11. *The Times*, October 16, 1924.

8

The British Protectorate in Egypt, 1914–38

Although the British had been in de facto control of Egypt since 1882, at the outset of World War I the country was still under de jure Ottoman suzerainty. Under pressure from the British Agency, the Egyptian Council of Ministers issued a virtual declaration of war against Germany on August 5, 1914, notwithstanding that Turkey, which was theoretically responsible for Egyptian foreign affairs, was still neutral. The British army and navy were granted belligerency rights on Egyptian territory, including its ports. German ships were declared to be enemy vessels and all forms of collaboration with German citizens and resident aliens were outlawed. On August 13, the same restrictions were imposed on Austrian and Hungarian shipping and citizens.

After Turkey entered the war on the side of Germany on November 5, the British commander in Egypt, Lieutenant General Sir John Maxwell announced the following day: "Great Britain is now fighting both to protect the rights and liberties of Egypt, which were originally won upon the battlefield by Mehemet Ali."[1] On November 7, Maxwell issued a proclamation declaring Turkey an enemy country, subject to the August 5 declaration of belligerency against Germany. In effect, the British had Egypt declare war against its nominal suzerain, thereby repudiating its former relationship with Istanbul.

Britain considered formally annexing Egypt, but was dissuaded from doing so because, from the standpoint of international law, Egypt was legally enemy territory, and under the Hague Convention of 1907, enemy territory could not be annexed by a belligerent during hostilities. Instead, it decided to establish a protectorate over the country, which went into effect on December 18, 1914. That same date, the khedive of Egypt, Abbas II, was deposed and the throne was offered to Prince Hussein Kamil, with the more exalted title of sultan to reflect the severance of the relationship to the Ottoman throne. As far as Lord Cromer, one of the original architects of British policy with regard to Egypt, was concerned, Egypt had finally become part of the British Empire. He wrote in 1915, "After hanging in the balance for a period of 33 years the political destiny of Egypt has at last been definitely settled. The country has been incorporated in the British Empire. No other solution was possible."[2]

The establishment of the protectorate had an unanticipated effect on the nationalist movement in Egypt, giving it new direction and focus. Until the very last moment of Ottoman suzerainty, the nationalist leaders "were unable to conceive of an independent Egypt completely detached from the Ottoman Empire."[3] The nationalist movement now shed its pan-Islamic orientation, enabling it to gain non-Muslim adherents, and began to work for the complete independence of Egypt.

Egyptian nationalists began to actively oppose the protectorate, and two unsuccessful attempts on the life of the new sultan were made in April and July 1915. The British hounded the nationalists, arresting many and exiling some. As one writer put it, "So heavy was the hand of military authority and so long the arm of their secret service, that prisons were soon full of political suspects."[4] In general, however, the Egyptians were fairly complacent about the change in political status, their passivity undoubtedly conditioned in part by the imposition of martial law in the country in November 1914, accompanied by press censorship and the prohibition of public meetings.

Nonetheless, resentment of the British mounted substantially during the war years as the Egyptian economy and populace were drawn into support of the war, in which they had little stake and less interest. Both people and animals were requisitioned for service in the Labour Corps, and about 100,000 men were aggressively recruited into the Camel Transport Corps in 1917. Of the latter some 23,000 were sent to serve in France. Moreover, the price of cotton had more than doubled between 1916 and 1919, but only a few Egyptians benefited from the trade in the commodity. Landowners ignored government restrictions and switched to planting cotton instead of wheat. As a result of this, and the general unavailability of food imports from abroad because of the shortage of shipping, food became scarce and expensive. All this was grist for the nationalist mill.

The British high commissioner in Egypt, Sir Reginald Wingate, sensitive to the mounting discontent, kept the Foreign Office informed of what was happening in the country. He emphasized "the need to define the meaning of the Protectorate, and the unanimous wish on the part of all Egyptians from the Sultan to fellah for a return to the autonomy promised since 1883."[5] His views were discounted.

Sultan Hussein died on November 9, 1917, and the sultanate was offered by the British to his brother Ahmad Fuad, after Hussein's son Kamal ad-Din declined the position. To Britain's surprise, Fuad was not as compliant as expected and, when he was denied the ability to change some of his ministers, the sultan and his government began to lend support to the nationalists. Following the armistice in 1918, the latter began to agitate actively for the realization of Egyptian national aspirations.

The acknowledged leader of the nationalists was Saad Zaghlul, a former minister of education and later of justice. He approached Wingate with a request that they be allowed to send a delegation (*Wafd*) to London to negotiate Egypt's future directly with the government. Their plan was to go from London to the Peace Conference in Paris to table their demands for independence. The request was rejected. Then, seeking to outflank his nationalist opposition, the Egyptian prime minister Hussein Rushdi Pasha requested that he be allowed to go to London to confer with the British authorities prior to the opening of the peace conference. His request was rejected as well, and he subsequently resigned along with his entire cabinet on March 1, 1919.

In the meanwhile, on December 6, 1918 Zaghlul sent a memorandum to the representatives of the Great Powers demanding Egypt's independence. At the same time, he indicated a willingness to continue to respect the Capitulations that were still in effect, to arrange for the neutrality of the Suez Canal, and to accept foreign control of Egypt's international debt. He similarly addressed an appeal to President Woodrow Wilson asking for the latter's help in arranging for the Egyptian delegation to attend the Peace Conference. It was at this time, however, that the nationalist initiative was sidetracked by internal Egyptian politics. Zaghlul had become too popular and his group, the Wafd, too powerful as far as the sultan was concerned. Fuad began to see him as a threat to his own position, and gave his support to the British. On March 8, 1919, Zaghlul and three associates in the Wafd were deported to Malta.

The following day, a series of demonstrations began with continually broadened participation from students to lawyers and then to strikes by railway workers that brought transportation to a standstill, isolating Cairo from the rest of the country. British military personnel became subject to frequent attacks, and much public property was destroyed. The British response was vigorous. Suspicious gatherings were attacked from the air and armored cars fired on any suspicious groups in the vicinity of railways and major roads. Order was restored in the Delta region within a few days. However, it took about a month to pacify Upper Egypt, where the insurrection was the most formidable. Special military tribunals were set up to try the principal offenders in the rioting. More than 2,300 cases were heard and some 1,600 persons were convicted. Of these, 102 were sentenced to death, 55 of these sentences being commuted later by the high commissioner.

British Prime Minister Lloyd George, upset about the unrest there, decided to recall Wingate and to send General Allenby back to Egypt as a "special high commissioner," which meant, in effect, to become the country's dictator. His specific instructions were "to exercise supreme authority in all matters military and civil, to take all measures necessary and expedient to restore law and order, and to administrate in all matters as required by the necessity of maintaining the King's protectorate over Egypt on a secure and equitable basis."[6] To the surprise of all but a few, Allenby seemed to actually believe in the principle of self-determination and proceeded to attempt to mollify the nationalists, hoping thereby to obtain their cooperation. On April 7, Allenby announced the release of Zaghlul from his confinement in Malta. Zaghlul and his colleagues, however, did not return to Egypt but headed for Paris and the Peace Conference. Lord Curzon then denounced Zaghlul in Parliament as irresponsible and ruled out any negotiations with him. To restore order in Egypt, Allenby imposed martial law in the country.

The granting of true independence to Egypt was not a serious consideration at the time. The existence of a British military base in Egypt at the outset of the recent war was instrumental in preventing a Turkish seizure of the Suez Canal. Geostrategically, Egypt was not only on the route to India but was also the key to Africa, where Britain had just dramatically enlarged its holdings as a result of the dismantling of Germany's East African Empire. Nobody of any consequence in the British government was prepared to abandon British control of this geopolitically valuable asset. At best, they might consider conditional self-government adorned in the trappings of political independence.

In Paris, Zaghlul and the Wafd delegation met with great disappointment. They not only were denied a hearing at the Peace Conference, they were flabbergasted by President Wilson's recognition of the British protectorate on April 23, 1919, considering his earlier public statements advocating the principle of national self-determination. It appeared at first that the Egyptian nationalist cause was lost. However, Zaghlul and the Wafd remained determined to continue the struggle for Egypt's independence.

Continuing pressure by the Wafd, and growing support for their efforts coupled with the British desire to bring an end to the state of siege in the country, caused the British government to send a commission of inquiry under Lord Milner to Egypt. However, the mission was to be predicated on the assumption that doing away with the protectorate was not on the table. Lord Balfour had made this quite clear to the House of Commons on November 17. "The question of Egypt, the question of the Sudan, and the question of the Canal, form an organic and indissoluble whole, and that neither in Egypt, nor in the Sudan, nor in connection with Egypt, is England going to give up any of her responsibilities. British supremacy exists, British supremacy is going to be maintained."[7]

The Milner Mission arrived in Egypt in December 1919 and left the country in March 1920, submitting its report in December of that year. The report, which was finally published in February 1921, recommended that a settlement should not be imposed but that negotiations on a bilateral agreement in the form of a treaty of alliance should be undertaken. Zaghlul, after being assured that the proposed talks with the British would not compromise his position, accepted the recommendations of the Milner Mission. The negotiations over the proposed alliance had actually begun with informal discussions in June 1920, but were not finally concluded until 1936.

Notwithstanding Zaghlul's earlier assertions that the Sudan was an inseparable part of Egypt, the agreement between Zaghlul and Milner contained no mention of the vast territory. Indeed, Milner made it clear that the Sudan was outside the scope of the negotiations. "The scheme embodied in the memorandum deals only with Egypt. It has no application to the Sudan, a country entirely distinct from Egypt in its character and constitution, the status of which is not, like that of Egypt, still indeterminate, but has been clearly defined by the Anglo-Egyptian Convention of January 19, 1899. For that reason the subject of the Sudan was deliberately excluded from all our discussions with the delegates."[8]

It turned out that a major sticking point in the preliminary discussions that took place in London was in fact the Sudan. The principal Egyptian concern was control of the Nile waters that flowed through the Sudan, which constituted the lifeblood of Egypt. Milner, expressed sensitivity to this concern in an August 18, 1920 letter to Adli Yeghen, a moderate Egyptian politician who sought to reconcile the interests of the British and Egyptians. The Milner Mission, he assured Adli, "fully realize the vital interest of Egypt in the supply of water reaching her through the Sudan, and we intend to make proposals calculated to remove any anxiety which Egypt may feel as to the adequacy of that supply both for her actual and her prospective needs."[9]

However, those proposals were not included in the proposed draft agreement and the Egyptians wanted it to be revised. Although both Milner and Lord Curzon favored changing the draft treaty, the British Cabinet refused to go along with their recommendations. As far as they were concerned, immense concessions had already been made and they would go no further. On November 9, Milner was forced to explain to the Egyptian delegation that it was pointless to attempt to work out the details of the agreement in advance of formal negotiations between Britain and Egypt. The informal discussions were suspended and the Egyptian delegation left London two days later. Milner subsequently resigned and negotiations were resumed by Lord Curzon in July 1921, without being constrained by anything previously agreed on. Once again agreement was impeded by Britain's reluctance to make any substantial concessions regarding Egyptian independence. One major point of contention was the Egyptian demand that all British forces in Egypt be withdrawn to the Suez Canal Zone. Britain rejected this demand and insisted on the freedom to occupy militarily any part of Egypt that it deemed appropriate. A second crucial issue was the British insistence on control of Egypt's foreign affairs, something that negated the very idea of independence. Further compounding the problem was the inability of the Egyptians to gather the necessary internal support to reach a satisfactory compromise on this and other issues. Having again reached an impasse, negotiations were suspended in November.

In a misguided effort intended to gain Egyptian support for Curzon's draft treaty, on December 3, 1921 Allenby outlined to the sultan the principles governing British policy towards Egypt. These included that Egypt was an integral part of the British Empire's system of communications, the national movement headed by Zaghlul was a disruptive force, and that Britain was committed to maintaining Fuad's authority in Egypt. This communication aligned Britain with the sultan in his struggle with Zaghlul and the nationalists, and effectively made Fuad dependent on the British for his continued rule.

With the publication of Curzon's draft treaty and Allenby's communication, coupled with the arrest and exile of Zaghlul on December 22 to the Seychelles, a series of strikes and demonstrations took place throughout Egypt, creating a chaotic situation in the country. To restore order, Allenby concluded that it would be advisable to unilaterally terminate the protectorate and to recognize the independence of Egypt, in advance of the final negotiation of a treaty of alliance. Exerting his considerable influence on the British government, including an implicit threat to challenge Lloyd George's already shaky government by an attack on it in the House of Lords, a unilateral declaration ending the protectorate and recognizing the independence of Egypt was issued on February 28, 1922.

However, the declaration contained a critical reservation that substantially reduced the significance of the concessions it proclaimed. It

absolutely reserved to the discretion of His Majesty's Government until such time as it may be possible by free discussion and friendly accommodation on both sides to conclude agreements in regard thereto between His majesty's Government and the Government of Egypt:

a. The security of the communications of the British Empire in Egypt;

b. The defence of Egypt against all foreign aggression or interference, direct and indirect;

c. The protection of foreign interests in Egypt and the protection of minorities;

d. The Sudan."[10]

Two weeks later, Sultan Fuad assumed the title of King Fuad I of newly independent Egypt. However, pending the conclusions of the agreements referred to, the status quo was to prevail. The resentment of the Egyptians continued unabated and British officials continued to be assassinated. Martial law continued in effect until July 5, 1923. It was abolished only after the Egyptian government promulgated an Act of Indemnity that pardoned all prior illegal measures and actions on the part of the authorities. As a result of the reservations specified in the declaration of February 28, 1922, the formal unilateral termination of the protectorate produced little change in Egypt's de facto status. It remained, for all practical purposes, a British protectorate. This fact, widely resented by the Egyptians, gave Zaghlul, who returned to Egypt in September 1923, a resounding victory in the elections that were held in January 1924. On January 27, the king had no choice but to ask Zaghlul to form a new government.

At the opening of the new Egyptian parliament on March 15, King Fuad stated to the assembled delegates: "You have before you one of the most grave and delicate tasks upon which the future of Egypt depends, the task of realising her complete independence in the true meaning of the word. . . . My Government is ready to enter into negotiations, free of all restrictions, with the British Government, so as to realise our national aspirations with regard to Egypt and the Sudan."[11] Fuad had unequivocally reasserted Egypt's demand for complete independence from Britain, effectively rejecting the de facto protectorate established by the February 28, 1922 declaration. Moreover, he had also renewed Egypt's claim to the Sudan, a matter that Britain had long considered settled and which it had refused to even consider in the negotiations.

Zaghlul had clearly chosen a policy course designed to press the British into further concessions, and to give effect to this approach, his administration began to take measures designed to restrict the ability of European officials to influence and intervene in Egyptian domestic affairs. Although Allenby remained optimistic about coming to a satisfactory agreement with Zaghlul that would ensure British interests, the new British prime minister, Ramsey MacDonald, was clearly frustrated by the situation and made his views known to Allenby in unequivocal terms. "The position of Great Britain in Egypt, whatever Egyptians try to make out, is juridically and internationally perfectly legal. Egypt was *de jure* and *de facto* a British protectorate. For reasons of their own and of their own motion His Majesty's Government modified that status and granted a measure of independence. His majesty's Government alone were able or had the right to do this, and Egyptian independence, so far as it exists, is the direct consequence of action of His Majesty's Government."[12] Accordingly, he did not see much value in negotiating with Zaghlul, who categorically rejected this position.

In the meantime, the Egyptians undertook a range of activities in the Sudan that were clearly subversive of British rule there. In June 1924, a political demonstration in Omdurman organized by Egyptian agitators erupted into violence, followed by a series of demonstrations and other acts there throughout that summer. In Egypt, tensions between the government and the British continued to rise, reaching a critical point on November 19, 1924 with the assassination in Cairo of Sir Lee Stack, sirdar (commander-in-chief) of the Egyptian army and governor-general of the Sudan. There seemed to be little doubt that the act resulted from incitement by Zaghlul, who repeatedly stated in public that the fact of a British commander-in-chief of the Egyptian Army was an insult to the independence of Egypt.

The British response was swift. Among other things, it was demanded that all Egyptian troops and disaffected officials be withdrawn from the Sudan, and that the Egyptian government formally signify its recognition of the Anglo-Egyptian condominium in Sudan in accordance with the Anglo-Egyptian agreement of 1887. The challenge this presented to Zaghlul was dramatic albeit of little tangible significance to Egypt. As a practical matter, few Egyptians had any interest whatsoever in the Sudan, despite its having served as a rallying cry for the Egyptian nationalists. The Sudanese themselves, at least most of them, despised the Egyptians and had no wish to be affiliated with them politically or in any other manner. Nonetheless, Zaghlul had made an issue of the Sudan, an issue punctuated by the assassination of its governor-general.

At this critical juncture, Zaghlul and the Wafd came under considerable pressure from Allenby, who had placed the Alexandria customs under military occupation and seemed determined to force a solution acceptable to the British government. Zaghlul concluded that discretion at this point was indeed the better part of valor, and he avoided having to deal with the problem he created by tendering his resignation on November 24, 1924. With Zaglul out of the way, at least temporarily, the crisis was soon defused. The new non-Wafdist prime minister, Ahmed Ziwar Pasha, accepted all of Allenby's demands. Egyptian troops were withdrawn from the Sudan, and the country became relatively quiet once more, albeit briefly. The British clearly remained in control for the time being.

Parliamentary elections were delayed until March 1925 in an attempt to assure that the new parliament would be supportive of the policies of the Ziwar government. However, at the very first sitting of the new parliament, Zaghlul was overwhelmingly elected its president, a highly unsatisfactory result from the British perspective. Parliament was dissolved that same day and new elections were set and then postponed indefinitely on the pretext that a better electoral system was required to assure that the parliament was truly representative of the country. For a year, Egypt was effectively ruled as a dictatorship. New elections were finally held in May 1926, and to British dismay, Zaghlul and the Wafd received an overwhelming majority. Zaghlul, as leader of the majority party and the governing coalition should have become prime minister, but the high commissioner, Lord George Lloyd, would not permit it and turned instead to Adli Yeghen

Pasha to form a government. Zaghlul remained president of the parliament until his death on August 23, 1927.

At the beginning of 1928 pressure began to build for the conclusion of a new Anglo-Egyptian treaty that would give Egypt the effective independence that had been promised for so long. Mainly, the Egyptians wanted the British occupation to end and British troops to be withdrawn. The British, however, had little interest in doing anything that would diminish its ability to maintain military forces in the country to protect the lines of communications between England and India. At the same time, the British were interested in a treaty that would legitimate their legally questionable presence in Egypt. Accordingly, a draft treaty was presented by the British in February 1928 but was unanimously rejected by the Egyptian parliament. On March 4, Prime Minister Sarwat Pasha presented Lord Lloyd with the official response of his government rejecting the treaty and resigned.

The British response was to take steps to nullify the constitutional basis for Egyptian self-rule and, with the collaboration of King Fuad, to institute another dictatorship in the country. On July 19, 1928, the king and his new prime minister Muhammad Mahmud Pasha, with Lord Lloyd's full support, carried out a *coup d'etat* from above. A royal rescript suspended the constitution for at least three years, and freedom of the press was abolished.

The situation changed significantly in 1929 with the assumption of power by a Labour government in Britain. The new foreign secretary Arthur Henderson repudiated Lord Lloyd's autocratic approach to his responsibilities and promptly replaced him with Sir Percy Loraine. Henderson soon presented the Egyptian government with a new draft treaty on August 3, 1929 that would have effectively put an end to the veiled protectorate as well as an end to the British military occupation.

Negotiations over the treaty took place in London in April and May 1930, but eventually broke down over the seemingly intractable issue of the Sudan. For Egypt, whose lifeline was the Nile River, control of the Sudan was considered absolutely essential. Whoever controlled the Sudan, for all practical purposes, could also control Egypt. For Britain, control of the Sudan was essential for its strategic position with regard to Egypt and the Red Sea, and as the northern anchor of its series of possessions in East Africa. Moreover, the more freedom and independence Britain was prepared to concede to Egypt, the more it felt the need to guarantee its position in the countries bordering the Suez Canal and in the Upper Nile region. There did not appear to be a way to reconcile these diametrically opposed interests.

The failure to come to terms on a treaty resulted in the imposition of yet another dictatorship in June 1930, this time under Ismail Sidki Pasha. This time, however, the British stood aside and a power struggle between the king and the Wafd soon erupted in violence. Bloody encounters took place between Egyptian troops and demonstrators, especially in Mansuriya on July 8 and in Alexandria on July 15. A new constitution that greatly restricted the rights of the parliament and strengthened those of the monarchy was promulgated by decree in the fall of 1930, and met with the adamant opposition not only of the Wafd but also of Egypt's two previous dictators, Ziwar Pasha and Muhammad Mahmud Pasha.

The apparent stalemate, which effectively left Britain in control of Egypt, was ultimately broken as a consequence of the Italian invasion of Ethiopia in 1935. The Egyptians, including the most extreme Wafdists, concluded that it was in their own interest to reach an immediate accommodation with Britain. They recognized that Italian penetration of Ethiopia posed a direct threat to the sources of the Nile, three of which originated in Ethiopia. Moreover, Britain now began pouring troops and air squadrons into Suez to block any further Italian advance, without any consultation with the Egyptian government. It became painfully obvious to Egyptian politicians that any future negotiations for real Egyptian independence would only become more difficult, especially if Egypt became directly involved in a widening conflict.

With both parties now ready to discuss a new arrangement, negotiations soon began, King Fuad dying in the meantime and succeeded by his son Farouk in April 1936. A treaty of alliance was finally signed on August 26, 1936 that declared the British occupation of Egypt to be at an end. Britain recognized the sovereignty of Egypt, the high commissioner became Britain's ambassador, and the British agreed to withdraw their troops from the principal population centers, especially Cairo and Alexandria. The sensitive and volatile issue of the status of the Sudan was effectively ignored, except for some minor alterations in the existing arrangements under which that country was governed.

In return, Britain was granted unrestricted access to Egyptian airspace as well as to the harbor at Alexandria. As many as 10,000 troops were to be permitted to take up positions on either side of the Suez Canal, the entire canal zone including its ports remaining effectively under British control, and British officers would continue to direct the Egyptian army. Although Egyptian independence, as a practical matter, was still hampered in significant ways by the military clauses of the agreement, politicians across the political spectrum experienced a collective sigh of relief that 54 years of British military occupation had come to an end. The treaty was ratified by the Egyptian parliament on December 22, 1936. On May 26, 1937, Egypt was admitted to the League of Nations.

One internal consequence of the treaty was that it undercut the popularity of the Wafd, which had thrived on the basis of its antagonism to Britain. King Farouk dissolved the Wafd-dominated parliament in February 1938, and the elections that were held the following month put a non-Wafdist coalition in power for the next four years.

NOTES

1. *British and Foreign State Papers, 1915*, vol. CIX, p. 434.
2. The Earl of Cromer, *Abbas II*, Preface, p. xvii.
3. Zaheer Masood Quraishi, *Liberal Nationalism in Egypt*, p. 34.
4. G. Young, *Egypt*, p. 218.
5. Ronald Wingate, *Wingate of the Sudan*, p. 220.
6. Peter Mansfield, *The British in Egypt*, p. 227.
7. Ibid., p. 231.
8. George Lloyd, *Egypt Since Cromer*, vol. 2, p. 389.
9. Ibid., p. 390.
10. Lloyd, *Egypt Since Cromer*, vol. 2, p. 64.
11. Ibid., p. 83.
12. Ibid., p. 89.

9

Turmoil in Transcaucasia, 1917–21

The collapse of the Tsarist government in Russia in March 1917 and its replacement by the social democratic regime of Alexander Kerensky left Russia's southern border regions in a confused state. The various entities that had been gobbled up by the Russian Empire over a period of centuries were immediately faced by the need to make one of two critical choices. They could opt for complete independence from Russia, or they could maintain some links with it as autonomous political entities, the precise nature of which would be determined through negotiation. As long as the new provisional government was committed to democracy and respect for the rights of the minorities that populated the vast region, most local political leaders, who quickly organized themselves in executive committees, were inclined to opt for autonomy rather than independence. As a practical matter, there could be significant economic and other advantages of intimate association with a major power.

In Transcaucasia, the region of the southern flank of the Caucasus Mountains, the viceroy Grand Duke Nicolas was expelled from Tiflis on March 19, 1917, two days after the revolution. The new Russian government made a good will gesture toward the region by appointing a Georgian Social Democrat as high commissioner for Transcaucasia, which included Georgia, Azerbaijan, and Armenia, and expectations for an amicable relationship with Russia were high. These hopes were soon to be dashed when the Bolsheviks overthrew the provisional government in November 1917. One almost immediate consequence was the virtual disintegration of the Russian Caucasian Army, which threatened the collapse of the front, and the rapid replacement of the regular Russian forces with indigenous troops hobbled together to prevent the Turks from overrunning the region. Moreover, the Russian troops, anxious to go home, began a disorderly with-drawal that threatened chaos and caused an outbreak of fighting between them and the Transcaucasian forces. On the political level, the Social Dem-ocrats in the region reacted to these events by taking steps to sever the re-maining ties between Transcaucasia and the Bolshevik regime in Russia.

The withdrawal of the Russians from the Transcaucasian front left it in the hands of the Armenians in the south and the Georgians in the north. The Turks quickly sought to bring the fighting on that front to a close by making an overture to the newly autonomous Transcaucasians that invited them to consider how a separate peace between them might be achieved. The Transcaucasian Commisariat was still ambivalent about a permanent break with Russia because there were still those in leadership positions who believed that the Bolshevik regime would be short-lived. Nonetheless, on December 4, 1917, the commissariat decided to accept an armistice along the Caucasus front proposed by the Turkish military commander, Ferik Vehib Pasha, which went into effect the following day. The Turks, however, were impatient to bring about a peace treaty because in the areas conquered by the Russians, who were replaced by Armenian and Georgian troops, Armenians seeking vengeance for past repression carried out atroc-ities against the Muslim population, several hundred being killed in Erzincan between January 15–16, 1918.

Finally, on March 1, the Trancaucasian Seim (parliament) and the com-missariat jointly agreed to negotiate a peace with Turkey based on the res-toration of the frontiers of 1914. The following day, as the negotiators were preparing to leave for Trebizond, where the peace talks were to take place, a message was received from Brest-Litovsk advising that Russia had de-cided to accept the German conditions for peace. Among other things, Rus-sia agreed to concede the territories of Kars, Ardahan, and Batum to Turkey, effectively incorporating most of Armenia into the Ottoman Em-pire. It thus seriously undermined the Transcaucasian negotiating posi-tion. It maintained that, since the Bolshevik coup in November of the preceding year, Russian central authority had ceased to function in Transcaucasia and an independent government had been established. In-deed it was as such that it accepted the Ottoman invitation to negotiate a peace treaty. The Transcaucasian Commissariat immediately sent protests to the capitals of all the belligerents stating that the concessions in Transcaucasia made by the Russians at Brest-Litovsk should not be consid-ered binding on them. Nonetheless, the political damage that had been done proved irreparable.

By the time the long-delayed peace conference took place in Trebizond on March 14, 1918, the Turkish position with regard to Transcaucasia had hardened considerably—they would not retreat from the Russian conces-sions made at Brest-Litovsk, and demanded the immediate evacuation by Transcaucasia of the ceded territories. Since Transcaucasia was not formally independent at the time that the Treaty of Best-Litovsk was signed, its post facto attempt to nullify the Russian concessions made with regard to Armenia was considered by the Turks as having no foundation in international law. To make matters worse, the Transcaucasian delegation to the talks was evasive about who they actually represented, because Transcaucasia in fact had not formally seceded from Russia.

Moreover, Vehib Pasha made it clear that because of the allegedly continuing Armenian atrocities, which effectively constituted a breach of the armistice, Turkish troops would continue to advance into Transcaucasia, where massacres of Armenians soon took place. There they found active support from indigenous Muslims, who destroyed bridges and railway depots, and disrupted communications behind the Transcaucasian lines. By March 19, Ardahan had been taken and the Armenian military units there disarmed, as the Turkish army continued to penetrate the region.

There is no little irony in the fact that as the Turkish army was moving forward on the ground, the Transcaucasian delegation to the peace talks at Trebizond continued to focus exclusively on challenging the legitimacy of the concessions made by Russia at Brest-Litovsk. By their procrastination and refusal to acknowledge the realities of the situation, the Transcaucasians had managed to maneuver themselves into a dead end. One of those realities was that the Transcaucasians were in no position to pressure the Turks into relenting. Another was that the Turks would have welcomed an independent Transcaucasia, which would serve as a buffer between Turkey and Russia. In fact, it was the Turkish delegation to the peace talks that expressed, on March 20, "the desire that Transcaucasia decide to proclaim its independence."[1] However, because of their uncertainty as to whether Transcaucasia would be able to hold out against Russia, the Turks insisted on retaining control of Kars and Batum. Only the Azerbaijanis, who viewed the Turks as fellow Muslims and expected special treatment from them, saw nothing amiss in their demands, an attitude that disrupted the cohesion of the Transcaucasian delegation.

Under continuing pressure from the Turks, who finally tired over the endless haggling over what they considered a dead issue and issued an ultimatum to the Transcaucasian delegation, the latter accepted the Brest-Litovsk treaty as the basis for peace negotiations on April 10. Nonetheless, the Transcaucasian Seim remained fundamentally opposed to such a step and on April 14, after ordering its delegation to leave the peace talks, it unanimously declared war on Turkey. Batum fell the next day, with the assistance of the Muslim Georgians who conducted guerilla operations that created chaos behind the Georgian lines.

The remaining key position in Transcaucasia was Kars, which was still held by its indigenous forces. A Turkish assault on the city on April 19 was repulsed, and the Turks were uninterested in placing it under a costly and time-consuming siege. Thus, on April 22, Vehib Pasha sent a message asking whether Transcaucasia was prepared to reopen peace talks, an offer that was accepted by the Seim. That same day, the Seim finally declared independence from Russia as well as the establishment of a Transcaucasian federation under the leadership of Akakii Chkenkeli of Georgia, who became its prime minister. The Ottoman Empire recognized the new Democratic Federative Republic of Transcaucasia on April 28, 1918, and a new round of peace talks opened in Batum on May 11.

The Turks now took the position that because it was Transcaucasia that had violated the agreement reached at the Trebizond negotiations, Turkey was no longer satisfied with the territorial gains it received at Brest-Litovsk and now demanded additional territorial concessions as compensation. These included the districts of Akhaltsikh and Akhalkalaki, the city and most of the district of Alexandropol, and the Kars-Alexandropol-Julfa railway that led to Persia. In effect, agreement to these demands would have meant giving all of Armenia to Turkey.

The Azerbaijanis pressed for Transcaucasia's acceptance of the Ottoman demand for territorial concessions, virtually all of which would come at the expense of the Armenians, something that was not really surprising given the long history of the enmity between the two peoples. However, this was a position that clearly meant the untimely death of the new federation, since it pitted Armenia and Azerbaijan against one another in an irreconcilable conflict.

Faced by the prospect of an imminent dissolution of the federation, its Georgian prime minister and the Georgian delegates promptly began separate negotiations with the German General von Lossow, who was present at the conference to protect the interests of his country. On May 24, an agreement was reached between von Lossow and the Georgians to the effect that Germany would oppose a Turkish invasion of an independent Georgia. Two days later, the Ottomans issued an ultimatum to the Transcaucasian leaders, this time demanding still more territory. That same day, May 26, 1918, Georgia withdrew from the federation and declared its sovereign independence. The justification for its defection from the federation was stated in the Act of Independence. "The present position of the Georgian people imperatively dictates to Georgia the necessity of creating her own state organization in order to save herself from enslavement by hostile forces and to lay a firm foundation for free development."[2]

Abandoned to the Turkish onslaught and without allies, Armenia had no choice other than to declare its independence on May 28 and pray for the best. Azerbaijan similarly declared its independence the same day.

Peace treaties between the Ottoman Empire and the republics of Georgia, Armenia, and Azerbaijan were signed on June 4, 1918. Under the Turko-Georgian treaty, the independent state of Georgia lost much of its newly proclaimed independence. The size of its army was to be determined jointly with Turkey, all foreign military and civilian officers of states at war with Turkey were to be expelled from the country, and the Turks were to have unrestricted use of Georgia's railways. The Turko-Armenian treaty was even more one-sided. Armenia lost Kars, Ardahan, and a large part of Nakhichevan. The treaty with Azerbaijan was rather different, since Azerbaijan was already a de facto ally of Turkey. This became patently clear when the two joined forces in an attempt to seize the major oil port at Baku, which was still under Soviet control.

There were expectations that the British would come to the defense of Transcaucasia to prevent a Turkish-German attempt to bypass western Persia and invade India through Transcaspia, Khorasan, and Afghanistan. This assessment, however, failed to recognize that the British were not in a position to commit sufficient forces to the region to do any such thing. This became clear when, after almost two months of fighting and political maneuvering, the Soviet government of Baku fell and was replaced by the so-called Centro-Caspian Directorate, which invited British help in the defense of the city.

In the meantime, the British dispatched a military mission to determine the situation and, if the German and Turkish forces were able to reach the Caspian Sea, to organize local resistance to hamper their advance eastward. A force of some 1,400 men under General Lionel C. Dunsterville left Baghdad, via Kermanshah and Hamadan, for the Persian port of Enzeli in January 1918, following in the wake of the withdrawing Russian forces that were heading for Baku, which was under threat of a siege. His primary mission, however, was to secure the road to Enzeli and report on any enemy moves in the direction of Tabriz. Dunsterville seized all Russian ships in Enzeli and established his headquarters aboard the *President Kreuger*. To display his neutrality with respect to internal Russian affairs, the general removed the red flag and flew the tsarist flag, but upside down, which made it identical to the flag of Serbia. It was only in June that emissaries from Baku finally managed to make contact with Dunsterville in Enzeli, asking him to help relieve the siege of Baku. Action was delayed, however, because of the reluctance of London to authorize operations beyond Persia's frontiers. It was only at the end of July that Dunsterville was authorized to enter into discussions with the Centro-Caspian Directorate about an agreement to assist them in the defense of Baku. Dunsterville subsequently described himself as "a British General on the Caspian, the only sea unploughed before by British keels, on board a ship named after a South African president and whilom enemy, sailing from a Persian port, under the Serbian flag, to relieve from the Turks a body of Armenians in a revolutionary Russian town."[3]

The first British elements arrived at Baku on August 4, followed by Dunsterville and reinforcements on August 17, disappointing the defenders with its size, about 900 men, which was too small to be of much military significance. Moreover, strong disagreements soon emerged between

Dunsterville and the Centro-Caspian Directorate over the military organization of the defense and its leadership. In the meantime, the British became aware that the Turks were preparing for an all-out attack on Baku and, indeed, broke through the city's defenses early in the morning on September 14. Before midnight that same day, the British force embarked and put out to sea under cover of darkness. The city fell the next day as Azerbaijani troops burst into the city, the Turks remaining outside for three more days, and massacred a large number of Armenians, nearly 9,000 by Armenian accounts. On September 17, the government of Azerbaijan arrived in Baku, establishing it as its capital, with the sultan's approval.

Although the Ottoman Empire recognized the independence of Georgia on June 4, Germany did not do so until after the conclusion of a new German-Russian treaty on August 27, 1918. This was a supplement to the Brest-Litovsk agreement in which, among numerous other matters, Russia stipulated that it had no objection to German recognition of the independence of Georgia. The value of this concession could not be assessed as being very high. On July 8, Joseph Stalin sent a message to the Bolsheviks in Baku stating: "Our general policy in the Transcaucasian question is to compel the Germans to acknowledge officially that the Georgian, Armenian, and Azerbaijani questions are internal Russian questions, in the solutions of which they should not participate. It is for this reason that we do not recognize Georgian independence recognized by Germany."[4]

In the meanwhile, German troops arrived in Georgia, at the invitation of its government, to help protect its frontiers from Turkish encroachment. Despite the fact that Germany and Turkey were allies, their relations in fact were far from harmonious. This was clearly reflected in the Russian-German treaty, which included a provision to the effect that Germany would not assist any third power, meaning Turkey, in possible military operations in the Caucasus. A line was drawn on a map along the southern frontier of Georgia, that included Baku, and Germany agreed to use its influence to prevent a crossing of that line by Turkey. General E. von Ludendorff made the reasons for this, and the entry of German troops, bluntly clear. "It had become essential for us to show a strong hand in this district—not merely because we hoped to secure some military assistance from this quarter, but also in order to obtain raw materials. That we could not rely on Turkey in this matter had been once again demonstrated by her conduct in Batum, where she claimed the right to retain all the stocks for herself. We could expect to get oil from Baku only if we helped ourselves."[5]

The region was thrown into renewed chaos with the capitulation of Germany and its allies in November 1918. Russia immediately announced its repudiation of the Brest-Litovsk treaty, which meant that Georgia and Armenia could attempt to reclaim Kars, Ardahan, and Batum. However, it also meant that Soviet Russia would not abide by the supplementary treaty of August 27, which implicitly acknowledged the independence of Georgia. To make matters worse, following the withdrawal of German forces from Transcaucasia, uprisings broke out across the region making the future of Georgia, Armenia, and Azerbaijan as uncertain as they had been six months earlier.

Within days of the Turkish announcement that they were withdrawing from Azerbaijan, British General Sir William M. Thomson, commander of the allied forces in Persia, declared that all Turkish as well as Azerbaijani troops were to evacuate Baku by the morning of November 17, 1918. He also announced that the troops under his command would occupy Baku and the surrounding oilfields. The remainder of Azerbaijan would remain under control of the Azerbaijani government, which would be given de facto but not de jure recognition by the governments of England, France, and the United States. At this point in time, Russia was still considered an ally and Azerbaijan was still being treated as an integral part of Russia. However, the situation changed over the next several weeks. On December 28, Thomson issued a proclamation stating: "In view of the formation of a coalition Azerbaijani Government under the presidency of F. Kh. Khoiski, I hereby declare that the Allied Command shall accord full support to the said Government as the only legal power within the limits of Azerbaijan."[6]

The stage seemed to be set for formal British recognition of Azerbaijan as an independent state. However, the common perception in Western capitals was that Russia was a beleaguered ally that needed help in overcoming the chaos resulting from the war and the revolution. As a result, few Western statesmen were prepared to entertain seriously the aspirations of the Transcaucasian peoples for self-determination and independence. Moreover, when the British Foreign Office was persuaded by representatives of Georgia to indicate the British government's sympathy for Georgian independence and its willingness to help it gain recognition at the Paris Peace Conference, the position was clearly contradicted by General Thomson in the field. Thomson made it clear to Georgian Prime Minister Noi Jordania that the Allied Powers did not recognize any independent political entities on Russian territory, and that their mission in the region was to restore the former viceroyalty of Transcaucasia to Russian authority.

At about the same time, a long-simmering territorial dispute between Georgia and Armenia erupted into a war between the two nascent republics in December 1918. Although the Armenians made some initial gains, reaching close to the Georgian capital at Tiflis, they were defeated at Shulaveri on December 29 and forced to withdraw. Armenia, under British pressure, agreed to bring an end to the conflict at midnight on December 31. The Armenian-Georgian war did great damage to the cause of independence for the Transcaucasian republics. The ancient hostility of the Georgians toward the Armenians precluded a coordinated approach to the Paris Peace Conference, at which their fate was to be decided, and boded ill for their future as independent republics.

Georgia seemed to have become obsessed with a virulent nationalism that was manifested by external imperialism and internal suppression of non-Georgians. An English observer noted: "'The Free and Independent Social-Democratic State of Georgia' will always remain in my memory as a classic example of an imperialist 'small nation.' Both in territory-snatching outside and bureaucratic tyranny inside, its chauvinism was beyond all bounds."[7] Its rejection of the idea of self-determination when applied to others became clear with regard to the question of the so-called South-Western Caucasian Republic.

The majority of the people in the southwestern part of Transcaucasia were Muslim and therefore quite understandably sought to affiliate with Azerbaijan. However, Georgia prevented this from happening by blocking Azerbaijan's incorporation of the Muslims of the southwest, which would have extended its frontiers to the Black Sea. As a result, the Muslims of the southwest formed an independent South-Western Caucasian Republic and laid claim to the districts of Kars, Batum, Akhaltsikh, Akhalkalaki, Sharur, and Nakhichevan, a claim supported by Azerbaijan. The new republic extended full rights to all except Armenians, and appealed to the Entente Powers for recognition. In response, the British indicated that they would protect the new republic from counterclaims on its territory from both Georgia and Armenia until the question would be decided by the Paris Peace Conference. The British commitment, however, was soon ignored as fighting broke out between the South-Western Caucasian Republic and both Georgia and Armenia. On April 10, 1919, General Thomson disbanded the new republic's national council, and nine days later Armenian forces entered Kars. Similarly, on July 7, 1920, the Georgian army entered Batum on the heels of the departing British, who had occupied it since the Turkish withdrawal.

As the principal power in the region, the British sought to use it as a vehicle for dealing with some problems among the Entente Powers regarding the distribution of the spoils of the late war. The Italians were particularly upset about the small gains they had garnered as one of the victor states, and the British proposed that they be given a League of Nations Mandate for Transcaucasia. On May 10, 1919, General Thomson notified the government of Azerbaijan that the British troops there would be replaced with Italian forces. Six days later, the Prince of Savoy arrived in Baku, followed a week later by an Italian military mission. However, as preparations for the Italian takeover were being made, a change of government took place in Rome and the new prime minister, Francesco Nitti, saw Italian involvement in the Caucasus as a mindless adventure and the whole matter was quickly dropped. Overextended, the British withdrew from Azerbaijan in August 1919, leaving it to the mercies of the Russian, highly nationalistic and anti-Soviet, Volunteer Army of General Anton I. Denikin that was ensconced across the border in Daghestan, which it had invaded in the spring.

As a Great Russian nationalist, Denikin's attitude toward Transcaucasia was straightforward. As he put it, "the main, or rather the only cause, of struggle in the Caucasus was the conflict between the idea of a unified Russia and the idea of a complete independence of the new Caucasian formations."[8] It seemed clear that it was only a matter of time before his forces marched south.

To preclude this from taking place, the British commander in the region drew a line that meandered across the Caucasus which Denikin would not be permitted to cross, giving both Georgia and Azerbaijan a temporary reprieve. The threat of invasion by Denikin's forces, notwithstanding the British position, brought the two countries together in a mutual defense alliance on June 16. Armenia was invited to join the alliance as well, but refused to do so since it expected the Western alliance to protect its interests, at the same time that it cooperated secretly with Denikin, who surreptitiously supplied it with arms.

The situation altered dramatically toward the end of 1919, when Denikin's army began to suffer defeats by the newly constituted Red Army of Soviet Russia. By February 1920, Denikin was no longer a threat to Transcaucasia. Indeed, he now sought its support and recognized "the independent existence of the *de facto* governments of the border areas which struggle against Bolshevism."[9]

TRANSCAUCASIA AT THE PARIS PEACE CONFERENCE

No one had placed greater hopes for realizing their national aspirations at the peace conference than the Armenians. In reflecting on the conference, Winston Churchill later wrote, "Now was the moment when at last the Armenians would receive justice and the right to live in peace in their national home.... The greatest nations in the hour of their victory were their friends and would see them righted."[10] Indeed, Armenian expectations of favorable treatment were so great that they misled themselves into making exorbitant demands, some of which were prompted by the Russian minister Sazanov, who still had hopes that the Bolshevik regime would collapse and that this would return things to normal in the former Russian empire.

The Armenian position was reflected in the claims made on Armenia's behalf by the Armenian National Union of America, its principal voice in the Western world. "The Armenians demand the redemption of their national heritage from alien rule, and its constitution into a free, self-governing, and independent state of Armenia. That is, they do not want to become an autonomous member of a confederation; they do not want international control; they do not want to have even a suggestion of any direct or indirect political connection with any neighboring nation or racial entity. Armenia demands unconditional liberation at the hands of the Allies."[11] What was being claimed as the Armenian "national heritage" was all the territory from the Caspian Sea to the Black Sea and the northern Mediterranean. The territorial demands made in the formal Armenian submission to the peace conference included the seven eastern vilayets of Turkey, Van, Bitlis, Diarbekir, Kharput, Sivas, Erzerum, and Trebizond, which represented almost half of Anatolia. In addition, it demanded all of Cilicia, including Adana and Alexandretta on the Syrian frontier. All this was to be in addition to the territory of the Armenian Republic of the Caucasus and the provinces of Kars and Erivan. All in all, what was being demanded was a reconstitution of the Kingdom of Armenia as it was at its height some two thousand years earlier, a relatively vast territory in which Armenians now constituted only a small part of the population.

As might have been expected, the Armenian demands could not be taken seriously by anyone other than the Armenians and some of their supporters, who seemed to be out of touch with the political realities of the day. Demanding eastern Anatolia at the same time that Kemal Ataturk was reconstituting the Turkish state there seemed rather senseless and the Armenians were essentially ignored by the Western statesmen at the conference. At last, recognizing that the forthcoming British withdrawal from the Caucasus would leave them at the mercy of Denikin's army, the Armenians began to seek a League of Nations mandate that might be awarded to the United States, where there was a good deal of sympathy for Armenian national aspirations. However, even in this their expectations of the mandatory power were excessive, amounting to what would today be referred to as an ethnic cleansing of the region. Nonetheless, the United States did send General James G. Harbord to Turkey and Transcaucasia to determine the practicability and desirability of taking on a mandate for Armenia.

Harbord's report to the president was unfavorable to the idea of a mandate. Perhaps most important, from a strategic perspective, Armenia was effectively surrounded by Russia, Persia, and Turkey. As a practical matter, for an American mandate over Armenia to be viable the United States would have to have control of Constantinople (Istanbul) in order that it not be cut off from the West, and this was quite out of the question. Nonetheless, on May 24, 1920, President Wilson informed Congress that he wanted the United States to accept a mandate over Armenia, a move that the U.S. Senate rejected overwhelmingly on June 1.

In the meanwhile, in January 1920 the Supreme Council of the Allies agreed to extend de facto recognition to the government of Armenia, making it de jure eight months later. Armenia thus became a signatory to the peace treaty signed at Sevres on August 10, 1920 between the countries of the alliance and Turkey. Under its terms, Armenia was given the vilayets of Erzerum, Trebizond, Van, and Bitlis, and Turkey agreed to abide by the decision of the U.S. president regarding the final frontier between Turkey and Armenia. That November, President Wilson announced his decision regarding the frontier, confirming the award of Erzerum and Trebizond and a good part of Eastern Anatolia to Armenia. The problem was that while the Supreme Council and Wilson were busy giving away parts of the former Ottoman Empire, Kemal Ataturk was even busier establishing new facts on the ground in Anatolia, re-occupying Kars, Ardahan, and Alexandropol.

Moreover, Russia and Turkey, longstanding foes, now found that their interests coincided and they came to a rapprochement beginning in November 1919 that effectively precluded the survival of the independent Transcaucasian republics. That which brought these former enemies together was a common hostility to the Western powers, as well as their need of each other's help. The Kemalists needed money and arms, and the Russians needed an ally that would effectively give them a foothold in the Middle East. As long as Turkey and Russia were enemies, the republics could maintain the hope of viability by playing off one against the other. Once they became allies, Armenia, Azerbaijan, and Georgia were doomed. For one thing, they now constituted obstacles on the supply route from Russia to Turkey. For another, because Kemal had renounced any interest in Transcaucasia, he had no objection to its reconquest by Russia.

Abandoned by its supposed Western allies, Armenia concluded that it had run its course in its attempt to hold on to the predominantly Armenian-populated parts of eastern Anatolia and agreed to an armistice with Turkey on November 18, 1920. Eleven days later, a Bolshevik Military Revolutionary Committee crossed into Armenia from Azerbaijan and triggered an uprising that brought down the nationalist Armenian government and the establishment of a Soviet regime on November 29. By a treaty signed at Erivan on December 2, Armenia was declared a Soviet Republic. Notwithstanding the Treaty of Sevres, the Armenian Republic survived less than two weeks following President Wilson's decision on its frontiers.

Azerbaijan and Georgia both received *de facto* recognition at the same time as Armenia in January 1920. It seems clear that the reason for the Supreme Council of the Allies taking these steps was directly related to the fact that the Volunteer Army of Denikin was being routed by the Red Army. By recognizing the Transcaucasian republics, the West hoped to strengthen its position in dealing with Soviet Russia. Beyond such diplomatic support, little else was done. The United States ignored the Azerbaijani and Georgian requests to establish diplomatic relations. By the middle of April, the Eleventh Red Army was concentrating at Derbent, along the narrow strip of land separating the mountains of Daghestan from the shores of the Caspian Sea, ready to strike across the essentially undefended Azerbaijani frontier. Most of the Azerbaijani army had earlier been shifted to the southwest to fight the Armenians. On April 27, the Azerbaijani government was given an ultimatum by the Central Committee of the Communist Party of Azerbaijan demanding that power be turned over to them within 12 hours. However, hours before the deadline Soviet troops had already crossed the frontier and were advancing rapidly toward Baku. The Azerbaijani government surrendered power to the local Bolsheviks that same day, followed shortly by a treaty of military and economic union between Soviet Azerbaijan and Soviet Russia.

The bolsheviks in Georgia had hoped to repeat the success that had been achieved in Azerbaijan, with the Red Army crossing the Azerbaijani-Georgian frontier, thereby forcing the Georgian government to capitulate. An uprising was staged in Tiflis on May 2, 1920, but it failed to topple the government. This left the government in a position to concentrate all its forces on blocking the advance of Soviet troops, which it did successfully, even counterattacking. Soviet Russia was not really in a position at the time to commit its forces to a full-scale conflict in Transcaucasia because it was expecting war to break out with Poland. It therefore pretended that the conflict was between Georgia and Azerbaijan, and did not involve Russia. A peace treaty between Russia and Georgia was negotiated and signed in Moscow on May 7, giving unconditional recognition to the independence of Georgia. All of this, however, was merely a delaying tactic on the part of the Russians who had no intention of allowing Georgia to be independent in fact.

Beginning on February 11, 1921, a series of communist uprisings took place in Georgia. In Shulavery, a revolutionary committee proclaimed a Soviet regime and appealed to Russia for help. Russia responded favorably and dispatched an army that invaded Georgia a few days later. By February 17, the Georgian government had left Tiflis, which fell to the Red Army after a valiant defense on February 25. Fierce resistance continued around the country for another two weeks before the Georgian government capitulated. A Russian-Georgian peace treaty was signed at Kutais on March 18, and Georgia, the last of the Transcaucasian republics, entered into the Soviet embrace, where it remained for the next six decades.

NOTES

1. Firuz Kazemzadeh, *The Struggle for Transcaucasia (1917–1921)*, p. 96.
2. Ibid., p. 121.
3. Ibid., p. 140.
4. Richard Pipes, *The Formation of the Soviet Union*, p. 202.
5. Erich von Ludendorff, *Ludendorff's Own Story*, vol. 2, p. 302.
6. Kazemzadeh, p. 167.
7. C. E. Bechofer, *In Denikin's Russia and the Caucasus, 1919–1920*, p. 14.
8. Kazemzadeh, p. 242.
9. Ibid., p. 249.
10. Winston S. Churchill, *The Aftermath*, p. 432.
11. *The Case of Armenia*, p. 3.

10

Developments in Iran, 1914–37

Almost simultaneously with the declaration of war by Great Britain, France, and Russia on the Ottoman Empire at the beginning of November, 1914, Iran formally declared its neutrality in the conflict. Russia and Britain, which had effectively partitioned Iran into Russian and British spheres of interest by the Anglo-Russian Agreement of August 31, 1907, both supported Iranian neutrality, principally for strategic reasons. It was to their mutual advantage to have Iran serve as a neutral buffer zone between Turkey and both Russian Central Asia and British India. The German and Ottoman generals, on the other hand, took a rather different view of the Iranian declaration. For the Central Powers, Iran could serve as the primary route for an assault on Russian and British interests in Asia. In any case, once war broke out, the long standing presence of Russian troops in the country constituted a clear violation of Iranian neutrality, and the Turks quickly exploited the opportunity to introduce their own forces into the country, after formally protesting the Russian military presence there. Britain urged the Russians to withdraw from Iran to undercut the justification for a similar Turkish violation of Iranian neutrality, but the Russians refused to comply. On December 29, Turkish forces crossed into Iran and seized Tabriz 10 days later. However, they failed to consolidate their position there and were driven out of Iran by the Russians by the end of January 1915.

In June 1916, the Iranian government headed by Sepahdar-i Rashti signed a treaty which, although never ratified by the Majlis, effectively transformed Iran into a British and Russian protectorate. The agreement empowered the two protecting states to create an army of 22,000 men officered by their own citizens. As soon as the agreement was signed, Sir Percy Sykes began raising the 11,000 men that were allocated to the British and that were constituted as a force called the South Persia Rifles, and took control of all southern Iran. The Russians already had a sizeable force in northern Iran.

Following the March 1917 revolution in Russia, the Kerensky government ordered the withdrawal of Russian troops from Iran, a process that took a relatively long time because of logistical problems. Most of these troops were already Bolsheviks and communist sympathizers and, together with segments of the local populations, created soviet-like entities in the districts of Iranian Azerbaijan and Gilan. The policy of withdrawal was both confirmed and expanded following the Bolshevik revolution of November 1917. On December 5, 1917, V.I. Lenin and Joseph Stalin (at the time commissar of nationalities) published an open letter to "all the toiling Moslems of Russia and the East," announcing that "the treaty for the partition of Persia has been torn up and destroyed. As soon as hostilities cease, the troops will be evacuated from Persia and the Persians will be ensured the right freely to determine their own destiny."[1] On January 14, 1918, Leon Trotsky, the Soviet commissar for foreign affairs, went farther and informed the Iranian government that not only would Russia withdraw its troops as soon as possible, it would also attempt to persuade the British and the Turks to so as well. The Soviet goal in this period was to do everything possible to make sure that no other power would achieve a position of hegemony in the country, and thereby preclude its use as an anti-Soviet base.

It was not long, however, before the posture of the Soviet government with regard to these and other international commitments became radically altered. With the subsequent collapse of the Central Powers on November 13, 1918, Russia declared the peace treaty of Brest-Litovsk to be null and void. As a de facto corollary to this, Soviet Russia also effectively repudiated its solemn undertakings to respect the political and economic independence of Iran, as well as its territorial integrity. It quickly became evident that, notwithstanding their pious declarations to the contrary, the Soviet heirs of tsarist imperialism continued to attach great strategic importance to Iran, geopolitically as well as ideologically. Iran, it was believed, could serve as a key to the revolutionary transformation of all of Asia. Thus, the Bolshevik ideologist Konstantin Troyanovsky wrote that same year:

India is our principle objective. Persia is the only path open to India. The Persian revolution is the key to the revolution of all of the Orient, just as Egypt and the Suez Canal are the key to the British domination of the Orient. Persia is the Suez Canal of the revolution. If we shift the political center of gravity of the revolutionary movement to Persia, the Suez Canal loses its strategic value and importance. . . . For the success of the oriental revolution Persia is the first nation that must be conquered by the Soviets. This precious key to the uprising of the Orient must be in the hands of Bolshevism, cost what it may. . . . Persia must be ours; Persia must belong to the revolution.[2]

Officially, the Soviet government continued to appear committed to rectifying the wrongs perpetrated against Iran by the tsarist regime. It announced the cancellation of all outstanding Iranian debts to Russia and renounced all Russian concessions and privileges in Iran. It seems clear, however, that the primary Soviet motivation for renouncing Russian imperialist aims in Iran was to generate sufficient popular resentment against the British to force them to withdraw their forces from the country and from Russia's volatile and turbulent southern frontier.

To the extent that the Soviets expected that their apparent selflessness and generosity toward Iran would be rewarded by a gratitude that could later be exploited for revolutionary purposes, they were to be sorely disappointed. The Iranian government correctly perceived the Soviet actions as a result of their intrinsic weakness, a direct consequence of the civil war that was raging in Russia. Instead of becoming infatuated with the ostensible friendliness of the Soviet regime, the Iranian government sought to exploit the opportunity presented to settle some old grievances engendered by tsarist imperialism.

An Iranian delegation, headed by Foreign Minister Mushavir al-Mamalek, was sent to the Paris Peace Conference to present Tehran's claims for a restoration of Iranian sovereignty over a number of territories previously seized from it by Russia. The territories claimed included Transcaspia, Merv, Khiva as far north as the Oxus River, and Nakhichevan. They also made a claim on Turkish Kurdistan as far to the west as the Euphrates River. However, primarily because of British objections, Iran was denied participation in the Peace Conference on the basis that it had formally maintained its neutrality during the course of the war. As a result, the Supreme Council ignored its territorial claims.

British interests in Iran, understandably, were diametrically opposed to those of Soviet Russia. When Russian forces were withdrawn from the country in 1918, the British promptly moved in to fill the vacuum, occupying Enzeli and Rasht in June. Once the war was over, the British government generally favored a prompt reduction of military commitments in the Near and Middle East, including Iran. However, Lord Curzon had become acting foreign secretary during the period when Lord Balfour attended the Paris Peace Conference. He began to pursue, as characterized by Harold Nicolson, his imperial dream "of creating a chain of vassal states stretching from the Mediterranean to the Pamirs and protecting, not the Indian frontiers merely, but our communications with our further Empire. . . . In this chain of buffer states . . . Persia was to him at once the weakest and the most vital link."[3] Thus, instead of withdrawing British forces from Iran, beginning in the spring of 1919, the country was transformed into a forward base for British and White Russian intervention in the Caucasus during the civil war in Russia.

Britain did whatever it could to establish its hegemony over Iran. This was evident in the treaty, the brainchild of Curzon that was signed on August 9, 1919, between Britain and the government of Vossuq al-Dawleh, the path to which was paid for in hard cash. Under the terms of the treaty, in exchange for a loan of two million pounds, Britain received control over the Iranian army, the country's finances, and its tariffs. The Russians were furious and Foreign Commissar Georgi V. Chicherin announced on August 30 that they would not "recognize the Anglo-Persian Agreement, which will lead to the slavery of the Persians." They viewed the agreement "as a scrap of paper having no legal validity."[4] The United States was also visibly annoyed about not having been consulted about the agreement and Secretary of State Robert Lansing expressed his anger at what he described as "a secret negotiation to obtain at least economic control" of Iran.[5]

Soviet Russia was particularly upset because its interest in Iran at the time transcended the matter of its territory being used as a base for the support of counterrevolutionaries. The Soviets had their eye on northern Iran for other reasons as well. Indeed, early in 1920, notwithstanding the assurances of the British government to the contrary, the *London Times* predicted the forthcoming Soviet invasion of Iran. "Mr. Lloyd George tells us that the Bolshevists will never invade the Middle East, and had nothing to gain thereby, yet Bolshevist Turkestan is starving while Persian Khorasan, Mazanderan, Gilan and Azerbaijan are fat and full of grain."[6]

By the end of April 1920, the counterrevolutionary armies of General Anton Denikin were defeated, the independent Azerbaijan Republic collapsed, and the Bolsheviks retook Baku. The remnants of Denikin's forces boarded vessels and escaped to the Iranian port of Enzeli, where they were ostensibly interned and placed under Iranian and British protection. Pursuit of those troops provided the Soviets with the occasion and rationale for crossing into Iran.

On May 18, a Soviet Caspian fleet of some 13 warships bombarded Baku, inflicting many casualties and causing considerable destruction. However, according to the commander of the Soviet fleet, F. F. Raskolnikov, it was only the Kazian area, where the British forces were located, and not the city itself that was actually shelled. On May 21, Vossuq al-Dawleh, appealed to Curzon for help, but to no avail. The following day, Bonar Law observed in a statement made in the House of Commons that "His Majesty's Government was under no obligation under the Anglo-Persian Treaty to defend Iran."[7] In any case, it was apparent that the British forces in Iran were outgunned and outmanned, and could not offer serious resistance to the Soviet forces. The British therefore withdrew from Enzeli without having fired a shot, first to Qazvin and subsequently from Iran entirely, once again reneging on their commitments and abandoning the Iranians at a time of need.

What the Soviets had failed to achieve by their diplomacy of calculated generosity toward Iran, they now accomplished by force of arms. Red Army units took over Enzeli and soon became entrenched in the province of Gilan. Tehran vigorously, but fruitlessly, protested this violation of Iran's territorial integrity both to Moscow and the League of Nations. Chicherin's response left little hope for a quick resolution of the problem. "The Persian Government may rest assured," he stated, "that the Soviet detachment has been ordered to leave Persian territory as soon as military requirements permit, and after re-establishing free and safe navigation of the Caspian."[8] Moscow later resorted to the patent fiction that the independent Soviet Republic of Azerbaijan was occupying Gilan as a necessary security measure, and that the government of Soviet Russia had no influence over the latter's decisions.

No sooner had the Soviets occupied Enzeli than they made contact with Mirza Kuchik Khan, Ekhsanulla Khan, and other leaders of the rural and radically pan-Islamic Jangali guerrilla movement, which was dedicated to bringing about radical social change in Iran and the overthrow of the existing regime. The movement had been engaged in an open rebellion against the Iranian central government and the British occupation since the collapse of the Russian army in Iran in 1917. The Jangali movement had also spread to Mazanderan, Astarabad, and other regions along the Caspian. However, the rebellion was eventually brought under control by the central government in the summer of 1919.

The Jangali leaders concluded from this experience that a successful revolution in Gilan could only be carried out with substantial assistance from the Soviets. Accordingly, they spent the next several months establishing contacts with the Bolshevik leaders across the border. In the early spring of 1920 they received a letter from the Bolshevik commander in the Caucasus advising them that Baku would soon fall. It was evident that the Soviets were seeking contacts with the Iranian rebels in anticipation of their forthcoming intervention in Iran. Now that the British had withdrawn and the Soviets were in effective control of northern Iran, there were no longer any significant obstacles to the establishment of an independent Iranian Socialist Soviet Republic of Gilan, which was duly proclaimed in Rasht on June 4, 1920.

The new republic soon extended its effective jurisdiction to Mazanderan as well. Kuchik, who became president and war commissar, promptly sent a telegram to Lenin asking for help. "In the name of humanity and the equality of all nations the Persian Socialist Soviet Republic asks you and all the socialists belonging to the Third International for help in liberating us and all weak and oppressed nations from the yoke of Persian and English oppressors. Bearing in mind the establishment of brotherly union and full unanimity between us, we expect from the free Russian nation the assis-

tance that may prove indispensable for the stabilization of the Persian Socialist Soviet republic."[9]

The Soviets clearly had little real trust in Kuchik, who was fundamentally a Muslim religious leader. Even while accepting Raskolnikov's help
he insisted that there should be no dissemination of communist propaganda in Iran, since communism was fundamentally incompatible with the
traditional religious sensibilities of the people. However, as far as the Soviets were concerned, Kuchik's primary value had always rested precisely in
his use as an instrument for communist revolutionary propaganda rather
than in his military or political leadership abilities. They argued that
"Kuchik is important as a socialist agitator not so much because he is a
leader of a guerrilla war but because he is a bearer of social slogans, which
he advanced even before the coming of the British to Gilan. His work which
is so closely connected with communism, although it is interpreted by the
Persians in a different sense, represents a seed which, once it is carefully
and skillfully cultivated, will produce a good harvest of revolutionary pre-
paredness among the Persian masses."[10]

Accordingly, following a pattern of Soviet takeovers that became classic,
Raskolnikov brought in his own trusted native agents to take control of the
critical levers of power. Thus, Jaafar Pishevari was appointed to take control of the Gilan Commissariat of Interior, giving the communists control of
internal security, and several Russians were placed in his service as advisers, and in some cases as executives. The latter occurred in Rasht where
Commissar Abrahamov fired the governor of the city and took over the position himself. In addition, in June 1920, the radical nationalist Adalet
moved to Rasht from Baku and helped form the Iranian Communist Party
(Bolshevik), which joined forces with the Jangalis. Before long, the pro-Soviet elements began to fill all positions of prominence, thereby threatening
to completely dominate the Jangali movement. This soon led to a power
struggle for control of the movement between Kuchik and the communists.
The matter at issue was the insistence of the communists, openly supported
by Soviet troops and political agents, on a ruthless expropriation and redis-
tribution of all existing landholdings, a step that was opposed by Kuchik.
In this struggle, Kuchik managed to retain the upper hand by contriving to
have virtually the entire communist leadership slaughtered at a feast
where the issue was to be resolved. Nonetheless, these developments,
which clearly reflected the Soviet determination to radically change the
economic and social structure of the Caspian provinces, greatly alarmed
Tehran. To help secure their gains, the Soviets placed heavy pressure on the
central government, notwithstanding the latter's inability to do anything
tangible about the problem, and helped precipitate the fall of the Vossuq
regime.

However, Vossuq's successor, Mushir al-Dawleh (later known as
Hassan Pirnia), was, if anything, at least as determined to resist Russian en-

croachment. The new prime minister made this quite clear. "The Iranians wished to live in friendship with Russia, but the attempt to use Iran as a springboard for the Bolsheviks in the interests of World Revolution, would be resisted even if the bloody insurgents of Gilan inaugurated their fresh victories on the bodies of our people."[11]

Surprisingly, Moscow was also disturbed by events in Iran, but for rather different reasons than Tehran. The Gilan initiative appears to have been undertaken unilaterally by local Soviet leaders on Stalin's authority, and was not looked on with favor by all in the Kremlin. Chicherin, for one, had earlier told Ekhsanulla that, from a Marxist standpoint, it was premature to attempt to take over and establish a soviet in northern Iran in view of the absence of serious preparatory work having been done among the masses. Indeed, the entire Soviet adventure drew a rebuke from Lenin. Viewing events in Iran from the perspective of furthering the spread of Soviet influence, Lenin was concerned that an attempt "to start revolution in any part of Persia would immediately throw it into the arms of the British, who would be received as the Saviors of the Fatherland."[12] Soviet actions in Gilan might therefore spur the British to remain in Iran and proceed with their idea of establishing a South Persian Federation, which would in effect be a British protectorate. This would ultimately make it more difficult for the Soviets to consolidate their position in Central Asia. Furthermore, it would exacerbate relations with Britain at a time when the Kremlin was negotiating for loans in London that it sorely needed to help rehabilitate Soviet industry. Accordingly, it was decided, if necessary, to abandon the Gilan initiative for the sake of broader Soviet interests.

It was soon evident that the Soviet position in Iran was becoming increasingly tenuous as a consequence of the dissension within the Jangali ranks that resulted from a split between Kuchik and Ekhsanulla. The government in Tehran took advantage of the disarray in the dissident ranks and prepared to move against them. Mushir al-Dawleh appointed a White Russian officer, Colonel Starosselski, to be commander of the Iranian Cossack Division and ordered him to undertake the reconquest of Mazanderan and Gilan. The former was quickly retaken, and was followed by the fall of Rasht on August 24, 1920. The Iranian forces then marched on Enzeli, but were stopped outside the city by fresh Soviet troops that had just arrived in the port with heavy mortars and artillery.

It was at this point that the Kremlin decided that the Gilan Republic was not viable without an extended Soviet occupation, and that was clearly inexpedient at the time. That same summer, Moscow notified Teheran that Leon Karakhan, deputy commissar for foreign affairs, was authorized to negotiate a new bilateral treaty with the Iranian government. It was understood by all that a minimum requirement of such a treaty would be a total withdrawal of Soviet troops from Iran. An Iranian mission headed by

Mushavir al-Mamalek arrived in Moscow in October and spent the next several months hammering out an acceptable agreement.

The British were greatly disturbed by these developments and sought to gain even greater influence and control over the Iranian government and its army. They had a deep distrust of the White Russian officers who commanded the army. On November 1, 1920, the commander of British forces in Iran, General Edmund Ironside, successfully pressured the Iranian government as well as the Iranian monarch, Ahmad Shah, to dismiss Starosselski and the other Russian officers and replace them with British officers. In Starosselski's place, Ironside appears to have promoted the rise of an ambitious Iranian Cossack colonel from Mazanderan, Reza Khan Savad-Kouhi.

Pressures were mounting on Britain either to significantly bolster its forces in Iran to deal with the problems of pacifying the country, thereby greatly increasing its financial commitment or to effectively sacrifice the Anglo-Persian Agreement and withdraw its forces from the country. Ironside, who operated with a free hand in Persia and tended to ignore the Foreign Office, favored withdrawal. He wrote in his diary on December 24, 1920: "The more I consider this show, the more I think we ought to get out of it. The state of affairs which allows us to be opposed in a state of actual war to a greatly inferior Bolshevik Army, without being allowed to deal with it, is unsatisfactory. The Bolshevik says that he is only helping the would be Soviet element in Persia while we are helping the old corrupt capitalist system. We cannot complain about his backing Kuchek Khan if we back the shah. We are both mixing in the internal politics of Persia. We want a *status quo ante* and they want a revolution."[13]

The problem, however, was how to insure against a Soviet takeover following the British withdrawal. Ironside evidently believed that what Britain needed in Iran was a strong indigenous military dictatorship to establish the desired *status quo ante*, and that Reza Khan was the man for the job. The latter soon formed an alliance with Sayyid Zia ed-Din Tabatabai, an anglophile newspaper editor and staunch anti-communist, who had strongly supported the 1919 Anglo-Iranian agreement. On February 21, 1921, Reza Khan's Cossack troops took control of Tehran, deposed the existing government, and forced Ahmad Shah to appoint Zia as prime minister and Reza as commander of the armed forces. At the same time, the British also armed the highly conservative Shahsavan tribesmen along the Azerbaijan-Gilan border to harass the forces of the Gilan Soviet. They also sent a British intelligence officer to the south to lay the groundwork for a South Persian Confederation that would be built out of the Bakhtiaris and other southern tribes, should Reza Khan lose control of the country. This latter idea was part of a contingency plan for protecting British interests in Iran conceived by Curzon as early as 1892.

The coup mounted by Reza Khan proved to be double edged as far as British interests were concerned. It did create a strong military dictatorship that was able to mobilize sufficient forces to deter a Soviet intervention following the British withdrawal. However, it also dramatically reduced British influence over the Iranian government. It did this first by effectively abrogating the 1919 Anglo-Persian agreement, a move that British policymakers agreed was essential if they were to remove a powerful propaganda tool from the Soviets that could be used to undermine the Iranian government. Second, the Reza-Zia regime turned out not to be as pro-British as had been expected of them. It quickly signed the treaty of friendship negotiated by the former Iranian government with the Soviet Union on February 26, 1921, that cancelled the Iranian debt to the tsarist regime, and annulled almost all concessions granted to Russia over the preceding century.

Under the terms of the 1921 Soviet-Iranian treaty of friendship, the central government in Tehran was to regain control over Gilan, although it remained unclear as to just when the Soviet forces would be withdrawn. Iran also received an assurance of the Soviet desire to abstain from any intervention in its internal affairs. However, the treaty also included two articles that would plague future governments, since the treaty was for an indefinite period and contained no provisions for its termination. Article 5 provided that both Iran and Soviet Russia undertake to prohibit the formation or presence within their respective territories of any organizations or groups of persons, whose object is to engage in acts of hostility against either Iran or Russia and its allies. They also obligated themselves to prohibit the formation of armed forces within their respective territories for such a purpose. Moreover, they also agreed to prevent, by all means in their power, the presence within their territories or that of their allies all military forces of a third party, when such forces might be regarded as a menace to the frontiers, interests, or safety of the other state.

Article 6 went even further and was, at the time, probably intended as a hedge against the possibility that Britain might establish a base in southern Iran. It granted Soviet Russia a unilateral right to intervene in Iran whenever it considered events in that country to represent a threat to its national security. The article stipulated:

If a third Party should attempt to carry out a policy of usurpation by means of armed intervention in Persia, or if such Power should desire to use Persian territory as a base of operations against Russia, or if a Foreign Power should threaten the frontiers of Federal Russia or those of its Allies, and if the Persian Government should not be able to put a stop to such menace after having been once called upon to do so by Russia, Russia shall have the right to advance her troops into the Persian interior for the purpose of carrying out the military operations necessary for its defence. Russia undertakes, however, to withdraw her troops from Persian territory as soon as the danger has been removed.[14]

Understandably, these provisions were seriously questioned in the Majlis when the government submitted the treaty for its ratification. The foreign minister wrote to Theodore A. Rothstein, the Soviet ambassador in Tehran, on December 21, 1921 noting the vagueness of Articles 5 and 6, and requested written clarifications. Rothstein responded the same day, "I have the honour to inform you that Articles 5 and 6 are intended to apply only to cases in which preparations have been made for a considerable armed attack upon Russia or the Soviet Republics allied to her."[15] This assurance appears to have satisfied the Iranian government, even though the text of treaty was never amended to incorporate this understanding.

With respect to Article 6, the Soviet negotiator, Leon Karakhan, had insisted that Russian troops would remain in Iran until after the withdrawal of British forces was completed. This did not take place until May 1921. However, the de facto Soviet occupation of much of northern Iran continued for some time after the British withdrawal. In June, Kuchik's troops, augmented by Soviet contingents from Georgia, began to march on Teheran. Soviet reinforcements were still landing at Enzeli in July. The Iranian Cossack Division managed to hold the forces of both Kuchik and the Soviets outside Teheran while the Iranian government protested vehemently.

It was now indisputable that the blatant Soviet intervention had made Iran the innocent victim of unprovoked Soviet aggression and imperialism, at a time when, as Lenin believed, it ill-served Soviet interests. Accordingly, the Soviets ultimately decided to give up their Gilan adventure, to which Lenin had never given his imprimatur in the first place, and withdrew their forces on September 8, 1921, allowing the Iranian army to proceed to restore order in the province. By October, the Jangali rebellion was over. Kuchik attempted to flee to northern Azerbaijan, but was later found frozen to death in the mountains of Talysh.

Having failed to obtain a permanent foothold in Iran through direct intervention, the Soviets reverted to more subtle methods in pursuit of their aims. Moscow now once again sought the establishment of warm relations with Tehran, preferring to rely on the use of more indirect means of infiltration and penetration to radicalize and ultimately gain effective control of the country. It was not deflected from this course by its failure to employ these methods successfully in connection with the noncommunist-inspired separatist revolts of Sheikh Muhammad Khibiani and Khoda Verdi Khan, that took place in Azerbaijan and Khorasan respectively during the same period, which were crushed by the Iranian army.

A major Soviet propaganda machine was organized in Iran, initially under the leadership of Rothstein, a former editor of the *Manchester Guardian*. Under his influence, some two dozen newspapers began to appear, most of them strongly anti-government and anti-British in orientation. At the same time, the Soviet embassy became a center of intrigue against the Iranian government. Things reached the point under Rothstein's successor, Boris

Shumiatsky, that Lord Curzon issued a "cease and desist" demand to the Soviet government on May 2, 1923. He demanded that there be an end to the anti-British activities of Soviet agents in Afghanistan, India, and Iran, which were clear violations of the non-propaganda clause of the Soviet-British Trade Agreement of March 16, 1921. To illustrate the basis for his concern, Curzon cited an intercepted message sent by Shumiatsky to the Kremlin the previous month: "Our mission, in putting into practice the instructions indicated in your telegram, has decided to follow those political directives especially in northern Persia and in Tehran. There has been organized a good group of propagandists who will be able to develop a really effective anti-British action."[16] Although Curzon's protest ultimately resulted in the recall of Raskolnikov from Afghanistan, Shumiatsky remained in Tehran.

It appears that during the 1920s the Soviet leaders had adopted the view that Soviet geopolitical interests no longer required that that there be a communist upheaval in Iran. As rationalized by Karl Radek in 1923: "For the Soviet government it is completely unnecessary to create in Persia artificial Soviet republics. Its real interests in Persia consist in the fact that Persia should not become a base for an attack on Baku. If the Persian government obligates itself to demand the withdrawal of the English forces, and England rejects this demand, in spite of the promise of Lloyd George, then the Red forces will make their appearance in Persia, not as conquerors but as allies."[17]

As already indicated, the coup d'etat staged by Reza Khan on February 21, 1921 took place to no small extent because the British wanted an indigenous military dictator to hold together what appeared to be a rapidly disintegrating Iran. Reza assured the Qajar monarch Ahmad Shah that the coup was designed to save the monarchy from revolution and to rid the country of foreign occupation. In response to his request, the shah appointed Sayyid Zia as prime minister and created the post of Sardar Sepah (Army Commander) for Reza.

In May 1921, Reza took control of the War Ministry and began to consolidate his control over the military, soon exercising a force monopoly in the country. He transferred the gendarmerie from the Interior Ministry to the War Ministry and replaced the remaining foreign officers with colleagues from the Cossack Division. Gendarmerie mutinies in Tabriz and Mashad were soon suppressed, and the Jangali movement was defeated handily once Soviet forces withdrew from Gilan. By December, Kuchik Khan's head was on display in Teheran, and order was clearly being established in the country.

Reza integrated the 7,000 Cossacks and the 12,000 gendarmes into a new 40,000 man army with which he mounted a series of expeditions over a period of four years against rebellious tribes from Azerbaijan to Khorasan, and from Fars to the frontier of Baluchistan. Having fired Sayyid Zia a few months after coming to power, he made and unmade a series of cabinets until October 1923, when he appointed himself to be prime minister. By December 1925, he was strong enough to convene a constituent assembly that deposed the Qajar dynasty and offered him the throne. In April 1926, Reza Khan, following the procedure of his hero Napoleon Bonaparte, crowned himself as the shah of Iran.

Reza Shah sought to stabilize his frontiers, and entered into a Turkish-Iranian pact of friendship and non-aggression on April 22, 1926, and an Afghan-Iranian treaty of friendship and collaboration on May 25, 1928. The emergence of Iraq as an independent state in 1932 gave new impetus to a regional politics that was independent of European machinations. Although Turkey had approached Iraq for a bilateral pact of friendship as early as November 1928, Iran initially showed little interest in doing likewise. In January 1932, however, the situation was quite different and Turkey and Iran both issued an invitation to Iraq to join in a tripartite agreement. Negotiations on a tripartite nonaggression pact began in earnest after King Feisal's visit to Tehran in April. The evident purpose of the pact was to lay the groundwork for Persian and Turkish neutrality in the event of Soviet involvement in a general war.

Progress on the tripartite agreement was impeded by Iran's position with regard to the Iran-Iraq frontier. In May 1934, Iran formally refused to accept the legitimacy of the frontier, particularly in the Shatt al-Arab, an issue that would escalate into a major war a half century later. Iraq appealed to the Council of League of Nations in November 1934 and a conciliation commission was set up to resolve the dispute. Iran, assuming that Iraq would do whatever the British wanted, focused its efforts on getting Britain to persuade Iraq to concede Iran's claims. The British were concerned that there should be no settlement of the Shatt al-Arab issue on terms that would leave Iran in control over access to Basra from the sea, or exclude Britain from a seat on the board that was to oversee control of the silting of the waterway.

Turkey was increasingly anxious to achieve the tripartite pact, to provide cover for its assertive position with regard to the neutrality of the Turkish Straits and the future of the sanjak of Alexandretta. It eventually persuaded Iraq, by promises of Turkish support of Iraqi supremacy in the Arab world, to give in to Iran on the Shatt al-Arab question. An Iranian-Iraqi frontier treaty that appeared to settle the Shatt al-Arab dispute was signed on July 4, 1937 followed by the signing of a non-aggression pact between Turkey, Iraq, Iran, and Afghanistan at Saadabad on July 8.

NOTES

1. V.I. Lenin and Joseph Stalin, *The Russian Revolution*, p. 275.
2. George Lenczowski, *Russia and the West in Iran, 1918–1948*, p. 10.

3. Harold Nicolson, *Curzon: The Last Phase, a Study in Post-War Diplomacy*, pp. 121–122.

4. Rohan Butler et al. eds., *Documents on British Policy Oversees*, vol. 4, p. 1208.

5. U.S. Department of State, *Foreign Relations of the United States 1919*, vol. 2, p. 700.

6. Nasrollah S. Fatemi, *Diplomatic History of Persia 1917–1923*, p. 196.

7. Ibid., p. 201.

8. *Times of London*, June 3, 1920.

9. Lenczowski, *Russia and the West in Iran*, p. 57.

10. Xenia Joukoff Eudin and Robert C. North, *Soviet Russia and the East: 1920–1927*, p. 177.

11. Fatemi, *Diplomatic History of Persia*, p. 239.

12. Louis Fischer, *The Soviets in World Affairs*, vol. 1, p. 430.

13. R. H. Ullman, *Anglo-Soviet Relations, 1917–1921*, vol. 3, p. 384.

14. Text of treaty in J. C. Hurewitz, *Diplomacy in the Near and Middle East*, vol. 2, pp. 90–94.

15. Fatemi, *Diplomatic History of Persia*, p. 287.

16. Lenczowski, *Russia and the West in Iran*, p. 67.

17. Ivar Spector, *The Soviet Union and the Muslim World 1917–1958*, pp. 95–96.

11

The World War II Period, 1939–45

As the British and the French prepared to challenge the Axis powers on the traditional battlefields of Europe, they also took steps to assure their continued dominance of the Mediterranean region, the soft underbelly of the continent. Britain and Turkey issued a "declaration of mutual guarantee" on May 12, 1939, which was followed on June 23 by a non-aggression pact between Turkey and France. The 1925 Treaty of Neutrality and Non-Aggression, which was renewed for an additional 10 years in 1935, governed Turkey's relations with the Soviet Union. Subsequently pressed by both the Allies and the Axis to cooperate in their war efforts directly or indirectly, Turkey managed to maintain its troubled neutrality throughout the conflict.

The Franco-Turkish rapprochement was facilitated by France's agreement on July 3, 1938 to allow limited numbers of Turkish troops to enter the sanjak of Alexandretta to assist in maintaining order there, an act that gave Turkey de facto control of the contested district. The Turkish majority of the population soon elected a Turk-led provincial government and transformed the former sanjak into the autonomous Republic of Hatay on September 2, 1938. Turkey subsequently annexed Hatay in the spring of 1939 with France's consent, at the time of the conclusion of the non-aggression pact of June 23. This betrayal of Syrian interests further fueled the growing anti-French sentiment in Damascus that led the new high commissioner Gabriel Puaux to suspend the Syrian constitution, to dissolve the chamber of deputies, and to establish rule by decree in July of that year. Similar measures were taken in Lebanon on September 21.

In the British sphere in the region, more subtle steps were taken to bolster British security interests. In volatile Palestine, the British sought to limit the effects of Axis propaganda by making concessions to the Arabs at

Jewish expense. This was a safe albeit cynical policy, because the British knew for a certainty that the Jews could not possibly align with the Axis against them in the war that could be clearly seen on the horizon, whereas this was hardly the case with the Arabs. Accordingly, at a time when Jews were desperately trying to find refuge outside Europe, the British issued a White Paper on May 17, 1939 that effectively restricted Jewish immigration to Palestine to a trickle. They also prohibited any further land sales in the country to Jews. Although there were rumblings in the Arab world that the White Paper did not go far enough, it was sufficient to achieve the British purpose at the time.

In Egypt, the onset of the war was met with considerable ambivalence. On the one hand, there were large numbers of British forces in the country, which urged cooperation with Britain even as the Egyptians wanted very much to rid themselves of the British presence. On the other hand, there were some 60,000 Italian residents in the country who had considerable influence because of their involvement in commerce and banking. Moreover, both Germany and Italy had been active in Egypt for some time preceding the outbreak of war, both diplomatically and propaganda-wise.

Britain invoked the security provisions of the 1936 treaty and all the country's ports and communications facilities came under direct British control. However, when Italy declared war on the Allies in June 1940, and Britain asked the Egyptian government to declare war on Italy, Prime Minister Ali Maher refused to do so and was subsequently dismissed by the king at British insistence. Nonetheless, his successors similarly refused to declare war against the Axis, even after Italian troops crossed the Egyptian border in August 1940 followed by the German Afrika Korps in April 1941, but did break diplomatic relations.

Concerned by the extent of pro-Axis sentiment in the country, the British decided it was in their best interest to restore the Wafd to power as a means of preventing their undermining the existing government and fostering further unrest. The king, however, was adamantly opposed to seeing Nahas Pasha, the Wafd leader, back in power. This led the British to surround the royal palace in Cairo with armored units on February 4, 1942, while the British ambassador and the commander of British forces presented Farouk with an ultimatum, to either nominate Nahas Pasha or be deported from the country. By the fall of 1944, when the Axis threat to the region was no longer a serious consideration, the British withdrew their support from Nahas and Farouk dismissed him, bringing the Saadist party back into office. The new premier, Ahmed Maher Pasha, was a realistic statesman and was concerned about Egypt's place in the post-war world. Since the Yalta Conference of the Big Three had made a declaration of war on the Axis a prerequisite for attendance at the United Nations founding conference in San Francisco, Egypt declared war on February 24, 1945. A fanatical student assassinated Ahmed Maher as he was reading the royal decree.

In Iraq, the pro-British government of Nuri as-Said, in conformity with the requirements of the 1930 Anglo-Iraqi Treaty, severed diplomatic relations with Germany in September 1939. In March 1940, however, Nuri was replaced by the anti-British Rashid al-Gailani, and his government began to move in the direction of neutrality. It simply ignored Italy's declaration of war on Britain and France and continued to permit the Italian minister in Baghdad to spread anti-British propaganda for more than a year after Italy entered the war, despite protestations by the British government.

At the outbreak of the war, France had an army of some 100,000 well-trained troops in Syria and eight divisions in Tunisia, superior to the forces of its British ally, and of higher quality than the Italian armies in Tripolitania and Cyrenaica. With a combined Anglo-French blockade that severed the lines of communication between Italy and the North African coast, it appeared that the Allies would retain control of the soft underbelly of Europe. It was even speculated that because the Italians did not seem to pose a significant threat to the Middle East, the French army in Syria might spearhead an attack on Germany through the Balkans.

However, neither the British nor the French anticipated or were prepared for the blitzkrieg that Germany launched on May 10, 1940 through Belgium and the Netherlands. Within a week and a half the German armies broke through to the English Channel and soundly defeated both the French army and the British expeditionary force, leaving some 340,000 of their troops to be evacuated by sea from the port of Dunkirk. France soon capitulated, signing an armistice agreement with Germany on June 22, 1940 that left the status of the French army in Syria unclear, since General Charles De Gaulle refused to accept the French surrender and formed a Free French resistance and later a government-in-exile. After some hesitation, the French mandatory regime in Syria decided to abide by the demands of the Vichy government and to reject any further cooperation with the British forces in Palestine and Iraq.

The decision of French High Commissioner Puaux to side with Vichy against the Free French was apparently prompted to a significant extent by a concern about the perceived readiness of Britain to support Turkish claims to Aleppo and the Jazirah. Presumably, Britain was prepared to do this as a means of ensuring Turkish adherence to the June 1939 non-aggression pact. As Puaux put it after the war:

I feared, without the support of the fleet or the rest of the empire, finding myself alone with the British, dependent on them for everything, in the midst of a Middle East entirely under their influence. Conversations that I had had with their local representatives led me to think that Britain would not have hesitated in supporting Turkish claims, or those of the neighboring Arab states under their protection, for a portion of Syria. I considered it my duty to guard for France the integrity of the territories that had been entrusted to me.[1]

The Vichy government was ostensibly neutral, but found itself unable to prevent Axis influence from penetrating the region, especially after the arrival in Beirut of the Italian and German armistice commissions in August 1940. Anti-British propaganda among the Arabs was stepped up with good results, Syria and Lebanon becoming bases for guerrilla activities against the British.

With an essentially hostile government in power in Baghdad, the character of Anglo-Iraqi relations was contingent on perceptions of how well the British were doing against the Axis. As a result of internal political machinations, Rashid Ali al-Gailani was ousted as premier in January 1941 and replaced by a more amenable General Taha al-Hashimi. Then, in the spring of 1941, Britain experienced serious defeats in the Balkans and an Italian-German offensive in Libya that threatened the British hold on Egypt. These events, coupled with pro-Axis intrigue and propaganda, further heightened anti-British sentiment in the country. Rashid Ali led a coup d'etat on April 3, ousting Taha al-Hashimi and forcing Nuri as-Said and the regent, along with most of the members of the cabinet, to flee to Transjordan.

Notwithstanding Rashid Ali's professed willingness to abide by the terms of the Anglo-Iraqi Treaty, the British became determined to restore the previous government and landed a British-Indian military contingent at Basra at the end of April. When a second British contingent arrived, the government decided to take action and fighting broke out on May 1. Iraqi forces surrounded the British air base at Habbaniya as well as the British embassy compound in Baghdad, and Rashid Ali sought to obtain Axis military assistance. The Germans, however, were preoccupied in Greece and were preparing for the invasion of Russia. As a result, they were not inclined to send any significant assistance to Iraq. Moreover, because Turkey refused to allow the transit of troops and supplies through its territory, whatever materiel aid Germany was prepared to send to Rashid Ali could only reach him through Vichy-controlled Syria.

The already testy relations between the Vichy government and Britain in the region reached a crisis point in May 1941. The new high commissioner in Syria, General Henri-Fernand Dentz, permitted German use of the Aleppo-Mosul railway and allowed German aircraft to land and refuel at Syrian airfields en route to Iraq with supplies for Rashid Ali. Despite this, the Rashid Ali rebellion was put down by the end of the month with troops from Palestine and Transjordan, in conjunction with the British-Indian forces already debarked at Basra. Rashid Ali escaped and eventually made his way to Berlin, along with a number of pro-Axis colleagues, including the exiled mufti of Jerusalem, Haj Amin al-Husseini, where they remained until the end of the war. Nuri as-Said was returned to the premiership of Iraq in October 1941 and remained in office until 1944. With a pro-Allies government in power, British troops began pouring into the country and a

Polish army was transferred to the area to help protect the northern frontiers against a possible German attack through the Caucasus. Iraq subsequently declared war on Germany, Italy, and Japan on January 16, 1943, and signed the United Nations Declaration on January 22.

At the same time, the British response to the blatant Vichy breach of its neutrality was to attack the French in Syria with forces from Palestine, Transjordan, and Iraq, accompanied by Free French troops. The invasion, which began on June 8, 1941 under the command of General Sir Henry Maitland Wilson, came to an end with an armistice on July 14. Syria and Lebanon were now placed under the British Middle East Command and occupied by the Ninth Army and Free French forces.

On the day of the invasion, the French commander General Georges Catroux proclaimed that the Free French authorities intended to abolish the mandate and to grant independence to both Syria and Lebanon. Although this proclamation seemed unequivocal, it soon became a matter of contention with the British, who took it at face value, and De Gaulle, who both procrastinated in carrying out the promise and insisted on a privileged French position in both countries once independence was granted. Finally, on September 27, 1941, Catroux proclaimed the independence of Syria with all the trappings of sovereignty, but required that Syria provide aid and facilities for the Allies during the war. These stipulations were to be formalized as soon as possible "in the form of a Franco-Syrian Treaty which will definitely guarantee the independence of the country."[2] Lebanese independence, under similar terms, was announced on November 26, 1941. Sheikh Taj ad-Din al-Hasani was invited by Catroux to become president of Syria and Alfred Naqqash to remain in office as president of Lebanon.

Despite the proclamations of independence and the de jure recognition of both governments by Britain, France refused to transfer the major functions of government to the new republics, the constitutionality of whose regimes was in doubt since elections were never held and De Gaulle was opposed to holding them. Under the pressure of an increasingly hostile populace, the French finally relented and permitted the holding of elections in March 1943. In both Syria and Lebanon pro-French politicians were turned out of office to be replaced by anti-French nationalists. Shukri al-Quwatli became president in Damascus, and Bishara al-Khuri became president and Riyadh as-Sulh became prime minister in Beirut.

The results of the elections further exacerbated tensions with the French who still effectively ruled by decree and were in virtual control of the security police, tribal affairs, and censorship of the press. The nationalists were furious and, on November 8, 1943, the Lebanese parliament adopted a resolution that would have eliminated from the constitution all articles that acknowledged France as the mandatory power. The French responded two days later by suspending the constitution, deposing the president and prime minister, arresting most of the cabinet, and appointing Emile Edde to be head of both state and government. This, however, was more than the British, who were in military control of the region, could accept and the French were compelled by the outbreak of anti-French violence and British pressure to release the elected Lebanese leaders and return them to office. An agreement was concluded with the French Committee of National Liberation on December 22, 1943 that provided for the transfer of almost complete power to the governments of both Lebanon and Syria.

Notwithstanding the December agreement, the French continued to insist that Syria and Lebanon conclude treaties with France that would tie both countries to it as a condition for French relinquishment of its mandatory responsibilities. Of particular concern was French insistence that the treaties acknowledge France's strategic interests in the area, provide for the maintenance of its naval and air bases, and affirm its right to organize and command the armies of Syria and Lebanon. Negotiations were scheduled to begin on May 19, 1945, but the French preempted them by landing reinforcements at Beirut several days earlier, precipitating violent anti-French outbursts in both Lebanon and Syria. Britain intervened once again, Prime Minister Winston Churchill effectively demanding that De Gaulle order a cease-fire and the return of his troops to their barracks. Faced by the British ultimatum, De Gaulle backed down and complied. This solved the immediate problem, but the treaty negotiations were never resumed. With British support, on June 21, 1945, Lebanon and Syria issued a joint declaration that dismissed all French citizens from government services and the transfer to their authority of the special forces that had remained under French control. France formally consented to the latter on July 7. Even so, French and British troops were not completely withdrawn from Syria before April 1946, and from Lebanon by December 31, 1946.

In Iran, the onset of the conflict created a new geopolitical environment. With the German invasion of Russia in June 1941, the Allies were confronted with the dilemma of how to deliver massive amounts of supplies to the beleaguered Soviet forces. There were four possibilities, but two of them, the route through Murmansk on the Arctic Circle or through Vladivostok at the eastern end of Asia, were ruled out because neither port could handle the quantity of supplies required. A third option was through the Turkish Straits. However, Turkey was a nonbelligerent ally and had closed its waterways; any attempt to force them open would likely have triggered a war, something no one in the West wanted. The only remaining practical route to the Soviet Union was overland through Iran, and the Allies decided to use it, without regard to Iran's neutrality, which it had declared formally on September 4, 1939.

For one thing, the long-planned Russian railway from the Caspian Sea to the Persian Gulf, from Bandar Shah to Bandar Shahpur, had actually been built by Reza Shah for the expressed purpose of reducing northern Iran's economic dependence on the Soviet Union for its markets and trade. Thus, the critical basic infrastructure for a supply corridor to the Soviet Union was already in place. In addition, Iran also provided a position from which a German advance towards India could be blocked. Furthermore, the oil wells and refineries in Iran and the Persian Gulf region were of vital importance to the British navy, which drew most of its required petroleum from these sources, and these had to be protected. This led Britain to approach the Soviet Union once again, as it had some forty years earlier, with a proposal to establish British and Soviet zones of influence in Iran. Churchill later wrote:

The need to pass munitions and supplies of all kinds to the Soviet Government and the extreme difficulties of the Arctic route, together with future strategic possibilities, made it eminently desirable to open the fullest communication with Russia through Persia. The Persian oil fields were a prime war factor. An active and numerous German mission had installed itself in Teheran and German prestige stood high. The suppression of the revolt in Iraq and the Anglo-French occupation of Syria, achieved as they were by narrow margins, blotted out Hitler's Oriental plan. We welcomed the opportunity of joining hands with the Russians and proposed to them a joint campaign. I was not without some anxiety about embarking on a Persian war, but the arguments for it were compulsive.[3]

In mid-July 1941, Britain and the Soviet Union concluded an Anglo-Soviet Agreement for Mutual Assistance and soon began pressing the Iranian government to expel the numerous German nationals from the country. The German-supported takeover of Iraq by Rashid Ali al-Gailani in April 1941 provided unmistakable evidence of Berlin's influence in and plans for the Middle East, most particularly the Persian Gulf region. Moreover, there was a concern that some of the Germans in Iran might, on instructions from Berlin, be in a position to sabotage the Soviet re-supply effort.

Tehran, however, was reluctant to comply with this demand. Since the outcome of the war was by no means certain at the time, it did not wish to risk antagonizing Germany, which, if it defeated the Anglo-Soviet alliance, might later retaliate against Iran. Tehran's reticence brought a strong response from the Soviets which indicated that, unless Iran complied, the Soviet Union might be compelled to send its own forces into the country under the provisions of Article 6 of the 1921 Treaty of Friendship. On August 17, Britain and the Soviet Union delivered formal notes to the Iranian government demanding expulsion of German technicians and experts. Both countries considered the Iranian hedged response on August 22 to the demand unsatisfactory and relations between the Allies and Iran reached a critical point. Reza Shah, however, appeared to be convinced that the British would not violate Iranian neutrality and that the Soviets were too preoccupied with the German advance into Russia to mount an invasion of Iran. What the shah failed to realize was that his continuing negotiations with the Allies did not reflect the reality of the situation. Britain and the Soviet Union had already decided to take direct action in Iran. Indeed, as Churchill later revealed, as early as July 22 the British commander in Iraq, General Quinan, "had been ordered to be ready to occupy the oil refinery at Abadan and the oil field, together with those two hundred and fifty miles farther north near Khanigan."[4]

Unknown to Reza Shah, the British and Soviet demand of August 17 was intended to be their final word prior to taking military action. Before dawn on August 25, the ambassadors of Britain and the Soviet Union informed Iranian Prime Minister Ali Mansur that their forces had entered the country in order, as the British explained, to forestall the "attempts of the Axis powers to establish their control on Iran."[5] The Soviets, as they had threatened to do, justified their intervention in Iran by reference to Article 6 of the 1921 Treaty. Their formal note of August 25 stated:

The situation in Iran . . . is fraught with extreme dangers. The Soviet Government is thus obliged to carry out immediately all measures which it is not only entitled to take but is bound to take for self-defense in strict conformity with Article 6 of the Treaty of 1921. . . . The Soviet Government has no designs affecting the territorial integrity and the independence of the Iranian State. The military measures which the Soviet Government is undertaking are directed exclusively against the danger created by hostile activities of Germans in Iran. As soon as this danger, threatening the interests of Iran and the USSR has been removed, the Soviet Government, in compliance with its obligation under the Soviet-Iranian Treaty of 1921 will immediately withdraw Soviet troops from Iranian territory.[6]

The Allied invasion met with some initial token resistance from Reza Shah's forces that was easily overcome. The shah, however, could not reconcile himself to what had happened and became an irritant to the Allies. His continued defiance soon brought about his forced abdication as Allied forces marched on Tehran on September 15. The following day Churchill told Stalin: "I am anxious to settle our alliance with Persia. . . . There are in Persia signs of serious disorder among tribesmen and of breakdown of Persian authority. Disorder, if it spreads, will mean wasting our divisions holding down these people. . . . Our object should be to make the Persians keep each other quiet while we get on with the war."[7] Reza Shah, who was succeeded by his son Muhammad Reza, went into exile in South Africa where he died in 1944.

The constitutional monarchy was restored in Iran on September 20, 1941, and the country was subsequently divided into British and Soviet zones. It is estimated that the number of Soviet troops brought into Iran were between 85 and 100 thousand. The area occupied by these forces was approximately 250 thousand square miles of northern Iran that included the provinces of Azerbaijan, Gilan, Mazanderan, Khorasan, Zanjan, Gorgan, and Qazvin.

The Allied powers understood and agreed that their presence in Iran was simply a matter of military expediency and conferred no territorial rights there. However, although both Churchill and Stalin had given their personal assurances to President Franklin Roosevelt that they would respect Iran's territorial integrity, Secretary of State Cordell Hull was unsatisfied and sought a formal public commitment from the Allies to this effect. Given the history of British and Soviet imperialist designs on Iran, there was a concern that the present occupation of the country would be perceived in that light, raising questions about the true character of their war aims. He noted, as early as August 27, two days after the Anglo-Soviet entry into Iran, that he had advised the Soviet ambassador that Soviet Russia and Great Britain should give this same assurance to all nations opposed to aggression. Hull believed that a formal declaration to this effect "would have a very healthy and wholesome effect on the entire Moslem world as it would be stimulating to the peoples of small countries everywhere."[8]

The formal undertaking to respect the territorial integrity and the sovereignty of Iran sought by Hull was affirmed in the Tripartite Treaty of Alliance of January 29, 1942 between Britain, Iran, and the Soviet Union. Article 1 stipulated unequivocally that Britain and the Soviet Union "jointly and severally undertake to respect the territorial integrity, sovereignty and political independence of Iran." Article 5 further specified: "The forces of the Allied Powers shall be withdrawn from Iranian territory not later than six months after all hostilities between the Allied powers and Germany and her associates have been suspended by the conclusion of an armistice or armistices, or on the conclusion of peace between them, whichever date is earlier."[9]

However, if there were any expectations that Soviet actions in Iran would be constrained by these provisions of the treaty, they were to be grossly disappointed. In fact, Iranian sovereignty and political integrity were consistently violated by the Soviets from the moment of the arrival of their forces. With the Soviet army occupying northern Iran, only the British forces to the south prevented Moscow from realizing the traditional Russian imperialist dream of direct access to the warm waters of the Indian Ocean. Once having gained a foothold only a relatively short distance from the Indian Ocean coast, the Soviets began to take advantage of the situation to consolidate their presence in the country. They did everything they could to destabilize Iran and to establish conditions for an upheaval that would bring the entire country under effective Soviet control.

According to Article 4 of the 1942 Tripartite Treaty, "the presence of Allied forces on Iranian territory does not constitute a military occupation and will disturb as little as possible the administration and the security forces of Iran, the economic life of the country, the normal movements of the population and the application of Iranian laws and regulations." Notwithstanding the clear language of the treaty, the Soviets virtually sealed off the northern provinces of Azerbaijan, Khorasan, Mazanderan, and Kurdistan from access by Iranian officials. They had in fact placed these territories under military occupation, and no one, including British and American nationals, could enter them without Soviet permission. Moreover, and of considerable significance for the future, the outlawed Communist Party reappeared under the name of the Tudeh (masses) party, and received the virtually open support of the Soviet forces in the country.

As early as September 23, 1941, Anthony Eden had cabled the British representative in Moscow, Sir Stafford Cripps, indicating his concerns regarding Soviet actions in Azerbaijan. "I understand that there had been a movement, especially among the Armenian minority, in favor of the separation of that province from Iran and its eventual federation with the Soviet Union. Considerable apprehension appeared to exist lest these separatist tendencies should be encouraged by the Soviet military authorities in Tabriz. . . . About first September, a large open air meeting had been held at Tabriz which was chiefly attended by Armenians, who demanded independence for Azerbaijan and its federation with the Soviet Union."[10] The Soviet hand in the open meeting was so blatant that they deemed it wise to ban a second such demonstration, although the separatist campaign was allowed to proceed by the circulation of petitions. Several days later, the American minister in Tehran reported that a Soviet paper printed in Farsi, *Thoughts of the People*, was "disseminating Russian propaganda."[11] Cordell Hull made note, on October 3, 1941, of "a recent suggestion of the Russian Ambassador in Teheran to the Iranian Government that special elections should be held and a greater degree of autonomy granted to certain areas in Iran."[12]

Moscow's expansionist interests in Iran were heightened by a general concern about the vulnerability of the Soviet southern flank. While still allied with the Axis powers, in June 1940 the Soviets became aware of British and French plans to attack the oil fields at Baku from both Turkish and Iranian territory. Then, after having been attacked by Germany and forced to switch sides, Moscow learned of a German scheme for fomenting a revolt of Armenians and Azerbaijanis within the Soviet Union. As a result, there was great interest in transforming northern Iran, at the least, into a secure buffer zone.

From the first, the Soviets virtually sealed northern Iran against entry from the south. Although they cooperated closely with their allies in operating the supply line from the Persian Gulf to the Caspian as long as the flow of materiel was critical to stemming the German offensive, this changed after the battle of Stalingrad in November 1942. As the tide of battle turned against the Germans, the Soviets directed their attention in Iran to further entrenching themselves in the north, giving every indication that they intended, in one way or another, to retain control there permanently. They took over the press in the areas under their occupation and used it to attack the Iranian government and promote separatism. As already indicated, this was particularly the case in the northwestern Iranian province of Azerbaijan, which was a territory of considerable strategic and economic value for the Soviets. Located at the junction of the Soviet Union, Turkey and Iraq, under Soviet control it would drive a wedge between Turkey and Iran, providing ready access to western Turkey through the road to Erzurum. As a forward base, it would have positioned Soviet forces on the Iraqi frontier only about 100 miles from the Kirkuk and Mosul oil fields.

The seriousness and extent of Soviet involvement in northern Iran was pointed out by John D. Jernegan of the State Department in a memorandum of January 23, 1943, in which he offered the following assessment of events in the country:

Apart from the general situation in Iran, I believe we should be fully alive to the character of the present Russian occupation of the northern provinces. In Azerbaijan, the Soviet authorities have greatly restricted the operations of the Iranian civil authorities and have virtually immobilized the small Iranian military forces which they reluctantly permitted to return to the area. They have alternatively encouraged and discouraged the restive Kurds, always a thorn in the flesh of the local government. More important still, they have been so successful in propagandizing the population that our Consul at Tabriz has reported that a soviet could be established overnight in Azerbaijan if the Russians gave the word. In this connection, it is well to remember that Azerbaijan is inhabited largely by a Turkish-speaking population whose cultural ties with Soviet Transcaucasia and Turkish Kurdistan are almost as strong as those with the rest of Iran. It is also the most important grain-producing area of Iran and would be a welcome addition to the food resources of Transcaucasia.[13]

It was becoming abundantly evident that the Soviets saw and treated Iran generally as a sheep to be fleeced for the benefit of the Soviet homeland, and had no intention of relinquishing its foothold there.

BIRTH OF THE ARAB LEAGUE

As early as 1941, with a threat of an imminent assault on the region by the Axis powers, Britain sought to gain allegiance among the Arabs by appealing to pan-Arab nationalist sentiment, implicitly urging their unity, and proffering support for pursuing such a goal. Thus, on May 29, the British foreign secretary Anthony Eden declared:

The Arab world has made great strides since the settlement reached at the end of the last war, and many Arab thinkers desire for the Arab peoples a greater degree of unity than they now enjoy. In reaching out towards this unity, they hope for support. No such appeal from our friends should go unanswered. It seems to me both natural and right that the cultural and economic ties, too, should be strengthened.

His Majesty's Government for their part will give their full support to any scheme that commands general approval.[14]

Eden's speech aroused considerable concern in Zionist circles because it made no reference to the British promise regarding a Jewish national home in Palestine. However, as Colonial Secretary Lord Moyne explained to a Zionist representative, Eden had stated to him that the phrase "general approval" used in the speech was meant to cover "Jewish rights."[15] This implied that the Jews would have a voice in the deliberations regarding the formation of an Arab union, a notion that was disingenuous at best.

Britain continued to maintain the policy favoring an Arab union even after the Axis military threat to the region began to dissipate in 1942 and effectively vanished after the battles of Al-Alamein and Stalingrad. It was perceived as being in Britain's interest to support the formation of an inter-Arab federation or at least an alliance, under British tutelage, that might serve to stabilize the region by subduing the prevailing inter-Arab rivalries. Eden made this clear on February 24, 1943, when he told the British parliament that "the British Government would view with sympathy any movement among the Arabs to promote economic, cultural or political unity," and lamented that "no such scheme which commands general approval has yet been worked out."[16]

The reactions to this prospect in the Arab world were mixed. Two principal advocates of unity were Nuri as-Said of Iraq and Emir Abdullah of Transjordan, both of whom envisioned the emergence of a Hashemite kingdom consisting of Iraq, Syria, Lebanon, Transjordan, and Palestine, lands claimed by the Hashemites during the previous war. Both would have excluded Egypt from the alliance, at least initially. Abdullah, in particular, disliked the Egyptians and did not consider them Arabs at all.

The Lebanese, on the other hand, were hesitant about joining such a scheme, and Saudi Arabia had little interest in anything that would support Hashemite ambitions in the region. After all, the Saudis had ejected the Hashemites from Arabia less than two decades earlier and saw no point to enhancing their status as possible alternatives to Saudi rule in the peninsula. Moreover, Abdullah was widely perceived as a British puppet and Transjordan as an artificial entity created to provide overland access for Britain from Egypt to Iraq.

Ironically, it was Egypt that, with British encouragement and support, soon emerged as the driving force behind Arab unity. Under British prodding, Nahas Pasha and Nuri as-Said, prime ministers of Egypt and Iraq, sought to find a compromise between a general union of Arabs led by Egypt and the Hashemite scheme proposed by Nuri. An ardent proponent of Arab unity, Abd al-Rahman Azzam Pasha, assumed the task of mediation. With the British applying pressure behind the scene, Azzam succeeded in gaining the support of King Farouk of Egypt and King Abd al-Aziz ibn Saud of Saudi Arabia. Following the lead of the two monarchs, other Arab leaders accepted the Egyptian invitation to attend an organizing conference in Alexandria that began on September 25, 1944.

The objective of the conference was to be the organizing of an all-encompassing Arab union. This objective, however, was met in only a limited sense. The conference produced a protocol that, despite paying lip service to the spirit and ideals of pan-Arabism and unity, looked toward a league of independent Arab states rather than a federation. Each of the member states was assured that its sovereignty would in no way be impinged by participating in a league that would work toward inter-Arab political coordination and social, economic, and cultural cooperation. The protocol also specifically endorsed the goal of Lebanese independence and the right of the Arabs of Palestine to a state of their own in that country. The protocol was soon transformed into the Pact of the Arab League, which was signed on March 22, 1945 by Egypt, Saudi Arabia, Iraq, Transjordan, Syria, and Lebanon, followed by Yemen on May 10.

Although the pact did create a regional forum for discussion of a range of issues and for cooperation between states on a number of issues, it failed to create an entity of political weight capable of creating a united front in the pursuit of pan-Arab interests. One of the principal weaknesses of the pact was that it made no provision for the unification of the foreign policies of the member states. It therefore did not preclude a member state from pursuing a foreign policy detrimental to the League as a whole or to any of its constituent members. Abdullah, whose ambitions were thwarted by the outcome of the negotiations, subsequently described the pact with some evident bitterness. It was, he said, "a sack into which seven heads have been thrust . . . with remarkable haste and at a time when Syria and Lebanon were still under a French mandate, Transjordan under a British mandate, and Iraq and Egypt bound by still valid treaties with Great Britain. Nonetheless, the Arab countries were content both with the veil concealing that which they wish to hide and with the vainglorious boasting about what they wish to advertise."[17] It was, as Elie Kedourie characterized it, "a device designed not so much to bring about Arab unity, as to keep the so-called Arab states at arm's length from one another."[18]

Indeed, weeks before the pact was signed opinion of its value in British policy circles was decidedly skeptical. As pointed out in a minute of January 28, 1945 by R.M.A. Hankey of the Foreign Office:

There is a unity about the Middle East which all Arabs feel but it is very easy to overstate the practical applications of this feeling. Egypt with its semi-African population and peculiar traditions, Syria so much the intellectual centre of Arabia, the Lebanon with its Christian population, Palestine with its Jews, the fanatic Nejdis in Saudi Arabia, and the population of Iraq scattered over such a colossal area and having such different problems that even though they feel in a similar way about a number of subjects, one cannot for the purposes of Government easily treat them on a parallel basis.[19]

Nonetheless, the pact became a reality and on March 30 Hankey wrote another minute suggesting that the Arab League be viewed as a vehicle for promoting British interests in the Middle East. "I suggest that there will be real advantages in the future in promoting solidarity among the Arab states and in encouraging them to look to us for leadership and help, as there is a strong tendency for them to do."[20] Getting the Arabs themselves to sustain Britain's preeminent position in the region was an ingenious notion and became a cornerstone of British policy in the immediate postwar years.

However, and contrary to British hopes and expectations, the formation of the Arab League did not well serve their interests. One unanticipated consequence of London's gamesmanship in promoting Arab unity was to give Egypt sufficient prominence to become the leading state of the Arab world, giving it international prestige and leverage in its campaign to rid itself of Britain and to project its influence throughout the Middle East.

NOTES

1. Howard M. Sachar, *Europe Leaves the Middle East, 1936–1954*, p. 116.
2. Albert H. Hourani, *Syria and Lebanon: A Political Essay*, p. 245.
3. Winston S. Churchill, *The Grand Alliance*, p. 477.
4. Ibid., p. 481.
5. *New York Times*, August 26, 1941.
6. Alvin Z. Rubinstein, ed., *The Foreign Policy of the Soviet Union*, pp. 183–185.
7. Churchill, *The Grand Alliance*, p. 484.
8. *Foreign Relations of the United States* (1941), III, p. 435.
9. J. C. Hurewitz, *Diplomacy in the Near and Middle East*, II, pp. 232–234.
10. *Foreign Relations of the United States* (1941), III, p. 468.
11. Ibid., p. 465.
12. Ibid., p. 467.
13. *Foreign Relations of the United States* (1943), IV, p. 333.
14. Vernon McKay, "The Arab League in World Politics," p. 209.
15. Ahmed M. Gomaa, *The Foundation of the League of Arab States*, p. 104.
16. Majid Khadduri, "Towards an Arab Union," p. 90.
17. Gomaa, *The Foundation of the League of Arab States*, p. 265.
18. Elie Kedourie, *The Chatham House Version*, p. 228.
19. Wm. Roger Louis, *The British Empire in the Middle East, 1945–1951*, p. 132.
20. Ibid.

12

The Geopolitics of Oil, 1914–47

The initial impetus for British involvement in the Middle East and especially the Persian Gulf region in the nineteenth and early twentieth centuries was primarily geostrategic, safeguarding the overland lines of communications and the sea routes to India. It was only in the years shortly before the outbreak of World War I that the future economic potential of the region, in terms of its oil wealth, began to come into the view of British financiers.

Shortly after the turn of the century, an Australian investor, William Knox d'Arcy obtained a concession from the shah of Iran to search for oil in the southern part of the country. His interests in the concession were subsequently sold in 1908 to a consortium of British and Dutch investors who organized the Anglo-Persian Oil Company and constructed a refinery at Abadan on the Persian Gulf. By 1914, the Abadan refinery was shipping oil at the astounding rate, at the time, of some 250,000 tons annually. Coincidentally, it was at the same time that the British navy completed the transition from coal-burning vessels to oil-burners. Only a few days before the outbreak of World War I, Winston Churchill, first lord of the admiralty, convinced the British parliament to authorize the government to increase its share in the Anglo-Persian Oil Company to allow it to have effective control of the company. From that moment, oil became a major factor in the geopolitics of the region.

In 1914, with the approval of the Ottoman government, the soon to be renamed Anglo-Iranian Oil Company (AIOC) reached an agreement with the Royal Dutch Shell Corporation, which was itself 40 percent British-owned, and a German company to explore for oil in the Ottoman vilayets of Mosul and Baghdad. The primary shareholder in the new Turkish Petroleum Company (TPC) was the AIOC, the second largest share-holder being Royal Dutch Shell. In other words, the British government controlled most of the oil of the region, either directly or indirectly. By 1934, with the completion by the TPC, now renamed the Iraq Petroleum Company, of a pipeline to the Mediterranean, the oil fields of Mosul became a major supplier for the world's growing and seemingly insatiable appetite for oil. Eventually, two pipelines were constructed in 1934, one going through French-mandated territory to Tripoli in Lebanon, and the other through British-mandated territory to Haifa in Palestine, where refineries were also built.

The British also established their preeminence in the Persian Gulf region by using their diplomatic muscle to prevent other outsiders from obtaining controlling interests in the Gulf oil fields. Thus, the American Gulf Oil Corporation was prevented from outbidding the British for a major concession in the sheikdom of Kuwait until 1934. It was then agreed that the American group would form a full partnership with the AIOC and that the new Kuwait Petroleum Company would be registered as a British enterprise. By the end of World War II, oil from the Middle East became the one truly bright spot in an otherwise faltering British economy, drained to the limit by the enormous costs it bore during the war and equally great burdens of reconstruction and rehabilitation. As one historian of the period put it: "In sum, at the end of the war no other investments in the world offered Britain's straightened economy the proved and estimated future income of this far-flung network of desert wells. London was determined to protect it as it protected the mines and factories of the home island itself."[1]

Despite the fact that British treaties with the several Gulf sheikdoms precluded "outsiders" from obtaining oil concessions, the Americans found a way to overcome the British restriction. A British group obtained a concession for oil exploration in the Bahrein Islands off the coast of Saudi Arabia in 1925, which was purchased a few years later by the Standard Oil Company of California. Standard Oil then went around the British restriction by registering in Canada as the British-owned Bahrein Petroleum Company. From Bahrein, the Americans began eyeing possible oil deposits in Saudia Arabia. Although it too was nominally bound by an agreement with the British not to allow "outsiders" in, its ruler, Abd al-Aziz ibn Saud, was in need of additional income and opened the door to exploration by an American petroleum engineer, Karl S. Twitchell, in 1931. The test drillings showed promise and Twitchell convinced Standard Oil of California to bid on the concession. To everyone's surprise, especially the British who were not even offered a share, Abd al-Aziz approved the American offer in 1933 and what would later be known as the Arabian American Oil Company (Aramco) came into being. The giant conglomerate would soon give the Americans preeminence over the British in the Middle East and would have significant influence on American Middle East policy.

Fearful that the British government was working behind the scenes to undermine Aramco's foothold in Arabia, the company began assuming responsibility for increasing the amount of the British wartime subsidy to Abd al-Aziz to offset the loss of revenue from the pilgrimage to Mecca caused by the war. By 1943, however, Aramco had advanced as much as they dared against future royalties, some $3 million, and appealed to the U.S. government for relief, arguing that without direct government intervention Abd al-Aziz might cancel the American oil concessions and turn them over to the British. On February 16, 1943, Harold Ickes, U.S. secretary of the interior and petroleum administrator, persuaded President Franklin Roosevelt to provide Lend-Lease aid directly to the Saudi monarch instead of funneling it through the British as in the past. Washington thus signaled to London that it considered Saudi Arabian oil to be its exclusive preserve.

The British, understandably, had no intention of simply acceding to American desires and continued to exert influence in the country both through its subsidy to Abd al-Aziz and other activities. Lord Moyne, the British Minister Resident in the Middle East, succinctly articulated British concerns about the American approach to the Arabs, with whom they had little experience, to Anthony Eden in September 1944. "There is a serious risk of their adopting an excessively paternal and patronising attitude to Saudi Arabia from a failure to understand that a fanatical Muslim population does not take the same view of the blessings of American civilisation as they do themselves." He cautioned the foreign secretary, "If the results of misguided American benevolence should be to undermine the independence of the country and make it a satellite of the United States, it would have serious reactions throughout the Moslem world and gravely prejudice British interests."[2]

The American perception from the region, on the other hand, was clearly set forth in a message from the U.S. minister in Egypt, Alexander Kirk, to Secretary of State Cordell Hull in April 1944. "Saudi Arabia is rapidly becoming an active battle ground in the implementation of two systems of foreign policy—the British which in the past has aimed to make countries in which they are interested dependent in perpetuity ... economically upon the Empire, and the American system which is based on the intent to help backward countries to help themselves in order that they may lay the foundation for real self dependence. Needless to say a stable world order can only be achieved under the American system."[3] That same spring, Hull was to complain that the British minister in Riyadh was "doing his level best to injure the United States Government's relations with King Ibn Saud, and was endeavoring in other ways to undermine our position in Saudi Arabia."[4]

Although efforts were subsequently made to formalize an agreement that would protect both American and British oil interests in the Middle East, the U.S. Senate rejected the proposed treaty on the grounds that it constituted a cartel. This development was not particularly disturbing to the British who still hoped to salvage their influence among the oil sheikdoms in the Persian Gulf region.

The emergence of Middle East oil as a significant factor in the world economy had a number of geopolitical consequences, one of which concerned the security of the means of making the oil accessible. As noted earlier, the Iraq Petroleum pipelines to Tripoli and Haifa were completed in 1934. After the war, Aramco organized a Trans-Arabian Pipeline Company in 1946 and began planning a major pipeline from the vast Abqaiq field on the Persian Gulf coast of Saudi Arabia to the port of Sidon in Lebanon, a distance of some 1,068 miles. This so-called Tapline was completed in 1950. In 1947, the Anglo-Iranian Oil Company announced plans for the construction of an even larger and longer pipeline, the so-called Mepline, from the Persian Gulf to Tarsus on the Syrian coast.

The growing network of pipelines crisscrossing the Middle East created a new geopolitical environment. The pipelines, which became of increasingly greater economic importance to both Britain and the United States, crossed vast stretches of desert and were particularly vulnerable to sabotage and disruption. Patrolling the pipelines was impractical and their security became increasingly dependent on the state of relations and the security of the host countries. Assuring the stability in the region that would facilitate the uninterrupted flow of oil became principally a British preoccupation in the post-war period, primarily because Britain had staked out its predominant role on the ground in the region. Britain's post-war policies in the Middle East were shaped in large measure by its perceived need to preserve its position there. However, other developments were already taking place that, within a few years, would relegate Britain to a minor role in the Middle East. One of these was the reassertion of Soviet imperialism in the region.

Soviet oil production in the Baku fields had declined significantly during the war and Moscow cast an envious eye at oil-rich Iran, the south of which was being exploited by British interests with the cooperation of the Iranian government. Moreover, it appeared that Iran was favorably considering additional applications for concessions that were made in the fall of 1943 by the Anglo-Dutch Shell oil company, and by two American oil companies, Standard-Vacuum and Sinclair, in the spring of 1944.

The Soviets perceived these developments as a challenge to their ambitions in the country, and decided to take steps to secure their interests in Iran. In mid-September 1944, Moscow sent Sergei I. Kavtaradze, Assistant Commissar for Foreign Affairs, to Tehran where he submitted a note complaining about Iran's negotiations with the British and American oil companies without giving comparable consideration to the interests of the Soviet Union. The note virtually demanded that Iran grant the Soviet Union oil concessions in the provinces of Astarabad, Azerbaijan, Gilan,

Khorasan, and Mazanderan for a period of 75 years, and that the details concerning the concession be worked out after the grant was approved by the Majlis.

It was soon clear that Iranian Prime Minister Muhammad Saed had no intention or wish to grant any oil concessions to the Soviets. The government informed the American, British, and Soviet embassies on October 14 that all negotiations concerning oil concessions would be postponed until after the conclusion of the war. It was evident that Saed had no desire to negotiate concessions with the Soviets while they were in effective military occupation of the territories concerned. Saed tried to put the best face possible on the matter when he told the Majlis, "The Soviet Mission was also informed that the Iranian government would like to postpone discussions on oil concessions to the period after the war. But unfortunately some newspapers and political circles have interpreted this decision as an anti-Soviet act. This is not true. Iran has been a strong and loyal ally of the Soviet Union in the prosecution of the war against Nazi Germany and in the future will strive to strengthen this friendship and cooperation between the two governments."[5]

Saed's attempt to placate the Soviets was unsuccessful and relations between the two countries began to deteriorate very rapidly. This was especially so because both the British and the Americans, who were now intensely involved and concerned with Iranian affairs, supported the Iranian decision not to grant any concessions to alien interests as long as foreign troops were stationed in the country. This suggested multilateral collusion against Soviet interests. In a sharp attack on Iranian policy in its edition of October 22, the Soviet trade newspaper *Trud* accused the Saed government of not taking steps to oppose "the present intensification of subversive work by pro-Fascist elements in Iran." It then noted "because of Mr. Saed's policies, Iranian relations with the Soviet Union have become tense and strained," and that many Iranians were asking Saed to resign because his policies were harmful to the interests of the country and the people.[6] The following day, Kavtaradze held a large press conference at the Soviet embassy in Tehran at which he indicated unequivocally that Saed's unfriendly attitude towards the Soviet Union precluded the possibility of further Soviet cooperation with him. He then made a blatant appeal to the Iranian public to put pressure on the government to force a change of policy. Massive demonstrations against the government soon broke out in the Soviet occupation zone.

As Soviet propaganda intensified, Saed called a press conference of his own to explain why he would not negotiate a concession with the Soviet Union. He made it clear that as long as foreign troops were in Iran, any concessions awarded would have been granted under duress. Furthermore, given the unstable world political and economic situation, it was unwise to negotiate something as far-reaching as oil concessions until the implications were better understood. Once again, his efforts were of little avail. The Soviet propaganda war against him and his government only became shriller and more vindictive. *Izvestia* joined the campaign claiming that "criminal and pro-Fascist elements" had influenced Saed's decision to refuse to negotiate with regard to the oil concessions and alleging that he was apparently determined to cause a rupture in relations between Iran and the Soviet Union.[7] The Soviet campaign against the prime minister soon bore fruit. In the wake of mounting unrest in the country, Saed felt compelled to resign, and did so on November 9. Morteza Qoli Bayat succeeded him on November 20. However, the fall of Saed did not resolve the issue.

On December 2, 1944, Muhammad Mossadeq, the veteran politician of Tehran, introduced a private bill in the Majlis that, in his view, would prevent the de facto partition of the country. It would have prohibited any Iranian government official from negotiating or concluding an agreement with any foreign government or company regarding any oil concessions that might incur legal obligations on the part of the Iranian government, without the prior authorization of the Majlis. The avowed purpose of the law was to exclude the Soviets, as well as the British, from obtaining what Mossadeq feared might become permanent foreign footholds in Iran. His argument was sufficiently persuasive to gain the overwhelming support of the Majlis, overriding the ineffective opposition of the communist Tudeh deputies, who numbered only eight out of a total of 130.

The Soviets, however, saw this nationalist move as directed particularly against them. Kavtaradze met with Prime Minister Bayat on December 8 and took strong exception to the new law. Kavtaradze pointed out that since the law was only concerned with new concessions, it gave the British, who already had concessions in the south, a privileged position in the country relative to the Soviets. Therefore, the law could only logically be interpreted as anti-Soviet. Bayat, however, was no more forthcoming on the issue than Saed had been, and Kavtaradze returned to Moscow in a huff. The Soviets would soon once again try to consolidate their position in northern Iran, this time relying more on the Red Army than on the Tudeh and its sympathizers.

The Soviets continued to tighten their grip on their zone of occupation, increasingly and portentously referring to the Soviet-Persian Treaty of 1921, rather than the Tripartite Treaty of 1942, as the basis for the presence of their forces in the country. Churchill was evidently disturbed by the extent to which the Soviets were entrenching themselves in Iran. He sent a secret telegram to Roosevelt on January 15, 1945, in anticipation of the Yalta Conference, suggesting that it did not appear that Stalin was willing to abide by his commitment to respect Iranian sovereignty and territorial integrity. He wrote:

You will have seen reports of the recent attitude of the Russians in Persia. . . . They have refused to accept the Persian decision to grant no concessions until after the war: and have brought about the fall of a Persian Prime Minister who, believing that there could be no free or fair negotiations so long as Russian (or other foreign) troops were in Persia, refused the immediate grant of their oil demands. . . . This may be something of a test case. . . . If the Russians are now able not only to save their face by securing the fall of the Persian Prime Minister who opposed them, but also to secure what they want by their use of the big stick, Persia is not the only place where the bad effect will be felt.[8]

At Yalta, the question of Iran first came up for discussion at the foreign ministers' meeting on February 8, 1945. Anthony Eden took the lead and set forth what he considered to be an acceptable basis for Allied policy in Iran. He argued that the Iranian government should be left as master in its own house and that the Allies should desist from interfering in the country's internal affairs. He took note of the Soviet Union's understandable desire for Iranian oil, since it was a natural market for it. Nonetheless, he argued that the Allies should not press for oil concessions until after their armed forces were withdrawn from the country. He suggested that such a withdrawal could begin as soon as the supply route through Iran to Russia was shut down. Soviet Foreign Minister Molotov was determined to forestall any decision on the question and urged that the discussion of the question be suspended for the time being. In his view, the Iranian decision not to grant any oil concessions until after the conclusion of the war constituted a reversal of their earlier assurances.

The question of Iran came up again at the Potsdam Conference on July 21, 1945, once more with Eden taking the lead. He proposed that British and Soviet troops should be withdrawn immediately from Tehran, and then, in gradual stages, from the rest of the country. When the matter was brought before the Heads of Government, Stalin agreed to the immediate withdrawal from Tehran, but was less forthcoming on the matter of an overall withdrawal. He again took the position he wanted to give the matter more consideration. Stalin suggested that it might be desirable to let the troops remain in Iran for six months after the end of the war with Japan. Although it had generally been assumed that the six month period provided for in the Tripartite Treaty related to the end of the war in Europe, neither Britain nor the United States objected to extending the period of occupation until a half year after the end of the war with Japan.

It is noteworthy that at the time Stalin made this proposal, the Soviet Union had not yet declared war on Japan and therefore had no justification for delaying its withdrawal from Iran once Germany had been defeated. Churchill, however, was interested in retaining effective British control over the oilfields and refineries of Iran for as long as possible, and was therefore not averse to Stalin's suggestion. He therefore readily agreed to the delay in the withdrawal schedule. President Harry Truman, while indicating his intention of going ahead with the withdrawal of American forces from Iran in order to transfer them to the Pacific theater of war, also took no issue with the proposed delay in the British and Soviet withdrawal. To assuage any concerns that Truman might have about what the Soviets might do in the absence of American forces in Iran, Stalin remarked: "So as to rid the United States of any worries we promise you that no action will be taken by us against Iran."[9] This was a promise that Stalin surely made tongue in cheek.

Sensing the reluctance of the Western powers to intervene on behalf of Iran, the Soviets saw the moment as ripe to begin to take control of the country. Azerbaijan soon became the target of a Soviet-inspired and communist-dominated separatist revolt. Reza Shah had outlawed the Communist Party in 1937, as part of a crackdown on all organized political opposition to his rule. However, under a general amnesty granted in 1941, 52 leading communists were released from prison. Well-known communists who had lived in the Soviet Union such as Jaafar Pishevari and Salamollah Javid were soon given control of the regional government in Azerbaijan.

Pishevari was a veteran communist who had earlier played a leading role in the autonomous government set up by the Soviets in Gilan in 1921. When the Soviets withdrew and the separatist movement collapsed, Pishevari went to the Soviet Union. Upon his return to Iran in 1936 he was imprisoned. However, he and other communist leaders that were released from jail by the general amnesty soon reorganized the Communist Party, renaming it the Tudeh at the end of January 1942, with its headquarters in Soviet-occupied Azerbaijan. The change in name was a purely tactical move calculated to avoid alienating those Iranians who were not communists but believed in drastic social and economic reforms, and who might be exploited for communist purposes. Although elected to the Majlis in 1943, that body rejected Pishevari's credentials the following year.

On August 26, 1945, Pishevari and the Tudeh took temporary control of Tabriz, under the protection of Soviet troops. The Soviets attempted to keep a low profile in the affair, preferring that it be seen as a purely indigenous uprising, although Soviet occupation forces were reinforced in October to insure its success. All communications with Tehran were cut off. The Iranian government decided to send a military force to Tabriz to restore order, and so informed the Soviet Embassy in Tehran on November 17. The advance of the Iranian troops was blocked by the Soviets at Sharifabad, near Qazvin, well outside the border of Azerbaijan. Moscow rejected the vigorous protests by the Iranian government and expressions of concern by the United States. It insisted that the Soviets were acting "with respect to the assurance of the democratic rights of the Azerbaijanian population of Northern Iran which is seeking national autonomy within the limits of the Iranian State which has this particular language different from the Persian language."[10] Consequently it was felt that the arrival of Iranian troops there would further aggravate the situation. This in turn would force the Soviet government to supplement its own forces there to maintain order, something it was not willing to do. At the same time, armed partisans, including *muhajirin* (immigrants), arrived from Soviet Azerbaijan to help take control of the province.

On November 24, 1945, Washington sent a note to Moscow questioning the role of Soviet forces in preventing Tehran from reasserting its authority in Azerbaijan. In its response, the Soviet government denied that it was interfering with the movement of Iranian military and gendarme forces operating in the north. It went on to state: "The Soviet Government opposed the dispatch of new Iranian troops to northern districts of Iran and informed the Iranian Government that the dispatch of further Iranian forces to northern Iran could cause not the cessation, but the increase, of disorders and likewise bloodshed, which would compel the Soviet Government to introduce into Iran further forces of its own for the purpose of preserving order and of insuring the security of the Soviet garrison."[11]

The Soviets effectively took a major step toward the eventual annexation of northern Iran on December 12, 1945, when the Autonomous Republic of Azerbaijan was proclaimed in Tabriz, with Pishevari as its prime minister.

The Soviets had also maintained an interest in the Kurdish problem since the early 1920s. The traditional homeland of the Kurds straddled the borders of Turkey, Iran, and Iraq, and was thus strategically located for the purposes of spreading Soviet influence and projecting power throughout the Middle East. Furthermore, the route to the Persian Gulf from the Soviet Union passed through Kurdistan.

The Soviet-British occupation of Iran had important effects on the Kurds of the northwest. The Soviet sphere of influence extended far enough to the south to include Mahabad. While Mahabad was relatively stable as a consequence of the presence of respected Kurdish religious and civil leaders there, the region north of it to Rezaiyeh was in a state of anarchy. The Soviets, however, would not permit Iranian army units to enter the zone to restore order. Although the Soviets were committed to maintain peace and security in the volatile tribal area, they were at the same time dedicated to a policy of retaining the good will of the tribes by encouraging their Kurdish nationalist aspirations. The Soviet presence thus presented an opportunity to lay the groundwork for a pro-Soviet autonomy movement. However, their approach to the Kurds had to be somewhat different than was the case in Azerbaijan. In attempting to establish their influence in the region, the Soviets had to overcome the traditional distrust of the Kurds. After all, for more than a century Russia had been pushing back the frontiers of Islam in the Caucasus while presenting itself as the protector of the native Christians against the Kurds of Azerbaijan and Turkey. Furthermore, the communist-dominated Tudeh Party had little following in Kurdistan. It was thus incapable of serving as an instrument for galvanizing the Kurds for effective political action. A more direct approach seemed necessary. Accordingly, in late 1941, an invitation was extended to some 30 prominent tribal leaders, including Qazi Muhammad of Mahabad, to visit the Soviet Union escorted by General Salim Atakchiev. The purpose of the visit, of course, was to convince the tribal leaders of Soviet interest in their national aspirations.

Almost simultaneously, but quite independently and with the assistance of a Kurdish officer in the Iraqi army, on September 16, 1942 a small group of middle-class citizens of Mahabad formed a clandestine Kurdish nationalist committee for the resurrection of Kurdistan, the Komala i Zhian i Kurdistan. Within six months the membership of the Komala grew to about 100. By 1944, it had extended its influence throughout northern Kurdistan and had become a major factor in regional politics. In October of that year, Qazi Muhammad, although he held no formal position, became the guide and spokesman of the party. It was now clear to the Soviets that Qazi Muhammad was the Kurdish proxy they sought.

It is noteworthy that the Komala had no qualms whatever about collaboration with the Soviets. It was, after all, the latter who were in actual control of Kurdistan and who were keeping the Iranians from reasserting their domination of the region. The Soviets had also conveyed the clear impression that they would support Kurdish independence once the war was over. However, in fact, the indigenous Komala was too nationalistic for Soviet purposes. Accordingly, in September 1945 a group of Komala leaders, including Qazi Muhammad, were invited to Tabriz by General Atakchiev to witness the formal conversion of the regional Tudeh Party into the popular front Democratic Party of Azerbaijan. Just as the Soviets were moving to detach Azerbaijan from Iran, they thought the time was ripe for a similar move in Kurdistan. Atakchiev told Qazi Muhammad that it would be desirable for a group of prominent Kurds to visit the Soviet Union once again to discuss the future of Kurdistan. It was clearly the Soviet intent to prepare such a delegation to assume the leadership of a distinctly pro-Soviet Kurdish party that would be tied to the communist-nationalist effort that was under way in Azerbaijan. Qazi Muhammad participated with the Soviets in selecting the delegation, which included the most important and amenable Kurdish tribal leaders.

The Kurdish leaders were simply invited to Tabriz for a meeting. Only Qazi Muhammad knew the final destination. Upon their arrival, they were bundled on to a train and taken across the Soviet border to Baku. There they met, as had the 1941 delegation, with the Soviet Azerbaijani Prime Minister Jafar Baghirov, who declared to them that "as long as the Soviet Union exists the Kurds will have their independence." Qazi Muhammad responded by declaring that a weak nation would welcome any helping hand: "Not only will we shake it, we will also kiss it."[12] Baghirov then proceeded to convince them that the Komala could not succeed in its current form. Given the general triumph of democracy in the West and in the Soviet Union, he argued, the Kurdish national movement would be successful only if it would create a new democratic party under Soviet sponsorship. Most of the Kurdish leaders returned to Iran convinced that Soviet hegemony in the region was a prerequisite to an independent Kurdistan. That November, the Democratic Party of Kurdistan was duly organized under the leadership of Qazi Muhammad, who promptly called for the autonomy of Kurdistan. Although the Soviets tried to accommodate Kurdish autonomy within the framework of the larger and more important Azerbaijani republic, the movement for Kurdish independence had already gone too far to turn back. On January 22, 1946 the diminutive Kurdish People's Republic was formally established in the towns of Mahabad, Bokan, Maqadeh, and Ushnuyeh.

A few days later, U.S. Secretary of State James F. Byrnes confronted Stalin in Moscow on the matter of the continued presence and actions of Soviet forces in northern Iran. Stalin insisted that under the Soviet-Iranian Treaty of 1921, the USSR had the right to send troops into Iran if it determined that there was a threat to Soviet security emanating from the country. Byrnes later wrote:

The more I thought about Generalissimo Stalin's excuse for retaining troops in Iran, the less confidence I had in the Soviet position. It was absurd to claim, as he had, that the Red Army of 30,000 well-trained and fully equipped troops must stop the poorly trained and inadequately equipped Iranian force of 1,500 from marching toward Azerbaijan on the public highway because it feared a disturbance would be created.... And his admission that the question of withdrawal would be examined on the evacuation date showed that our worries about his fulfilling the Teheran declaration were justified.[13]

Under the provisions of the Tripartite Treaty, all Allied forces were to be withdrawn from Iran within six months after the end of the war. As anticipated, the Soviet forces were not withdrawn as agreed, and Iran soon brought the issue before the UN Security Council, despite Soviet objections. Moscow took the position that the end of the war did not refer to the war with Germany only, but to that with Japan as well. Since the latter conflict ended with the signing of the Instrument of Surrender on September 2, 1945, the Tripartite Treaty did not obligate the Soviets to withdraw their forces until March 2, 1946. Indeed, Stalin had raised this point at the Potsdam Conference and neither Churchill nor Truman raised any objections.

The Iranian government charged that the Soviets were interfering in Iran's internal affairs and asked the Security Council for help. Andrei Vishinsky, the Soviet representative, freely admitted that Soviet troops had blocked the Iranian government from sending its forces into Azerbaijan, but argued that it was inappropriate for the Security Council to take up the matter. He insisted that what was happening in Azerbaijan had nothing whatever to do with the presence of Soviet troops there, but was actually evidence of the legitimate demands of the people of Iran's northern provinces for national autonomy. The Security Council, in view of the Soviet Union's ability to veto any proposal not to its liking, could only pass a bland resolution on January 30, 1946 that called for the Soviet Union and Iran to enter into bilateral negotiations to resolve the problem.

Soviet-Iranian negotiations were subsequently held between February 19 and March 11 in Moscow. Iranian Prime Minister Ahmad Qavam es-Saltaneh, who took office on January 26, 1946, had been chosen to head the Iranian government primarily because he was known to be on relatively good terms with the Tudeh. This, it was believed, would please the Soviets and make negotiations with them easier. Nonetheless, the talks ended without any concrete results. According to the Iranian ambassador to the United States at the time, Hossein Ala, the Soviet leaders were pressing Qavam to accept the following proposals: (1) Soviet forces would remain in some parts of Iran for an indeterminate period; (2) the Iranian government would recognize the autonomy of Azerbaijan. In return, the Soviets would undertake to assure that 30 percent of local revenues would be paid to the central government in Tehran. The latter would maintain control of the province's defense and foreign affairs; (3) the Soviets would give up their demands for oil concessions in exchange for a joint Iranian-Russian stock company that would be set up with the Soviets owning 51 percent of its shares.[14]

On March 1, 1946, the day before the six month period from the Japanese surrender ended, Radio Moscow announced: "On 25th February, during discussions with the Persian Prime Minister Qavam es-Saltaneh, he was informed of the decision of the Soviet Government that, with effect from 2nd March, Soviet troops would begin their evacuation of the areas of Meshed, Shahrud and Semnan, in eastern Persia. The Soviet troops in other areas of Persia will remain there pending clarification of the situation."[15] It was clear that the Soviets intended to remain in Azerbaijan and Kurdistan.

The continued Soviet occupation of northern Iran was leading to a Soviet-American confrontation, as President Truman became increasingly disturbed over Soviet behavior. The United States delivered a note to the Soviets on March 6, stating that "the decision of the Soviet government to retain Soviet troops in Iran beyond the period stipulated by the Tripartite Treaty has created a situation with regard to which the Government of the United States, as a member of the United Nations and as a party to the declaration regarding Iran, dated 1st December, 1943, cannot remain indifferent."[16] Stalin responded to Walter B. Smith, the American ambassador to Moscow: "You don't understand our situation as regards oil and Iran. . . . The Baku oil fields are our major source of supply. They are close to the Iranian border and they are vulnerable. Beria [the head of the M.V.D.] and others tell me that saboteurs—even a man with a box of matches—might cause us serious damage. We are not going to risk our oil supply."[17] Nonetheless, it soon became clear to Stalin that he would have to relinquish direct control in Iran in the face of the adamant U.S. stance on the issue. Truman's view was quite unequivocal. "Russian activities in Iran," he later wrote, "threatened the peace of the world. . . . If the Russians were to control Iran's oil, either directly or indirectly, the raw material balance of the world would undergo serious damage, and it would be a serious loss for the economy of the Western world."[18]

Stalin could not afford the risk of a showdown confrontation with the American president. Truman was, after all, the man who decided to use atomic weapons to force Japan to the surrender table less than a year earlier, and who now seemed intent on getting the Soviets to withdraw from Iran. Nevertheless, the Soviets wished to be sure that the political arrangements they had set up in the north remained intact after their departure, and that they at least reap some economic advantages as part of the price of their withdrawal. This led to a good deal of maneuvering and negotiations.

Stalin sent Ivan V. Sadchikov to Tehran as the new Soviet ambassador, and empowered him to negotiate an accommodation with Qavam. On April 4, Qavam and Sadchikov issued a joint communique announcing that an agreement had been reached. The agreement included a pledge by the Iranian government to grant the Soviets a major oil concession in the form of a joint Iranian-Soviet company, to be established in the north, in return for a Soviet withdrawal of its forces within one and a half months from March 26, 1946. That same day, in an exchange of letters, it was agreed that the Soviet Union would get 51 percent of the shares of the proposed joint company, as they had proposed earlier. The agreement was to last for 25 years after which Iran and the Soviet Union would have equal shares of the company's stock. The agreement would then be in effect for another 50 years. It appeared to be a clear victory for the Soviets.

This assessment of the situation proved quite wrong. Qavam shrewdly made his commitment on the part of Iran subject to the approval of a new Majlis. However, he made clear that the elections for the Majlis could not take place while the north was under Soviet occupation. This was justified on the basis of the resolution passed by an overwhelming majority of the Majlis on October 14, 1945 that forbade the holding of elections until after the Allied troops had departed from the country. It was thus in the Soviet interest to withdraw their forces sooner rather than later. It was also in the Soviet interest to bring about a reconciliation of Azerbaijan and the central government in Tehran. Once this was accomplished, Azerbaijan, as an autonomous province of Iran, would be able to send sufficient delegates to the Majlis that, together with other pro-Soviet deputies, would constitute the majority required to guarantee ratification of the oil agreement. Soviet troops were finally pulled out on May 9, 1946, leaving behind their puppet governments in Azerbaijan and Mahabad to reach an accommodation with Qavam.

Negotiations between Tehran and the Azerbaijanis, led by Pishevari, began on April 28, before the Soviet withdrawal, but collapsed on May 13, with Pishevari returning to Tabriz. The talks resumed again two days later in Tabriz under the eye of the Soviet consul general. The subtle Soviet pressure that was brought to bear resulted in a June 13 agreement that was signed by Pishevari and Muzaffar Firuz, a member of Qavam's cabinet known for his pro-Soviet sympathies. The 15-point agreement was very favorable to the Tudeh, and was what the Soviets had hoped for. Things took another turn for the better, from a Soviet perspective, when Qavam shuffled his cabinet on August 2, included three Tudeh members for the first time, and appointed Firuz to be Vice Premier. The prospects for a communist takeover in Iran never seemed better. The Tudeh, however, having become somewhat overconfident as a result of its success in negotiating the status of Azerbaijan, turned its attentions to Khuzistan to the south. It soon provoked a number of violent riots, including one that accompanied a general strike in the concession owned by the Anglo-Iranian Oil Company.

This precipitated a new crisis with Britain as troops were quickly moved from India to Basra, and positioned to cross into Iran. Simultaneously, and evidently as a consequence of British influence, a number of tribal leaders began to actively oppose the communist influence in the south. This development came as a surprise to the Soviets who had opened two consulates in the region during the first half of 1946, and had been courting the Qashqai, Iran's largest tribe. In return for their allegiance, the Soviets had offered them large quantities of small arms as well as full tribal autonomy. However, contrary to Soviet expectations, the Qashqai, who had recently entered into an agreement with another major tribe, the Bakhtiari, demanded that Qavam fire the Tudeh ministers in his cabinet, purge the bureaucracy in Fars of Tudeh members, and grant local autonomy to the southern provinces peopled by the Qashqai.

Qavam rejected their demands and, on September 23, an open rebellion broke out that resulted in the occupation of some Gulf ports and the siege of Shiraz. The Muslim clergy of the south also supported the demands of the Qashqai. A full scale crisis developed which soon forced Qavam to dismiss the government on October 17, and then form a new cabinet two days later without any communist ministers. The expansion of Tudeh influence in the south was effectively blocked. While Qavam protested the role of the British, working through their consuls at Ahwaz and Isfahan, in the affair, his hand was significantly strengthened thereby in asserting Teheran's control over the country, notwithstanding the ominous specter of the Soviet presence hovering across the border.

Qavam's resolve to confront the Tudeh was bolstered further by an increasingly assertive American policy with regard to Iran that served to offset the lingering Soviet threat. In mid-November, Qavam arrested 100 leading communists in Tehran and, on November 24, ordered central government troops to march into Azerbaijan to supervise the elections for the new Majlis. When the Soviet ambassador hinted that this was not a good idea and should be abandoned, the American ambassador, George V. Allen, countered on November 27 that, in his view, "The announced intention of the Iranian Government to send security forces into all parts of Iran . . . seems to me an entirely normal and proper decision."[19]

A few days later in Washington, Under-Secretary of State Dean Acheson expressed a similar view. Qavam went ahead with the troop movement and by December 14 the communist-dominated regime of Azerbaijan collapsed, as Iranian army units occupied Tabriz. Having seen the Soviets permit the destruction of its creation in Azerbaijan, Qazi Muhammad and his colleagues in Kurdistan quickly gave up any thought of seriously opposing the central government. A few days later, government troops entered Mahabad bringing an end to the fledgling Kurdish republic. The American ambassador in Moscow noted on December 27: "Collapse of Azerbaijan house of cards was a major victory for UN—and for a firm policy toward USSR. It must not be thought, however, that Kremlin will resign itself to this humiliating reverse. It will continue to maneuver not only for oil concessions but also for political (and strategic) ascendancy in Iran."[20]

With the dissident provinces back under Tehran's control, the elections for the new Majlis began on January 11, 1947, although it took until the middle of August until it was officially inaugurated. It had generally been expected that, notwithstanding the communist defeats in Azerbaijan and Kurdistan, the oil agreement with the Soviets would be quickly ratified. However, to everyone's surprise, there was substantial opposition to ratification. There was also an emerging outcry against Qavam for having agreed to it in the first place. The Soviets were outraged and began to apply heavy pressure on Qavam. However, the public stance taken by the American ambassador served as an offset to the Soviets, while significantly bolstering the opposition to the agreement. Speaking to the Irano-American Cultural Relations Society on September 11, Allen declared:

The United States has no proper concern with proposals of a commercial or any other nature made to Iran by any foreign government as long as these proposals are advanced solely on their merits, to stand or fall on their value to Iran. We and every other nation in the world, however, do become concerned when such proposals are accompanied by threats of bitter enmity or by a statement that it would be dangerous for Iran to refuse. The United States is firm in its conviction that any proposals made by one sovereign government to another should not be accompanied by threats or intimidation. When such methods are used in an effort to obtain acceptance doubt is cast on the value of the proposals. . . . Patriotic Iranians, when considering matters affecting their national interest may therefore rest assured that the American people will support fully their freedom to make their own choice. Iran's resources belong to Iran. Iran can give them away free of charge or refuse to dispose of them at any price if it so desires.[21]

The Majlis subsequently approved the establishment of an American military mission on October 6. By time the vote came up on October 22, 1947, the Majlis, bolstered by the increasing U.S. role in Iran and the failure of Qavam to even press for its approval, rejected the oil agreement with the Soviets by a margin of 102 to 2. Moscow was furious. The Iranians had proved to be wily antagonists who had outfoxed the Soviets. Moscow vigorously denounced the Iranian decision as incompatible with the maintenance of normal relations between the two countries, but was unable to do much about it at the time without running the unacceptable risk of provoking a major confrontation with the United States. Seeing Iran slip into the Western orbit, at a time when Washington was already pursuing an active policy of containment of the Soviet Union, was a severe blow to the Soviet leadership. For the moment, however, Moscow could do little beyond lick its wounds and increase its clandestine support for the Tudeh and other anti-government groups in Iran.

NOTES

1. Howard M. Sachar, *Europe Leaves the Middle East, 1936–1954*, p. 390.
2. Wm. Roger Louis, *The British Empire in the Middle East, 1945–1951*, p. 182.
3. Kirk to Hull, April 25, 1944, *Foreign Relations of the United States 1944*, vol. 5, p. 690.
4. Cordell Hull, *The Memoirs of Cordell Hull*, vol. 2, p. 1516.
5. Faramarz S. Fatemi, *The U.S.S.R. in Iran*, p. 38.
6. *New York Times*, October 23, 1944.
7. *New York Times*, November 5, 1944.
8. Text in J.C. Hurewitz, *Diplomacy in the Near and Middle East*, II, pp. 244–45.
9. Herbert Feis, *Between War and Peace: The Potsdam Conference*, p. 304.
10. *Foreign Relations of the United States 1945*, VIII, p. 468.
11. *New York Times*, December 9, 1945.
12. William Eagleton, *The Kurdish Republic of 1946*, pp. 44–45.
13. James F. Byrnes, *Speaking Frankly*, p. 119.
14. *New York Times*, March 20, 1946.
15. A.H. Hamzavi, *Persia and the Powers*, p. 58.
16. Ibid., p. 61.
17. Walter B. Smith, *Moscow Mission 1946–1949*, p. 40.
18. Harry S Truman, *Memoirs*, vol. 2, *Years of Hope and Trial, 1946–1952*, p. 95.
19. Robert Rossow, Jr., "The Battle of Azerbaijan 1946," p. 29.
20. *Foreign Relations of the United States 1946*, pp. 566–67.
21. *New York Times*, September 12, 1947.

13

Prelude to the Arab-Israeli Conflict, 1945–48

The constellation of forces in the Middle East and its periphery at the conclusion of the war in Europe in 1945 set the stage for a fundamental restructuring of the region. For one thing, as discussed in the preceding chapter, the Soviet Union had begun to make its presence felt, and although foiled in its attempt to establish a foothold in Iran, there was little reason to believe that its retreat was anything but a tactical move. Strategically, the Soviets were looking southward at Turkey and Iran, considering both as being in their security zone, and as their potential gateways to the Mediterranean and the Indian Ocean. Soviet Foreign Minister V.M. Molotov made this clear on November 25, 1940 to the German ambassador in Moscow, at a time when the two countries were still allies. Discussing the draft German-Soviet agreement, he commented that it would have to be amended "so as to stipulate the focal point of the aspirations of the Soviet Union south of Batum and Baku in the general direction of the Persian Gulf."[1]

It was evident that following the war the Soviets were determined to build a ring of buffer zones around the Soviet heartland, and that in the Middle East this meant Turkey and Iran. Indeed, by the beginning of 1946 Soviet actions with regard to Turkey were such that President Truman wrote in confidence to his secretary of state: "There isn't a doubt in my mind that Russia intends an invasion of Turkey and the seizure of the Black Sea Straits."[2] Nonetheless, the emerging Soviet threat was, generally speaking, poorly perceived and understood, although within a few years it would become a dominant factor in the politics of the region.

In the meantime, the principal factor in the Middle East was the still massive British presence there. To all appearances, the British troops that appeared to be everywhere in the region were capable of keeping a lid on the nationalist restiveness that seemed to be growing rapidly since the end of the war. Moreover, the British expected a favored position in the region because of its promotion and sponsorship of the Arab League. The reality, however, was quite different. Britain was in a serious economic bind and in a poor position to maintain its empire intact. Its already severe domestic economic problems were seriously compounded by the abrupt cancellation of American Lend-Lease at the end of the war with Japan. Retrenchment and conservation of resources now became the leitmotif of British foreign policy. Moreover, expectations that the Arab League would respond favorably to Britain's security needs quickly proved to be wishful and perhaps overly naïve thinking. In this environment, particularly in view of the looming Soviet ambitions in the Middle East, the security of British oil interests in and the critical lines of communication crossing the region took on renewed importance to London.

It was these considerations that led Britain to vacillate with regard to fulfilling its obligation to remove its troops from the Nile Valley and into the Suez Canal Zone, as required by the 1936 treaty with Egypt. The Egyptians wanted the British out. Indeed, by January 1946 all parties and groups in the country had been agitating for the abrogation of the 1936 treaty. A massive demonstration of university students in Cairo on February 6 demanded a more assertive stance against Britain by the government. This soon led to its collapse on February 15, with a new government under Ismail Sidki coming into power two days later. A similar situation prevailed in Iraq, where the Iraqis wanted to be rid of the British military presence that belied their nominal sovereignty.

For their part, the British recognized that their bargaining position had seriously deteriorated because of their economic problems. In fact, at war's end, Britain owed Egypt some 400 million and Iraq about 70 million pounds. It was also not in a position to supply the level of arms that might have fed the growing ambitions of the region's political leaders. Nonetheless, the growing disparity between Soviet and Western forces in Europe and the continued presence of the Red Army in northern Iran were matters of great concern to the government in London. Britain felt an urgent need to retain its military bases in the Middle East or, at the least, to obtain the right to return to them in the event of any danger to British economic or security interests in the region.

From March 1946, when Britain first began to deal with the problem of post-war alignments in the Middle East, to January 1948, attempts at treaty renegotiation failed everywhere except in impoverished Transjordan. There, in a treaty for which Abdullah was severely criticized by his colleagues in the Arab League, he agreed to allow British troops to remain in the country for another 25 years in return for a relatively small subsidy.

In Egypt, for a moment, it seemed as though a draft treaty negotiated by Ernest Bevin and Egyptian Prime Minister Sidki in the autumn of 1946 would result in the complete evacuation of British troops by September 1949, providing two conditions were met. The first was the establishment of an Anglo-Egyptian military alliance that would go into effect in the event of war. The second was that any change to the 1899 Condominium arrangement for the Sudan should be subject to the consent of the Sudanese, a condition that negated the previous Egyptian position, which demanded the unity of the Nile Valley. However, both the proposed treaty and Sidki were promptly disavowed, the latter's government falling in December 1946. The Egyptians wanted the British out without conditions. A similar development took place in Iraq in January 1948. Iraqi nationalists repudiated the Portsmouth Treaty, which would have given the British some continuing military rights in the country. They too demanded unconditional British withdrawal.

The British military leaders had agreed, at the beginning of May 1946, to withdraw their troops from Egypt because, at the time, alternative comparable bases were available to them. British-controlled Cyprus was favored by the Royal Air Force, but it was Palestine, preferred by the army, that was expected to replace Suez as Britain's principal base in the region. Palestine soon proved to be an extremely poor choice. A rebellion against the British was already in progress both because of the restriction of Jewish immigration in deference to Britain's ultimately ineffectual pro-Arab policy, and because of Britain's cynical betrayal of its commitments to the Jews contained in the Balfour Declaration and the League of Nations Mandate. Once the war was over, even the moderate majority among the Jews of Palestine, who had long considered Britain their protector and sponsor, notwithstanding repeated betrayals of that trust, soon reached the conclusion that the time had come for Britain to get out.

The idea of partitioning Palestine between the Jewish and Arab communities began to gain ground in international circles as a means of resolving the seemingly intractable problem facing the country. In such a scheme, however, there was little if any role for Britain beyond putting the partition into effect. This put the notion of using Palestine as the principal alternative to Egypt as the primary British military base in the region in jeopardy, because of the categorical Arab rejection of the idea of partition. Except for the Suez Canal zone, most of Egypt was being evacuated and there was no other area that could serve as a base for a Middle East reserve force that was considered necessary to deter any threat to the canal or to the oil installations in the region. On January 13, 1947 Field Marshal Montgomery, chief of the Imperial General Staff, advised Prime Minister Attlee that it was "essential to retain the right to station forces in Palestine."[3] Lord Tedder, chief of the Air Staff seconded his view, adding, "Our whole military position in the Middle East depended on the cooperation of the Arab states."[4] That cooperation would be scuttled by British consent to a partition of Palestine, whereas the Palestinian Arabs had promised that, if they were assisted in attaining independence and majority rule in Palestine, they would grant Britain the military facilities that it sought. It thus seemed that only a solution to the Palestine problem that suited Arab purposes would serve British interests.

On January 14, Bevin completed a policy paper in which he spelled out his intention of developing a proposal that would give the Arabs majority rule in a unitary state, with local autonomy and some Jewish cantonal enclaves. Bevin was fully convinced that the Arabs would reject any partition proposal and, he suggested, "There can be little doubt that in this event the Soviet group would align itself with the Arabs." He then concluded: "I cannot conceive of the British government, even aided by the United States, being able to carry partition with the requisite majority."[5] He also anticipated that the announcement of this policy would precipitate a major rebellion by the Jews in Palestine. However, in his view, this too would serve British interests, because it would happen during the transition to Arab majority rule, while Britain was still responsible for maintaining order. The British army would have to bring the situation under control, further enhancing its position with the new Arab state.

Bevin's argument against partition was recapitulated by one of his deputies, Robert Howe, in a memorandum of January 21: "To how great an extent partition would result in an estrangement between Great Britain and the Arab peoples it is not possible to estimate. But the consequences of such an estrangement would be so grave that the risk of it should be a major consideration in the examination of partition as a possible policy. The loss of Arab good will would mean the elimination of British influence from the Middle East to the great advantage of Russia. And this in turn would greatly weaken the position of the British Commonwealth in the world."[6]

In the opinion of the British military chiefs, partition of Palestine would destroy the British military position in the Middle East. It would create indefensible borders. Moreover, although British troops could impose a solution by force on one of the two contending communities in Palestine, they could not do so on both simultaneously. Strategic requirements dictated that Britain retain a commanding position in the country. They argued: "It was essential to our defence that we should be able to fight from the Middle East in war. . . . In future we should not be able to use India as a base for . . . deployment of force: it was the more essential, therefore, that we should retain other bases in the Middle East for this purpose. Palestine was of special importance in this general scheme of defence. In war, Egypt would be our key position in the Middle East; and it was necessary that we should hold Palestine as a screen for the defence of Egypt."[7]

It was shortly after these discussions that Bevin's plans for Palestine received a lethal blow from a most unexpected source—the Soviet Union. Soviet opposition to Zionism was a predicate of Bevin's strategy. He had every reason to believe that Soviet opposition to partition was unshakable.

As late as April 27, an article in Moscow's *Red Fleet* dismissed partition as a bourgeois Jewish aspiration and called for an independent Arab Palestine. Then, on May 14, Andrei Gromyko addressed the General Assembly and argued that the Jewish aspiration to have a state of their own was a consequence of the failure by Western Europe to guarantee their elementary rights. Accordingly, "It would be unjustifiable to deny this right to the Jewish people, particularly in view of all they have undergone during the Second World War."[8] Gromyko took the position that if it were not possible to establish a unitary state in Palestine that would assure equal rights to both Arabs and Jews, then perhaps the only viable alternative might be to consider a partition of Palestine into separate and independent Arab and Jewish states.

Although Gromyko avoided definitively committing the Soviet Union to the support of partition, the fact that he opened the possibility of such support had far reaching consequences. Bevin, who had been so certain of Soviet opposition and had sold his plan for turning to the UN to the British cabinet on the basis of that certainty, was flabbergasted. Of course, what he failed to grasp was that the Soviets understood that the creation of a Jewish state in Palestine meant a significant loss of British prestige in the Middle East. It also assured a British withdrawal from Palestine and the loss of the strategic benefits afforded by bases and facilities there. The Soviets were fully prepared to yield their intrinsic opposition to Zionism for the opportunity of forcing a British withdrawal in the Middle East. This unanticipated turn of events gave special significance to the United Nations Special Committee on Palestine (UNSCOP), which was formally constituted on May 15th, and its subsequent recommendations to the General Assembly.

The majority report of the UNSCOP, given to the General Assembly on August 31, proposed partition of the country. The Jewish territory was to include the eastern Galilee, the central coastal plain, and the Negev. The Arabs were to receive the western Galilee, central Palestine, and the northern and southern ends of the coastal plain. Jerusalem and the surrounding area were to become an international zone. The minority report, which essentially proposed a cantonization scheme with a single capital at Jerusalem, also called for a three-year period of United Nations administration.

Three days after the UN session began in September 1947, the Arab League held a secret meeting at Sofar, Lebanon, at which it was agreed that the Arab states would intervene in Palestine if the General Assembly voted for partition. The secretary-general of the Arab League announced at a press conference in London on September 15, "a solemn warning that any attempt to impose the committee's [UNSCOP] recommendations, or any similar scheme, would be implacably resisted by the Arabs. . . . Let there be no doubt that the Arabs, if compelled, would fight for Palestine."[9] The Arab Higher Committee for Palestine swore that the "Arabs would never recognize the validity of partition or the authority of the United Nations to implement it."[10] On September 23, Arthur Creech-Jones blithely informed the General Assembly that Britain would not carry out the recommended partition of Palestine. The adoption of partition, without a British commitment to assure its peaceful implementation, raised the prospect of direct military intervention by the armies of the Arab states.

As the debate over partition continued at the UN, it became increasingly evident that the British were not acting in good faith or responsibly as a major power. Although the British spokesmen declared their opposition to partition, they offered no alternatives. They also made clear that they would not undertake to implement any solution that was not acceptable to both Arabs and Jews. Given the categorically intransigent position of the Arabs, this meant that Britain would do nothing at all to help resolve the problem. Moreover, there was increasing evidence that the British intended to stay in Palestine for a long time to come. In Britain, a vigorous campaign to recruit candidates for service in the Palestine police continued unabated.

At the UN, the subcommittee on partition labored to make the partition proposal acceptable to a two-thirds majority of the General Assembly. In the process, the size of the proposed territory to be allocated to the Jews was whittled down from some 6,000 square miles to about 5,500 by the removal from the plan of part of the Negev and the city of Jaffa. The subcommittee proposed that the mandate be brought to an end on May 1, 1948, and that the transfer of power to the Arabs and Jews take place on July 1. Once it became clear that the Soviets and Americans had mutually agreed to back partition, the British cabinet gave Attlee, Bevin, and Creech-Jones blanket authority to establish a timetable for the inevitable British withdrawal. On November 13, the British ambassador to the UN, Alexander Cadogan, announced that British troops would not leave until August 1, and that until that time the United Nations would not be permitted to exercise any jurisdiction in Palestine. The subcommittee revised its timetable accordingly and proposed that the mandate end on August 1, but it also suggested that a UN commission should administer the mandate during the period of transition. Cadogan then announced that Britain alone would determine when the mandate would come to an end. The reason for Britain's unwillingness to cooperate with the UN went beyond mere peevishness. It appeared that Bevin was in fact engaged in plotting a virtual total collapse of order in Palestine, with or without partition, to justify continued British intervention.

Finally, after some hectic maneuvering by the Zionists and their supporters to influence the General Assembly vote, on November 29, 1947 the proposal for a partition of Palestine passed by a vote of 33 to 13 with 10 abstentions. In effect, the United Nations had given its blessing to the creation of a Jewish ministate in Palestine. Immediately after the vote, Saudi Arabia announced "that it does not consider itself bound by the Resolution adopted today by the General Assembly. Furthermore, it reserves to itself the full right to act freely in whatever way it deems fit, in accordance with the principles of right and justice."[11] Iraq took an even more extreme position, asserting that the injustice of the Assembly's decision absolved it in advance for any actions it might take to prevent implementation of the resolution. "Iraq does not recognize the validity of this decision, will reserve freedom of action toward its implementation and hold those who were influential in passing it against the free conscience of mankind responsible for the consequences."[12] Syria, if anything was even more blunt: "Let the consequences be on the heads of others, not on ours."[13] In Cairo, King Farouk told the American ambassador that the Arab states were prepared to resist partition by force of arms.

The United Nations resolution calling for the partition of Palestine gave new immediacy to the expectation of a war between the Jews and the Arab states. Among the latter, it was Transjordan that had the most to gain or to lose. It was also the only one of the Arab states that had any clear view of what its objectives would be in a general Palestine war. The British had already dissuaded King Abdullah from actively pursuing his dream of a Hashemite Greater Syria, and he made an announcement to that effect on October 14, 1947. He now turned his attention to the more immediate prospect of creating a Greater Transjordan following the withdrawal of the British from Palestine. According to a Palestinian friend of the king, Abdullah explained his position to him on October 1, 1947, before the UN vote took place: "The Mufti and Kuwatly want to set up an independent Arab state in Palestine with the Mufti at its head. If that were to happen I would be encircled on almost all sides by enemies. This compels me to take measures to anticipate their plans. My forces will therefore occupy every place evacuated by the British. I will not begin the attack on the Jews, and I will only attack them if they first attack my forces. I will not allow massacres in Palestine. Only after quiet and order have been established will it be possible to reach an understanding with the Jews."[14]

The British government, for its part, sought to be as obstructive as possible. It informed Parliament in mid-December that the mandate would be terminated on May 15, 1948. However, it refused to allow the members of the Palestine Commission appointed by the United Nations to enter the country before May 1. It also refused to accede to the requests made by the commission, in accordance with the requirements of the partition resolution, with regard to matters such as the delineation of frontiers, immigration, and the establishment of armed militias. The British reluctantly admitted that hundreds of armed Arabs were entering Palestine from nearby states. They excused their failure to stop this by contending that the character of the terrain made the detection and prevention of such infiltration difficult, especially at night. The commission subsequently reported that, to some extent, the Palestine administration was arming the Arabs.

The United States also retreated from its support of partition and a Jewish state almost as soon as the resolution passed. Within days, reacting to pressures on and by American oil companies and other private commercial interests in the Middle East, the State Department announced an embargo on shipments of arms to the Near East, an ostensibly evenhanded approach to limiting potential violence in the volatile area. Of course, the State Department was well aware that, since the Arabs were receiving arms from the British, the embargo was in effect directed primarily against the Jews.

The U.S. representative to the UN Security Council, Warren Austin, stated on February 24 that while the United States would consider the use of armed force to restore order in Palestine, it would not agree to such in order to enforce partition, thereby seconding the obstructionist British position. Then, on March 19, Austin proposed that further action on implementing partition be suspended and that the General Assembly be called into special session to consider the establishment of a temporary trusteeship over Palestine, "without prejudice . . . to the character of the eventual political settlement."[15] This American betrayal of its undertakings to the Zionists, had it been carried through, would have meant the aborting of the Jewish state. There is more than a little irony in the fact that it was the Soviet Union that effectively blocked it, availing itself of the opportunity to assail the Western Powers for undermining the authority of the United Nations.

At the same time, the British were pursuing a new understanding with Transjordan that would continue to ensure the protection of some of their interests in the region. Negotiations on a new Anglo-Transjordanian treaty opened in London in March 1948. The Transjordanian delegation included Prime Minister Tawfiq Abul Huda, Foreign Minister Fawzi al-Mulqi, and Brigadier John Bagot Glubb, the British commander of the Arab Legion. After the treaty negotiations were completed, Abul Huda and Glubb met privately with Bevin to discuss the question of the Arab state that would arise in the territory of Palestine designated for the Arabs.

Abul Huda made the argument that, as soon as the British withdrew in May, the Jews would immediately establish a state. The Arabs of Palestine, however, were too disunited and unprepared to establish an Arab state. In Abul Huda's view, the vacuum that would occur in the Arab zone after British withdrawal might tempt the Zionists to ignore the boundaries set forth in the partition plan and to occupy the territory, perhaps as far east as the Jordan River. The other possibility was the seizure of control of the territory by the mufti. Neither situation would serve British or Transjordanian interests. Abul Huda therefore suggested that the easiest way to assure that neither of the two possibilities took place would be for the Arab Legion to quickly occupy the territories assigned to the Arabs under the partition scheme. Glubb, aware of the limitations of the Arab Legion, interjected that it would prove impractical for the legion to attempt to occupy either the

Upper Galilee or the Gaza area. It could only take effective control of the areas immediately adjacent to the existing frontier along the Jordan. Abul Huda agreed to these constraints. Bevin's reply, as recorded by Glubb, was: "It seems the obvious thing to do, but do not go and invade the areas allotted to the Jews."[16]

The prime ministers of the seven member states of the Arab League met in Cairo on December 7, 1947 and announced that they would back the Palestinian Arabs with arms, money, and troops. They promised that their armies would be committed to the struggle against the Jewish state as soon as the mandate came to an end. In the meanwhile, an Arab army of liberation was being formed in Damascus under the command of Fawzi al-Qawkaji, and was being trained by the Syrian army. At the same time, there was still very little evidence that the British really expected to withdraw from Palestine in the near future. As late as December 1947, the British continued constructing military bases in the southern part of the country.

The Arab strategy in the opening phase of the Arab-Israel conflict that would afflict the region for more than a half century was determined from the outset by the character and pattern of Jewish settlement in the country. The Jewish population was concentrated for the most part in the cities of Tel Aviv, Jerusalem, and Haifa, and in some 700 settlements spread throughout the country, many of them in predominantly Arab areas. Consequently, the coherence of the Jews as an organized community depended heavily on control of the roads connecting the many points of population concentration. The Arabs were similarly concentrated in some 760 villages and 25 towns, in addition to their relatively large populations in Haifa, Jaffa, Safed, and Tiberias.

Operating in an offensive mode, the Arabs were well positioned to interrupt vital road communications links in many parts of the country. By occupying positions on the heights and hillsides commanding the roads, small forces and snipers could effectively cut off and isolate whole Jewish areas of settlement, which could be choked out of existence later. As a result, there was a good deal of Arab sniping at virtually anything that moved through the countryside. It was expected that one by one the remoter settlements in the Galilee and the Negev would have to be abandoned or surrendered. A similar fate would await Jerusalem, which was particularly vulnerable because the roads that connected it to the rest of the Jewish areas meandered through winding passes where they were readily subject to interdiction. The struggle with the Arabs thus became one primarily for control of the network of roads.

The situation around Jerusalem was particularly grim. The Arab Legion, under British command, was intervening in an attempt to clear out a bloc of four settlements that commanded the road from Jerusalem to Hebron. The apparent aim was to create a situation in which the Arab Legion, as a British force, would withdraw a day before the end of the mandate, as promised by the colonial secretary. It would then return unimpeded the following day as an "independent" Arab force, still under Glubb's command, to complete the conquest of Jerusalem, even though this went beyond the understanding reached with Bevin in March.

However, events in the previous two months had radically changed the situation, precluding the peaceful takeover of central Palestine by the Arabs. First, the attempts of the Palestinian Arabs to close the road to Jerusalem had brought Jewish forces into areas assigned to the Arabs under the partition plan in order to keep the road open. It was hardly likely that the Jews would simply turn these strategically vital footholds over to the Arab Legion. Second, notwithstanding his repeated assurances to the Jews, by the first week of May, Abdullah had already committed himself to joint military action with the Arab League. Several days before the mandate was to come to an end, the political committee of the Arab League convened in Amman to work out final arrangements for inter-Arab coordination during the coming war. Abdullah tried once more to convince the other Arab leaders that a war with the Jews, whom he considered to be better prepared for it, was overly risky. His colleagues, however, were determined to resolve the problem by force. He told Glubb immediately after the meeting: "If I were to drive into the desert and accost the first goatherd I saw, and consult him whether to make war on my enemies or not, he would say to me, 'How many have you got, and how many have they?' Yet here are these learned politicians, all of them with university degrees, and when I say to them, 'The Jews are too strong—it is a mistake to make war,' they cannot understand the point. They make long speeches about rights."[17]

Abdullah nonetheless sought to reach some sort of accommodation with the Zionists that would satisfy the other Arab states and thereby avoid the coming conflict. Abdullah inquired if "the Jewish leaders would be prepared to cede to him some of the land allotted to them in the partition scheme, so as to persuade the Arab world to accept the division of Palestine." This sort of tactic did not sit very well with David Ben-Gurion and his colleagues. Even the staunchest Zionist advocates of partition had accepted it as the only practical means of obtaining international support for a Jewish state in Palestine. However, it was one thing to appease the United Nations and quite another to appease the Arab states that had no legitimate claim on Palestine in the first place. The kind of bargain that Abdullah sought was out of the question. In fact, Ben-Gurion, as well as some of the other leaders, had concluded that if the Arabs did not accept the partition scheme as it was, he would not be bound by it either. In such a case, he would feel free to re-divide the country in accordance with the opportunities that were presented by the impending military struggle. Accordingly, the Zionist response to Abdullah was "that the acceptance of the boundaries described in the plan approved by the United Nations Organization was subject to the partition scheme being implemented as a whole and in a peaceful fashion. If the Arabs went to war the Jews would retain anything they could win."[18]

On May 14, 1948, the British reluctantly withdrew from Palestine, the State of Israel came into being, and the Arab-Israel conflict began.

NOTES

1. George Kirk, *The Middle East in the War*, p. 449.

2. William Hillman, ed. *Mr. President: The First Publication from the Personal Diaries, Private Letters, Papers and Revealing Interviews by Harry Truman*, p. 23.

3. Nicholas Bethell, *The Palestine Triangle*, p. 292.

4. Ibid.

5. Ibid., p. 293.

6. Wm. Roger Louis, "British Imperialism and the End of the Palestine Mandate," in Wm. Roger Louis and Robert W. Stookey, *The End of the Palestine Mandate*, p. 17.

7. Ibid., p. 16.

8. Bethell, *The Palestine Triangle*, p. 313.

9. Jon and David Kimche, *A Clash of Destinies*, p. 64.

10. Bernard Postal and Henry W. Levy, *And the Hills Shouted for Joy*, p. 109.

11. *Official Record of the Second Session of the General Assembly*, 2, p. 1425.

12. Ibid., p. 1427.

13. Ibid.

14. Jon Kimche and David Kimche, *A Clash of Destinies*, p. 59.

15. J.C. Hurewitz, *The Struggle for Palestine*, p. 312.

16. John B. Glubb, *A Soldier with the Arabs*, p. 63.

17. Ibid., p. 152.

18. Alec Kirkbride, *From the Wings: Amman Memoirs, 1947–1951*, pp. 21–22.

14

The First Arab-Israeli War and Its Aftermath, 1948–52

On May 15, 1948, the day after the declaration of the independence of Israel, the Arab states made good on their threats and the armies of Egypt, Iraq, Lebanon, Syria, and Transjordan invaded Palestine. That same day, the secretary-general of the Arab League sent a cablegram to the UN secretary-general, justifying the invasion. He asserted disingenuously that the purpose of the intervention of Arab States in Palestine was "to restore law and order and to prevent disturbances prevailing in Palestine from spreading into their territories and to check further bloodshed."[1]

On May 17, the United States argued before the Security Council of the UN that the fighting represented a breach of the peace within the meaning of Article 39 of the UN Charter and that the council should order an immediate cease-fire. The British representative, Sir Alexander Cadogan, asserted the following day that it was unclear that a breach of the peace had taken place, notwithstanding the reports confirming the advance of the Arab armies, and blocked any UN action. It quickly became abundantly clear that Britain was deliberately preventing the council from acting in the expectation that the Arabs would destroy the fledgling Jewish state within days. Moreover, on May 21, Sir John Balfour, minister at the British embassy in Washington, told U.S. Under-Secretary of State Robert Lovett that because the Arab territories in Palestine had been promised to Abdullah, any reverses suffered by the Arab forces would precipitate a British intervention on their behalf.

It soon became apparent, however, that the Arab states had not launched a coordinated military effort. Farouk refused to place Egyptian troops under anyone else's command, and Abdullah would not turn over the Arab Legion, the only credible fighting force in the Arab world and the basis of his power in Transjordan, to foreign control. The Arab Legion was under the command of John B. Glubb, the only significantly experienced general among the lot, but the other Arab military leaders would not place their forces under his direction because they distrusted the British. As a result, coordination between the several Arab armies became dependent on liaison officers assigned to a joint operations center near Amman. The war did not go as the wishful thinking of the Arab leaders, perhaps excluding Abdullah, had led them to expect.

Abdullah was particularly distressed by the realization that events would not unfold the way he had imagined. He had thought that if the partition plan was implemented, the other Arab states would first declaim loudly against it and then reluctantly, and under protest, accept it as a fact. Then, given his understanding with the British, he would add the territory envisioned for the Arab state in Palestine to his domain. For the most part, he was little concerned with precisely which tracts of territory were to become his as long as he would be able to expand the borders of his realm. As noted with bitterness by Nasir ad-Din al-Nashashibi of Jerusalem, who became his private secretary after the war, "Palestine was to King Abdallah nothing more than a piece of earth on which stood the al-Aqsa Mosque and, buried beside it, the remains of his father, King Husayn. That is all he saw in it. That was the limit of his understanding of it. . . . As to the homeland, the coastal plain, the wealth, the property and the cities—they did not interest King Abdallah at all."[2]

The Arab states had deluded themselves and it was the Arabs of Palestine who had to pay for their folly. The only Arab leader of any consequence who understood the extent of the risk they were taking was Abdullah. He had consistently advised against overconfidence. As Glubb later explained: "One of the major causes of the Arab failure in 1948 was their unwillingness to face facts. Not only did they neglect to study the potential military strength of both sides, but they accused of treachery any man with a courage to speak the unpalatable truth."[3] Abdullah's own assessment was both more blunt and more profound: "My conclusion from all this is that the Arabs must give up day-dreaming and apply themselves to realities."[4]

When a truce agreement brought an end to the fighting several weeks later, only Transjordan emerged with substantial territorial gains. Egypt occupied the Gaza strip, which was of strategic value but not much else. Abdullah was in control of almost all the territory allocated to the Arabs under the partition scheme in the central part of the country. Perhaps most important, he had achieved control of the Old City of Jerusalem which had great symbolic significance as well as political importance.

The final truce lines bore little resemblance to those envisioned under the partition scheme. The Israelis had taken the western Galilee, and the towns of Jaffa, Ramle, Lydda, and Nazareth, all of which had been assigned to the Arabs under the partition plan. The Egyptian army cut off the Negev, assigned to Israel, and Abdullah's Arab legion was in control of eastern Jerusalem. UN mediator Folke Bernadotte proposed, in effect, that the clock should be turned back and the partition be implemented once again from a clean slate. Under his British-inspired scheme, which departed significantly from the partition plan, he proposed "that in view of the historical connexion and common interests of Transjordan and Palestine, there would be compelling reasons for merging the Arab territory of Palestine with the territory of Transjordan." Furthermore, "the port of Haifa, including the oil refineries and terminals, and without prejudice to their inclusion in the sovereign territory of the Jewish State . . . should be declared a free port, with assurances of free access for interested Arab countries."[5] Jerusalem was to be placed under UN control, with local autonomy for the Jewish and Arab sections of the city. Finally, in the event that the Jews and Arabs could not reach an agreement, he proposed that the UN impose it own solution. Bernadotte submitted his recommendations to the UN secretary-general on September 16, and was assassinated in Jerusalem the following day by Jewish extremists.

As widely anticipated, on December 11, 1948, the General Assembly failed to adopt a resolution supporting the Bernadotte plan. The British, however, still attempted to implement the provision in it that called for the unification of Arab Palestine with Transjordan. Britain, considering its own interests in the region, did not want the southern Negev to become part of Israel. It much preferred to see it transferred from Egyptian control and incorporated within Transjordan for at least two reasons. First it would provide a direct land bridge between Egypt and the rest of the Middle East, thereby ensuring territorial contiguity between all the members of the British-backed Arab League. Second, in the event of problems with Egypt, it would provide a suitable alternative location for the large British military infrastructure in the Suez Canal zone. It was this latter consideration that probably most accounts for the strong British support of the Bernadotte plan. It also explains Britain's eagerness, at every opportunity, to charge Israel with violation of Transjordan's territorial integrity, presumably to justify British intervention and the dispatch of military forces to the territory in accordance with the provisions of the Anglo-Transjordanian treaty. Nonetheless, after a number of unsuccessful attempts of this sort that were in clear violation of the truce, the British were embarrassed into halting their transparent support of Abdullah's attempt to seize the Negev region. The Transjordan-Israel armistice agreement was finally concluded on April 3, 1949.

Abdullah now had no recourse other than to take the practical steps necessary to ensure that the part of the projected Arab state that was under his military control would become part of his new and expanded kingdom. It was abundantly evident that the Arab states were utterly opposed to any extension of Hashemite power in the region, and determined to thwart any illusions he may have entertained about creating a Greater Hashemite Syria. Indeed, his Arab allies had already taken steps to insure that Transjordan would reap no lasting benefit from being the only Arab state to emerge from the conflict in control of a sizeable tract of land originally intended to become part of the Arab state in Palestine. As early as April 12, 1948 the Arab League passed a resolution that precluded any of the Arab states that would send armies into Palestine from taking possession of any lands they might conquer. All such lands were to be turned over to the Palestinian Arabs. Abdullah's rejection of this proposition was reflected in Transjordan's vote against the resolution.

With encouragement from the member-states of the Arab League, an Arab Government of All Palestine, headquartered in Egyptian-occupied Gaza, was proclaimed on September 20, 1948 under the premiership of Ahmad Hilmi Pasha. A week later, Haj Amin al Husseini, the mufti of Jerusalem, was elected president of an Arab Palestine National Assembly, also in Gaza, that claimed jurisdiction over all of Palestine. Within a month all the members of the Arab League, with the exception of Transjordan, extended formal recognition to the new regime of a Palestine it did not control. The obvious purpose of this charade was to prevent Abdullah from annexing those parts of Palestine under his control. It was believed that the mere existence of such a shadow indigenous Palestinian government would serve to constrain Abdullah's freedom of action. Abdullah could simply have ignored the All Palestine government's existence, had he chosen to do so, since its writ only covered Gaza, and even there only to the extent that the Egyptians would permit it to exercise any authority. He elected, instead, to take more active though cautious steps to assert his authority in Palestine.

On October 1, 1948 some 5,000 Palestinian Arab notables convened in Amman at a Palestine refugee conference at which they repudiated the mufti's government and, as might have been expected given the venue of the gathering, urged Abdullah to extend his protection over the country. Then on November 15, Abdullah paid a visit to the Coptic convent in Jerusalem's Old City where the Coptic bishop crowned and proclaimed him king of Jerusalem. Then, on December 1, an Arab Congress of the national leaders of Arab Palestine under Transjordanian control convened in Jericho. The Congress adopted a resolution proposing that "Palestine and the Hashemite Kingdom of Transjordan be united into one Kingdom and that King Abdallah ben el-Hussein be proclaimed constitutional King over Palestine."[6] The resolution was promptly sent to the United Nations General Assembly and to the Arab League. It was then submitted to the Transjordanian Cabinet, which gave its approval on December 7 and then presented it to the parliament in Amman, which gave its assent on December 13. It was expected that Abdullah would soon name himself king of Palestine.

Abdullah's opponents in the Arab world began to react in unproductive attempts to forestall what was to prove inevitable. King Farouk of Egypt sent a letter dated December 13 to all Arab heads of state rejecting the resolutions of the Jericho congress as unrepresentative of the majority of Palestinian Arabs, and therefore invalid. The Arab League similarly attacked the resolutions. Even the Council of Ulemas of al Azhar University in Cairo denounced the prospective annexation of Palestine as "violating Islam's pledge to Allah."[7]

Abdullah responded to these challenges in kind, not personally but through Palestinian Arab spokesmen. Sheikh Muhammed Ali al-Jabari broadcast an open letter to King Farouk reminding him of his utter failure to redeem his promise to liberate Palestine by force. Since he had failed, it would be better if he kept out of Palestinian affairs in the future. "Let us, the people of Palestine, save at least what is left of our country by peaceful means." To the Ulemas of al Azhar, Sheikh Suleiman Taji al-Faruqi of the Palestine Muslim Ulemas responded that what took place in Palestine was simply none of their business.[8]

In the meantime, the United Nations, apparently unconcerned by what was actually happening in Palestine, was busily engaged in pushing a resolution calling for the internationalization of Jerusalem. This was part of the original partition resolution that was vehemently opposed by all the Arab states. Now, however, these same Arab states became zealous supporters of internationalization, to deprive both Israel and Abdullah of their holds on the city. With regard to Abdullah, it was believed that without Jerusalem, and particularly control of the great mosques in the Old City, he might not be able to consolidate his position in Palestine. Accordingly, in October 1949 the Arab League Council adopted a resolution calling for the long rejected internationalization of the city. This had the peculiar effect of making Transjordan and Israel allies in their joint opposition to the proposal. The Arabic newspaper of Jerusalem, *Falastin*, commented: "How can we adequately express our hatred for those Arab delegates at Lake Success who sacrificed Arab interests in Jerusalem for the sake of their political speculations and personal ambitions? It was the disunity and lack of public spirit on the part of those same Arab states that caused the loss of a large part of Palestine to the Jews a year ago. Now they want to be instrumental in losing the Mosque of Omar also."[9]

In face of the mounting opposition to his control of the West Bank, Abdullah began to move more decisively. From December 16, 1949 onward, all governmental affairs in the West Bank were conducted from Amman. The Transjordan Parliament was dissolved on December 27 and elections to a new Parliament covering both Transjordan and Palestine were called for the following April. To assure stability on his meandering frontier with Israel, as he moved to annex the West Bank, Abdullah proceeded to accelerate the secret negotiations with Israel on a security agreement, and intensive discussions were held between November 1949 and March 1950. One of the major concessions offered by Israel was to grant Jordan an outlet to the Mediterranean by means of a corridor that would run across Israeli territory connecting Jordan with the coast at Gaza. However, Abdullah would have to convince Egypt to turn Gaza over to him.

A draft treaty was prepared and initialed, but Abdullah buckled under the rising pressure from both Arab and British opposition to it. As recorded by Moshe Dayan, one of the participants in the discussions with Abdullah:

We pursued this idea, and at one of our last meetings in Shuneh, on December 17, 1949, when I saw the king together with Reuven Shiloah, we reached the stage of drafting the terms of a peace treaty. The king was wary of the explicit term "peace treaty," but agreed to call it a "paper" on which were inscribed "Principles of a Territorial Arrangement (Final)." This "paper" was initialed by the king and Reuven Shiloah. I do not know whether the Israeli government would have ratified this agreement. Ben-Gurion did not reject it, but he wrinkled his nose when he read it. At all events, when we returned to the king to continue the negotiations, he informed us that his friend Sir Alec Kirkbride, Britain's minister to Transjordan, did not agree that Jordan should enter into such a treaty with Israel while other Arab states, mainly Egypt, had not done so. The king therefore asked us to regard the "paper" as cancelled.[10]

The outcome of the negotiations confirmed Ben-Gurion's judgment on the extent of Abdullah's freedom of action, when he told Dayan a year earlier to go ahead and try to negotiate with the king. "Our future need is peace and friendship with the Arabs," he said. "Therefore I am in favor of talks with King Abdulla, although I doubt whether the British will let him make peace with us."[11]

When word of the proposed agreement eventually leaked out, the opponents of peace with Israel reacted with virulence. Prime Minister Abul Huda felt obligated to resign, and stepped down on March 2, 1950, but was soon recalled when his replacement, Samir Pasha ar-Rifai, could not form a new government. Under the mounting pressure, including that provided from his influential British advisers, Abdullah quietly allowed the chance for peace with Israel to lapse. It appears that the British Foreign Office made the assessment that the advantages that Abdullah might reap from a normalization of relations with Israel were not commensurate with the risks involved for him and the Hashemite dynasty, and consequently for the security of Britain's own position in Transjordan.

The cessation of the peace initiative had virtually no impact on the anti-Hashemite campaign that had been set in motion. On March 19, the Cairo al-Masri proclaimed: "The time has come for the Arab League to cut off relations with Transjordan, a country that has betrayed Islam and Arab unity and the Arab cause. The time has come to sever this decayed member from the body of the Arab world and to bury it and heap dung thereon."[12] At its 12th meeting, which convened a few days later, the Arab League took steps to block the no longer pending treaty with Israel as well as the annexation of the West Bank by Abdullah. On March 27, the All Palestine Government, now headquartered in Heliopolis near Cairo, was invited to attend the meetings of the Council. This led to a de facto boycott of the meetings by Transjordan, which sent no delegation from Amman, but permitted its representative in Cairo to attend. The Council reaffirmed its resolution of 1948, which precluded any Arab country from annexing any part of Palestine. The Transjordanian representative abstained from taking part in the vote.

A general election for the new Jordanian parliament was held on April 11, providing for equal representation from both the East and West Banks. Eleven days later Abdullah commented publicly on the Arab League's threat to expel Transjordan if it went ahead with annexation. "If expulsion comes as a result of unifying the two parts of this besieged nation," he said, "it will be welcome. We do not wish to be of those who oppose unity in the name of the Arab League, from which we had hoped good would come."[13]

On April 24, 1950, at the inaugural session of the new Parliament, Abdullah lashed out at the Arab League once again. "My Government considers the resolution adopted by the Political Committee of the Arab League Council of April 12, 1948 as invalidated by the conclusion by the Arab states of a permanent truce and acceptance of the partition resolution, thereby contradicting the aforementioned . . . resolution." Both houses of the Parliament, in joint session, then passed a Resolution of Unity, which was signed into law by Abdullah the same day. "Approval is granted to complete unity between the two banks of the Jordan, the eastern and the western, and their amalgamation, in one single state: the Hashemite Kingdom of the Jordan, under the crown of His Hashemite Majesty King Abdallah ben el-Hussein the Exalted. This will be upon the basis of parliamentary constitutional rule and complete equality in rights and duties of all the citizens."[14]

The Council of the Arab League subsequently maintained that the annexation was illegal but it could not get the unanimity necessary to take effective action against Jordan. Finally, a face saving formula was arrived at that Abdullah was able to accept in the interest of maintaining the facade of unity in the Arab world. The Arab League passed a resolution on June 12, 1950 declaring that the annexation of the West Bank was simply a measure necessitated by immediate practical considerations and was not intended to be permanent in character. It further stated that Jordan would simply hold the territory in question in trust until a final disposition of the Palestine problem was achieved, and that Jordan committed itself to accept, with regard to the future of Palestine, whatever might be decided unanimously by the other member states.

Following the annexation of the West Bank, Abdullah's enemies in the Arab world characterized him as a British puppet and instrument of continued British control in the Middle East. Since the British were now being blamed for the Arab defeat in Palestine, notwithstanding Britain's notorious anti-Israel behavior, the responsibility for the disaster was to be shared by Abdullah. Consequently, it became an imperative of Arab nationalism to get rid of both the British and their Arab lackey. As a result, Abdullah's relations with some of the Arab leaders on the West Bank became increasingly strained.

Abdullah was warned repeatedly that he was becoming a target for assassination by Palestinian extremists, but he does not appear to have taken such warnings seriously enough. On Friday, July 20, 1951, he was shot to death as he was entering the Al Aqsa Mosque in the Old City of Jerusalem. His death brought an end to the longstanding dream of a Greater Syria under Hashemite leadership. His successors would be preoccupied with trying to hold on to what he had achieved by expanding Hashemite rule to the West Bank.

After more than a year of maneuvering over the succession to Abdullah, his eldest son, Talal, was dethroned on August 11, 1952 by a unanimous decision of both houses of the Jordanian parliament which proclaimed his minor son Hussein as king in his place. At the time of Hussein's ascension to the throne, the Jordanian population of some two million was two-thirds Palestinian. One-third consisted of refugees housed and fed by the United Nations refugee relief organization (UNRWA) in camps on both sides of the Jordan. Another third were West Bankers, who viewed themselves as Palestinians rather than Jordanians. Many of these tended to look upon Hussein and the Jordanians as alien usurpers of their patrimony and remained unreconciled to Amman's authority over their affairs. The remaining third were indigenous East Bankers, mostly Bedouins, who by now had developed a loyalty to the Hashemite dynasty. These demographic facts promised to create serious problems for any attempt to develop an integral Jordanian state under Hashemite rule. In 1954, the Jordanian parliament tried to mitigate the problem of the Palestinian majority in the country by passing a Nationality Law that granted Jordanian citizenship to anyone, except Jews, of Palestinian origin residing in Jordan. This offer was subsequently extended on February 4, 1960 to all Palestinians living abroad who wished to acquire Jordanian citizenship.

The British withdrawal from Palestine under the unrelenting pressure of the revolt against their rule, and their demonstrated inability to bring about the results they wished as a result of the first Arab-Israeli war, had consequences in other parts of the region as well, especially in Arabia and in Egypt. In August 1952, the Saudis made a move toward the British protected sheikhdoms in the Persian Gulf, launching an expedition that seized the oasis at Buraimi, about 100 miles closer to the coast than the maximum line claimed by Abd al-Aziz ibn Saud in 1935. Resolution of the issue was long and drawn out and relations between Britain and Saudi Arabia turned cold.

In Egypt, the perception of growing British weakness helped precipitate a series of events that soon led to the Suez crisis discussed in the chapter that follows.

NOTES

1. John N. Moore, ed., *The Arab-Israeli Conflict*, vol. 3, p. 353.

2. Clinton Bailey, "Changing Attitudes Toward Jordan in the West Bank," p. 155.

3. John B. Glubb, *A Soldier with the Arabs*, p. 79.

4. Abdullah, *My Memoirs Completed*, p. 30.

5. Moore, ed., *The Arab-Israeli Conflict*, vol. 3, *Documents*, p. 353.

6. Hussein A. Hassouna, *The League of Arab States and Regional Disputes*, p. 33.

7. Benjamin Shwadran, *Jordan a State of Tension*, p. 282.

8. Ibid., pp. 282–283.

9. Ibid., p. 286, n.9.

10. Moshe Dayan, *Moshe Dayan*, pp. 143–144.

11. Ibid., p. 133.

12. Shwadran, p. 292.

13. Ibid., p. 296.

14. Marjorie M. Whiteman, *Digest of International Law*, vol. 2, p. 1166.

15

The Suez Crisis,
1951–57

The Anglo-Egyptian treaty of 1936 converted the British protectorate in Egypt into an alliance between the two countries. The treaty limited British rights in Egypt to the area of the Suez Canal Zone. The presence of British troops in the zone was not to be construed as an occupation or an impingement on Egyptian sovereignty. They were there to ensure free navigation through the canal and were to be removed at any time after 20 years when the Egyptian army was considered capable of assuming responsibility for protecting the waterway, which was a vital link connecting the far-flung British Empire. If, after 1956, there were disagreement between Britain and Egypt over the competence of the Egyptian army to assume the defense of the canal, the matter was to be submitted to arbitration.

However, as already indicated, by the end of World War II, the Canal Zone had become the primary military base for securing Britain's interests in the Middle East. Moreover, with the emergence of the Cold War between the Soviet Union and the West, the base became an important point in the Western defense system protecting the vital supply of oil from the region to Europe. This new function for the Canal Zone went far beyond the stipulations of the Anglo-Egyptian treaty, causing Egypt to become directly involved in a conflict in which the country had little interest and even less say. The Egyptians wanted the British out of their country completely. As long as there were foreign troops on their soil serving the interests of others, the notion that such a presence did not impinge on Egypt's sovereignty was seen by many as patently absurd. The last of the Wafd governments came into power in Egypt in October 1951 by unilaterally repudiating the 1936 treaty.

It was at about this time that the Western powers sought to enlist the Middle Eastern countries in the struggle to prevent the expansion of Soviet power into the region. It was proposed to Egypt and other countries of the region that they join in a comprehensive military alliance, the Middle East Defense Organization (MEDO), that would be modeled after the North Atlantic Treaty Organization (NATO), of which it would be an extension. The inducement for Egypt would be that it would supersede the despised Anglo-Egyptian treaty. The proposal, however, was viewed in Egypt and in the other Arab countries as a scheme to transform them into Western puppets, and was generally rejected in favor of an increasing neutralism.

Having turned down the MEDO plan, the Egyptians resolved to force a British withdrawal very much along the lines used successfully by the Zionists in Palestine. The Wafd, which was well organized and had cells in the towns and large villages in the Canal Zone, assisted by the Egyptian police, began a campaign of harassment of the British. Government ministers whipped up anti-British sentiment in Cairo and, in January 1952, a large mob attacked British buildings and residents in the city. The rioting was checked only when King Farouk called in the Egyptian army out of a fear that the mob might turn against the throne. He also dismissed the Wafd government. There is some irony in the fact that the army suppressed the rioting only because its own plans for overthrowing Farouk had not yet been completed. It would take several more months before it acted.

The group of army officers, known as the Free Officers, who concocted the plan to overthrow the government were all relatively young men of middle rank who had fought in the war with Israel and were disenchanted with the corruption at home that hampered their effectiveness as soldiers. The Free Officers, nominally headed by General Muhammad Neguib, a likeable figurehead, but actually led by Colonel Gamal Abd al-Nasser, struck on July 23, 1952 in an almost bloodless coup. The government of Nagib Hilali was dismissed and Ali Maher was asked to form a new government of civil servants. On July 26, Farouk was ordered to abdicate and to leave the country. His infant son, Ahmad Fuad, was proclaimed king and a Regency Council was established. However, it soon became clear that the Free Officers intended to rule the country themselves when a Revolutionary Command Council was formed under the chairmanship of Nasser.

The Free Officers had some concern about what the British might do, perhaps intervene on behalf of Farouk. The British, however, were hardly upset at seeing Farouk go. They were weary of dealing with the corrupt and wily Egyptian politicians and thought it might be to their advantage to deal with soldiers. However, their expectations in this regard were soon to prove frivolous.

The officers of the Revolutionary Command Council were ardent nationalists, and the campaign against the British presence in the Canal Zone increased in intensity following the Egyptian revolution. Nasser laid out the strategy to be pursued. "Not formal war. That would be suicidal. It will be a guerrilla war. Grenades will be thrown in the night. British soldiers will be stabbed stealthily. There will be such terror that, we hope, it will become far too expensive for the British to maintain their citizens in occupation of our country."[1]

On January 17, 1953, the junta effectively ruling the country dissolved and banned all political parties. A three-year transition period was announced, during which the Revolutionary Command Council would formally rule Egypt, with a provisional constitutional charter proclaimed on February 10. Then, on June 18, the Command Council abolished the monarchy and declared Egypt a republic, with Neguib as both president and prime minister, and Nasser as deputy premier and minister of the interior. This arrangement lasted until February 24, 1954 when Neguib resigned and Nasser became chairman of the Command Council and prime minister. A new constitution was promulgated on January 16, 1956, which eliminated the parliamentary system and provided for a presidential republican form of government. Nasser became president of Egypt on June 29.

Compounding the problem of Anglo-Egyptian relations, in addition to the British presence in the Canal Zone, was the Egyptian demand that Britain also withdraw from the Sudan, a vast territory that Britain governed as though it were a crown colony even though it was supposed to be an Anglo-Egyptian condominium. Egyptian nationalists wanted the status of the Sudan to return to that which prevailed prior to the British intervention in the nineteenth century, namely, to an Egyptian dependency. However, this aspiration was preempted by the emergence of parties and groups in the Sudan which, with British encouragement, sought to establish an independent and sovereign Sudanese state. Negotiations with the Egyptian military regime led to an Anglo-Egyptian agreement on February 12, 1953 that provided for a three-year transition period during which the Sudanese would prepare for independence, at the end of which the Anglo-Egyptian condominium would come to an end. Sudan duly achieved its independence in 1956.

By 1954, the campaign of anti-British harassment achieved its purpose. The British base in the Canal Zone was devoid of Egyptian labor, forcing the British to rely on their own troops for all services behind barbed wire enclosures that reminded them of their comparable earlier experience in Jerusalem. The maintenance of the British base clearly became counterproductive, even a liability, leading to the Anglo-Egyptian agreement, initialed on July 27 and signed on October 19, 1954 that resolved the problem on essentially Egyptian terms, but included some significant concessions to Britain.

The agreement, which superseded the 1936 treaty, called for the evacuation of British troops from the Canal Zone within a period of 20 months after signature, and the last British troops left Port Said on June 13, 1956.

However, the agreement still provided for the maintenance of the canal base in usable military condition, for possible use by Britain in the event of external aggression against any member state of the Arab League and Turkey. In such a case, Egypt was to help the British reactivate the base on a war footing. In addition, Egypt agreed to recognize the Suez Canal as an international waterway, with right of passage guaranteed to all states in accordance with the Istanbul Convention of October 29, 1888.

Although Nasser did succeed in getting the British to withdraw from Egypt, the character of the agreement he had signed fell short of popular expectations. Seen by some as insufficiently nationalistic, he was accused of having conceded too much and was almost assassinated in Alexandria a week after the agreement was signed. Nasser resolved that any future military pacts that Egypt entered into would only be with other Arab countries. It was his intention "to make the Arab Collective Security Pact the sole authorized instrument of defense of the Arab states."[2] As he explained to a Lebanese reporter, "From the very first moment I explained to the British and Americans that the responsibility for the defense of the Middle East rests on the shoulders of the Arab states alone, and that neither Egypt nor the Arab states will allow any outside state to interfere with the defense of the Middle East."[3] This approach, designed to enhance Egypt's status as the leader of the Arab world, placed it on a political collision course with Iraq.

The prime minister of Iraq, Nuri as-Said, who returned to power in 1954 as the result of a rigged election, had a rather different outlook on the world than his younger Egyptian counterpart. Nuri had few illusions about Arab military power and, being physically much closer to Turkey, Iran, and the Soviet Union, could ill afford the nationalistic posturing for which Nasser was admired. Moreover, Nuri was concerned that Turkey might still want to take Mosul from Iraq as it had earlier managed to obtain Alexandretta from Syria, and he needed to strengthen Iraq's military capabilities. As he told Nasser's representative, "There is no hope whatsoever of getting more arms and of building up a real army except by concluding a pact with the West as Pakistan and Turkey have done."[4]

On January 12, 1955, Iraq announced its intention to conclude a mutual defense pact with Turkey. Nasser called an emergency meeting of Arab prime ministers on January 22, at which he accused Iraq of violating the Arab Collective Security Pact and threatened to withdraw from it if Iraq went ahead with the Turkish treaty. Nuri was not dissuaded and a Turco-Iraqi Pact was signed in Baghdad on February 24, 1955, with Britain joining it on April 5, followed by Iran on October 11. Nasser was livid, seeing the Baghdad Pact as a deliberate challenge to his leadership of the Arab world, and from that point onward he resolved to remake the Arab world in his own image. "Nasserism" was on the march and its first major confrontation was to be with Israel.

Egypt's continuing hostility to Israel became evident following the armistice agreement when, in violation of international law, it hindered the passage of Israeli ships and Israel-bound cargoes through the Suez Canal. In the fall of 1949, Egypt placed guns at Sharm al-Sheikh, commanding the straits at the mouth of the Gulf of Aqaba and proclaimed a blockade of the gulf for Israeli or Israel-bound vessels. The matter was ultimately referred to the UN Security Council, which passed a resolution on September 1, 1951 calling upon Egypt "to terminate the restrictions on the passage of international commercial shipping and goods through the Suez Canal wherever bound and to cease all interference with such shipping beyond that essential to the safety of shipping in the Canal itself and to the observance of the international conventions in force."[5] Egypt rejected the Security Council's position, insisting that notwithstanding the extended armistice it was still at war with Israel. As expected, the council took no action against Egypt.

Nonetheless, during the two years when Nasser and the Revolutionary Command Council were preoccupied with consolidating their position in Egypt, their primary concern being with getting rid of the British, the situation along the Israeli-Egyptian frontier was relatively quiet. This was to change significantly in 1954, when there was a marked upsurge in incidents of Palestinian Arab infiltration across the armistice line followed by relatively minor Israeli retaliations. It seemed clear that Nasser was deliberately fanning the flames, announcing that "nobody can force the Arabs to accept peace with Israel or to recognize her as an established state. We believe we can reverse the position in Palestine to its natural state and return the land to its people and owners. I believe in the rights of Arabs in Palestine and I have faith in Arab Nationalism which shall triumph over borders and artificial lines."[6]

Then, on January 21, 1955, nine days after Iraq announced its intention of entering the mutual security pact with Turkey, an Egyptian army unit crossed the armistice line and attacked an Israeli military outpost. After another such assault three days later, the Mixed Armistice Commission called on the Egyptian authorities to "terminate immediately these aggressive actions by Egyptian military patrols and the continuous infiltration into Israel."[7] The plea was ignored an another raid took place, reaching some 30 miles into Israel. This precipitated a major retaliatory raid by Israel on the Egyptian headquarters in Gaza on February 28 that reflected its growing impatience with Egyptian and Egyptian-sponsored violations of the armistice agreement. For its part, Egypt escalated the propaganda war to a fever pitch with Cairo's *Voice of the Arabs* calling for "the extermination of Zionism in the second round of the Palestine war."[8]

It was not long before a new and potentially more volatile issue arose with regard to the area of al-Auja or Nitzana, which was of considerable strategic importance because it stood astride one of the two major invasion routes from Egypt to Israel. Although the territory was within Israel's borders, Israel agreed to its demilitarization as part of the armistice accord. However, the Mixed Armistice Commission agreed to the presence of Israeli civilian police there to maintain public order. Egypt now insisted on the right to maintain border checkposts in the demilitarized zone, something that Israel considered a violation of the armistice. Then, on October 26, Egyptian forces moved into the al-Auja area, attacked the Israeli police checkpoint, and established defensive military positions there. This led to an Israeli retaliation two days later at the Egyptian base at Kuntilla in the southern Negev. Egypt then brought up reinforcements to al-Auja, and Israel retaliated with an assault on the Egyptian positions at al-Sabha on the Egyptian side of the demilitarized zone.

The escalation of tension over the demilitarized zone raised concerns in both London and Washington about the outbreak of another war in the region. Anthony Eden proposed a compromise that would establish the Arab-Israeli borders somewhere between the 1947 partition plan boundaries and the additional territory that had subsequently come under Israeli control. While the proposal had some appeal to Nasser, since it involved an Israeli withdrawal from territory taken in battle, it made little sense to Ben-Gurion. The Arab states started the war because they refused to accept the existence of Israel within the 1947 partition lines. Since they had not even attempted to help the local Arabs to establish their own state in Palestine, and had no legitimate claims of their own to any of its territory, it was absurd to reward their aggression with additional territory. Eden's proposed compromise, which helped establish the pattern of all subsequent compromise plans conjured up by outside powers, was for Israel to cede the tangible for the ephemeral, land for peace.

While the controversy over the al-Auja demilitarized zone was heating up, Egypt announced on September 27, 1955 that it had concluded a major arms deal with Czechoslovakia. This was an unequivocal sign that the Soviet Union was now attempting to bring the Arab world into its sphere of interest through becoming a patron of Egypt. The upgrading of the Egyptian army, coupled with Nasser's unmistakable intentions, was correctly seen in Israel as a prelude to an Egyptian attack and the renewal of war. As the Israeli Chief of Staff General Moshe Dayan put it: "The decisive intimation to Israel of approaching Egyptian attack was the arms deal concluded between Czechoslovakia and Egypt in September 1955. . . . She also judged that the very possession by the Arabs of arms superior in quality and volume to those available to Israel would spur them to exploit this military advantage and hasten their attack."[9] This assessment was well founded. On December 18, Nasser made it clear to an American visitor that one of his principal concerns about Israel was strategic in nature. "Israel forms a wedge between the two halves of the Arab world, the Arabs of Africa and the Arabs of Asia. When the Israeli army occupied Umm Rashash, the southernmost tip of Palestine on the Gulf of Aqaba, which they have now turned into the port of Eilat, they completed this separation, which now runs from the Mediterranean to the Red Sea."[10] Israel stood in the way of the contiguity of the Arab world and Nasser was going to eliminate the anomaly. On February 15, 1956 a "top secret" order was given to the commanders of the Egyptian forces in Palestine to prepare their troops "for the unavoidable war with Israel, in order to achieve our supreme objective, namely annihilation of Israel and its complete destruction in as little time as possible."[11]

With the Soviets backing Egypt, the only place Israel could get advanced arms was from the West. However, Britain, still smarting from Israel's disruption of their schemes for the Middle East, and as sponsor of Jordan's Arab Legion, would not countenance helping Israel, and the United States had declared an arms embargo on the Middle East. This meant, in effect that, since both Britain and the Soviet bloc were supplying the Arabs, the U.S. embargo was directed at Israel. As Golda Meir noted, despite "the unconcealed Soviet-Arab preparations for another war—the United States and Britain refused to sell us arms. It didn't matter how often or how loudly we knocked on their doors. The answer was always negative."[12] The hypocrisy of the U.S. position on the embargo became apparent when the press reported on February 16, 1956 that the United States was about to ship 18 M-41 tanks to Saudi Arabia, apparently as part of the price it had to pay for the renegotiation of base rights at Dharan. Fortunately for Israel, Arab League support for the rebellion against French rule in Algeria had soured Franco-Arab relations, and on April 15 France announced that it would sell Israel 12 advanced Mystere jet fighters, originally designated for delivery to NATO, followed by another such sale in early May. Other high quality weapons were also transferred from France to Israel, significantly enhancing the ability of Israel's forces to contend with the Soviet-equipped Egyptian army.

Nasser soon gave his increasing bellicosity an international dimension with his announcement on July 26, 1956 that he had nationalized the Universal Maritime Suez Canal Company. Both Britain and France saw Soviet-backed Egyptian control of the canal as a threat to their economic security as well as that of Western Europe, and Britain made it clear that it would act to protect its interests. As Anthony Eden put it, "failure to keep the canal international would inevitably lead to the loss, one by one, of all our assets in the Middle East, and even if Her Majesty's Government had to act alone, they could not stop short of using force to protect their position."[13]

France, although less affected than Britain by Egyptian control of the canal, was concerned that Nasser's success in confronting the Western powers would lend additional encouragement to the Algerian nationalists and contribute further to the deterioration of the French position in North Africa. From Israel's standpoint, if Nasser got away with standing up to both Britain and France, his prestige in the Arab world would surge to the point where a general war against it would become inevitable. As a result, all three countries, each reflecting different primary concerns, soon found common cause in preventing Nasser from making Egypt the dominant force in the Middle East.

In the meantime, Nasser's influence throughout the Arab world was growing rapidly. A stream of anti-imperialist propaganda coming out of Cairo and intrigues carried out by pro-Nasser elements put enormous pressure on Jordan, which was still highly dependent on Britain, the Anglo-Jordanian military alliance remaining in effect until March 13, 1957. When Sir Gerald Templer, chief of the British general staff, visited Amman at the end of 1955 to encourage Jordan to join the Baghdad Pact, pro-Nasser rioting broke out and King Hussein declined to do so. By March 1, 1956, Hussein felt compelled to unceremoniously dismiss General Glubb from command of the Arab Legion, which he had led since 1939. It appears that Glubb was too much of a symbol of Jordan's dependence on Britain for its security.

Following Glubb's dismissal, violations of the armistice along Jordan's border with Israel increased dramatically, with Israel registering as many as 59 complaints with the Mixed Armistice Commission between July 29 and September 25. This soon led to Israeli retaliations and a serious battle at Qalqilya, in which the defending Arab Legion took relatively heavy casualties. This led Hussein to demand British military intervention in support of Jordan in accordance with the Anglo-Jordanian Defense Treaty of 1948. Given the emerging Suez crisis, this left Britain in a quandary, which it tried to resolve by encouraging Hashemite Jordan to reopen negotiations with Hashemite Iraq to form a joint army.

Israel quickly let it be known that it would consider the movement of Iraqi forces into Jordan as undermining the armistice agreement and posing a direct threat to its security. The implication was that in response to such an Iraqi move, Israel would feel free to attack Jordan, if necessary, to mitigate the threat. At that point Britain warned Israel not to attack Jordan, threatening to go to the latter's assistance under its 1948 treaty. Considering the mutuality of interest between Britain and Israel at the time with regard to Egypt, the British seemed to be acting somewhat irrationally. Moshe Dayan wrote in his dairy on October 21:

I must confess to the feeling that, save for the Almighty, only the British are capable of complicating affairs to such a degree. At the very moment when they are preparing to topple Nasser, who is a common enemy of theirs and Israel's, they insist on getting the Iraqi Army into Jordan, even if such action leads to war between Israel and Jordan in which they, the British, will take part against Israel. The result will be that instead of bringing down Nasser and safeguarding Britain's position in the Middle East . . . they will leave Nasser gobbling his prey while they rush off to start a new Israel-Britain-Jordan conflict. I doubt whether anyone can explain why Britain does not hold off her Iraqi plan until after the Suez campaign.[14]

As it turned out, the Jordanians themselves foiled the British scheme when their parliamentary elections held on October 21 resulted in a pro-Nasser victory, despite British efforts to prevent it. As a result, Iraq promptly dropped the idea of sending its troops into Jordan and the threat of war with Israel dissipated.

On October 23, 1956, Ben-Gurion and Moshe Dayan went to Paris to clarify the roles that each of the participants were to play in the forthcoming operation against Egypt. Ben-Gurion was especially concerned about the possibility that Russians might pilot Egypt's Soviet-built planes. He wanted assurances that the British and French would neutralize the Egyptian air force. Britain agreed to bomb the Egyptian airbases as long as it could be seen as part of Britain's effort to protect the Suez Canal against both the Egyptians and the Israelis. This put Israel in an awkward position since its own war plans did not include a drive to the canal. From Israel's standpoint, because its shipping was prevented from using the canal when the British were in effective control, it made little sense for them to fight to restore British control of the canal. Nonetheless, Israel was so concerned about removing the air threat to its population centers that it agreed to the British proposal. In other words, Israel would attack the canal, in which it had no interest, in order to provide a justification for the British and French to intervene to protect the international waterway. Israel's strategic aims were to defeat the Egyptian army, to gain control over the Gaza Strip, and to break through to the Straits of Tiran and thereby put an end to the Egyptian blockade of the Gulf of Aqaba. However, to accommodate Britain and France, it would first launch an assault toward the Suez Canal, creating a threat to the international waterway that would justify an Anglo-French ultimatum to Egypt and Israel to cease fire. When, as anticipated the ceasefire did not happen, the Anglo-French intervention would take place. This strategy was originally devised and presented by French General Maurice Challe to Eden on October 14.

The British, understandably, refused to put the agreement they and the French had reached with Israel on paper. As British Foreign Secretary Selwyn Lloyd later stated: "Ben-Gurion said that he did not trust us to act as we said we would. Throughout I tried to make it clear that an Israeli-French-British agreement to attack Egypt was impossible. We had thousands of British subjects in Arab countries with valuable property, and oil installations of great strategic importance. If there were a joint attack, there might be wholesale slaughter of British subjects and destruction of our installations."[15] The absurdity of the British position in the region, which aligned Britain and Jordan against Israel and Britain and Israel against Egypt, became patent on October 24, when Egypt, Jordan, and

Syria announced an agreement that placed the armies of all three under the overall command of General Abd al-Hakim Amer of Egypt.

Faced with the prospect of a coordinated three-front war, Israel began mobilizing for a preemptive strike, notwithstanding a warning from President Dwight Eisenhower on October 27 against taking any offensive action. Ben-Gurion responded to Eisenhower that Israel's mobilization was a direct consequence of Arab actions. "In view of the establishment of the Joint Command of Egypt, Syria, and Jordan, the decisive influence of Egypt in Jordan, and the renewed penetration by Egyptian bands into Israel, my government would be betraying its principal responsibility if it did not take all possible measures to ensure the frustration of the declared policy of the Arab rulers—the liquidation of Israel."[16] Indeed, the same day that the exchange of communications between Israel and the United States took place, the official organ of the Egyptian military government, *Al Gomhouria*, stated that the unified command with Jordan and Syria had been established "in a supreme effort to tighten the death noose" around Israel. A day later, the Syrian chief of staff affirmed that the purpose of the agreement was "to unify Arab military action against the common enemy."[17]

Israel struck on October 29, and the British and French made good on their promise and demolished the Egyptian air force the following day. Gaza was overrun on November 3. Although Saudi Arabia, Syria, and Iraq sent forces into Jordan, they took no action against Israel, effectively abandoning Egypt notwithstanding the existing mutual security treaty obligations. The war was over in five days. For the time being, the capture of Sharm el-Sheikh by Israel broke the Egyptian stranglehold on the Straits of Tiran and the Gulf of Aqaba, permitting Israeli and Israel-bound shipping access to and from the Indian Ocean.

Because of British and French involvement, the Security Council was prevented from taking up the issue of Suez. The matter was addressed, however, by the UN General Assembly, which not only called for a ceasefire on November 2, but also insisted that all parties to the armistice agreements immediately withdraw behind the armistice lines. A United Nations Emergency Force (UNEF) came into being on November 7 to ensure and supervise the cessation of hostilities. Under tremendous international pressure, especially from the United States, Israel reluctantly announced on December 2 that its forces would begin withdrawing from Sinai, a withdrawal that was mostly completed by January 22, 1957. Israel balked, however, at returning Gaza to Egyptian control, since Egypt had no legitimate presence there in the first place. It also insisted that it would not withdraw from Sharm el-Sheikh without an international guarantee of free passage through the Straits of Tiran, itself an international waterway. The UN rejected the Israeli position, and the General Assembly demanded an unconditional withdrawal on February 2. The United States, pursuing its own international and regional interests, essentially ignored Israel's security needs and pressured the country, threatening sanctions, to restore the status quo ante by what amounted to a unilateral withdrawal from both Gaza and Sharm el-Sheikh. The only concession Israel was able to obtain was that both places would come under the control of a UN force following the Israeli withdrawal, which took place by March 6, 1957.

For a while, at least, the Gulf of Aqaba was opened to Israeli shipping, and an international force was stationed along the Israeli-Egyptian frontier to prevent border clashes. Although Israel rested easy for the moment, Ben-Gurion remained concerned about his Egyptian nemesis. He told Israel's Knesset on April 2, 1957: "I always feared that a personality might rise such as arose among the Arab rulers in the seventh century or like him [Kemal Ataturk] who arose in Turkey after its defeat in the First World War. He raised their spirits, changed their character, and turned them into a fighting nation. There was and still is a danger that Nasser is this man."[18]

NOTES

1. Interview with Marguerite Higgins, *The New York Herald Tribune*, November 21, 1952.

2. *Jewish Observer and Middle East Review*, June 11, 1954.

3. Ibid.

4. Patrick Seale, *The Struggle for Syria*, p. 202.

5. John N. Moore, ed., *The Arab-Israeli Conflict*, vol. 3, *Documents*, pp. 581–582.

6. *Jewish Observer and Middle East Review*, June 11, 1954.

7. *Jerusalem Post*, January 25, 1955.

8. *Jewish Observer and Middle East Review*, June 17, 1955.

9. Moshe Dayan, *Diary of the Sinai Campaign*, p. 4.

10. Mohammed H. Heikal, *Cutting the Lion's Tail*, p. 92.

11. Harold Wilson, *The Chariot of Israel*, p. 320.

12. Golda Meir, *My Life*, p. 295.

13. Anthony Eden, *Full Circle*, p. 475.

14. Dayan, *Diary*, p. 59.

15. Selwyn Lloyd, *Suez 1956: A Personal Account*, p. 184.

16. "Israel's Security and Her International Position before and after the Sinai Campaign," p. 31.

17. Walter Eytan, *The First Ten Years*, p. 103.

18. Donald Neff, *Warriors at Suez*, pp. 439–440.

16

The Nasserist Era, 1952–67

The ascension to power in the Soviet Union of Nikita Khrushchev in February 1955 marked a new era of Soviet involvement in the Middle East. Previously, Soviet expansionism had been primarily in areas contiguous to its borders, and the Western powers sought to contain its movement southward through promoting and supporting a series of alliances involving the countries of the so-call "northern tier," Turkey, Iraq, Iran, and Pakistan. Turkey had also become a member of the North Atlantic Treaty Organization (NATO) in 1951, leading Moscow to protest Turkey's attempts "to involve the Near and Middle East in the military maneuvers of NATO aggression," effectively extending NATO's influence in the Arab world.[1]

Khrushchev took the audacious step of leapfrogging the "northern tier" directly into the Arab world. Division among the Arab states over whether to align with the West, as Iraq had done by joining the Baghdad Pact, or to remain neutral as Egypt insisted that the Arab world should, provided fertile ground for the Soviets to cultivated the uncommitted. Khrushchev's signal achievement in this regard was Moscow's sponsorship of the arms deal between Egypt and Czechoslovakia in the fall of 1955 that helped precipitate Israel's preemptive strike against Egypt in October 1956.

However, even before the arms deal with Egypt, the Soviets had begun to cultivate Syria. Following the crisis over the Baghdad Pact in February 1955, Turkey and Iraq reacted very strongly to the announcement of the Egyptian-Syrian-Saudi alliance and began to pressure Syria. There were reports on March 20 about concentrations of Turkish armor on the Syrian frontier. Syria complained bitterly two days later about the harsh notes it had received from Ankara "which give no consideration at all to Syria's natural right as an independent and sovereign state to follow the policy dictated by its national interest."[2] This provided an opportunity for the Soviets to intervene on Syria's behalf. Soviet Foreign Minister Molotov advised the Syrian envoy in Moscow that "the USSR supports Syria's attitude and is willing to extend to it aid in any form whatsoever for the purpose of safeguarding Syria's independence and sovereignty."[3] The Molotov guarantee was loudly proclaimed throughout the region.

The Soviets soon started pouring vast amounts of arms and equipment into Syria, arousing Turkey's concern that the arms were intended for use by Soviet troops. In December 1956 the Turkish foreign minister confirmed the concern that Syria had received more Soviet arms "than she could use given her present capabilities."[4] Viewing the buildup of what was now perceived as a Soviet surrogate to its south, Turkey began concentrating its forces on the Syrian frontier in the spring of 1957, and NATO gave notice that it would conduct an exercise in the eastern Mediterranean. On September 10 Moscow issued a warning through one of its press organs that "in encroaching against the security of her southern neighbor, Turkey would undoubtedly expose her own security to a direct blow. The Soviet Union, whose frontiers are near the threatened area, cannot adopt the attitude of a spectator to the situation there."[5] The following day an agreement was reached in Cairo with the Syrian chief of staff, Major General Afif Bizri, for Egypt "to reinforce [Syria's] forces and strengthen her defensive capabilities."[6] By mid-October, more than 1,000 Egyptian troops were in position at Aleppo, some 30 miles from the Turkish frontier. That same month, the Syrian government accepted a Soviet offer to build a deepwater naval base north of Latakia.

In the meantime, the United States, which had replaced Britain as the principal Western power in the region, announced the Eisenhower Doctrine, approved by Congress in a joint resolution of both houses on March 9, 1957. That doctrine stated that the United States might use its armed forces to protect any Middle East state requesting assistance "against overt armed aggression from any nation controlled by International Communism."[7] In late October 1957 Washington reaffirmed its commitment to come to the defense of Turkey in the event of an attack resulting from "Soviet infiltration of Syria."[8]

The crisis came to an end rather quickly that same autumn, since Khrushchev evidently saw little value in protracting or escalating it. It had well served the Soviet interest in establishing that, as Andrei Gromyko made clear at the UN on September 20, 1957, because of its close proximity to the Soviet Union, the Middle East was an area of Soviet security concern. The Soviet Union had established its presence in the Arab world and would remain a potent factor in regional geopolitics throughout most of the remainder of the century. On October 16 Syria requested the General Assembly to set up a commission to investigate the Syrian-Turkish border situation, a move supported by the United States. Turkey agreed two days later to a UN debate and the crisis fizzled.

At the height of the Syrian crisis of 1957, it seemed that Syria was destined to become a Soviet satellite, or at least a client state. However, there were other forces at work that prevented this from happening at the same time that the Soviets continued to be its principal source of arms and advocacy in the international arena. The spoiler of Soviet aspirations in Syria was that other recipient of Soviet assistance, Egypt.

One of the two most dynamic political forces in Syria at the time was Gamal Abd al-Nasser, who was immensely popular because of his successfully standing up to Britain and France, and who was seen as acceptable to the Soviet Union. The second was the Baath (Resurrection) Party, a small elite group of ardent pan-Arab nationalists that controlled only a little more than 10 percent of the seats in the Chamber of Deputies. The Baath, by themselves in no position to take effective control of the country, saw their opportunity to do so in an alliance with pro-Nasser elements. In retrospect, this seems to have been a somewhat bizarre conclusion since, although both Nasser and the Baath knew more or less exactly what they wanted, they did not want the same thing.

The Baathists were advocates of a progressive social system that would herald an Arab renaissance in modern times. They wanted to liberate the Arab world from foreign influences and to bring about Arab unity in a unitary state that would encompass that world. They held that unity, freedom, and socialism were interdependent and essential to an Arab revival. The Baathists placed little value on existing political institutions, which they saw as incapable of breaking out of their molds, kept in place by established interests. They were in a revolutionary frame of mind, and Nasser was perceived as the instrument that could reshape the Arab world. Moreover, it was not only Nasser's policies and personality that attracted them, but also the fact that he was the leader of the most populous and most powerful Arab country. As one of the founders of the Baath, Michel Aflaq, put it: "We had the conviction that there could be no Arab unity without Egypt. This was not because we believed she was destined to be the Prussia of the Arab world, uniting it by force; nor because we thought that no other country could serve as rallying centre. It was more because we had seen at work Egypt's powers of obstruction: she could and would successfully oppose any movement towards Arab unity which excluded her."[9]

The problem was that Egypt under Nasser was not interested in a unitary Arab state at the time. Egypt was a principal sponsor of the Arab League, which it considered a major victory against Hashemite Jordan's plans for a Greater Syria and Hashemite Iraq's scheme for a Fertile Crescent union. The basic premise of the Arab League was not Arab unity but the defense of the existing frontiers that divided the Arab world. Egypt wanted to dominate the Arab world by controlling the Arab League and not by submerging itself into a larger entity.

These differences in basic conception would become contentious in the future. However, in the heady days after Nasser's successful nationalization of the Suez Canal, the Baathists became staunch advocates of union between Syria and Egypt, a position echoed by the politically conservative Syrian premier Shukri al-Quwatli. For Nasser, who had struggled mightily against the Baghdad Pact, Arab unity meant Arab solidarity in the face of imperialism under his leadership, and not necessarily in a territorial or constitutional sense. Nonetheless, he needed Syria to follow his lead if his foreign policy, and the inevitable renewal of conflict with Israel, were to succeed. If constitutional unity with Syria were the price he had to pay, he was prepared to set aside his fundamental opposition to it.

With Syria, plagued by internal political problems, in a state of virtual disintegration, the strong hand of Nasser was seen by many as essential, and on February 1, 1958 he agreed to unity with a country he had never visited. After a considerable amount of intrigue and infighting in Damascus, and approval by an Egyptian-Syrian plebiscite on February 21, the new United Arab Republic (UAR) came into being the following day. Nasser became its president, with virtually plenipotentiary powers that appear to have altered his views about the benefits of a unitary Arab state. The proclamation announcing the formation of the UAR included an open invitation for membership to any Arab state on the basis of union or federation. Shortly afterward, the new republic entered into a federation agreement with Yemen that allowed the ruling Imam Ahmad bin Yahya to retain his absolute powers. The federation afforded Ahmad the Egyptian military and economic aid he needed to deal more effectively with the troublesome British colony of Aden, as well as internal opponents of the monarchy. It also provided for the establishment of unified armed forces and foreign policies, both of which would be under Nasser's presidential control. The federation, named the United Arab States, came into being on March 8, 1958. It is noteworthy that the agreement put together over 4 million Yemenis, 4 million Syrians, and more than 23 million Egyptians in a federation without common frontiers.

The emergence of the UAR also had immediate repercussions in Iraq and Jordan, where the two Hashemite monarchs, Feisal and Hussein, had close political ties, sharing a pro-British orientation that earned them denunciation by Arab nationalists. On February 14, Hussein announced the union of the two kingdoms in the Federal Arab Union of Jordan & Iraq. The new entity was to have one parliament, one army, and one diplomatic service. Feisal was to be its head of state and Hussein his deputy. However, events in Iraq were soon to put an end to the new anti-Nasser entity.

The successful 1952 revolution of the Free Officers under Nasser's leadership that toppled the Egyptian monarchy inspired a Free Officers group in Iraq to plan a similar upheaval in their own country. Pro-Nasser elements opposed to the government of Nuri as-Said had roundly condemned Iraq's entry into the Baghdad Pact as a sellout to Nuri's British masters. When Egypt came under attack in 1956, a minor pro-Nasser uprising took place in Mosul, Kirkuk, and Basra that was quickly suppressed. The fractious opposition then concluded that bringing about change would require a cohesive force and it formed a United National Front that included the pan-Arab Istiqlal and Baath parties, as well as the Communists. At the same time, the military similarly came to the conclusion that the time for action against the existing political system had arrived and it carried out a coup on July 14, 1958, under the leadership of Brigadier Abd al-Karim Qasem and Colonel Abd as-Salam Arif. King Feisal, the crown prince, and Premier Nuri as-Said were killed, and the 12, 000 Iraqi troops that were stationed in Jordan as part of the Federal Arab Union's army were withdrawn.

On the same day as the coup in Iraq, Hussein made public his request to friendly governments to send military aid to Jordan "as a temporary measure to protect our borders from surrounding enemies."[10] Four days later, some 2,000 British paratroopers arrived in Amman from Cyprus in response to Hussein's request. Jordan's relations with the UAR remained testy, particularly after Nasser predicted in a speech on June 24 that Hussein would be assassinated as had his grandfather, Abdullah. Hussein subsequently severed diplomatic relations with the UAR after the Jordanian premier Hazza Majali was assassinated on August 29, 1960. On September 5, Hussein charged that the assassination of Majali was part of a plot against the stability of Jordan hatched by UAR officials in Syria, with the knowledge of Nasser.

The leaders of the Iraqi coup soon turned out to be strange bedfellows. Qasem was a nationalist and opposed to pan-Arabism, whereas Arif was an ardent Islamic-oriented pan-Arabist. Nonetheless, they had worked together with the Free Officers in the framework of a National Pact that committed them to establish a republic, representative government, land reform, and support for Kurdish national aspirations within the context of a decentralized Iraqi state. However, once in power, the vast differences in outlook between Qasem and Arif, as well as those between the pan-Arab and the nationalist parties in the National Front, rose to the fore. The pan-Arabist Baath called for an immediate merger between Iraq and the UAR. The pan-Arabists argued that Iraq was a British creation and had no basis in history as a nation. In their view, the revolution that had just taken place was merely a stage in the struggle for the resurrection of the Arab nation. The nationalists, on the other hand, argued that a unitary Arab nation was antithetical to Iraqi national interests, with serious economic implications. A merger with the UAR would have essentially created an open market in which Iraq would be unable to compete successfully with more technically advanced Egypt. This would have the effect of retarding Iraq's development, turning it into an Egyptian hinterland.

The nationalists, with Qasem at their head, refused to go ahead with the proposed merger, causing a major split in the country. Qasem had no intention of subordinating himself or his country to Nasser and Egypt. Arif was removed as Qasem's second in command on August 28, 1958, and was sent to an effective exile in Germany as Iraq's ambassador. When he returned several weeks later he was arrested, tried, and sentenced to death for treason, a sentence that Qasem demurred from carrying out because of Arif's popularity.

Nasser was frustrated in his efforts to bring Iraq under his wing, and saw the communists, who had thrown their support behind Qasem, as the underpinning of the latter's regime. On December 28, 1958 Nasser launched a verbal attack on the Syrian communists, charging them with working against Arab interests. His primary target, however, was the Iraqi communists because of whom the Soviet Union had extended its support to Qasem. Subsequently, the UAR radio and press launched a major and vitriolic propaganda campaign against Qasem and the Iraqi communists as enemies of Arab unity.

With the implicit support of Nasser, the pan-Arabists under the leadership of the imprisoned Arif began plotting a takeover of the government, and a limited army revolt took place in Mosul in March 1959. This was followed by an attempt on Qasem's life on October 7, the responsibility for which was laid at the feet of Nasser. The chief of Iraq's Special Supreme Military Court, Colonel Fadil Abbas al-Mahdawi, declared on Radio Baghdad that the attempted assassination was one of the "reactionary plots of the U.A.R.—those which are hatched by the miserable criminal, Jamal Abd an-Nasir, the docile slave of imperialism."[11] Had the assassination been successful, it was expected there would have been an invasion from Syria as a pro-Nasser coup took place in Baghdad. It was alleged that the UAR had massed troops along the Syria-Iraq border just prior to the attack on Qasem. The attempt on his life apparently convinced Qasem that Nasser and the UAR were the principal obstacles to his ambitions for Iraq, and he became determined not only to prevent the UAR from expanding, but also to try to destroy it by "liberating" Syria.

Syria had long been seen in Baghdad as a thorn in its side. It not only blocked Iraqi access to the Mediterranean, the pipelines that carried the oil wealth of the country ran through Syria. During the Suez Canal crisis, Syria had cut the pipelines and stopped the flow of oil from the British concessions, causing serious financial problems in the country. For decades, Iraq had schemed to annex Syria but was always blocked one way or another by Egypt. Consequently, when the UAR came into being, Iraq, under Nuri as-Said, would not extend recognition to it. Following the revolution, annexation schemes and plots were put aside in the interest of a new era of cooperation between Egypt and Iraq. In fact, the first group of officials of the old regime was sentenced to death on the charge of plotting to annex Syria. However, once relations soured, Qasem reverted to the original Fertile Crescent scheme of Nuri as-Said that encompassed Jordan, Syria, and Lebanon. Following the assassination attempt, the Fertile Crescent scheme became an element of Iraq's national policy, although it does not seem that Qasem actually had any real plans to march into Syria. However, the fact that he indicated that if the Syrians were interested, he would be happy to oblige them, severely irritated Nasser who was already having problems with the Syrians. One immediate effect of Iraq's implied threat against Syria was that, despite Nasser's continuing taunts to force Qasem to nationalize the Iraqi oil industry, Nasser never attempted to tamper with the Iraqi pipelines, knowing that such an act would surely bring Qasem to invade Syria.

As Qasem tightened his control over Iraq, many of the ideals of the revolution fell by the wayside. One of the more volatile of them dealt with the perennial problem of the Kurds, who began demanding fulfillment of the promises of national autonomy made to them in the National Pact, and who were increasingly being seen as a threat to the internal cohesion of Iraq. Qasem launched a campaign against them in 1961 that proved inconclusive and alienated a good part of the army, which did not like being forced to suppress the Kurds.

With the Kurdish campaign having backfired politically, Qasem turned his attention to what he believed would be taken by the Iraqi public as a popular cause. He resurrected the claim that Kuwait was really an extension of the Iraqi nation and should be returned to it. In fact, Kuwait had been part of the vilayet of Basra during the Ottoman period and had become a British protectorate in 1913. When the protectorate ended on June 19, 1962 with a British withdrawal, Kuwaiti ruler Abdullah al-Sabah declared independence and immediately applied for membership in the United Nations and the Arab League. Qasem, however, rejected the notion of Kuwaiti sovereignty and demanded the immediate merger of the territory with Iraq. Had he been able to force this, he would have solved one of Iraq's major geopolitical problems. The British-drawn borders between Kuwait and Iraq left the latter effectively landlocked, without direct access to a deepwater port in the Gulf. This hampered Iraq's ability to move its petroleum to market efficiently and was a continuing bone of contention in the country.

The British, who had very significant economic interests in Kuwait, were not prepared to let Qasem have his way and, on July 1, 1962 British and Saudi troops moved into Kuwait to forestall a possible Iraqi attack. They remained in the country until Qasem relented under pressure from Arab and other governments. The affair proved disastrous for Qasem who had managed to make enemies everywhere including the army, which was his power base. Qasem was overthrown on February 8, 1963 and replaced by his former colleague Arif.

The reverberations from the formation of the UAR were also felt in pro-Western Lebanon, where the government claimed that an insurrection of Muslim, Druse, and socialist dissidents in May 1958 had received support from the UAR, a charge that was never fully substantiated. On May 21 Lebanese President Camille Chamoun told the press: "The United Arab Republic is still strongly interfering in our internal affairs, with the aim of effecting a radical change in our basic political policy. . . . The United Arab Republic wants our national policy to be in accord with its policy, or parallel to it. This is a thing which we cannot do. . . . In other words, we are determined to remain independent."[12]

A statement by the opposition parties made clear what Chamoun meant by his assertion that the UAR was demanding that Lebanon conform to its Nasserite policy. "The President's statement at his press conference for foreign correspondents has confirmed the fears of the Lebanese public that the Lebanese leaders are inclined towards the Baghdad Pact, the Eisenhower doctrine, and the policy of military pacts and international blocs, which have been repudiated by the Arab people of the Lebanon since 1954."[13] Lebanon appealed to the UN Security Council that same day and, after the Arab League failed to resolve the matter to Lebanon's satisfaction, the Security Council took up the complaint of UAR interference in Lebanon's internal affairs with similar result.

Chamoun repeated his charges to a press conference in Beirut on June 25: "The situation now developing in Lebanon is far from being a domestic issue. It involves the stability and peace of the Middle East. Interference by the UAR is but one milestone of its desire to dominate the Arab world. An earlier milestone was in April 1957, when an attempt was made to overthrow the legal authority in Jordan. We knew then that Lebanon would be the next victim of a similar attempt."[14] Although Washington was aware that a great deal of Lebanon's problems derived from internal factors, it was also widely held that these factors alone would not have precipitated the current crisis. A joint message issued on July 4, 1958 by the Department of State and the U.S. Information Agency asserted that while there was "no doubt violence manifested in Lebanon is, in large part, civil strife, . . . this strife would not be prolonged and might not have erupted into violence without intervention from [the] UAR."[15]

Chamoun subsequently appealed to the United States for military assistance on July 14, 1958, the same day that the Iraqi monarchy was overthrown. The United States responded affirmatively and quickly. The following day, 1,500 marines landed near Beirut. By July 20 there were more than 10,000 American troops in and around the Lebanese capital. Nasser loudly denounced the American intervention, comparing it to the imperialist attempt by Britain and France to seize control of the Suez Canal in 1956. Whatever aspirations Nasser may have entertained with regard to Lebanon were thwarted as a state of tenuous order was soon restored in the country.

It was not to be long before the Arab nationalist enthusiasm that brought the UAR into existence began to wane. The Syrians soon discovered that they were becoming second class members of the union; Syria was being transformed into a de facto province of Egypt. Nasser was employing his virtually uncontested power to effectively "Egyptianize" Syria by placing Egyptians in all positions of significant responsibility in the country. Moreover, on August 16, 1961 he abolished the regional cabinets for Egypt and Syria and their functions were consolidated into a single central cabinet that sat in Cairo. This move, which was strongly resented by Syrian political and military leaders, since it put many of them out of a job, was probably the proverbial straw that broke the camel's back.

On September 28, 1961 a column of troops, tanks, and armored vehicles entered Damascus on the orders of a so-called Higher Arab Revolutionary Command of the Armed Forces and seized the Damascus radio station and other key points. Surrounding the army headquarters, they trapped the UAR commander in chief, Field Marshal Amer, but allowed him to fly to Cairo that same day. Nasser's initial reaction was to order the UAR forces in Syria to crush the rebellion and ordered an airlift of some 2,000 paratroopers to Latakia, Syria's main port, but soon countermanded his orders. As he explained the following day, he had decided not to shed Arab blood and would seek other ways to resolve the crisis. He was to prove unable to do so.

In the meantime, on September 29, the Syrian Revolutionary Command installed Dr. Mahmoun al-Kuzbari, a law professor, as head of an all-civilian cabinet. Kuzbari immediately proclaimed Syria's secession from the UAR. Jordan and Turkey promptly extended recognition to the interim government, which led Nasser to sever diplomatic relations with both on October 1. As one of its first acts, the interim government ordered the deportation of all Egyptian civilian and military personnel, which began on October 2. That same day, Kuzbari announced that his government would follow a policy of nonalignment in foreign affairs.

Nasser's flirtation with pan-Arabism had proved a disaster and an embarrassment. After four years of work, the net result of his efforts was the official change of name from Egypt to the United Arab Republic. He was also disenchanted with Yemen because of its opposition to his socialization program, and derided both Imam Ahmad and King Saud of Saudi Arabia as reactionaries, descrying conditions in their countries in a radio broadcast on December 23. At that point, he saw no further utility in the federation of the UAR and Yemen in a United Arab State and unilaterally dissolved it on December 26, 1961. The reason for the step, as announced by Abd al-Kader Hatem, was that there was nothing in common in the nature

of Egypt and Yemen "to make the federation between them an effective political instrument able to contribute positively in strengthening the Arab
struggle."[16] Indeed, the federation between the revolutionary UAR and the
theocratic monarchy of Yemen in March 1958 made little real sense from
the very outset; it was consummated only because Nasser believed it
would enhance his prestige.

On March 28, 1962, the interim civilian government of Syria was ousted
by a military coup and the provisional constitution suspended. Three days
later, pro-Nasser army officers in northern Syria revolted. The uprising began in Homs and then spread to Aleppo and Hama. One of the principal demands of the rebels was a renewal of the union between Syria and Egypt.
The revolt came to an end on April 3 with an agreement that met a number
of the rebel demands. On June 6, Syrian premier Bashir al-Azmah proposed
an arrangement whereby Syria would retain its sovereignty within the
UAR and announced that negotiations with Egypt would begin on that ba-
sis. Turbulent negotiations regarding a rapprochement between Egypt and
Syria went on for some ten months, until a pro-Nasser coup overthrew the
government of Khaled al-Azm in Damascus on March 8, 1963. Then, on
April, 11, an agreement to form a new United Arab Republic merging
Egypt, Syria, and Iraq was announced in a communique signed in Cairo by
Nasser, Louai al-Attassi, president of the Syrian National Revolutionary
Council, and Iraqi premier Ahmed Hassan al-Bakr.

The proposed federation was to go into effect following plebiscites in all
three countries on September 27, 1963. These plans soon fell apart, however, as a result of a growing and increasingly acrimonious conflict between Nasser and the Baathists in Syria, Nasser apparently demanding
that the Baathists and Syrian Nasserites form a single unified political
camp before Egypt would join the federation. The Baathists would have
none of this and instigated a purge of pro-Nasser officers following reports
of a Nasserite attempt to assassinate Louai al-Atassi on May 3, 1963. A similar development took place in Iraq, where the Revolutionary Command
Council reported on May 25 that it had smashed a pro-Nasser conspiracy to
arrest the Baathist president, Abd as-Salam Arif, and to dismantle the
Baathist militia. Four Nasserite political parties were implicated in the conspiracy and some 50 alleged conspirators were executed in Baghdad in the
following weeks. Then, on July 18 the Syrian army thwarted an attempt by
pro-Nasser forces led by Lieutenant Colonel Jasm Alwan, who was also
leader of the March 28, 1962 coup attempt, to overthrow the Baathist government in Damascus. Numerous pro-Nasser government and military
leaders were implicated and 20 were executed the following day. By July
22, 1963, it was apparent even to Nasser that his aspiration to bring both
Syria and Iraq under his wing was unrealistic and he publicly renounced
the April agreement to form the new UAR.

THE INTERVENTION IN YEMEN

Although Nasser had unilaterally dissolved the federation with Yemen at the end of 1961, his involvement in Yemini affairs deepened once again following the overthrow of the monarchy and the emergence of a revolutionary regime. On September 26, 1962, a week after Imam Ahmad died, a clandestine group calling itself the Liberal Revolutionary Army mounted a coup against the new ruler Muhammad bin Ahmad al-Badr and proclaimed a Free Yemeni Republic. Both the Soviet Union and the United Arab Republic recognized the new government of Colonel Abdullah as-Salal on September 29.

Believing his nephew Imam Muhammad to have been killed, Prince al-Hassan bin Yahya established his headquarters in Jeddah, Saudi Arabia, where he began mobilizing an army of some 100,000 Yeminis resident in the country to retake control of Yemen. On October 2 the revolutionary government warned that it would bomb tribal villages that gave support to the royalists. Following reports that regular Saudi troops were massing along the Yemen frontier, it also threatened to carry the struggle into Saudi Arabia to attack Yemini royalist forces there. The UAR had begun to provide military supplies to the revolutionary government immediately after it took power and the first ship carrying "technicians" and "medical supplies" arrived in Hodeida on October 5. Two days later, fighting between the forces of the republicans and the royalists broke out in northern Yemen, and the Salal government announced on October 15 that Saudi and Jordanian troops were fighting on the side of the royalists. On October 29 Sana radio acknowledged that UAR troops were actively engaged in the conflict. By the end of the month, the Salal government appeared to be in relatively firm control of the country and warned that its forces were prepared to move north against Saudi Arabia unless the latter and Jordan ceased their aggression against Yemen. Saudi Arabia severed relations with the UAR on November 6 after announcing that UAR warships and aircraft had bombarded Muwassam, a Saudi port on the Red Sea near the Yemini border. Four days later, Yemen and the UAR entered into a mutual defense pact.

With both Soviet and Chinese Communist aid pouring into Yemen in support of the republican regime, the United States felt it necessary to have an offsetting presence in the country and attempted to settle the civil war through negotiations, an effort that was rejected by the Saudis. Washington subsequently formally recognized the republican government on December 19, 1962, after the Salal regime promised to honor the 1934 British-Yemini treaty regarding the British protectorate in Aden as well as the 1951 agreement that demarcated the Aden-Yemen border. In addition, Cairo had announced on the previous day that the UAR would withdraw the 12,000 troops it had sent to Yemen to assist the republican forces, one of the short-term goals of U.S. policy in Yemen.

Notwithstanding what was taking place on the diplomatic front, the civil war in Yemen seemed to be expanding. UAR aircraft had bombed the Saudi oasis town of Najiran for three consecutive days at the turn of the year, and Mecca announced a Saudi mobilization against the UAR on Jan 4, 1963. The following day, reports from Cairo indicated that Nasser had reversed his decision to withdraw UAR troops from Yemen. On January 8 the U.S. State Department made public a letter dated October 26, 1962 from President John F. Kennedy promising "full U.S. support for the maintenance of Saudi Arabia's territorial integrity."[17]

A number of clashes took place in February 1963 between Yemeni forces and those of the Federation of South Arabia, a British protectorate, and on February 27 Salal called on the southern Yeminis of Aden and the Federation of South Arabia to revolt against the British. The situation in the north also remained highly volatile, with UAR air and sea attacks in Saudi Arabia being reported in early March, attacks that the UAR asserted were aimed at destroying Yemeni royalist encampments and supply lines.

There seemed to be no end in sight for resolving the civil war in Yemen, which in many respects had become a proxy conflict between the UAR and Saudi Arabia that begged for international mediation. On April 30, 1963 UN Secretary General U Thant announced that both countries had accepted a UN plan to withdraw their forces from Yemen. The Saudis were also to cease their support of the Yemeni royalists and the UAR was to end its attacks on Saudi territory. In addition, a 12–mile demilitarized zone was to be established along the Saudi-Yemeni frontier. Notwithstanding their acceptance of the plan, both sides appear to have continued to violate it repeatedly. Indeed, Maj. General Anwar Qadi, commander of UAR forces in Yemen, stated in Cairo on May 28 that the UAR would not withdraw its troops from Yemen until its mission of stabilizing the revolution and building up the republican army had been accomplished, something that might take another five years. The UN dispatched a UN Yemen Observation Mission to help bring an end to the fighting and supervise the withdrawal of foreign forces, but it was essentially unsuccessful in doing so.

The deadlock in the fighting was exhausting both sides, with the republicans unable to dislodge the royalists from their strongholds in the northern part of the country. Saudi Arabia and the UAR agreed on September 14, 1964 to terminate their involvement in the Yemeni civil war and to seek a peace resolution of the conflict. A truce between the contending sides went into effect on November 8. However, sporadic clashes continued between the republican and royalist forces. The negotiations between the UAR and Saudi Arabia aimed at reconciling the Yemeni factions ended in deadlock on December 10, and the fighting soon resumed. By June 1965 the number of Egyptian troops in Yemen rose to between 50,000 to 60,000, with large shipments of tanks, armored cars, and artillery. Nonetheless, there was little change in the disposition of forces on the ground. The republican-UAR forces could not dislodge the royalists.

A new agreement to end the conflict was signed by Nasser and King Feisal in Jeddah on August 24, 1965. However, efforts to form a unity government and to hold a plebiscite to ratify a new regime again soon ended in deadlock and talks were postponed to February 1966. The talks never reconvened as fighting broke out again. The UAR was bogged down in Yemen at enormous expense and had no politically acceptable way out, as the royalists appeared to be making some gains at republican expense. Suffering increasing losses from guerrilla warfare, the UAR began using poison gas against the royalists throughout the following year. Nasser's direct military involvement in Yemen ended only following Egypt's defeat by Israel in the June 1967 war. The Yemen adventure was too costly to continue and most UAR troops were withdrawn by the end of the year, to be reassigned to the Suez front.

NOTES

1. *Pravda*, January 29, 1952.
2. Patrick Seale, *The Struggle for Syria*, p. 234.
3. BBC, no. 556, April 1, 1955.
4. Altemur Kilic, *Turkey and the World*, p. 96.
5. *Izvestiia*, September 10, 1957.
6. Dan Hofstadter, ed., *Egypt & Nasser, vol. 2, 1957–66*, p. 33.
7. *United States Policy in the Middle East, September 1956–June 1957*, p. 20.
8. *New York Times*, October 26, 1957.
9. Seale, *The Struggle for Syria*, pp. 310–311.
10. Hofstadter, ed., *Egypt & Nasser, vol. 2, 1957–66*, p. 50.
11. Benjamin Shwadran, *The Power Struggle in Iraq*, p. 48.
12. M.S. Agwani, *The Lebanese Crisis, 1958*, p. 75.
13. Ibid., p. 76.
14. Hofstadter, ed., *Egypt & Nasser, vol. 2, 1957–66*, p. 45.
15. Erika G. Alin, *The United States and the 1958 Lebanon Crisis*, pp. 75–76.
16. Ibid., p. 89.
17. Hofstadter, ed., *Egypt & Nasser, vol. 2, 1957–66*, p. 183.

17

Inter-Arab Rivalry and the 1967 War

Perhaps as a consequence of his adventures in the Arab world having gone awry, perhaps for genuine ideological reasons, Gamal Abd al-Nasser triggered a series of events in 1967 that resulted in disaster for Egypt and a good part of the Arab world. Moreover, it also involved the Middle East in the Cold War between the Soviet Bloc and the Western alliance in an unprecedented manner, significantly reducing the freedom of action of the states in the region.

The Suez crisis of 1956 had ended with Israeli forces in control of the Gaza Strip and Sharm el-Sheikh at the Straits of Tiran, determined to assert the right of Israel to unhindered passage to its southern port on the Gulf of Aqaba. Under extreme pressure from the United States, Israel agreed to withdraw from both in March 1957 with the understanding that they would be placed under UN control until a peace settlement was reached. Although this was a difficult pill for Nasser to swallow, it was clearly preferable to a continued Israeli presence there. However, Israel's foreign minister Golda Meir made it clear to the General Assembly of the UN that there was not to be a return to the status quo ante. The international intervention in the crisis was to assure that Egyptian aggression against Israel, either directly or indirectly through support of Palestinian infiltrators, was not to be renewed. With regard to Gaza, she told the forum: "It is the position of Israel that if conditions are created in the Gaza Strip which indicate a return to the conditions of deterioration which existed previously, Israel would reserve its freedom to act to defend its rights." And, with regard to Sharm el-Sheikh, she stated unequivocally: "Interference, by armed force, with ships of Israel flag exercising free and innocent passage in the Gulf of Aqaba and through the Straits of Tiran, will be regarded by Israel as an attack entitling it to exercise its inherent right of self-defence under Article 51 of the [UN] Charter and to take all such measures as are necessary to ensure the free and innocent passage of its ships."[1]

Nonetheless, the UN resolution did not expressly state that the UN force would remain at Sharm el-Sheikh to safeguard Israeli free passage until a final settlement was reached. According to a memorandum of February 26, 1957, a decision on withdrawal of the UN force or its replacement by an Egyptian force was left to an advisory committee appointed by the UN Secretary General, in the absence of a specific UN resolution to that effect. In other words, Israel's withdrawal was a gamble predicated on the hope that the international community would insist that the Straits of Tiran remain open to Israeli shipping. This aspiration was to be sorely disappointed a decade later.

In the meantime, while the Egyptian-Israeli borders remained generally quiet, the Syrian-Israeli border became increasingly volatile. Repeated incursions from Syria, often by regular army forces, took place between 1956 and 1962. In mid-January 1962 the Syrian army commander-in-chief, Zahr-e-din, told a graduating class of naval officers that it was necessary to choke Israel out of existence by cutting off its communications with the outside world, and declared the Mediterranean to be Israel's nautical front with the Arabs. "To strangle and destroy Israel, the Arabs must pluck out Israel's sea lung by means of a naval force that will constitute a wall of steel in the sea and deny air to this monstrous state."[2] Although this saber-rattling may have been part of Syria's attempt to wrest the leadership of the Arab world away from Egypt following the collapse of their union in the United Arab Republic, Israel could hardly afford to dismiss it as mere rhetoric.

As Syria continued to vie with Egypt for dominance over the Palestine question, the Israeli-Syrian border remained volatile but manageable for the next several years. However, matters took a clear turn for the worse following the military coup that toppled the Baath regime in Syria on February 23, 1966. The new neo-Baath government was constituted out of the more radical elements of the previous regime and the military, and was dominated by two competing factions, a civilian group headed by Salah Jadid and a military faction headed by Hafez al-Assad. Jadid, who held no significant governmental office, and Assad, who became defense minister, were both Alawi, a Shiite sect on the fringe of traditional Islam, a fact that alienated many Druse military officers as well as many among the predominantly urban Sunni majority. Although forced to cooperate because of the lack of public support for the narrow government, Jadid and Assad had very different perspectives on how to deal with Palestine and many other questions. With regard to Israel, Jadid and his radical socialist group were advocates of a people's liberation war, which was certain to provoke Israeli retaliation, whereas Assad did not want Syria directly engaged in that kind of low level conflict which he saw as counterproductive. Assad, recognizing Israel's military superiority, wanted a united front among the Arab states that could defeat Israel on the battlefield. It appears that whenever the factional dispute threatened to undermine the regime's control of the country, the specter of Israeli aggression was raised as a means of mobilizing public support.

It was against this background that the new president of Syria, Nur ad-Din al-Atassi, a member of the Jadid faction, began calling for the liberation of Palestine and the annihilation of the Zionists through a "people's war" involving sabotage and terrorism. The level of cross-border violence began to escalate, with intensifying attacks on Israeli settlements in the Jordan and Hula valleys from the Golan Heights. On May 11 al-Atassi declared: "We raise the slogan of the people's liberation war. We want a total war with no limits, a war that will destroy the Zionist base."[3] Again on October 13, as the Syrian representative to the UN gave a letter to the Security Council denying any responsibility for incursions from Syria into Israel, the Syrian chief of staff was announcing that "the war for the liberation of Palestine has begun."[4]

Tensions increased further as a consequence of meddling by the Soviet Union, which had adopted Syria as a client state and began to give public credence to the idea that Syria was under threat of attack from Israel. In October 1966 the Soviet ambassador handed a note to Israeli Prime Minister Levi Eshkol that claimed: "According to information in our possession, concentration of Israeli troops can be discerned along the Syrian frontier. Preparations are being made for an air attack, so that in its wake Israeli troops may penetrate deep into Syria."[5] Eshkol responded by inviting the diplomat, Dmitri Chuvakin, to get into a car with him and drive to the Syrian frontier to see for himself whether his information had any truth to it. Chuvakin declined the offer but continued to insist that the Soviet Union had proof of its assertions.

Tensions also increased along the Israeli-Jordanian frontier in late 1966 as a result of repeated incursions, leading Israel to retaliate with a substantial punitive raid against five villages in November, a fierce battle taking place with the defending Jordanian border guards and police. The Syrians sharply criticized Hussein for the poor showing by his forces and, with no little irony, demanded that Nasser take some punitive action against Israel. Nasser, however, was not about to be drawn into a premature war with Israel. He would only do so at a time of his own choosing.

Jordan, for reasons of its own, also began baiting Egypt to take action. Hussein had been the subject of a negative propaganda campaign coming out of Cairo, primarily because of his reluctance to allow Palestinian guerrillas to attack Israeli targets from Jordan. Nasser declared that Hussein "was ready to sell the Arab nation in the same manner as Abdullah sold it in 1948."[6] Hussein evidently wanted to turn the tables on Nasser by making him look foolish. Jordan claimed that Egypt, with the connivance of the So-

viets, "was preparing to sell out the West Bank to Israel in return for a separate peace settlement."[7] He wanted to show the Arab world that Nasser
couldn't be taken seriously by anyone, including the Israelis. On May 16,
Amman radio declared: "If the Egyptians really mean what they say, let
them demonstrate their real intentions by expelling the UN force."[8] The implication was that as long as the UNEF was still in place, Nasser could use
its blocking presence as an excuse for not taking any action. If he was serious, he would have to get rid of UNEF, something Hussein never expected
Nasser to do.

On April 7, 1967 several Israeli settlements in the north came under an
artillery, mortar, and tank cannon barrage from Syrian positions on the
Golan Heights, inflicting serious damage. Israel reacted immediately and
its air force quickly silenced the Syrian batteries, destroyed a number of
tanks, and shot down six MIG-17s in aerial combat. A few days later, the
commandant of the Egyptian air force, Marshal Muhammad Sidki
Mahmoud, offered to base some Egyptian squadrons, under Egyptian control, in Syria. The offer was rejected. However, Mahmoud warned the Syrians that Egypt would not allow itself to be dragged into a war by Syria and
that, if Syria wanted Egyptian help, it had best stop provoking untimely
clashes with Israel.

Syria once again raised the specter of Israeli mobilization for war on May
13 when it informed Egypt that Israel had positioned between 11 and 13
regiments along the Syrian frontier, in order to prod Egypt into activating
the Egyptian-Syrian defense agreement. It would seem that the internal crisis in Syria's ruling circles had heated up once again and the Soviets feared
that the current pro-Soviet regime might be toppled. A war scare served to
calm the internal waters. It was at this time that the Soviet Union, seemingly anxious to provoke a conflict, again began claiming that there was a
major buildup of Israeli forces along the Syrian frontier, confirming the
Syrian claims. Moreover, the Soviets told Damascus that Israel was going
to attack on May 17, 1967, and the same message was passed on to Cairo.
On May 14 the Egyptian chief of staff, General Muhammad Fawzi, arrived
in Damascus to coordinate a joint Egyptian-Syrian campaign against Israel.
The following day Egyptian armored columns began heading for Ismailia,
from where they crossed the Suez Canal into the Sinai. Air squadrons were
redeployed from fields along the canal to forward bases in the desert. That
same day Eshkol passed a message to Nasser through U Thant assuring
him that Israel had no intention of initiating any military action to alter the
status quo. It was to no avail.

On May 16 the following note from General Fawzi to General Indar Jit
Rikhye, commander of the United Nations Emergency Force (UNEF) in the
Sinai and the Gaza Strip, was handed to the latter by General Eiz ad-Din
Mokhtar. "To your information, I gave my instructions to all U.A.R. armed
forces to be ready for action against Israel, the moment it might carry out

any aggressive action against any Arab country. Due to these instructions our troops are already concentrated in Sinai on our eastern border. For the sake of complete security of all UN troops which install OP's [observation posts] along our borders, I request that you issue orders to withdraw all these troops immediately."

Rikhye replied that he would report to the secretary general for instructions, but Mokhtar was not satisfied with his response. He told Rikhye: "General, you are requested to order the immediate withdrawal of UNEF troops from El-Sabha and Sharm al-Sheikh tonight. Our Supreme Command anticipates that when Israel learns of our request to you, they will react immediately. In anticipation of any action they might take, our army must establish control over El-Sabha and Sharm el-Sheikh tonight." Rikhye noted that the letter from Fawzi made no mention of Sharm el-Sheikh, but Mokhtar assured him that it was the intent of his headquarters that the UNEF be withdrawn from all of Sinai.[9]

Apologists for Nasser have propounded the myth that he never really intended that UNEF should withdraw, that he expected that the secretary general would reject the request on the basis of the original understanding between Nasser and Dag Hammarskjold. Presumably, Nasser would then have no alternative but to back off. However, this was clearly not the case. The secretary general wrote in an *aide memoire* on August 5, 1957: "It would be obvious that the procedure in case of a request from Egypt for the withdrawal of UNEF would be as follows. The matter would at once be brought before the General Assembly. If the General Assembly found that the task was completed, everything would be alright. If they found that the task was not completed and Egypt, all the same, maintained its stand and enforced the withdrawal, Egypt would break the agreement with the United Nations."[10]

It is alleged that the purpose of the charade was to enhance Nasser's prestige in the Arab world, where he was being criticized for failing to assert his leadership. While this may be true to some extent, the fact is that Egyptian troops acting on Fawzi's orders occupied El-Sabha on May 17. They also forced the evacuation of members of the Yugoslav contingent of the UNEF from their posts at Kuntilla and El-Amr the following day, evidently to clear a path for an Egyptian advance. Similarly, a group of Egyptian officers arrived at Sharm el-Sheikh by helicopter and informed the UN commander there they had come to take over the position. Given the significance of these moves, it seems quite unlikely that Fawzi did all this on his own initiative and without Nasser's approval.

In any case, when U Thant received the Egyptian request he indicated to the Egyptian representative that a partial or temporary withdrawal was unacceptable. "A request by the United Arab Republic authorities for a temporary withdrawal of UNEF from the Armistice Demarcation Line and the International Frontier, or from any parts of them, would be considered by the Secretary-General as tantamount to a request for the complete with-drawal of UNEF from Gaza and Sinai, since this would reduce UNEF to in-effectiveness."[11] It was to be all or nothing. The Egyptian response came on May 18 in the form of a request that the UNEF be withdrawn from the terri-tory of the UAR and Gaza Strip. Understandably, Israel was furious since Hammarskjold had assured Ben-Gurion in March 1960 that the UNEF would not be withdrawn without the consent of the General Assembly. U Thant, however, refused to reconsider his highly contentious decision to withdraw the UNEF, and would only direct an appeal to Egypt to with-draw its request that he do so. However, Egypt's foreign minister, Mahmoud Riad, advised him that he "should not make an appeal to Presi-dent Nasser to reconsider the request for withdrawal of the UNEF and that, if he did so, such a request would be sternly rebuffed."[12]

In the meantime, UN observers could find no signs whatever of the claimed Israeli military buildup and U Thant so informed the Security Council on May 19, the same day he informed the General Assembly that the UNEF was to be withdrawn. Nonetheless, the Soviets had caused both Egypt and Syria to set forces in motion that soon got out of control and were destined to lead to full-scale war with Israel. That same day, Jordan once again was busy goading Egypt into taking further action, Amman radio raising doubts as to whether Egypt would take the next logical step and close the Straits of Tiran. It declared, "Logic, wisdom and nationalism make it incumbent on Egypt to do so, because closure of the Gulf of Aqaba to Israeli navigation will destroy the Negev reconstruction plan and pre-vent the immigration of millions of Jews to Israel."[13]

On May 22 Atassi clearly indicated that the moment for which the Arabs had been waiting had arrived. He stated over Radio Damascus: "In the light of the many authenticated reports concerning the Israeli troop con-centrations, it has been agreed between us and Egypt to take all necessary measures, not only to thwart the plot and repel the aggression, but to launch the battle of liberation, and to take the first step."[14] That same day Nasser made the fateful announcement that he would no longer permit the passage of Israeli ships, or ships with cargoes destined for Israel, through the straits. "The Aqaba Gulf constitutes our Egyptian territorial waters. Under no circumstances will we allow the Israeli flag to pass through the Aqaba Gulf. . . . This water is ours."[15] As far as Israel was concerned, and as they had made clear before turning over Sharm el-Sheikh to the UNEF, this was tantamount to a declaration of war.

On May 23 King Feisal of Saudi Arabia announced that Saudi forces would play an active role in the coming war with Israel. The following day, Jordan announced a general mobilization and that it had granted permis-sion for the Saudi and Iraqi armies to enter Jordan, and some 20,000 Saudi troops moved up to the Jordanian-Saudi border. The scene had been set for a three-front war. As Cairo radio announced on May 26, "We know that the blockade of the Gulf of Aqaba is a *casus belli*. Israel has two alternatives, either of which is drenched in her own blood. Israel can either strangle in the Arab economic and military noose, or be shot to death by the Arab forces surrounding her on the south, north and east."[16]

As late as May 29, notwithstanding the war drums being sounded in Cairo, Israeli Prime Minister Eshkol still hoped war could be avoided, placing his faith in U.S. President Lyndon B. Johnson's assurances. The president stated on May 23 that "the United States considers the Gulf to be an international waterway and feels that a blockade of Israeli shipping is illegal and potentially dangerous to the cause of peace. The right of free, innocent passage of the international waterway is a vital interest of the international community."[17] However, contrary to expectations, President Johnson did nothing to keep the straits open beyond some ineffectual approaches to Egypt. Since neither the British nor the French would take any naval action to keep the straits open, the United States was not going to do so unilaterally. As Johnson put it, "I want to see [Prime Minister Harold] Wilson and [President Charles] de Gaulle out there with their ships all lined up too."[18] The American pseudo-guarantee to Israel proved worthless. At the same time, Nasser raised the ante on the high stakes game by expanding the scope of the crisis. He told the National Assembly in Cairo that same day: "The issue now at hand is not the Gulf of Aqaba, the Straits of Tiran or the withdrawal of the U.N.E.F., but the rights of the Palestinian people . . . the aggression which took place in 1948."[19] In other words, the battle that was to ensue was for the complete eradication of Israel as a state.

Convinced that Jordan would become a primary target in the coming war, Hussein sent his chief of staff, General Amer Khammash, to Cairo to get briefed on Egypt's war plans. The general returned to Amman on May 28 with the news that the unified military command called for in the proposed defense pact with Egypt did not exist. Nasser snubbed Hussein, forcing him to make a number of political concessions before he was permitted to end his isolation in the Arab world in the event of the Israeli attack that Jordan had been provoking. On May 30, Hussein, accompanied by the top echelon of his government, went to Cairo to meet with Nasser and later with Ahmed Shukairy, leader of the Palestine Liberation Organization, a man with whom Hussein had repeatedly refused to deal. The result of this visit was the Egyptian-Jordanian Mutual Defense Treaty, which, in the event of war, would place Jordanian forces under the Egyptian chief of staff, General Muhammad Fawzi. This ended all hope of avoiding the war. As Abba Eban, Israel's UN ambassador at the time, noted: "By his journey to Cairo on May 30, Hussein made it certain that war would break out and that it would not necessarily be limited to the Egyptian-Israeli front. Israel's plans . . . had all made provision for leaving Jordan scrupulously alone. Hussein had now thoughtlessly renounced this immunity."[20]

Nonetheless, Israel made a last ditch effort to keep Jordan out of the war on June 5, the day hostilities broke out with Egypt firing the first shots with a bombardment of two Israeli settlements. From Israel's perspective, Jordan had little if anything to gain that was worth the risks it would take. In his broadcast to the people of Israel, Prime Minister Eshkol also directed a message to Jordan. He stated that Israel would not attack any state that did not enter the coming conflict, even though Jordanian forces had already begun shelling the Jewish sector of Jerusalem early that morning. Israel did not respond immediately to the Jordanian attack. Instead, Eshkol sent another urgent and more explicit message to Hussein through multiple channels, including the U.S. Embassy in Tel Aviv, and the UN truce supervisor, General Odd Bull. It stated: "We shall not initiate any action whatever against Jordan. However, should Jordan open hostilities, we shall react with all our might and he [Hussein] will have to bear the full responsibility for all the consequences."[21]

According to Hussein, when he received the message over the telephone from General Bull he rejected the Israeli overture, foolishly believing Nasser's assurances that the Egyptian army was marching on Tel Aviv and that the Egyptian air force would provide cover to protect Jordanian forces from an Israeli counterattack. He told Bull, "They started the battle. Well, they are receiving our reply by air."[22] What Hussein failed to realize was that the squadrons of warplanes sighted heading north from Egypt to Israel were not Egyptian planes en route to attack Israel. They were Israeli planes returning from the destruction of the Egyptian air force on the ground that morning. By the time the smoke cleared on the third day of the war, Hussein had lost all the territories in Palestine that his grandfather Abdullah had managed to occupy in 1948, with British assistance, and to annex in 1950. As Jordanian Prime Minister Wasfi al-Tal later put it: "We could have easily avoided this premature war. Of course, we hardly expected such a devastating defeat. But with the information we had, we didn't believe in the possibility of victory either."[23]

Hussein now faced a possible Israeli invasion across the Jordan River and quickly sent a message that morning to the Israeli defense minister, Moshe Dayan, requesting a negotiated cease-fire. Dayan responded: "We have been offering the King an opportunity to cut his losses ever since Monday morning. Now we have 500 dead and wounded in Jerusalem. So, tell him that from now on, I'll talk to him only with the gunsights of our tanks."[24]

When the UN Security Council convened shortly after the outbreak of hostilities, and U.S. representative Arthur Goldberg proposed that the council call for an immediate cease-fire, the Indian representative, acting on behalf of the Arab states, objected. "The Arabs will not accept a cease-fire resolution that does not include a demand for an immediate withdrawal of troops." Goldberg rejected this approach, arguing: "A return to the positions previous to those of June 4 means acknowledgment of the blockade of Aqaba. If a return to the *status quo ante* is desired, then the situation must be restored to what it was before the crisis began—namely, freedom of navigation in the Gulf of Aqaba and the restoration of the U.N. Emergency Force in the Sinai peninsula."[25] This, of course, was unacceptable to the Arab states and, ironically, the Soviet representative, evidently uninformed about what was happening on the battlefield, proposed that the council delay ordering a cease-fire until the following day, presumably to allow the Egyptians to consolidate their gains. Thus, while the Soviets were deliberately delaying a cease-fire, the Israelis were advancing deep into Sinai.

As their armies were being mauled, Nasser and Hussein concocted the fantasy that the United States and Britain were fighting on Israel's side. This fiction helped them explain to their bewildered people why, after years of preparation for the struggle with Israel, they were being soundly defeated. Thus, on June 6 Cairo radio announced: "We have proof that several British and American aircraft carriers are conducting wide scale operations off the coast of Israel. On the Egyptian front British and American planes are providing air coverage for the Israeli ground forces. On the Jordanian front those planes are engaged in direct attacks, as the radar stations have proved."[26]

The Egyptian, Syrian, and Jordanian ambassadors in Moscow approached the Foreign Ministry with messages from their governments denouncing American and British participation in the conflict. The Soviets reacted furiously, knowing full well that this was nonsense. The ambassadors were told in blunt terms that their claims were untrue and that the Soviet Union would not be drawn into a conflict with the United States on the basis of such spurious allegations. By the end of the day, June 6, the Soviets decided to press for a cease-fire in the interests of their Arab clients, whether the latter liked it or not. Soviet Prime Minister Alexei Kosygin sent a message to the White House stating that the Soviet Union would agree to an unconditional cease-fire, and the Security Council passed such a resolution that same evening.

Israel promptly announced that it would abide by the cease-fire if the Arabs did so as well. The latter, however, rejected the cease-fire and the fighting continued, with Israel chewing up the Arab armies. By the end of June 7, Nasser had a change of heart and asked the Soviet ambassador to get Moscow to take the steps necessary to get an immediate cease-fire in Sinai. The Security Council met in emergency session and ordered a cease-fire to go into effect that same evening. Incredibly, however, Nasser evidently changed his mind again and the Egyptian representative announced that his country would not accept the cease-fire.

By that same evening, Hussein's forces had been completely driven out of Palestine, and he eagerly accepted the cease-fire. In Sinai, the Israelis had already reached Sharm al-Sheikh and had cut off the Egyptian army's line of retreat, trapping it in the desert. In the absence of a cease-fire, the battle continued with Israeli forces reaching the Suez Canal, putting them in position to cross the canal into Egypt proper. On the night of June 8, Nasser, having run out of any other realistic options, finally agreed to the cease-fire.

Having disposed of the Jordanians and Egyptians, Israel turned its full force to the Syrian front, battling its way up the Golan Heights. By June 10 it appeared as though the Israeli army might march on Damascus. This, however, was totally unacceptable to the Soviets, who did not wish to see their client so abjectly humiliated. Moscow let it be known that it was prepared to take direct military action against Israel if it did not cease its advance. However, before the Soviets were able to issue their ultimatum from the floor of the Security Council, Israel had already agreed to a cease-fire on the Syrian front.

In his assessment of the conflict, Terence Prittie later noted, "The Six-Day War was a barren historical episode, except that it proved Israel's ability to defend herself in the face of ultimate pressure. Out of it emerged the sad truth that an area of the world which needs peace is not going to be helped to achieve that peace by great powers obsessed by their own rivalries."[27]

NOTES

1. Abba Eban, *An Autobiography*, p. 252.
2. David Ben-Gurion, *Israel: A Personal History*, p. 652.
3. Terence Prittie, *Eshkol: The Man and the Nation*, p. 248.
4. Ben-Gurion, *Israel: A Personal History*, p. 756.
5. Lester Velie, *Countdown in the Holy Land*, p. 92.
6. Malcolm Kerr, *The Arab Cold War*, p. 117.
7. Anthony Nutting, *Nasser*, p. 393.
8. David Kimche and Dan Bawly, *The Sandstorm*, p. 103.
9. Indar Jit Rikhye, *The Sinai Blunder*, p. 16.
10. *International Legal Materials*, May-June 1967, pp. 593–602.
11. *UN Monthly Chronicle* 4:7 (June 1967), pp. 135–161.
12. Gideon Rafael, *Destination Peace*, pp. 139–140.
13. Walter Laqueur, *The Road to Jerusalem*, p. 92.
14. Prittie, *Eshkol*, p. 248.
15. *New York Times*, May 26, 1967.
16. Ruth Bondy et al., eds., *Mission Survival*, p. 17.
17. Lyndon B. Johnson, *The Vantage Point*, p. 291.
18. Ibid., p. 292.
19. Eban, *An Autobiography*, p. 380.
20. Ibid.
21. Theodore Draper, *Israel and World Politics*, p. 115. See also Odd Bull, *War and Peace in the Middle East*, p. 113.
22. Hussein, King of Jordan. *My War with Israel*, p. 65.
23. Ibid., p. 126.

24. Ibid., p. 65n.
25. Michael Bar-Zohar, *Embassies in Crisis*, p. 222.
26. Ibid., p. 226.
27. Prittie, *Eshkol*, p. 278.

18

The Torturous Road to Camp David, 1967–79

The Six-Day War of 1967 was to prove to be, as Abba Eban put it, "the first war in history which has ended with the victors suing for peace and the vanquished calling for unconditional surrender."[1] In fact, the reach of Israel's armies created the dilemma for it of what to do with the conquered territories. It had neither the intention nor desire to make the Suez Canal the border between it and Egypt, or to expand into Syria. Because of this, Israel offered to sign peace treaties with both that would return the borders to the former international boundaries, subject to the demilitarization of the evacuated territories and a special regime for Sharm el-Sheikh to assure freedom of navigation in the Gulf of Aqaba.

The situation regarding the territories formerly under the control of Jordan was far more complex, and there was no consensus in Israel concerning their disposition. Given the level of guerrilla and terrorist activity that had its origins in the West Bank for two decades, there was not much support for transforming Judea and Samaria into an independent Arab state. Moreover, not a single Arab state recognized Abdullah's annexation of the territory. In fact, Britain and Pakistan were the only members of the international community that did recognize Jordanian sovereignty over the West Bank. However, there was also little enthusiasm in Israel itself for annexing the territories because it meant absorbing a large Arab population. The question of what to do with the territories of Judea and Samaria, which ironically constituted the heartland of ancient Israel, continued to trouble Israel and its relations with the Arab world for the remainder of the century.

This time, Israel was determined not to buckle under international pressure, including that of the United States, given the sorry nature of the latter's failure to carry out its commitment regarding freedom of navigation through the Straits of Tiran in 1967. Israel told the international community that it would not return to the status quo ante, to once again becoming a no-man's land wide open to infiltration and violence emanating from its neighbors. It wanted peace and would not withdraw from conquered territories until appropriate arrangements and guarantees were made.

Egypt and Syria, with Soviet support, promptly rejected Israel's overtures for peace and began demanding a unilateral withdrawal from all conquered territories. They viewed their defeats in the war as temporary setbacks in an ongoing conflict and evidently thought it reasonable that Israel should be forced to retreat to the status quo ante, to help facilitate its destruction in the next round of war. The Soviet Union began pouring arms and advisers into both Egypt and Syria in preparation for renewal of the struggle.

It was only a few days after the cease-fire went into effect that it began to erode. On June 18, 1967 Syrian forces crossed the truce lines and opened fire at Israeli positions on the Golan Heights. Then, an Egyptian force crossed the truce lines on July 1 and opened fire at Israeli troops south of Port Said. Following this, sniping across the canal became a daily routine. The Egyptians escalated the truce violations, starting on July 4, by using artillery, and then aircraft, provoking Israeli responses in kind.

The Soviet Union soon recognized that Israel's position was now considerably stronger than it had been in 1956, and that if the Arabs were to regain their lost territories, they would have to compromise. Moscow had come to the point where it was prepared to ask the Arab states to recognize the legitimacy of Israel as the price of an Israeli withdrawal. The Soviet representative at the UN, Jacob Malik, made such a proposal at a meeting of Algeria, Egypt, Iraq, Sudan, and Syria on July 14. Syria and Algeria refused to go along with the Soviets on this and demanded unconditional withdrawal before the matter of recognition might even be considered.

A summit meeting of Arab leaders was held in Khartoum on August 29 to arrive at a common Arab position regarding the conflict with Israel. There were essentially two options for consideration on the table. One was the acceptance of shared responsibility by the Arab world for the continuation of the struggle against Israel. The second, introduced by Nasser under pressure from Moscow, was a draft Soviet-American resolution to be submitted to the UN, but ultimately rejected because of the refusal of some Arab states to support it. It contained two principal provisions. First, it called for "Withdrawal without delay by the parties to the conflict of their forces from territories occupied by them, in keeping with the inadmissibility of conquest of territory by war." Second, it required "acknowledgement without delay, by all members of the United Nations in the area, that each enjoys the right to maintain an independent national state of its own and to live in peace and security; and renunciation of all claims and acts inconsistent therewith."[2]

The majority of the participants in the Khartoum conference considered the proposal to be unrealistic. First, they had little confidence that either of the sponsors would be able to force Israel to withdraw without achieving its stated aims. Second, most were not interested in negotiating a peace settlement with Israel. None of the Arab leaders was prepared to go before his own public and explain why they should now put aside two decades of anti-Israel diatribes that denied its legitimacy. One notable exception among the Arab leaders was Habib Bourguiba of Tunisia, who had publicly urged the Arab states to give up their "dead-end policy of belligerency." Several days before the conference, he stated: "The state of Israel has been recognized by both the United States and the Soviet Union . . . its existence is challenged only by Arab countries. . . . In these circumstances, it is useless to continue ignoring reality and to claim to wipe Israel off the map."[3] His efforts bore no fruit.

From an Arab nationalist perspective, the most the Arab states could gain from a settlement with Israel under existing circumstances was the return of territories taken from them. However, the reason they had gone to war was to destroy Israel and impose their own will on Palestine. To accept peace with Israel in exchange for their own territories but not for Palestine was considered unthinkable at the time by both Egypt and Syria. Jordan was in an even worse position because it had lost territories that it had previously seized and annexed in Palestine itself. Accordingly, a return to the armistice lines of 1949 seemed to them the minimum they required before they could even begin to seriously consider a negotiated settlement with Israel. The Khartoum conference resolved that there would be "no peace, no recognition, and no negotiations," until the Arabs had been restored to a position of strength.

Truce violations became routine and more intense. On October 21, 1967 the Israeli destroyer *Eilat* was hit and sunk by Egyptian missiles in international waters off the coast of Sinai, losing half the crew. Four days later Israel retaliated by shelling two large oil refineries and associated storage tanks near Suez that supplied most of Egypt's fuel. Following this the Suez front remained relatively quiet for more than a year, as the Egyptians established fortified positions and restructured their forces along the canal, under the direction of Soviet specialists.

By the end of October 1967, frustrated by Arab intransigence regarding a peaceful settlement, Prime Minister Eshkol told the Knesset that Israel had decided to consolidate its control on the occupied territories until a permanent peace had been negotiated:

The area that was under Jordanian occupation and the Gaza region, which the Egyptians ruled, were held by them not by right but by force, as the result of military aggression and occupation. This occupation was recognized, it is true, in the armistice agreement, but these agreements have been nullified by military provocation and aggression on their part. Moreover, it was agreed between the par-

ties in 1949 that the armistice lines had been determined only by military considerations and did not have the character of frontiers. . . . For these reasons, there is
ample justification . . . for Israel's attitude that the aim should now be to determine
agree-upon boundaries within the framework of peace treaties.[4]

At the UN, on November 22, 1967, after extensive debate and maneuvering the Security Council passed Resolution 242, based on the earlier Soviet-American proposal that was rejected by the Khartoum Conference.
The Resolution called for the establishment of a just and lasting peace in the
area based on application of two principles: (1) "Withdrawal of Israeli
armed forces from territories occupied in the recent conflict"; and (2) "Termination of all claims or states of belligerency and respect for and acknowledgement of the sovereignty, territorial integrity, and political
independence of every state in the area and their right to live in peace
within secure and recognized boundaries free from the threats or acts of
force." This established the so-called "land for peace" notion that served as
the basis for Arab-Israeli negotiations into the twenty-first century. Because the resolution was intended to provide a set of guidelines for negotiations between Israel and the Arab states, no mention of the Palestinian
Arabs was contained in the document, although the latter would continually try to insert themselves into its compass. Moreover, the meaning of the
principle concerning withdrawal was set forth in a manner that obfuscated
its real intent. The resolution, which in the official English version called for
an Israeli withdrawal "from territories" occupied in the 1967 war, was rendered as "from *the* territories" in the French version, which the Arabs consistently understood as meaning *all* the territories, a reading that Israel
equally consistently refused to accept.

It was generally assumed at the time that by accepting Resolution 242
the Arab states had agreed to settle the Arab-Israeli conflict in accordance
with its terms. However, this clearly was not the case in the years immediately following its adoption. In the Arab world, Resolution 242 was widely
held to apply exclusively to Israel's withdrawal from occupied territories
without regard to the matter of recognition of Israel's right to exist. For
Egypt, as indicated in *Al Ahram* on December 29, 1967, the issue was one of
"liquidating the results of the June '67 aggression without losing sight of
the aim of liquidating the results of the aggression of May '48," which
brought Israel into existence.[5]

Nasser repeatedly assured the Egyptian people that he would soon liberate the occupied territories, and there was no doubt in anyone's mind
that he was not merely referring to Sinai. As explained by Cairo radio on
March 17, 1968: "The real Palestine problem is the existence of Israel in Palestine. As long as a Zionist existence remains even in a tiny part of it—that
will mean occupation. The important thing is to liquidate the Israeli occupation, and there is no difference between the territories lately occupied
and those occupied before."[6]

Bravado aside, the most Nasser could actually do was to find a way of increasing pressure on the Israelis to force them to maintain an extended high level of mobilization, which would place heavy strains on its economy and ultimately force a unilateral withdrawal to conserve resources. This pressure was to be applied in a limited war of attrition along the Suez Canal that would drain Israel but would not be at a level that would justify a full-scale Israeli attack on Egypt proper. The strategy was explained by Mohamed Heikal, at the time a close confidant of Nasser. "Reliable authorities state that the enemy cannot stand the consequences of protracted war because the prolongation of general mobilization—given her limited resources in manpower—is liable to threaten her with complete internal breakdown." Moreover, because of its size, Israel could not accept a steadily increasing casualty rate for very long. Heikal pointed out: "If the enemy succeeds in inflicting on us 50,000 casualties in this campaign, we can go on fighting nevertheless, because we have manpower reserves. And if we succeed in inflicting 10,000 casualties, he will indisputably find himself compelled to stop fighting, because he has no manpower resources at his disposal. The moment we succeed in increasing the enemy's losses in lives above his capacity to replace them, we can count ourselves the victors."[7]

By September 1968 the Egyptians completed construction of a network of defensive positions along the west bank of the canal and began intensive artillery barrages and commando raids intended to weaken Israel's resolve to hold on to the Sinai. Instead of weakening, however, the Israelis adopted a retaliatory policy designed to convince the Egyptians that it would be more advantageous for them to observe the truce. Israeli aircraft destroyed a number of bridges across the Nile and paratroopers landed at Naj Hamadi, deep in Egypt, destroying the major power station there. These retaliatory raids brought a temporary quiet to the confrontation line. In January 1969 Egypt renewed the war of attrition.

On January 21, 1969 Nasser clearly reaffirmed Egypt's commitment to a military solution of the stalemate with Israel. He stated in an interview in *Al Ahram*: "The first priority, the absolute priority in this battle, is the military front, for we must realise that the enemy will not withdraw unless we force him to withdraw through fighting. Indeed, there can be no hope of any political solution unless the enemy realises that we are capable of forcing him to withdraw through fighting."[8] To some extent, Nasser's attrition strategy was working, albeit at heavy cost to Egypt, and Israel was tiring of it. On July 1 Prime Minister Golda Meir, who had replaced Eshkol, warned that continued Egyptian violations of the cease-fire would cause Israel to escalate its retaliation and that it would "hit back with seven blows for each one it receives."[9]

Israel was as good as its word. Continued Egyptian attacks brought a massive Israeli retaliatory air raid on July 20 that pounded the northern canal sector for some five hours. Its air force shot down 17 Egyptian aircraft and sank two torpedo boats, and a commando raid destroyed numerous ammunition dumps and other facilities. As a result of the increased levels of retaliation, about a half-million civilians had to be evacuated from towns on the canal's west bank. By the fall of 1969, with the attrition strategy backfiring, Egypt's military posture was deteriorating rapidly and Nasser appeared ready to reconsider the possibility of a political solution. Egypt indicated to the United States that it was ready to begin indirect talks with Israel.

Assistant Secretary of State Joseph Sisco and Soviet Ambassador Anatoly Dobrynin came up with a set of proposals in late 1969, from which the Soviets later distanced themselves, that subsequently became known as the Rogers Peace Plan. In effect, it sought to impose a solution to the Arab-Israeli conflict rather than prod the belligerents to negotiate a mutually acceptable arrangement. Although the plan had a number of troublesome provisions from the Arab standpoint, its approach made it categorically unacceptable to Israel. Abba Eban, Israel's foreign minister, made it clear that "Israel will oppose with all its strength every effort to fix restrictive conditions prior to negotiations directly with the Arabs."[10] Egypt also rejected the plan as conceding too much to Israel and as constituting an attempt to split the Arab world by dealing with Egypt and Jordan separately.

With movement on the political front at a standstill, Israel continued to escalate its retaliatory strikes. However, instead of attempting to come to terms with Israel, Nasser chose to go to Moscow on January 22, 1970 to request that the Soviet Union send forces to Egypt to aid in its defense. The Kremlin agreed and Soviet missile units began arriving in Egypt, followed on April 1 by three squadrons of Soviet-piloted fighter planes. The Soviets took over direction of the Egyptian air defense system. Confident that he now had the military upper hand, Nasser escalated the war of attrition and mounted a successful commando raid across the canal that wiped out an Israeli armored unit. Israel responded with some 500 air sorties within the space of a week, sinking an Egyptian destroyer and missile patrol boat. By June, Israel had shot down a total of 101 Egyptian aircraft and 23 Syrian planes, itself losing 20 aircraft, primarily while attacking Soviet surface-to-air missile emplacements along the canal. The following month there was a direct Soviet-Israeli clash in the air when an Israeli patrol was attacked by Eight Soviet-piloted MIG-21s over the northern sector of the Gulf of Suez. The net result was the downing of four Soviet planes, without any Israeli losses. To avoid embarrassing the Soviet Union, Israel made no public mention of the encounter.

To Nasser's disappointment, the Soviet military presence did not give him the edge in the confrontation with Israel. Egypt soon needed a respite from the fighting to rebuild its fortifications as well as its forces, and international calls for another cease-fire were shortly to be heard. Israel was very wary of creating yet another opportunity for Egypt to regain its strength for another round of fighting. Indeed, as Mohamed Heikal explained in *Al Ahram* on August 2: "Egypt risks nothing by attempting first of all to solve the first phase by political means. The same does not apply to Israel. If the Arabs wish to retract their agreement to the Security Council resolution, it is easy for them to do so by a single word. But if Israel should wish to retract the implementation of this resolution, it will have to fight a new war in order to occupy again the territories it will have evacuated in accordance with the resolution."

Under heavy pressure from Washington, Israel agreed to another 90-day cease-fire on August 7, 1970. One of the primary stipulations of the agreement was that "Both sides will refrain from changing the military status quo within zones extending 50 kilometers to the east and west of the ceasefire line. Neither side will introduce or construct any new military installations in these zones. Activities within the zones will be limited to the maintenance of existing installations at their present sites and positions and to the rotation and supply of forces presently within the zones."[11] As Israel fully anticipated, the Soviets and Egyptians immediately violated the cease-fire agreement and began to deploy missile batteries along the canal. For its part, anxious to keep its political efforts alive, the United States simply turned a blind eye to what was happening, pretending that it had no evidence that the violations charged by Israel had actually taken place. By thwarting Israel from taking action to stop the violations, the United States effectively allowed the Soviet-Egyptian buildup to proceed unimpaired. Once again, the U.S. State Department had intervened in the Arab-Israeli conflict in a manner that contributed to exacerbating rather than ameliorating it, a counterproductive pattern it continued to follow throughout the rest of the century. This put Israel and the United States on a collision course. As Prime Minister Meir put it at the end of August: "We are now in the midst of a strenuous dispute with the United States over Egyptian violations of the ceasefire. The U.S. government has guaranteed that neither side would improve its military position as a result of the ceasefire. But only a few hours had passed when the Egyptians began violating it. We cannot give in on this score. We cannot be weaker should the war along the Suez Canal resume."[12]

By September 5, 1970 at least 45 SAM (surface-to-air missile) sites, Israel claiming it was double that number, had been constructed within the canal zone and at least 30 of these had been made operational since the cease-fire. Fearful of jeopardizing its relations with the United States, the only major power ostensibly friendly to it, Israel was constrained from doing anything significant about the violations. For many in Israel, given Washington's previous failure to keep the Straits of Tiran open only a few years earlier, it raised the question of the value of any U.S. guarantee. The cease-fire violations also placed in great doubt the value of any agreement an Arab government might sign.

Nasser died unexpectedly on September 28, 1970 and was replaced by Anwar Sadat, who agreed to an extension of the cease-fire for another 90 days at its expiration at the end of November. Sadat was in no sense another Nasser. He had a mind of his own and a different perspective on Egypt's role and destiny. In essence, he saw Egypt's future as the leading state of Africa and wanted to reorient Egypt in that direction and away from the interminable conflict in the Middle East. However, he was constrained by the Nasserist legacy and had to proceed cautiously. He could not simply stop Egypt's role in the Arab-Israeli conflict at a point when Israeli troops were positioned along the Suez Canal and in control of Sinai. Nor could he simply abandon the Arab cause that had been underpinning Egyptian policy for more than two decades. Nonetheless, his desire to reorient Egyptian policy was evident as early as December 1970 when he indicated a retreat from the Khartoum policy during an interview in which he outlined Egypt's terms for a settlement of the conflict. First, "Israel must give up every inch of territory she captured from the United Arab Republic in the Six-Day War of June 1967." Subsequently, Egypt "will recognize the right of Israel as an independent state . . . and will welcome a guarantee" by the four big powers "of all Middle East borders, including [those of] Israel." Furthermore, Egypt was "prepared to negotiate Israel's right of passage through the Straits of Tiran and the Gulf of Aqaba, and this should be done at once. But Israel's right of passage through the Suez Canal depends on an agreement between Israel and the Arab countries on what is going to happen to the Palestinian Arabs; settlement of this refugee problem is a precondition to agreement on the passage of Israeli shipments through the Canal." However, he also stated that even if all these issues were resolved satisfactorily, "we would still not enter into normal diplomatic relations with them . . . leave it to the coming generations, not me."[13]

On February 4, 1971 Sadat announced that he was prepared to extend the cease-fire for another month, and issued a feeler for an interim solution to the impasse that would allow Egypt to reopen the Suez Canal to international traffic, a step important to Egypt's strained economy. He indicated his willingness to reopen the canal if Israeli troops would pull back from its east bank to a line stretching from El-Arish on the Mediterranean to Ras Mohammed on the Red Sea. He was further prepared to extend the cease-fire for another six months if such an interim agreement was reached. Israel too was interested in an interim arrangement that would lead to a separation of forces, as was made clear by Moshe Dayan, who had argued in January: "We have demanded total peace, and this the Arabs were not ready to grant us. The Arabs have demanded total withdrawal, and with this we are not willing to agree. So let us have an arrangement that would give us something less than total withdrawal."[14] The reasoning behind

Dayan's proposal was that if a limited withdrawal would allow Egypt to reopen the canal, the Soviets would have a vested interest in keeping it open to shorten its ocean supply route to its allies in Vietnam. It would serve Israel's interests by effectively creating a buffer zone not only between Israeli and Egyptian forces, but perhaps even more importantly between Israeli and Soviet forces.

Nonetheless, although Israel was interested in an interim agreement, it was not prepared to carry out a limited withdrawal on the terms proposed by Sadat, which included moving Egyptian forces to the east bank of the canal. This latter demand, which Sadat insisted on, was completely unacceptable to Israel. Given Egypt's record of cease-fire violations, lending little credibility to any of its assurances, Israel was not about to give Sadat a foothold in Sinai without a peace agreement. Moreover, Sadat's evident need to continually proclaim his support for a pan-Arab approach to Israel, such as his assertion that "there can be no partial solution to the aggression that was perpetrated against our nation as a whole,"[15] hardly instilled any confidence in his commitments to Israel.

In the meantime, international pressure was mounting on Israel to agree to a total withdrawal from territories taken in 1967 on the basis of a commitment by Egypt that it would agree to a general peace settlement with Israel. Egypt even indicated a willingness to bring the UN back to Sharm el-Sheikh. Israel, however, was unwilling to commit itself to a unilateral withdrawal in exchange for Arab promises, the value of which was dubious. After all, in the 23 years since the establishment of Israel, there had been 26 successful revolutions in Arab countries, and at least another 42 that were unsuccessful. What assurance could there be that an agreement signed by one Arab leader would be honored by his successor, especially if he came to power through a coup. Dayan put it plainly: "The Arabs have agreed to sign a peace accord with us not because they have come to terms with the existence of Israel but to induce Israeli withdrawal. We want security, not just peace documents, and would prefer that Israel hold sensible, effective lines for her defense, even if the Arabs refuse to regard them as permanent, rather than return to the 4 June borders."[16]

The trumpets of war were being sounded in Cairo once again in the latter part of 1971, with an announcement by the Egyptian vice president that "By the end of the year there will be either peace with justice or total war between Egypt and Israel."[17] Sadat, however, realized that, notwithstanding the improvement in Egypt's armed forces resulting from Soviet arms sales, the United States had been similarly upgrading the Israelis and that he would not really be ready for a full-scale war until the arms balance was tilted decisively in Egypt's favor. Sadat made this clear to his critics in the Arab world on January 30, 1972. "The decision concerning the war has been made.... The only change is that I have postponed the Zero-Hour, because all my calculations had been undone, and if I should go to war, I would be beyond the point of no return."[18]

Although Sadat evidently was ready for war in early 1972, the Soviets were not and the Kremlin applied pressure on him to delay further, in addition to placing restrictions on his use of advanced Soviet weapons. The Kremlin was actively pursuing détente with Washington at the time and a Brezhnev-Nixon summit meeting was scheduled for May 1972. Moscow did not want to see its global strategic interests placed in jeopardy by the untimely outbreak of a war in the Middle East that might trigger a great power confrontation as well. Sadat's frustration with Egypt's Soviet backers led him to decide to do without their direct help, thereby relieving him of some of the Soviet constraints on his freedom of action. He announced that he had terminated the role of Soviet advisers and experts in Egypt on July 17. This by no means meant a break with the Soviet Union, only that Soviet personnel were being removed from the battle zone.

Egyptian war planning entered a more definitive phase with the appointment of Marshal Ahmad Ismail as minister of war at the end of 1972, and serious negotiations with Syria began in January 1973. That same month, an Egyptian-Syrian Supreme Council, under Ismail's leadership, was established. It would take several more months before any serious joint planning began. The Supreme Council met in Alexandria toward the end of April and began discussing the timing of the forthcoming attack.

Jordan was a key element in their plans, both because it provided a direct link between Egypt and Syria and because its long border with Israel would tie down large numbers of Israeli troops even if Jordan took no overt action. Hussein was extremely wary of joining in the war effort. His failure to stay out of the fighting in 1967 cost him the entire West Bank and Jerusalem, and he feared that a miscalculation this time could cost him the East Bank as well. Nonetheless, he ultimately agreed to be involved in the war planning with the understanding that Jordan's mission would be only to tie down Israeli forces along its border and to prevent Israel from outflanking Syrian forces from the south. The agreement with Jordan, concluded at a meeting held in Cairo in September 1973, cleared the way for a three-front campaign against Israel.

Israel watched the growing buildup of Egyptian and Syrian forces with some concern, but without alarm. They knew, and were convinced that the Arabs knew, that the enemy did not have sufficient countervailing air power to enable their armies to succeed on the ground, and that it was therefore unlikely that they would launch a major war that they couldn't win. As a result, the Israelis did not react. What they didn't anticipate was that Sadat's basic expectation was not that he would decisively defeat Israel. His real aim was to be able to definitively alter the status quo in Egypt's favor, making it politically possible for him to reach an accommodation with Israel and thereby remove Egypt from the pan-Arab Palestinian quagmire.

It was not until just before dawn on October 6 that Israeli intelligence received reliable word from an Arab source that Egypt and Syria were going to attack that same day. The Israeli chief of staff immediately requested permission from the prime minister to mount a preemptive air attack. Mrs. Meir, however, was concerned about the international reaction to such a move, especially from Washington, upon which Israel might have to rely for additional military aid. It was reluctantly decided that Israel would have to absorb the first strike, and rely on its ability to confine the battle to the Sinai and the Golan so as to limit damage to Israel proper. Israel began a partial mobilization as Operation Badr, as the Egyptian-Syrian battle plan was known, was put in motion with coordinated attacks on Israeli positions on the east bank of the canal and in the Golan Heights.

Even though Egypt was clearly considered the primary adversary, Israel decided to give the Syrian front its initial highest priority, even though it would mean the loss of its advanced positions along the canal. This was deemed necessary because of the proximity of the Golan Heights to Haifa and other population centers in northern Israel. Once the north was secured, a counterattack would be mounted in Sinai that would drive the Egyptians back to the west bank of the canal. After two days of heavy fighting, the Syrian advance was stopped and the Israeli counterattack began. The Syrians were reinforced by Iraqi troops on October 10 and by Jordanians on October 13, but were nonetheless severely mauled. Israel then turned to deal with the Egyptians in the south. By October 16, it was evident that the Egyptian army no longer had any prospect of taking the vital strategic passes in Sinai. Sadat then proclaimed, for the first time, Egypt's limited aims in the war, which were, namely, not to destroy Israel but to recover territories lost in 1967 and thereby to restore Arab honor. Golda Meir later wrote about the apparent Arab obsession about the lines of June 4, 1967: "When Arab statesmen insist that Israel withdraw to the pre-June, 1967, lines, one can only ask: If those lines are so sacred to the Arabs, why was the Six-Day War launched to destroy them?"[19]

Although the United States sought to get the Security Council to call for a cease-fire the day following the outbreak of hostilities, the Soviet Union displayed no interest in such an intervention. Its clients were on the offensive and their patron did not want to curtail their successes. They did not do so even when Egypt's forces were pushed back to an enclave on the east bank of the canal. However, once Israeli forces crossed the canal into Egypt proper and cut the Ismailia-Cairo road, threatening to isolate the Egyptian army now trapped on the wrong side of the canal, the Soviets became anxious for a cease-fire. On October 22 the Security Council passed Resolution 338, which called for an immediate cease-fire in place, implementation of

Resolution 242, and the start of negotiations that would bring peace to the region.

This time, however, Israel's immediate reaction was to ignore the cease-fire resolution, the sole purpose of which was the Soviet desire to prevent the total collapse of the Egyptian army. Throughout the night of October 22 and the following day Israeli forces continued their drive into Egypt, taking control of the port facilities in Suez City, isolating the city and cutting off the 20,000 troops of the stranded Egyptian Third Army, and getting into position for an attack on Cairo. Under extreme pressure from Washington, Israel was then reluctantly forced to accept the cease-fire. The message to Israel was clear. The United States, which was concerned about the ramifications of possible direct Soviet intervention, might accept an Arab defeat of Israel, but it would not accept a decisive Israeli victory over the Arabs. Two days later, the Security Council adopted a resolution calling for the establishment of a UN peacekeeping force to supervise the cease-fire.

With the active intervention of Secretary of State Henry Kissinger, a cease-fire stabilization plan was agreed to on November 11. Kissinger subsequently undertook an unprecedented "shuttle diplomacy" that resulted in a further disengagement agreement between Egypt and Israel on January 18, 1974. By mid-1975, after more than a year of diplomatic fits and starts, Sadat announced that the Suez Canal would be reopened to international traffic, and that the mandate of the UNEF in Sinai was extended for an additional period. These were taken as indicators that Sadat was ready to negotiate a peace agreement with Israel. The onset of a fundamental shift of Egypt's orientation from the Soviet Union toward the United States gave new impetus to Washington's interest in demonstrating to Sadat that only the United States could help Egypt regain its territory. This meant, of course, that Israel was to come under intense American pressure to make greater accommodations to Egypt. These concessions were reflected in the Sinai II agreement signed in Geneva on September 4, 1975.

The Sinai II agreement had the odd result of making Israel increasingly dependent on the United States for its security. Since the cease-fire of 1973, some $3 billion in Soviet and French weaponry, most of it paid for by Saudi Arabia and the Persian Gulf states, came into Egypt and Syria. Israel, with limited resources, had to rely on Washington's commitment to supply it with the money necessary to keep up with the Arabs in the new Middle East arms race, a need that could be directly related to the inconclusive character of the termination of the 1973 war.

Since 1967, the notion of "territory for peace," the concept set forth in Resolution 242, had been the accepted policy of the Israeli Labor governments. Thus, when Menahem Begin, leader of the opposition Likud coalition became prime minister on June 21, 1977, it seemed clear that the "territory for peace" formula would undergo significant reinterpretation. The Likud categorically rejected the notion that any part of Palestine might be alienated from Israeli sovereignty, thereby dismissing out of hand the aspirations of the Palestinian Arabs for their own state in the country. This threw a proverbial monkey wrench into the plans of the U.S. administration of President Jimmy Carter for securing a comprehensive peace settlement, which in its view required an internationally recognized Palestinian Arab entity on the West Bank.

Begin arrived in Washington on July 15 and advised President Carter that Israel was prepared "to make a significant withdrawal of her forces in Sinai," within the framework of a peace treaty. As for the Israel-Syria border, Israel was determined to remain on the Golan Heights, but "within the framework of a peace treaty, we shall be prepared to withdraw our forces from their present lines and redeploy them along a line to be established as the permanent boundary." As for the West Bank and Gaza, Begin stated flatly that "Israel will not transfer Judea, Samaria and the Gaza District to any foreign authority."[20]

Carter had hoped to reconvene the Geneva peace conference in the fall, but was concerned, especially given the approach outlined by Begin, that the Arabs and Israelis were too far apart for the conference to achieve much unless he first narrowed the gap, which Washington attempted to do. Begin, however, was not willing to wait for Carter to dream up yet another peace formula that gave short shrift to Israel's interests as the preceding American administrations had. With Dayan as the new foreign minister, Israel began searching for a direct political way of resolving its confrontation with the Arab states. What Israel needed was an Arab broker who was not directly involved in the conflict who could serve as an intermediary. The Arab leader who was up to the task was King Hassan of Morocco.

Dayan made a secret visit to Morocco where he conferred with Hassan and explained what he had in mind. As Dayan saw it, there were two issues that had to be dealt with. The first was that no single Arab country was prepared to break ranks and unilaterally enter into a peace agreement with Israel, even if it were to its advantage. The second issue was that there was no realistic way that a comprehensive peace could be negotiated with all the Arab states at the same time. The only way out of the dilemma, he told Hassan, was to conclude a de facto peace agreement with one or more Arab states that would be made public only gradually as the problems entailed were resolved one by one. The commitments under such gentlemen's agreements could be spelled out in letters sent to President Carter. Hassan was taken with the idea and undertook to arrange a meeting for Dayan with a top Egyptian official.

Hassan delivered on his promise and Dayan met with Egyptian Deputy Prime Minister Hassan Tuhami in Rabat on September 16, 1977. Tuhami assured Dayan that Sadat was sincere about wanting peace with Israel, but asked that the United States be kept in the dark about their negotiations for the time being. Tuhami further proposed that only after agreement had been reached should they go to the Geneva Conference to sign the treaty and nothing more. Although he was convinced that Sadat would not sign such a treaty unilaterally, he also was convinced that once an Egyptian-Israeli agreement was reached, Jordan and even Syria would soon come to terms with Israel.

While both Israel and Egypt were considering the reports of the secret discussions in Rabat, Dayan met with President Carter on September 19 and again on October 4 to discuss the proposed Geneva Conference. Carter told him bluntly that the Palestinians would have to be represented at the conference and that Israel would ultimately have to accept a Palestinian homeland in the West Bank and Gaza. Dayan's response was equally blunt. Israel would never, at least under the Likud government, accept an independent Palestinian state or homeland in the West Bank and Gaza, nor would it remove any of its settlements in those territories. Moreover, he told Carter, Israel did not think reintroducing the Soviet Union into the peace process, after Kissinger had managed to exclude them, was a good idea.

It soon became clear that Sadat was equally concerned about Carter's bringing the Soviet Union back into the picture. It was unlikely to be helpful and might possibly prove an impediment because of its strong influence on Syria. He made this clear in an interview published on December 25, 1977. Sadat stated: "The Syrian Baath party will go to Geneva, and if it did the picture would be like this: The Soviet Union has the Syrians in its pocket and Syria has the Palestinians in its pocket also. . . . And the result would be that the Geneva Conference would greatly add to our level of disillusionment."[21]

Sadat also made clear, in an address to his parliament on November 9, his determination not to have Egypt's interests jeopardized by Carter's naïve notions regarding the value of bringing in the Soviets and moving the negotiations over peace back to Geneva. At that time he expressed his willingness to go anywhere, including to the Israeli Knesset, in the search for peace. After repeating this offer to a visiting delegation of U.S. congressmen, Israel began to take it seriously and Begin similarly made a number of public statements that included informal invitations for Sadat to come to Jerusalem as well as indicating that he was prepared to go to Cairo. A formal invitation to Sadat was received on November 15, and he arrived in Israel four days later.

In his address to the Knesset on November 20, Sadat made clear that he was not prepared to sign a separate peace treaty with Israel, or to negotiate over territory. "Therefore," he stated, "I have come to tell you that we insist on your total withdrawal from all territories conquered by Israel in 1967, including Arab Jerusalem." He also asserted that "the heart of the struggle is the Palestinian problem, and you must recognize the right of the Palestinians to their own State and their own entity. That is the first step along the only path leading to peace."[22] When asked by Dayan later that evening what he meant by "peace," Sadat responded that he meant that disputes between states should be settled peacefully rather than through war. That was as far as Egypt was prepared to go in its future relations. In other words, for Sadat, peace meant nothing more than a situation of continued nonbelligerency.

Although Sadat's visit did not close the distance between the stances of Egypt and Israel, the fact that Sadat took an enormous political risk in coming to Jerusalem to speak to Israel directly and publicly was in itself considered by Israel to be of major political significance. Moreover, Sadat had come to Jerusalem, where even American diplomats feared to tread lest it be considered as recognizing the reality of Israel's control of the city. Sadat also stated that although he could not reciprocate by inviting Begin to Cairo as long as Israel occupied Egyptian territory, he would invite him to Sadat's home in Ismailia, where Egyptian legislators would congregate to meet him. With Sadat's dramatic and unprecedented gesture, the psychological barrier that had prevented the Arab states from negotiating directly with Israel was broken, at least as far as Egypt was concerned.

Dayan met with Tuhami again in Marrakesh on December 2 and 3. The meeting was convened on Sadat's initiative to set forth Egypt's proposals for a peace agreement. The proposals did not strike Dayan as being sufficiently realistic, and he noted that he was uncomfortable discussing them with Tuhami because the latter did not seem to have the authority to do anything beyond deliver Sadat's message. Dayan recalled: "I also had an unhappy feeling about Sadat himself, in so far as what Tuhami and King Hassan told me reflected his policy. I did not think he would retreat from the course of peace on which he had embarked, but I suspected that he did not quite know how to advance. He knew what he wanted but not how to achieve it. I reached the conviction that unless the Americans could be involved and threw their weight behind the negotiations, the wheels of peace would remain at a standstill."[23] His misgivings were soon borne out as the negotiations ground to a halt, despite Begin's visit with Sadat at Ismailia on December 25. Sadat would not budge from any of his previously stated positions and Begin was not prepared to jeopardize Israel's security for an Egyptian promise of nonbelligerency.

Concerned about the possible consequences of a breakdown of contacts between Egypt and Israel, President Carter seized the initiative and called for a summit meeting with Begin, Sadat, and himself at the presidential retreat at Camp David, Maryland. Both leaders, wanting to find a way of breaking the deadlock, eagerly accepted the invitations tendered by Secretary of State Cyrus Vance in August 1978. The meeting convened on September 5 and lasted until September 17. As one of the Americans attending the discussions observed: "The thirteen days at Camp David were in some ways like a microcosm of the preceding year and one-half. The same issues were debated, often with little change in the script. Hopes rose, then fell, and then sober realism began to take hold. But everything happened so much more quickly, and the normal domestic political constraints that operated on all the parties were somewhat minimized by their remaining secluded from the public and conducting talks in almost total secrecy."[24]

Begin and Sadat signed two agreements on September 17, 1978. One was a statement of general principles that were to apply to the future of the West Bank. Israel agreed to provide Sadat with a partial pan-Arab fig leaf to cover his separate peace settlement by having the document refer to the legitimate rights of the Palestinian people and their right to choose their own form of government. However, it made no provisions for determining the final status of the West Bank and Gaza. There was no commitment to independence for the territories or an eventual Israeli withdrawal from them. The agreement said nothing about Jerusalem or Israeli settlements in Gaza, Samaria, or Judea. In other words, the first agreement primarily reflected Sadat's concessions, since Begin was prepared to see the negotiations collapse entirely rather than concede anything of substance on matters that, in Israel's view, were not really any of Egypt's business, pan-Arab rhetoric aside.

The second agreement dealt with a formula for achieving peace between Egypt and Israel. Here, Israel was willing to make far-reaching concessions for a peace treaty. These included, in addition to a withdrawal of troops, return of the oil fields developed by Israel, removal of the air bases (which had to be relocated to the Negev at extraordinary expense), and the abandonment of the Israeli settlements that had been built on the Egyptian side of the international boundary. Sadat had to agree to a three-year withdrawal period and definitive security arrangements to be overseen by both the United States and the UN, as well as a commitment to normalize relations with Israel upon completion of the first phase of the withdrawal. In terms of Egypt-Israel relations, the calendar was effectively returned to 1948, and Egypt had to decide once again whether its national interests required it to go to war with Israel in the name of an ephemeral Arab nationalism. Israel gambled that it would not.

On March 26, 1979 despite heavy pressures on Sadat from the Arab world that almost scuttled the peace, and President Carter's active intervention, Begin and Sadat signed an Egyptian-Israeli peace treaty in Washington. As expected by most realists, the notion of normalized relations between the two countries was not taken seriously in Egypt. In its view, as Sadat had clearly indicated in his address to the Israeli Knesset, the treaty, regardless of how optimists chose to interpret it, was a nonaggression pact and nothing more. From Israel's point of view, achieving a state of nonbelligerence with Egypt, even within what would be called a "cold peace," constituted a major achievement.

NOTES

1. Abba Eban, *An Autobiography*, p. 446.

2. Gideon Rafael, "U.N. Resolution 242: A Common Denominator," June 1973.

3. *Washington Post*, August 27, 1967.

4. *New York Times*, November 1, 1967.

5. Gil C. AlRoy, *The Kissinger Experience: American Policy in the Middle East*, p. 115.

6. Ibid., p. 114.

7. Yaacov Bar-Siman-Tov, *The Israeli-Egyptian War of Attrition, 1969–1970*, pp. 54–55.

8. Chaim Herzog, *The War of Atonement: October, 1973*, p. 15.

9. Foreign Broadcast Information Service (FBIS), July 3, 1969.

10. *Le Monde Weekly*, December 24, 1969.

11. John N. Moore, ed., *The Arab-Israeli Conflict*, vol. 3, *Documents*, p. 103.

12. *Washington Post*, September 1, 1970.

13. *New York Times*, December 28, 1970.

14. *New Middle East*, January 1971, pp. 6–7.

15. Anwar Sadat, *The Public Diary of President Sadat*, vol. 1, p. 34.

16. *New Middle East*, May 1971, p. 10.

17. Lawrence L. Whetten, *The Canal War: Four Power Conflict in the Middle East*, p. 209.

18. Sadat, *The Public Diary*, vol. 1, p. 155.

19. Golda Meir, *My Life*, p. 364.

20. Moshe Dayan, *Breakthrough: A Personal Account of the Egypt-Israel Peace Negotiations*, p. 20.

21. William B. Quandt, *Camp David: Peacemaking and Politics*, p. 146.

22. Dayan, *Breakthrough*, p. 81.

23. Ibid., p. 97.

24. Quandt, *Camp David*, p. 219.

19

Crisis and Conflict in Lebanon, 1970–85

Egypt and Syria, discounting their pan-Arab rhetoric, had always treated the Palestinians as an instrument in their struggle with Israel that they exploited to destabilize the enemy. At the same time, Egypt and Syria were well aware of Israel's retaliatory policy, which held the state from which terrorist activity originated responsible and accountable. They thus restricted cross-border raids originating in their territories. Instead, a number of guerrilla units trained in Egypt, as well as Palestinians who had served in the Egyptian army were sent to Jordan, where they were supervised by the Egyptian military attaché in Amman. During the Egyptian-Israeli war of attrition along the Suez Canal, from 1968 to 1970, there was a significant upsurge of guerrilla activity along the Israel-Jordan border, and Israel retaliated in Jordan, from where the attacks originated.

The guerrillas established a major base at Karameh in the Jordan Valley, which became the headquarters for Fatah and other Palestinian groups. On March 18, 1968 an Israeli school bus struck a mine laid near the border and Israel retaliated four days later with an armored force crossing into Jordan to attack the guerrilla base, which was destroyed with heavy loss of life. Guerrilla headquarters were then relocated to Salt, a town of some 30,000 that was out of Israeli artillery range, from which a new series of attacks were launched. In August, Israel struck back with a destructive raid on the guerrilla camp. Following the Salt raid, the guerrillas moved their bases into the refugee camps, where they knew they would be less prone to retaliatory attack. However, before long, the guerrillas began to act more as an army of occupation than tolerated guests in Jordan, and Hussein found himself in a virtual power-sharing arrangement with their leaders.

Hussein was severely constrained in his ability to bring the guerrillas under control due to the moral support they received from Jordan's predominantly Palestinian population, as well as the political support from Egypt. To further complicate matters, the guerrilla groups took over control of the Palestine Liberation Organization (PLO) and fundamentally changed the constitutional structure of the organization at a meeting of the Palestine National Council held in Cairo in July 1968. The PLO was originally an organization of individual Arab notables and others committed to a struggle against Israel. It now became an umbrella organization of the various guerrilla and other Palestinian groups. At the fifth council meeting held in Cairo in February 1969, Yasser Arafat of the Fatah was elected chairman of the PLO. Within a year, all remaining guerrilla groups of any consequence came under the PLO umbrella. With this concentration of Palestinian power, the PLO began to resemble an autonomous state within Jordan, and seemed to be ready to take over the country. There were soon a number of attempts on Hussein's life and by August 1970, open clashes between the guerrillas and Jordan's security forces had taken place.

In mid-September 1970 Hussein concluded that he had to act to bring the guerrillas under control, and on September 17 his forces attacked the guerrilla bases in the refugee camps, initiating a battle that lasted for 11 days. At the same time Syria decided to intervene directly, ostensibly to prevent the guerrillas from being wiped out, by diverting Hussein's attention. On September 18 a Syrian commando force attacked two villages in northern Jordan. The next day an armored column of some 300 tanks bearing the insignia of the "Palestine Liberation Army" crossed the Syrian-Jordanian border, taking Irbid after a battle in which the Syrians sustained heavy losses of armor, and started moving toward Amman, which it would have reached by September 20. Unable to stop the Syrians, and facing the prospect of losing his throne, Hussein appealed to the U.S. ambassador for help "from any quarter" to stop the Syrian invasion.

As a practical matter, the only country in a position to intervene effectively and in time was Israel. Henry Kissinger approached the Israeli ambassador in Washington, Yitzhak Rabin, and told him: "King Hussein has approached us, describing the situation of his forces, and asked us to transmit his request that your air force attack the Syrians in northern Jordan."[1] Israel's response was generally positive; it clearly preferred to have Hussein in control of its eastern frontier than the Syrians, but it sought assurances from Washington that the United States would prevent a Soviet intervention on behalf of its Syrian client. While waiting for the assurances it wanted, Israel took the preliminary step of redeploying two armored brigades to the Golan Heights, placing them in position to cut off the Syrian forces that had moved south in Jordan. This redeployment sent a clear message to Damascus that Israel was unwilling to accept the fundamental change in the regional balance of power that was implicit in their intervention in Jordan.

In Damascus, Hafez Assad, defense minister in the government controlled by Salah Jadid, had been reluctantly drawn into support of the intervention on behalf of the Palestinians. However, he refused to commit the Syrian air force, his power base in the military, to the venture. Thus, faced by the prospect of being cut off by Israeli forces and trapped in Jordan without air support, Syria had little choice other than to abandon the Palestinians and withdraw their forces from Jordan. On September 25 Kissinger called Rabin again to deliver a personal message from President Richard Nixon to the Israeli prime minister: "The president will never forget Israel's role in preventing the deterioration in Jordan and in blocking the attempt to overturn the regime there."[2]

Two days later, to forestall the anticipated onslaught against the guerrillas by Hussein, Nasser convened a meeting of Arab heads of state at which he pressured Hussein and Arafat into an agreement on a *modus vivendi*, although neither was really committed to making it work. It was immediately after Hussein left Cairo that Nasser suffered his fatal heart attack. With Nasser gone and the Arab world in sudden disarray, Hussein promptly repudiated the agreement and proceeded to wipe out the guerrilla presence in Jordan.

In Damascus, the debacle of the Syrian intervention in Jordan led to recriminations and renewed conflict between the ruling factions. Matters came to a head on November 13, 1970, when Assad led a military coup that overthrew the Jadid-controlled government and put Assad into power.

Hussein's struggle with the guerrillas turned into a full-scale civil conflict that lasted until July 1971. By that time, most of the guerrillas had been killed, arrested, or forced out of the country. The PLO infrastructure was relocated to Lebanon, with the net result that the immediate threat to security of Israel's borders shifted from its eastern frontier to the north, where it was concentrated in Syria and Lebanon.

As a practical matter, there was little that the Lebanese government could do about the influx of Palestinian guerrillas. Lebanon itself was sharply divided into religious and ethnic communities, and seemed on the verge of exploding into civil war once again. As the PLO began to increase the number of guerrilla attacks mounted from Lebanon, Israel began to retaliate in force against their bases in the southern part of the country. Israel's actions in Lebanon had the unintended consequence of further weakening the ability of the Lebanese government to impose constraints on the PLO's freedom of action. During the winter of 1975–76 civil war erupted in Lebanon and the country appeared on the verge of disintegration, with the PLO and its supporters increasingly assuming the role of a state within the state. Lebanese President Suleiman Franjieh accused the Palestinians of having conspiratorial objectives. "Their first objective was to obtain gradually full control over Lebanon by installing certain kinds of puppet rulers who will be in harmony with the Palestinians, the actual rulers. . . . Their second objective was to establish a Palestinian homeland, a part of which will be in the south of Lebanon, a size dependent on the magnitude of their victory over the Lebanese."[3] The civil war also raised the specter of a Syrian intervention in the country to preserve Damascus' interests there, if not to effectively take over the country as part of the Greater Syria to which Assad and the Syrian nationalists aspired.

Although the Lebanese Maronite Christian leaders asked Israel to intervene directly in their behalf, Prime Minister Yitzhak Rabin was reluctant to do so. At the same time, Israel did not want to see a Syrian takeover of Lebanon, which would have compounded its security concerns. What it decided to do was to accept a limited Syrian intervention in Lebanon up to a pre-established "red line." This required an arrangement with Syria in which Washington would serve as the intermediary. The ground rules that Israel insisted upon were communicated to Washington on March 24, 1976. They provided that Syrian forces in Lebanon might not exceed a single brigade that was not equipped with tanks, artillery, or surface-to-air missiles. In addition, Syrian warplanes were not to operate over Lebanon, nor were Syrian naval units to operate in Lebanese waters. Finally, Syrian units were not to be deployed south of a line 10 miles south of the Beirut-Damascus highway. It was also understood that the latter constraint also applied to PLO positions in the country. Israel made it clear that if Syria violated these ground rules, it would take the necessary action to take control of those strategic positions in Lebanon that it considered vital to the security of northern Israel. With some hesitation and some minor modifications, Syria agreed to abide by these ground rules to avoid a direct military confrontation with Israel in Lebanon. Syria then intervened militarily in Lebanon in June 1976 for the proclaimed purpose of preventing the Palestinian-leftist coalition from achieving a military victory in the civil conflict that might lead to a partitioning of the country.

Nonetheless, in 1977–78 Syria's relations with the PLO improved and the latter was permitted to extend its operation to the area south of the "red line," that is, the area south of the Litani River. Israel made it clear that this was unacceptable. As one official stated on behalf of the government on April 2, 1977: "Israel will not tolerate the penetration of Syrian or pan-Arab forces south of their existing positions . . . or tolerate activity against the Lebanese villages which are close to our border and considered by it to be friendly."[4] To deal with the increased threat to its security, Israel built an elaborate defense system along its border with Lebanon, and provided additional support to the primarily Christian militia, run by Major Saad Haddad, which controlled a number of enclaves close to the Israeli border. It also struck at Palestinian positions established in the area south of the Litani.

The volatile and often violent status quo that prevailed along the border was shattered in March 1978 following an attack by a Palestinian terrorist unit that originated in Lebanon. It managed to evade Israeli naval patrols and landed near the coastal highway south of Haifa, where it commandeered a civilian bus, and attempted to shoot its way to Tel Aviv. The heavy civilian casualty toll prompted Prime Minister Menahem Begin to take drastic measures to pacify southern Lebanon.

The initial Israeli plan called for an attack against the PLO forces along the entire 60-mile border that was expected to penetrate no further than six miles into Lebanon, avoiding, if possible, any clashes with Syrian forces, which should not have been in the area. The objective was to establish a security belt in southern Lebanon in collaboration with the friendly Christian militia forces operating there. The operation went smoothly. However, while the Israeli government was deciding what to do next, it learned that the Security Council was actively contemplating sending a UN peace force to southern Lebanon. At that point, Israel decided to quickly push farther north as far as the Litani. The rationale was that when the UN forces arrived, Israel would withdraw entirely and leave the entire zone south of the "red line" in UN hands, thereby solving the security problem in southern Lebanon.

The United Nations Interim Force in Lebanon (UNIFIL) came into being on March 19, 1978 with a three-fold mission: (1) to confirm the withdrawal of Israeli forces, (2) to restore peace and security in southern Lebanon, and (3) to assure that the area where UNIFIL had responsibility was not used for hostile activity. UNIFIL was only successful in accomplishing the first mission, and this was easy because Israel had no intention of remaining in Lebanon. Nonetheless, for a period of nine months, southern Lebanon was relatively quiet, as the PLO built up its infrastructure there. The lull came to an end on December 22, 1978 when the PLO fired a salvo of Katyusha rockets that hit the Israeli town of Kiryat Shemoneh. The war of attrition across the Lebanese-Israeli border was on again.

Israel retaliated by striking at PLO installations and on January 19, 1979 its forces crossed the Litani for the first time in pursuit of PLO guerrillas. Disturbed by the effect that PLO attacks were having in disrupting normal civilian life in northern Israel, in April the Israeli government decided on a change of policy from retaliation to preemption. The intent was to dramatically increase the pressure on the PLO by taking the initiative away from it, and impairing its ability to establish and maintain permanent bases and supply lines.

By 1980 sectarian politics and the increasingly destabilizing presence of the PLO in Lebanon converged to produce what appeared to be a major indigenous political force in Bashir Gemayel and the Maronite Christian Lebanese Forces. The principal component of the latter was the Phalange, a nationalist militia committed to achieving a Syrian withdrawal from the country and reining in the Palestinians. These goals provided a common ground between the Lebanese Forces and Israel.

Since Syria's intervention in the Lebanese civil war in 1976, its forces had taken over control of the Bekaa Valley, a region of strategic importance that Syria did not appear willing to surrender under any circumstances. The Bekaa, since remote antiquity, provided a route of attack between Syria and Palestine. In the event of a renewal of war between Israel and Syria, the former could attempt to outflank Syria's main defense line by taking either or both of two approaches. It could attack through northern Jordan, which was unlikely as long as Jordan stayed out of the conflict, or through the Bekaa, a far more likely prospect given the chronic instability of Lebanon and the military irrelevance of its small army. The Syrians thus decided to build a forward defense line in the Bekaa to protect the most direct approach from Israel to Damascus, or possibly as an advance position for a Syrian attack on Israel.

Toward the end of 1980 Bashir Gemayel decided to extend his political and military control to Zahle in southern Lebanon, linking it to the Maronite heartland in the north. The Syrians perceived this move as part of a coordinated plan between the Lebanese forces and Israel to undermine its position in southeastern Lebanon. The strategic assumption was that Israel might join up with the Lebanese Forces at Zahle, cut the critical Beirut-Damascus highway and establish a countervailing presence in the adjacent Bekaa.

Key to this scenario was control of the strategically important road from Zahle to Mount Lebanon. Both Syria and the Lebanese Forces wanted to take the dominating point along this road at Mount Sanin and a low-level struggle for the site began. Then, in March 1981 the Lebanese Forces trapped a Syrian military unit and inflicted many casualties. Syria retaliated with a heavy shelling of both the militia and the town of Zahle and landed commando units by helicopter on Mount Sanin, taking control of the important position.

Assad's decision to use helicopters in this operation created a far more serious problem because it constituted a deliberate violation of the "red line" ground rules established by Israel and tacitly accepted by Syria in 1976. It was taken in Israel as a clear indication that Syria, with a new treaty with the Soviet Union in hand and a large reequipped army, was ready to challenge Israel once again. The government of Israel ultimately concluded that it was necessary to take steps to convince Damascus that Israel would not permit any change in the status quo in southern Lebanon that it viewed as endangering its security. From this perspective, Syria's use of its air force in southern Lebanon was unacceptable. The Israeli air force was instructed to shoot down two helicopters carrying supplies to the new Syrian positions on Mount Sanin. Syria responded by establishing ground-to-air missile batteries in the Zahle area and also deployed long-range missiles in

Syrian territory along the Lebanese border. The former constituted a further violation of the "red line" rules and the latter a direct threat to Israel itself.

The Soviet Union defused the "missile crisis," which threatened to precipitate another round of war between Israel and Syria, at least for a while. Moscow was interested in a controlled crisis in the region to offset the anti-Soviet initiatives of the new administration of President Ronald Reagan, and was not about to draw the Soviet Union into a confrontation that might easily get out of control. Moscow advised Damascus that their treaty did not extend to Syrian operations in Lebanon, and that the Soviets would not intervene to prevent a military debacle there.

As the missile crisis continued to simmer through the summer of 1981, the PLO infrastructure in Lebanon underwent a massive buildup, indicating the potential for a sustained war of attrition along the Israel-Lebanon border. Beginning in May, the PLO began heavily bombarding Israel's northern towns, with 1,230 rocket and artillery attacks by July, that drove much of the population into air raid shelters for days at a time. Israel sought to stop the PLO by attacking its well-fortified positions in the south from the air and with artillery, but to little avail. Israel then took a different approach and began attacking PLO targets throughout the country, including its headquarters in Beirut. At that point, Washington intervened and managed to arrange a cease-fire between the PLO in Lebanon and Israel that went into effect on July 24, 1981.

Israel understood the cease-fire to require a cessation of attacks against Israel anywhere. However, as far as the PLO was concerned, the cease-fire only applied to the Lebanese border, and another 290 attacks against Israel that did not take place across the border occurred between July 1981 and June 1982. The United States, for purposes of its own diplomacy in the region, seemed inclined to accept the PLO position even though it would never accept such a position with regard to attacks against itself. On the contrary, Washington always considered attacks against U.S. installations and Americans abroad as attacks on the United States itself. It nonetheless placed heavy pressure on Israel not to react strongly to continuing PLO provocation. When Israel subsequently did react, it was accused of being the party to violate the cease-fire.

The PLO took full advantage of the respite provided by the cease-fire to further enhance its capabilities in southern Lebanon, and it amassed sufficient strength to paralyze northern Israel from its Lebanese bases. Since there was no basis for any possible political solution to the problem, given the fundamental goal of the PLO that called for the complete destruction of Israel, it became increasingly clear that it would require a military approach to deal with the PLO threat. It is noteworthy that the PLO threat was never perceived as a threat to the Israeli state or its institutions. It was the threat to the security of the civilian population of northern Israel that was at issue.

Eliminating the PLO threat from Lebanon required more than a large-scale military operation, it required the reconfiguration of the power balance in the southern part of the country. The approach taken by the Israeli government was based in part on the supposition that Bashir Gemayel and the Lebanese Forces were likely to become the dominant factor in Lebanon's political sphere. Accordingly, the Israeli plan proposed to link Gemayel's bid for power in the country to a large-scale Israeli military operation that would extend as far north as the southern suburbs of Beirut. The plan called for a penetration of Lebanon to a depth of 40 kilometers measured from Israel's most northern town of Metulla. The assumption was that if this happened, the Lebanese government would be sufficiently heartened to eliminate entirely the PLO's use of Lebanon as a base against Israel.

However, it had also become increasingly unlikely that the planned offensive against the PLO could be achieved without a confrontation with Syria, which had already increased its activity in southeastern Lebanon. Until May 1982, Israel was constrained from acting by pressure from Washington, which was concerned that an Israeli assault into Lebanon might jeopardize the fragile peace with Egypt and impede the scheduled Israeli withdrawal from Sinai. However, once the withdrawal was completed, Washington's attitude changed. This was signaled by Secretary of State Alexander Haig when he stated on May 26: "Lebanon today is a focal point of danger . . . and the stability of the region hangs in the balance. . . . The Arab deterrent force, now consisting entirely of Syrian troops . . . has not stabilized the situation. . . . The time has come to take concerted action in support of both Lebanon's territorial integrity within its internationally recognized borders and a strong central government capable of promoting a free, open, democratic, and traditionally pluralistic society."[5] With an effective "green light" from the United States, Israeli forces crossed into Lebanon on June 6.

The Israelis soon learned that there was a fundamental flaw in their plan for a limited operation to take control of a 40–kilometer belt across southern Lebanon, without a confrontation with Syria. In the central and eastern sectors of the country many of the PLO forces were concentrated under a protective Syrian missile umbrella, unacceptably close to the Israeli border. Moreover, unless the PLO was brought under strict Syrian control or was expelled from the Bekaa, the aims of the Israeli operation would not be achieved. To further compound the problem, Syria began to deploy additional missile systems in the northern part of the valley, preventing Israel's air force from providing close support to its ground troops. As a result, a limited war with Syria in Lebanon soon erupted.

By June 9, 1982 Israeli forces had outflanked the Syrian positions in the Bekaa and the Israeli air force had destroyed the Syrian missile batteries. It also shot down several dozen Syrian fighter planes. With the Israeli army once again within striking distance of Damascus, with a large force pinning down the bulk of the Syrian army on the Golan Heights, Syria pressed the Soviet Union to intervene politically and obtain a cease-fire. Washington supported the idea and prevailed on Israel to agree to it. An Israeli-Syrian cease-fire went into effect on June 11, leaving Israel free to move north in the western sector and link up with the Lebanese Forces of Gemayel near Beirut.

With the PLO ensconced in the western part of Beirut, it was Israel's expectation that Gemayel's forces would take on the job of ridding the city of the unwanted Palestinians. Gemayel, however, was reluctant to commit his forces to what would undoubtedly be a bloody campaign against thousands of PLO fighters trapped against the sea, without a line of retreat. He did not want to bear the political onus of having destroyed a good part of the city in order to oust the PLO. He was sensitive to the fact that there were some 90 private armies operating in Lebanon, most of which were Muslim or Druse, and feared that an attack by a Christian militia against the PLO, which was primarily Muslim, might cause them to unite in support of the PLO. It was therefore preferable, from his standpoint, that Israel bear the burden of cleaning up the western part of the city, correctly assuming that if he did not move against the PLO, the Israelis would have to. An Israeli withdrawal, which would have to come sooner or later, with Arafat's forces still intact in Beirut would be construed as a political victory for the PLO and a defeat for Israel, something that Israel could not permit. Within a few days, the Israeli army placed west Beirut under siege.

At this point the situation was further complicated by a wave of contradictory statements and leaks coming from Washington that suggested that Israel had no intention of actually moving into Beirut. This had the effect of convincing Arafat that he should hold on as long as possible in the expectation that he would eventually be rescued by either the United States or the UN, and he began casting about for international support for his plight. The Israelis, however, were seeking the annihilation of the PLO forces in Beirut. They wanted to prevent them from using Lebanon as a base. On June 29 Prime Minister Begin proposed that "the Lebanese army will go into West Beirut; the terrorists will hand over their arms to them, and we will let them go via one of three routes."[6] He was even prepared to allow them to take their personal weapons with them. Arafat, however, rejected these generous terms, expecting international political intervention to save him, and Israel began bombarding western Beirut.

Once again, Israel was prevented from achieving a decisive victory because of international pressure, its freedom of action in Beirut becoming increasingly constrained by Washington, which was actively arranging for the evacuation of the PLO from the city. The evacuation, which was completed on September 4, was accomplished on the same terms as those freely offered six weeks earlier by Begin.

Two days after the PLO evacuation began on August 21, Bashir Gemayel was elected president of Lebanon and his putative alliance with Israel began to unravel, the flimsy informal relationship coming apart completely when Gemayel was assassinated on September 15. Because no other Lebanese leader seemed capable of controlling the situation, let alone root out the approximately 2,000 armed PLO fighters that had remained in the city in violation of the evacuation agreement, the Israeli army was ordered into Beirut to maintain order. Although the Lebanese government of Shafiq al-Wazzan ordered the Lebanese army to cease its operations against the PLO after Gemayel's assassination, the Phalange agreed to enter the city under an Israeli security umbrella. The Christian militiamen exploited the opportunity to exact revenge against the Palestinians and massacred several hundred civilians in the neighborhoods of Sabra and Shatilla. Curiously, the subsequent international outrage over the incident was not directed against the Lebanese who actually committed the atrocities, but primarily against the Israelis for not preventing it from happening. Following this, Israel withdrew from Beirut in favor of an international peace-keeping force.

An Israeli-Lebanese treaty designed to satisfy Israel's security concerns and bring about its withdrawal from the country was signed on May 17, 1983, and was warmly endorsed by Egypt, whose foreign minister referred to it as "an important step along the path of a comprehensive Middle East settlement."[7] Syria, however, had a different perspective on the matter. As its foreign minister, Abd al-Halim Khaddam, put it, "Terminating the state of war is an Arab responsibility, and we believe that neither Lebanon nor the Lebanese government has the right to yield to Israeli pressure and terminate the state of war.[8] The irony of this position was compounded by Syria's position that one of the objections it had to the Israel-Lebanon agreement was that it constituted an infringement on Lebanon's sovereignty.

Assad rejected the treaty out of hand and refused to withdraw his forces from the Bekaa, which was now Syria's forward line of defense against Israel. Without Syria's cooperation the treaty became a worthless scrap of paper. Frustrated by its inability to achieve peace with Lebanon, Israel unilaterally withdrew its forces to the Awali River in July 1983 and again to the Zahrani River in February 1985. Israel formally ended its occupation of Lebanon in June 1985, after establishing a security zone along the international border under the nominal control of the predominantly Christian South Lebanese Army under General Antoine Lahad, who succeeded Saad Haddad after his death in January 1984. The security situation along the Israel-Lebanon border remained essentially unchanged over the remainder of the century. The rest of Lebanon came increasingly under Syrian domination, with Damascus in full control of Lebanon's foreign policy as well as the low-intensity conflict with Israel that continues to be conducted across the Lebanese-Israeli frontier by Lebanese and Palestinian surrogates to this day.

NOTES

1. Yitzhak Rabin, *The Rabin Memoirs*, p. 187.

2. Ibid., p. 189.

3. Wadi Haddad, *Lebanon: The Politics of Revolving Doors*, p. 52.

4. Yair Evron, *War and Intervention in Lebanon*, pp. 70–71.

5. *Department of State Bulletin*, July 1982, pp. 44–47.

6. *Towards a Safe Israel and a Free Lebanon*, Jerusalem, Israel Information Centre, September 1982.

7. Foreign Broadcast Information Service, *Middle East*, May 17, 1983, D1.

8. Haddad, *Lebanon*, p. 95.

20

Conflict in the Persian Gulf Region, 1973–99

The seeds of the struggle for hegemony in the Persian Gulf region that would trigger two major wars and a continuing crisis throughout the last two decades of the twentieth century were sown in part by the British as early as 1913. An Anglo-Ottoman agreement of that year awarded two small islands at the head of the Persian Gulf, Warba and Bubyan, to Kuwait, effectively giving the latter control of access to Iraq's only port on the Gulf at Umm Qasr. Moreover, the Iraq-Kuwait border was drawn in a manner that provided Iraq with a very short coastline of some 40 miles. This transformed it into a virtually land-locked country, heavily dependent on access to the Shatt al-Arab, the waterway that empties into the gulf and which constitutes the southern frontier between Iraq and Iran.

Iraq's strategic situation was further exacerbated by Iran's seizure, with Britain's blessing following its withdrawal from the region, of three strategically located islands, the Lesser and Greater Tunbs, that belonged to the sheikdom of Ras al-Khaima, and Abu Musa, which belonged to the sheikdom of Sharjah. These islands, in addition to three islands that were already in Iran's possession, Qeshm, Larak, and Hormuz, formed an arc that put Tehran in a position to control Iraq's maritime communications through the Straits of Hormuz into the Indian Ocean.

Under British pressure, Iraq had reluctantly accepted the border with Kuwait in 1923 and again in 1932, when it became a precondition for entry into the League of Nations. A year later, the government of King Ghazi began demanding the annexation of Kuwait to Iraq on the basis that the territory had been an Ottoman district nominally governed from Basra, ignoring the fact that Kuwait had been an autonomous region ruled by the house of Sabah since 1756. The demand never went beyond the rhetorical phase as long as Kuwait remained a British protectorate. However, when the protectorate came to an end and Kuwait became independent in 1961, the Qasem government in Iraq began preparing for an invasion of the country that was prevented only by a deployment there of British forces in 1963. Although Iraq once again accepted the border and recognized Kuwaiti sovereignty, boundary disputes continued for another decade. Iraqi troops crossed into Kuwait in 1973–74, but soon withdrew under pressure from both the United States and Iran that was manifested in part by their support of the Kurdish rebellion that erupted in Iraq in 1974 and overshadowed Baghdad's concern about Kuwait.

Control of the Kurds, who dominated most of northern Iraq, had been a problem that had plagued the successive governments in Iraq since independence. The Baath government that came into power in 1968 attempted to integrate the Kurds into the Iraqi state by force, but simply did not have the necessary military capability. A *modus vivendi* was arrived at that accorded the Kurds a measure of autonomy while the government built its forces to the point where it could enforce its will on them. That happened in 1974.

However, it soon became apparent that suppressing the Kurds was not going to be an easy task, notwithstanding the buildup of Iraq's military capabilities, because the Kurds were receiving support from both the United States and Iran, as well as some modest aid from Israel. As a result, although the Iraqis succeeded in reducing the size of the areas controlled by the Kurds, they did this at the cost of heavy casualties. Moreover, when they tried to crush the center of the rebellion, they were effectively precluded from doing so militarily because of the direct involvement by the more powerful Iranian army in the conflict. Iran not only provided the Kurds with American and Israeli arms, but also provided them with an anti-aircraft missile umbrella. In January 1975 the shah also sent two Iranian army regiments into the Kurdish held areas of Iraq, creating a standoff that set the stage for a major conflict between Iraq and Iran that would erupt within a few years, but not immediately. In the short run, Iraq's internal need to bring the Kurds under Baghdad's control took priority, and it was prepared to make significant concessions to Iran to remove it from the equation. Iran, which was becoming increasingly disenchanted with the Iraqi Kurds because their struggle was creating secessionist aspirations among the Kurds of Iran, was also amenable to a negotiated settlement on terms favorable to it.

Tehran's price for giving Iraq a free hand with the Kurds was the abandonment of Baghdad's claim to full sovereignty over the whole of the Shatt al-Arab and its agreement that the *thalweg* (or median line of the deepest channel) should constitute the boundary between the two countries. In return, Iran conceded some territory in the Qasr-e Shirin area to Iraq, but never actually transferred it to Baghdad. The agreement reached between

Iran and Iraq in Algiers on March 6, 1975 permitted Baghdad to crush the Kurds without Iranian interference, the United States similarly ceasing its support of the Kurds. It was clear from the outset, however, that the Iraqis, and especially Saddam Hussein who was in large measure responsible for the agreement, bore a deep resentment of being effectively coerced into acceding to it. As Saddam later put it: "We signed it, but the Iranians gained legal rights under unnatural circumstances and under conditions we could not control . . . the Iranians used military force against us."[1]

Over the next several years Saddam marshaled Iraq's strength for an eventual showdown between the aspiring autocrat in Baghdad and the shah in Tehran, who had humiliated him. Propitious events were to take place in both capitals in 1979. In January of that year, the shah was forced to leave Iran, the monarchy being replaced by an Islamic republic under control of the clergy. Simultaneously, Saddam succeeded in maneuvering himself into position to seize absolute power in Iraq. In July, Saddam was elected president of Iraq and chairman of its real ruling body, the Revolutionary Command Council. He also became commander in chief of the Iraqi armed forces.

Having attained absolute power in Baghdad, Saddam sought to demonstrate to Iran that Iraq could no longer be intimidated by it, especially in view of Iran's clandestine support of a potential insurrection against the Baathist regime by the overwhelmingly Shiite majority in Iraq. Saddam did this by attributing an attempted assassination of an insider in his regime, Tariq Aziz, in April 1980 to an Iraqi of Iranian origin, meaning a Shiite. He then summarily executed the leading Shiite cleric in Iraq, Muhammad Baqr as-Sadr, who had been held under house arrest for a year as an opponent of the regime, and made membership in the Shiite-based Al-Da'wa party retroactively punishable by death. Saddam also began rendering aid to minority communities in Iran, especially to the Arabs in the province of Khuzistan, which the Iraqis insisted on referring to as Arabistan. All this was intended to serve as a clear message to Ayatollah Ruhollah Khomeini's government in Tehran that the rules of the game between them had changed. It was but a short step to escalate the increasingly testy relationship into one of limited military confrontation, given that the Iranian revolutionary government was busy weakening itself through its widespread purge of the powerful military put in place by the shah.

Saddam demanded that Iran relinquish its claims to Abu Musa and the Tunbs, islands near the Strait of Hormuz the sovereignty over which was in dispute. More ominously, unilaterally abrogating the 1975 Algiers agreement, Iraq now again claimed sovereignty over the entire Shatt al-Arab. Khomeini's response to these rhetorical challenges was simply to ignore them. It would take more than threats to get Iran to acknowledge Iraq's claims, and Saddam decided to cross the threshold of armed conflict in the late summer of 1980. He issued an ultimatum to Tehran on September 6 demanding that Iran turn over the 150 square kilometers of territory in the Qasr-e Shirin area that it had promised to cede to Iraq in 1975, but had failed to do. When Iran did not respond to the ultimatum, Iraqi forces began to occupy the disputed territory, Saddam telling the Iraqi National Assembly on September 17: "We in no way intend to launch war against Iran or extend the circle of struggle beyond the limits of defending our rights and sovereignty."[2] Five days later, Iraq invaded Iranian territory at a number of points along the length of the border and attacked 10 Iranian airfields. The Iraqi minister of defense, General Adnan Khayrallah, provided the rationale for the evidently unprovoked attack. "We decided to lay our hands on points vital to Iran's interests inside Iranian territory to deter Iran from striking our national sovereignty and to make it recognize our full sovereignty over the Shatt al-Arab."[3] It appears that Iraq believed that, given Iran's perceived weakness, the limited strike it had initiated would merely result in a reversal of the situation it had faced in 1974, undo the concessions granted under pressure in the Algiers agreement, and restore the status quo ante. Saddam evidently did not take into consideration that Khomeini might not view it in this manner.

The ayatollah characterized the struggle with Iraq not as a territorial issue but as a fundamentally religious one. He told the Iranian people on October 20, 1980: "You are fighting to protect Islam and he [Saddam] is fighting to destroy Islam. . . . It is not a question of a fight between one government and another; it is a question of an invasion by an Iraqi non-Muslim Ba'thist against an Islamic country; and this is a rebellion by blasphemy against Islam."[4] Once having defined the conflict in these terms, there was no room for compromise because, while one might compromise over territory, it was extraordinarily difficult for an Islamic state to publicly compromise on the defense of the faith. This meant war until victory, even if victory was unachievable as a practical matter.

It quickly became evident, despite some early gains by Iraqi forces, that Baghdad had miscalculated the residual strength and determination of Iran to turn back the invaders. Having a far superior navy, Iran imposed a blockade of the Shatt al-Arab and effectively closed the port at Basra, bringing Iraqi oil shipments by sea to a halt by late September. The Iranians also had air superiority. When Iraqi artillery attacked the world's largest oil refinery at Abadan on September 25, causing Iran to suspend its oil shipments, Tehran retaliated with a massive air assault that devastated Iraq's oil facilities at Basra and Zubair in the south and Mosul and Kirkuk in the north. By the end of the month, the Iraqi advance had been stopped short of reaching its prime targets, the cities of Abadan, Ahvaz, and Dezful.

Seeking to consolidate his gains, Saddam announced that he had achieved his territorial objectives in Iran and was prepared to order a cease-fire, if Iran complied with the demands of Iraq's ultimatum of September 6. He again demanded that Iran acknowledge Iraqi sovereignty over the Shatt al-Arab and relinquish control of the Tunbs and Abu Musa. Iran's response was to intensify its efforts to hold and push back the Iraqis. On October 20 Saddam explained to the Iraqi public that victory had eluded them thus far because of Iran's military superiority, but that they had to press on because what he was leading was a jihad, a holy war, against the Persian infidels. And, to emphasize the new purpose of Saddam's cynical religious crescentade, pro-regime Sunni and Shiite clergy were enlisted in the war effort and sent to the front and occupied Iranian territory to affirm clerical support of the war against Khomeini's heretical interpretation of Islam.

Although Iraq was able to make some additional gains on the battlefield, reaching some 10,000 square miles of Iranian territory by November 1980, Saddam was concerned about the effects of heavy casualties on the Shiite majority in the Iraqi armed forces, whose loyalty to the regime was not considered reliable. He thus preferred to place Abadan under siege rather than attempt to take the city, which would have involved heavy losses, hoping to force the Iranians into a settlement. That hope proved to be vain. The siege of Abadan continued for a year and was finally broken by the Iranians on September 29, 1981.

A series of Iranian campaigns from mid-November 1981 to the end of May 1982 put Saddam on the defensive and concluded by driving the Iraqi forces out of Iran. Saddam's problems were compounded by an economic crisis brought on by his trouble-making in neighboring Syria, where he was providing aid to the dissident Muslim Brotherhood. In retaliation, Hafez Assad closed the Iraqi-Syrian border and shut down the pipeline carrying Iraqi crude oil to Mediterranean ports in Syria and Lebanon on April 10. This left Iraq with the Turkish pipeline as its only outlet. The result was a cut in Iraqi oil exports from 1.4 million barrels a day in August 1981, about half of its average 1980 figure, to a mere 600,000 a day, and a consequently enormous loss of income at a time when the costs of the war were mounting steadily.

The Iraqi retreat from Iran that began in mid-March 1982 was completed by June of that year. At that point, Iran considered the option of continuing the war into Iraq to punish Saddam Hussein. There was evidently a strong feeling among Iranian leaders that the war with Iraq had helped consolidate the Islamic regime and that the national unity created might begin to dissipate after a cease-fire, unless it was clearly perceived as a victory for Iran. Tehran's conditions for a cease-fire were announced on July 9, 1982. They included Iraqi reacceptance of the terms of the 1975 Algiers agreement, reparation of the more than 100,000 Iraqi Shiite citizens expelled by Baghdad, Iraq's public acceptance of its responsibility for the war, the payment of $100 billion for war damages, and the punishment of Saddam as a war criminal. These were in effect terms for an Iraqi surrender, something that was not going to happen.

At that point, the United States and the Soviet Union were both disturbed about the prospect of an invasion of Iraq by an Islamic fundamentalist Iranian regime, which could set the whole Middle East aflame and complicate the interests and policies of the superpowers in the region. With the encouragement of both Washington and Moscow, the UN passed a resolution on July 12 calling for a cease-fire and a withdrawal of the belligerents to the international border. Tehran rejected the resolution and launched an invasion of Iraq the following day.

One unanticipated consequence of the new phase of the Iran-Iraq war was the effect it had on the other states of the region. For the most part, the small states of the Persian Gulf, concerned about both belligerents, adopted a stance of neutrality. Only Kuwait, partly because of its fear of Iraq and partly because of a concern about what its large Shiite minority might do, openly lent its support to Iraq. The largest of the Gulf states, Saudi Arabia, was genuinely concerned about the implications of an Iranian victory for its own security and it became the principal supporter of Iraq, helping to finance the Iraqi war effort in a number of ways. Longstanding competitors for leadership of the Arab world, Iraq initiated a rapprochement with Egypt, which had effectively been isolated in the Arab world because of its peace treaty with Israel. Following the assassination of Anwar Sadat in October 1981, his successor, Hosni Mubarak, was anxious to reenter the pan-Arab arena and supporting Iraq was a good way to do it. Egypt soon became a significant source of arms and military instructors for Baghdad. Egypt's support of Iraq led its North African adversary Libya to side with Iran. Similarly, Iraq's adversary, Syria, also aligned itself with Iran, a relationship that would continue for the rest of the century with significant consequences for Lebanon, where Iranian-backed Shiite militants, with Syrian support, mounted and sustained a campaign of low level warfare along the Israel-Lebanon border. Israel, which had enjoyed reasonably good relations with Iran prior to the Islamic revolution, saw the Iran-Iraq war as an opportunity to come to terms with the new Iranian regime and to weaken Iraq, which it saw as a long-range danger to its security. Indeed, it was for the latter reason that Israel undertook, in a daring air assault, to destroy a nuclear reactor near Baghdad in June 1981. Israel also undertook, through intermediaries in countries such as Portugal, Italy, and Cyprus, to clandestinely supply Iran with a modest but not insignificant amount of arms and spare parts, that Iran, notwithstanding its anti-Israel rhetoric, was happy to accept as long as it was kept secret.

Faced by the prospect of a stalemate on the battlefield that would ultimately work to Iran's advantage, Iraq, which seemed to be in the Soviet camp, began making overtures to the United States, suggesting that it was in Washington's interests to be "present in the region when any other big or superpower is present."[5] This was perceived by the administration of President Ronald Reagan as an open invitation to intervene in the conflict at

Moscow's expense, one that it seemed unable to resist. By June 1983, despite the fact that the U.S. State Department listed Iraq as one of the nations that support international terrorism, the Reagan administration authorized the sale of 60 helicopters to Iraq that were ostensibly to be used for agricultural purposes, but which were easily convertible to military use. It also extended some $460 million in credit to Iraq for the purchase of American rice. This had the effect of significantly bolstering Iraq's international credit standing. Before long, a study by the U.S. National Security Council concluded that Iraq's defeat by Iran would have disastrous consequences for the Gulf region, which contained more than half of the world's known oil reserves. The United States henceforth became a de facto ally of Iraq.

By November 1983 Iraq was removed from the list of states supporting international terrorism, making it possible for it to legally receive U.S. arms shipments. Two months later, Iran was placed on the U.S. roster of pariah states, ostensibly as a result of alleged Iranian sponsorship of the October 23, 1983 bombing of the U.S. marine barracks in Beirut that took the lives of 259 men. Washington's barely concealed support for Iraq became evident in March 1984 when information was made public about an Iraqi chemical complex near Rutba manufacturing poison gas. Iraq, concerned about the real possibility of an Israeli attack similar to the one that destroyed its nuclear reactor less than three years earlier, sent its deputy foreign minister, Ismat Katani, to Washington to dissuade it from sanctioning such an operation. The chemical weapons plant was left untouched, only to become a source of major concern for the United States only a few years later.

Having lost the initiative on the ground, Iraq shifted its strategy to trying to force Iran into a cease-fire by attacking its economy through concentrating on the destruction of its port facilities and oil tankers in the Gulf. This posed a dilemma for Iran, because it could not retaliate in kind since Iraq was not shipping any oil by sea. Instead, Tehran decided to begin attacking the vessels of countries supporting Iraq, especially Kuwait and Saudi Arabia, thereby widening the war and increasing Washington's direct involvement in the conflict by sending military personnel to Kuwait to upgrade its anti-aircraft missile systems.

The rapprochement between Baghdad and Washington was viewed with some dismay in Moscow, which had been supplying as much as 70 percent of Iraq's arms by the end of 1984, as well as thousands of military advisers. The Soviets suspended talks about the sale of advanced fighters to Iraq at the same time that the other Warsaw Pact countries began cutting back on their arms shipments. The situation changed somewhat after the offensive mounted by Iran in March 1985 that broke through Iraq's defense lines. Tariq Aziz flew to Moscow pleading with the Soviets to begin an immediate airlift of critical supplies and weapons to block the Iranian advance. By mid-May, Tariq Aziz announced that the Soviets had fulfilled Iraq's military needs and that it would remain Iraq's primary source of support. That same December, Saddam Hussein made his first visit to Moscow since assuming power in 1979, urging the Soviet leaders to do whatever they could to bring the Gulf war to an end. At the same time, considering the possibility that Iran might actually prevail in the conflict with Iraq, high-ranking officials in Washington began a clandestine relationship with Iran, including the shipment of arms, that was to later emerge as the major political scandal known as Irangate.

The Iran-Iraq war continued on inconclusively until 1988, badly bleeding both countries, with the balance of power again shifting in favor of Iraq. Finally, on July 17 of that year Iran accepted Security Council Resolution 598, adopted a year earlier, to bring an end to the conflict. Iraq, feeling its new strength, now attempted to impose its own conditions for a cease-fire, demanding that all outstanding issues between the two belligerents had to be settled by direct negotiations before a cease-fire went into effect. And, to put a fine point on its ultimatum, Iraq mounted major offensives in three sectors of the front on July 22 that netted it some 920 square miles of Iranian territory. By August, however, it became evident that Saddam's ploy was backfiring. His attacks served to resuscitate the Iranian public and the military, and the possibility of renewal of all-out war became very real. On August 6 Saddam stepped back from the brink and withdrew his ultimatum, stating instead that Iraq was ready for a truce providing that "Iran announces clearly, unequivocally and formally its acceptance to enter into direct negotiations with Iraq immediately after a ceasefire takes place."[6] Iran agreed and the cease-fire went into effect on August 20, 1988.

The long conflict had the unplanned effect of militarizing Iraqi society. With almost a million men under arms in the regular military, and another half million in the popular forces, Saddam came to the realization that the armed forces were a more potent vehicle for integrating the Iraqi people and state under his control than the Baath Party. With a vast military establishment and intelligence apparatus at his disposal, Saddam was able to contain the ever present threat of Kurdish insurgency as well as to maintain tight control over the Shiite majority, which although proven loyal to Iraq during the conflict with Shiite Iran, required constant surveillance.

The United States, ostensibly appalled at Saddam's human rights record, including the use of chemical weapons to suppress the Kurds, adopted the position that his behavior could best be ameliorated by drawing Iraq closer to the West. In its strategic review of 1989, the administration of President George Bush concluded: "Normal relations between the US and Iraq would serve our longer-term interests in both the Gulf and the Middle East. The US government should propose economic and political incentives for Iraq to moderate its behaviour and to increase our influence with Iraq."[7] The naivete of Washington's perceptions of Saddam's Iraq soon became evident as the budding relationship with the dictator's regime turned into an embarrassment. On January 12, 1990 Under Secretary of State John Kelly was telling Saddam that he was a "force for moderation in the region, and the United States wishes to broaden her relations with Iraq."[8] Three days later, Saddam was being referred to by the Voice of America as a tyrant, and by late February Iraq was being condemned in the Foreign Affairs Committee of the Congress for its gross violations of human rights.

With the peace negotiations with Iran deadlocked, and Iraq unable to demobilize large numbers of troops into an economy that could not absorb them, Saddam decided to use the military assets he had in hand to resolve the country's rapidly evolving economic crisis that threatened to bring him down. In February 1990, Saddam asked King Hussein of Jordan and President Mubarak of Egypt to advise the Gulf countries, including Saudi Arabia, that Iraq required a total moratorium on its wartime debts and an immediate infusion of $30 billion in new funds. He warned, "Let the Gulf regimes know that if they do not give this money to me, I will know how to get it."[9]

Saddam turned to what he perceived as an easy target, wealthy Kuwait, to which Iraq had a longstanding claim and currently owed some $10 billion, and from which he now demanded an additional $10 billion as a grant. Moreover, Saddam demanded that Kuwait reduce its oil production quota in order to increase oil prices and thereby Iraq's oil revenues. The emir of Kuwait refused to agree to any of these demands, insisting that any support that Kuwait might grant to Iraq was contingent on a satisfactory resolution of the outstanding border issues between the two countries. He told Saddam's emissary, "Let's agree about our borders, and then we can talk about other things."[10]

Intimidation of Kuwait having failed, Saddam proceeded to build up his forces along the Kuwaiti frontier. By July 19, 1990 some 35,000 Iraqi troops, supported by hundreds of tanks, were arrayed as close as 10 miles from the border. That same day Secretary of Defense Richard Cheney affirmed that the United States would defend its interests and friends in the region, an implied threat of intervention should Iraq attack Kuwait. Saddam was duly concerned about the U.S. statement and sought clarification from the American ambassador, whose response evidently led him to believe that Washington would not interfere militarily. The Iraqi buildup continued, reaching 100,000 troops along the border by July 27. Washington, repeatedly asked by the Arab states to keep a low profile in the crisis, warned Saddam in a personal message from President George Bush not to pursue "threats involving military force or conflict against Kuwait," at the same time that it indicated a desire to improve relations with Baghdad.[11] Apparently convinced that the United States would not intervene militarily, Saddam ordered Iraqi forces into Kuwait on August 2, 1990 and took effective control of the entire country within 12 hours. That same day his spokesman told the extraordinary session of the Arab League, which convened in Cairo to consider the crisis: "What happened in the emirate was an internal affair. There had been a popular uprising against the treacherous al-Sabah regime, and the provisional revolutionary government requested Iraq's assistance. Naturally, Baghdad complied with the request."[12]

The Iraqi invasion nonetheless quickly became internationalized. It surprised Washington and dumbfounded Moscow, which was furious at Saddam for having taken such a destabilizing step that could upset the East-West balance of power in the region. The Soviets immediately took the position that "the sovereignty, national independence and territorial integrity of Kuwait must be fully restored and defended."[13] With both superpowers in rare agreement, it was only a matter of days before the Security Council Resolution 661 imposed an embargo on all trade with Iraq or Kuwait and any transfer of funds, except for medical and humanitarian assistance. It soon became clear that economic sanctions were not going to force an Iraqi withdrawal, and planning to use force to do so went into high gear. Nonetheless, it was to take months before President Bush could muster sufficient public and Congressional support for a war in which the United States would bear the primary burden, notwithstanding the broad alliance that was conjured up to give the forthcoming struggle a truly UN flavor.

Iraq was ultimately given a deadline of January 15, 1991 to comply with the UN demands, a deadline that passed without any response from Baghdad. War broke out the following day with a massive air assault against Iraqi targets, more than 1,300 sorties being flown in the first 24 hours, 97 percent of which were by U.S. forces. The UN coalition's intervention was limited to air attacks primarily because this was the only option available at the time. It would take almost half a year before Washington was able to transport sufficient troops and equipment to the Middle East to mount an effective ground campaign, which was the only realistic way of forcing Iraq to withdraw from Kuwait.

Iraq's only offensive response was to launch Scud missile attacks against Saudi Arabia and Israel, the former because of the concentration of American forces there, and the latter for political-strategic reasons. Because of Washington's concern to enlist as many of the Arab states as possible in the anti-Iraq campaign, Israel was specifically excluded from the coalition. Saddam, however, hoped to split the coalition by creating a situation in which Israel would feel obligated to retaliate against Iraq for its unwarranted attack on primarily civilian targets. If this happened, Saddam would succeed in linking the Kuwait crisis to the Palestinian problem, making it impossible for many of the Arab states to remain in the coalition in de facto alignment with Israel against a fellow Arab country. It would also have created problems among some Western members of the coalition with clearly pro-Arab policies concerning Palestine. The strategy failed only because of tremendous pressure brought to bear on Israel by Washington not to react to the wanton Iraqi aggression.

With the coalition holding together, a second deadline was given to Saddam; he was to begin to withdraw from Kuwait unconditionally by February 23, 1991. The land war began the following day. Less than 48 hours later, Baghdad radio announced that Iraqi troops in Kuwait had been ordered to withdraw across the border. Washington, however, was unwilling at this point to accept an Iraqi withdrawal as a close to the affair. There was a strong sentiment that Saddam would simply keep his forces in readiness to attack Kuwait once again at a later time. What Washington wanted was to undermine Saddam's position in Iraq by compelling him to publicly acknowledge that he had made a blunder, a humiliation that would seriously damage him politically. In the meantime the war went on and coalition forces crossed into Iraq, destroying a substantial part of the retreating Iraqi army. In about 100 hours the coalition forces had captured almost 74,000 square kilometers of Iraqi territory, some 15 percent of the country. However, international pressure for a cease-fire quickly began to mount, given that the primary objective of liberating Kuwait had been achieved. There was a widespread presumption that his defeat would topple Saddam, and there was little interest in having the U.S. army take Baghdad to oust him. A cease-fire went into effect on March 3, 1991.

Saddam was now faced with a Shiite rebellion in the south and a Kurdish rebellion in the north, which were expected to result in his overthrow by fractious elements in Baghdad. This, however, did not happen and assessments regarding Saddam's inability to survive the disaster of the war proved to be ill informed. Saddam unleashed a purge that removed at least 14 senior commanders of whose loyalty he could not be sure. The Republican Guard was unleashed on the rebellion in the south, where thousands of Shiite clerics were arrested and hundreds summarily executed. Similarly, a furious assault against the Kurds in the north soon produced some two million refugees along the Iranian and Turkish borders by the end of April.

Saddam's brutal campaign against the Kurds, who had mounted their rebellion in the expectation of help from the United States, which had clearly urged the Iraqi people to get rid of Saddam, soon aroused international indignation. Questions were being raised about Washington's evident abandonment of the Kurds for the second time in two decades, after encouraging them to rebel. President Bush, in a remarkably disingenuous response, stated: "Do I think that the United States should bear guilt because of suggesting that the Iraqi people take matters into their own hands, with the implication being given that the United States would be there to support them militarily? That was not true. We never implied that."[14]

One solution to the perennial Kurdish problem in Iraq would have been to have the international community support the partition of the country to provide for an independent Kurdistan. Turkey, however, with its own Kurdish problem, did not want a Kurdish state on its border with which its own Kurds could identify. As a result, it was not long before Washington policymakers were voicing concerns about the desirability of maintaining the territorial integrity of Iraq. Nonetheless, by mid-April 1991, at the prodding of the British government, Washington agreed with its proposal to establish safe havens under coalition protection in the north and south of the country to afford a measure of security for the Kurdish and Shiite populations of those regions. The situation on the ground in Iraq remained essentially unchanged throughout the rest of the decade.

Following the second Gulf war, under Washington's leadership, the UN sought to root out and eliminate Iraq's ability to produce weapons of mass destruction and imposed an inspection regime on the country. The Iraqi government's limited cooperation in the UN effort assured the continuation of the punishing international economic sanctions against the country. Moreover, Saddam's efforts to hide his chemical and biological warfare stockpiles and activities from the UN inspection teams led the United States to adopt an unprecedented stance toward Iraq in an Iraq Liberation Act that was signed into law by President Bill Clinton on October 31, 1998. The Act declared: "It should be the policy of the United States to seek to remove the regime headed by Saddam Hussein from power in Iraq and to promote the emergence of a democratic government to replace the regime." Washington did nothing of any consequence to carry out the declared policy. However, it did set the stage for a massive three-day aerial bombardment of Iraq that it launched on December 16, 1998, with the support of Britain alone, in an effort to bring Saddam's regime into compliance with UN demands for cooperation. As a practical matter, the attacks produced little result and essentially left the situation unchanged, except that an increasing number of countries were beginning to waver in their willingness to continue with the sanctions against Iraq.

NOTES

1. Shahram Chubin and Charles Tripp, *Iran and Iraq at War*, p. 23.
2. Ibid., p. 29.
3. Ibid., p. 30.
4. Ibid., p. 38.
5. Dilip Hiro, *The Longest War*, p. 119.
6. *Observer*, August 7, 1988.
7. Lawrence Freedman and Efraim Karsh, *The Gulf Conflict, 1990–1991*, p. 26.
8. Pierre Salinger with Eric Laurent, *Secret Dossier*, p. 4.
9. *Observer*, October 21, 1990.
10. Salinger and Laurent, *Secret Dossier*, p. 37.
11. *International Herald Tribune*, July 13–14, 1991.
12. Salinger and Laurent, *Secret Dossier*, p. 105.
13. Freedman and Karsh, *The Gulf Conflict*, p. 78.
14. Bush's News Conference, USIA, April 16, 1991.

21

At Century's End

By any measure, the twentieth century was one of extraordinary extremes. The pace and extent of technological progress during the period is mind-boggling, as is the unspeakable savagery and brutality of the Holocaust and the wanton slaughter of hundreds of thousands and even millions of Armenians, Biafrans, Cambodians, Russians, and others. From the standpoint of political history, however, and especially in the Middle East, the twentieth century seems to have ended, in a number of significant respects very much as it began.

The conflicting Arab and Jewish claims to the land of Palestine, the problem with which this book began, were hardly resolved at century's end, despite the intimations of progress that seem to be more illusion and wishful thinking than reality. The "bull in a china shop" approach of the Great Powers, regrettably including the United States, to the Middle East helped immeasurably in creating and sustaining the chaos in the region that had hardly changed by century's end. Suffice it to note that the last chapter of this book discussed the Persian Gulf wars, the United States becoming a de facto ally of Iraq in the first, and its arch antagonist in the second, both taking place within a single decade. Similarly, the century began with turmoil in the Balkans, and ended with turmoil in the Balkans, with the United States trying desperately to bring about peaceful resolution to a series of conflicts that it clearly does not appear to truly comprehend.

From a geopolitical perspective, Washington's engagement with and intervention in the Balkans betokens a dramatic shift in the political center of gravity in the wider region contiguous to the Middle East. This shift is due mainly to the geopolitical implications of the implosion of the Soviet Empire a decade ago, which had the unanticipated consequence of diminishing the relative importance of the Arab world and with it of the Arab-Israeli conflict to the United States and its allies. This is not to say that Middle Eastern oil has diminished in importance; it clearly has not, as evidenced by U.S. military involvement in the Persian Gulf. However, the Middle East, narrowly defined as the region of the Fertile Crescent, is no longer an arena for the NATO-Warsaw Pact Cold War to be fought by their respective proxies.

During the approximately two decades between 1970 and 1990, the East-West confrontation took place in a series of proxy conflicts, both hot and cold, around the globe. All of these conflicts, in Southeast Asia, Angola and Mozambique, the Horn of Africa, the Middle East, and elsewhere, had indigenous causes and would have been fought even if the Great Powers ignored them. However, the fact of Great Power involvement, directly or indirectly, raised the stakes for all concerned by contributing to escalating the lethality of the conflicts through arming the antagonists with increasingly sophisticated and deadly weapons. This in turn created dependency relationships between sponsors and clients that limited the freedom of action of the latter, transforming them into perhaps unwilling surrogates for policies that did not always serve their best interests.

The emergence of the East-West conflict in the wake of World War II gave the Middle East a geostrategic significance that has now diminished dramatically. The Western alliance, led by Washington, chose to defend Europe from the Soviet bloc through a policy of containment, building a virtual defensive wall through Europe from the Baltic to the Mediterranean. However, the weak link in NATO's defenses was the vulnerability of southern Europe from the Mediterranean. To offset this vulnerability, it was essential to deny the Soviets access to ports leading to the Mediterranean, and the security of Greece and Turkey, where the Soviets sponsored unsuccessful insurrections in the late 1940s as a prelude to seizing the region, became critical elements of the strategy. The other Soviet line of approach was through Yugoslavia, which, although communist, had managed to remain outside the Soviet grip and maintain a policy of armed neutrality.

With a containment line running from the Adriatic Sea through the Caucasus Mountains to the Caspian Sea, Moscow pursued an alternate breakout strategy of encircling Turkey through the support of anti-Western governments in Iraq and Syria. By squeezing Turkey between the Soviet Union to the north and hostile Arab states to the south, it was hoped that the Turkish link in the containment line would break. This stratagem gave new geostrategic importance to Israel, Saudi Arabia, and Iran, states on the peripheries of Iraq and Syria, each of which was in a position to draw the latter's troops away from the Turkish frontier, foiling the Soviet plan. As a result, the region south of Turkey became the focus of international geopolitics in the Middle East, with the Arab-Israeli conflict taking center stage.

The collapse of the Soviet Union eliminated the threat to Turkey from the north, with the result that Iraq was now wedged between an increasingly assertive Turkey to its north, U.S.-backed Saudi Arabia to the south, and Iran to the east. Syria was similarly caught between Turkey and Israel, which in the late 1990s formalized their alliance through a series of agreements, completely reversing the situation at the outset of the century, when Turkey was adamantly opposed to the Zionist enterprise in Palestine.

Although, for a variety of reasons, the United States remains intensely interested in the final resolution of the Arab-Israeli conflict, the conflict itself is no longer of global geopolitical importance. As suggested, the focus of international geopolitical interest has moved farther north, where a whole new array of issues has emerged in the region from the Adriatic through the Caucasus to the Caspian. These involve the anticipated reemergence of Russia as a major force in the region and the exploitation of the vast oil resources of Azerbaijan, against the background of an unresolved conflict between the latter and Armenia over the territory of Nagorno-Karabagh.

In a very real sense, as we enter the twenty-first century, it may no longer be useful to employ the designation Middle East to describe the region under discussion. The term, which clearly reflects a Eurocentric perspective, was coined at the beginning of the twentieth century by the American naval historian Alfred Thayer Mahan to designate the region centering on the Persian Gulf and stretching from Arabia to India, which at the time included Pakistan. The area originally encompassed by the term reflected Mahan's particular strategic interest, one that was not necessarily shared by other writers on the history and foreign affairs of that part of the world, who assigned to the term a different content. As a result, there was never any consensus regarding the precise delimitation of the territories that are included in the Middle East.

In the post-Soviet era, however, the topography of geopolitics has changed in highly significant ways. The line between Eastern and Western Europe has shifted substantially eastward with the extension of NATO to include Hungary and Poland, moving the West to the borders of Belarus and Ukraine. Turkey has long been part of the Western alliance (NATO), and Israel clearly has far more in common with the Western world than it does with its immediate geographic neighbors. Indeed, Israel truly stands today, as it has for decades, as a fortified Western outpost on the fringe of the Third World. As one perceptive Israeli analyst argues: "The aspirations [articulated by some Israelis] to integrate into the Middle East are a strategic, economic, and cultural folly. What can a bankrupt dictatorship such as Syria offer us? Do we really want to have close contact with a region where a tyrant such as Saddam Hussein is adored by the masses? . . . Politics makes strange bedfellows indeed, but our aim cannot be integration. If we wish to belong to the enlightened West, we need separation. Fortress Israel is unfortunately the correct vision."[1]

It is no longer clear what if any useful information is conveyed by considering Turkey and Israel as part of the Middle East, while excluding Greece, the Balkans, and Transcaucasia, all of which are interlocked geopolitically, as clearly demonstrated by the long complex history of the wider region. Perhaps the time has come to avoid a repetition of the semantic confusion and geostrategic misperceptions of the last century and to devise a new designation for the Third World region east of the present East-West divide. It would surely be most helpful in thinking about the region in more geopolitically realistic terms. However, coming up with such a designator is a task I gladly leave to others.

NOTE

1. Efraim Inbar, "The Eastern Mediterranean—The New Western Frontier," 1999.

Selected Bibliography

Abdullah, King of Jordan. *My Memoirs Completed.* Washington, D.C.: American
    Council of Learned Societies, 1954.
Abrahamian, Ervand. *Iran: Between Two Revolutions.* Princeton, N.J.: Princeton
    University Press, 1982.
Adams, Michael. *Suez and After: Year of Crisis.* Boston, Mass.: Beacon Press, 1958.
Adelson, Roger. *London and the Invention of the Middle East: Money, Power, and War,
    1902–1922.* New Haven, Conn.: Yale University Press, 1995.
Agwani, M.S. *The Lebanese Crisis, 1958: A Documentary Study.* New York: Asia Pub-
    lishing House, 1965.
Aldington, Richard. *Lawrence of Arabia, A Biographical Enquiry.* Westport, Conn.:
    Greenwood Press, 1976.
Alin, Erika G. *The United States and the 1958 Lebanon Crisis: American Intervention in
    the Middle East.* Lanham, Md.: University Press of America, 1994.
AlRoy, Gil C. *Behind the Middle East Conflict.* New York: Putnam's Sons, 1975.
———. *The Kissinger Experience: American Policy in the Middle East.* New York: Ho-
    rizon Press, 1975.
Amirsadeghi, Hossein, ed. *Twentieth-Century Iran.* New York: Holmes and Meier, 1977.
Amos, John W., II. *Arab-Israeli Military/Political Relations: Arab Perceptions and the
    Politics of Escalation.* New York: Pergamon Press, 1979.
Antonius, George. *The Arab Awakening.* New York: Capricorn Books, 1965.
Atiyyah, Ghassan R. *Iraq, 1908–1921: A Socio-Political Study.* Beirut: Arab Institute
    for Research and Publishing, 1973.
Bailey, Clinton. "Changing Attitudes Toward Jordan in the West Bank." *Middle
    East Journal,* Spring 1978.
Baker, Randall. *King Husain and the Kingdom of Hejaz.* Cambridge: Oleander Press,
    1979.
Baram, Amatzia and Barry Rubin, eds. *Iraq's Road to War.* New York: St. Martin's
    Press, 1993.

Barbour, Nevill. *Nisi Dominus: A Survey of the Palestine Controversy*. London: G.G. Harrap, 1946.

Bar-Siman-Tov, Yaacov. *The Israeli-Egyptian War of Attrition, 1969–1970*. New York: Columbia University Press, 1980.

———. *Linkage Politics in the Middle East: Syria Between Domestic and External Conflict, 1961–1970*. Boulder, Colo.: Westview Press, 1983.

Bar-Zohar, Michael. *Embassies in Crisis: Diplomats and Demagogues Behind the Six-Day War*. Englewood Cliffs, N.J.: Prentice-Hall, 1970.

Bechofer, C. E. *In Denikin's Russia and the Caucasus, 1919–1920*. London: W. Collins & Sons, 1921.

Bell, Lady Gertrude. *Letters*, 2 vols. New York: Boni and Liveright, 1928.

Ben-Gurion, David. *Israel: A Personal History*. New York: Funk and Wagnalls, 1971.

Benoist-Mechin. *Ibn-Seoud ou la Naissance d'un Royaume*. Paris: Albin Michel, 1955.

Bentwich, Norman. *My 77 Years*. Philadelphia: Jewish Publication Society, 1961.

Bethell, Nicholas. *The Palestine Triangle: The Struggle for the Holy Land, 1935–48*. New York: G.P. Putnam's Sons, 1979.

Blaxland, Gregory. *Egypt and Sinai: Eternal Battleground*. New York: Funk & Wagnalls, 1966.

Bleck, Edward C. and Edward Parkes, eds. *British and Foreign State Papers, 1915*. Vol. CIX. London: His Majesty's Stationery Office, 1919.

Boehm, Adolf. *Die Zionistische Bewegung, 1918 bis 1925*. Jerusalem: Hozaah Ivrith, 1937.

Bondy, Ruth, et al., eds. *Mission Survival*. New York: Sabra Books, 1968.

Bull, Odd. *War and Peace in the Middle East*. London: Cooper, 1976.

Bullard, Reader. *Britain and the Middle East: From Earliest Times to 1952*. London: Hutchinson House, 1952.

Burns, E.L.M. *Between Arab and Israeli*. London: George G. Harrap, 1962.

Busch, Briton Cooper. *Britain, India, and the Arabs 1914–1921*. Berkeley: University of California Press, 1971.

———. *Mudros to Lausanne: Britain's Frontier in West Asia, 1918–1923*. Albany: State University of New York Press, 1976.

Butler, Rohan, et al., eds. *Documents on British Policy Overseas*, 5 vols. London: Her Majesty's Stationery Office, 1984.

Byrnes, James F. *Speaking Frankly*. New York: Harper, 1947.

Calvocoressi, Peter. *Suez Ten Years After*. New York: Pantheon Books, 1967.

Carlton, David. *Britain and the Suez Crisis*. New York: Basil Blackwell, 1989.

The Case of Armenia. New York: Press Bureau of the Armenian National Union of America, n.d.

Chaqueri, Cosroe. *The Soviet Socialist Republic of Iran, 1920–1921: Birth of the Trauma*. Pittsburgh: University of Pittsburgh Press, 1995.

Chubin, Shahram and Charles Tripp. *Iran and Iraq at War*. Boulder, Colo.: Westview Press, 1988.

Churchill, Winston S. *The Aftermath*. New York: Charles Scribner's Sons, 1929.

———. *The Grand Alliance*. Boston: Houghton-Mifflin, 1953.

Cooper, Chester L. *The Lion's Last Roar: Suez, 1956*. New York: Harper & Row, 1978.

Cromer, Earl of. *Abbas II*. London: Macmillan, 1915.

Dan, Uriel, ed. *The Great Powers in the Middle East 1919–1939*. New York: Holmes & Meier, 1988.

Dawisha, Adeed I. *Syria and the Lebanese Crisis*. New York: St. Martin's Press, 1980.

Dayan, Moshe. *Diary of the Sinai Campaign*. New York: Schocken Books, 1967.

———. *Moshe Dayan: Story of My Life*. New York: William Morrow, 1976.

———. *Breakthrough: A Personal Account of the Egypt-Israel Peace Negotiations*. New York: Alfred A. Knopf, 1981.

Dockril, Michael L. and J. Douglas Goold. *Peace Without Promise: Britain and the Peace Conferences, 1919–1923*. London: Batsford Academic and Educational, 1981.

Documents on British Foreign Policy 1919–1939, first series, 27 vols. Butler, Rohan, et al., eds. London: Her Majesty's Stationery Office, 1949–1976.

Draper, Theodore. *Israel and World Politics*. New York: Viking Press, 1968.

Eagleton, William. *The Kurdish Republic of 1946*. London: Oxford University Press, 1963.

Eban, Abba. *An Autobiography*. New York: Random House, 1977.

Eden, Anthony. *Full Circle*. Boston: Houghton Mifflin, 1960.

Eisenhower, Dwight D. *The White House Years: Waging Peace, 1956–1961*. Garden City, N.Y.: Doubleday, 1965.

Ellis, C.H. *The British "Intervention" in Transcaspia 1918–1919*. Berkeley and Los Angeles: University of California Press, 1963.

Eudin, Xenia Joukoff and Robert C. North. *Soviet Russia and the East: 1920–1927*. Stanford, Calif.: Stanford University Press, 1957.

Evron, Yair. *War and Intervention in Lebanon: The Israeli-Syrian Deterrence Dialogue*. London: Croom Helm, 1987.

Eytan, Walter. *The First Ten Years: A Diplomatic History of Israel*. New York: Simon and Schuster, 1958.

Fatemi, Faramarz S. *The U.S.S.R. in Iran*. South Brunswick, N.J.: A.S. Barnes & Co., 1980.

Fatemi, Nasrollah S. *Diplomatic History of Persia 1917–1923*. New York: R. F. Moore, 1952.

Feis, Herbert. *Between War and Peace: The Potsdam Conference*. Princeton, N.J.: Princeton University Press, 1960.

Fischer, Louis. *The Soviets in World Affairs*, 2 vols. Princeton, N.J.: Princeton University Press, 1951.

Foreign Relations of the United States. Washington, D.C.: U.S. Government Printing Office, 1941–1947.

Freedman, Lawrence and Efraim Karsh. *The Gulf Conflict, 1990–1991; Diplomacy and War in the New World Order*. Princeton, N.J.: Princeton University Press, 1993.

Friedman, Isaiah. *The Question of Palestine, 1914–1918: British-Jewish-Arab Relations*. New York: Schocken Books, 1973.

———. *Germany, Turkey, and Zionism 1897–1918*. Oxford: Oxford University Press, 1977.

Frischwasser-Ra'anan, H.F. *The Frontiers of a Nation*. London: Batchworth Press, 1955.

Fromkin, David. *A Peace to End All Peace: Creating the Modern Middle East 1914–1922*. New York: Henry Holt, 1989.

Gelber, Nathan M. *Hatzharat Balfur veToldoteha*. Jerusalem: haHanhalah haTzionit, 1939.

Ghods, M. Reza. *Iran in the Twentieth Century: A Political History*. Boulder, Colo.: Lynne Rienner Publishers, 1989.

Glubb, John B. *A Soldier with the Arabs*. New York: Harper and Brothers, 1957.

Gomaa, Ahmed M. *The Foundation of the League of Arab States: Wartime Diplomacy and Inter-Arab Politics 1941–1945*. London: Longman, 1977.

Great Britain, *Palestine, Statement of Policy*. Cmd. 6019, 1939. London: H.M.S.O.

Gunther, John. *Inside Asia*. New York: Harper & Brothers, 1942.

Haddad, Wadi D. *Lebanon: The Politics of Revolving Doors*. Westport, Conn.: Praeger, 1985.

Haj, Samira. *The Making of Iraq, 1900–1963: Capital, Power and Ideology*. Albany: State University of New York Press, 1997.

Haldane, Aylmer L. *The Insurrection in Mesopotamia, 1920*. Edinburgh and London: W. Blackwood & Sons, 1922.

Hamizrachi, Beate. *The Emergence of the South Lebanon Security Belt: Major Saad Haddad and the Ties with Israel, 1975–1978*. New York: Praeger, 1988.

Hamzavi, A.H. *Persia and the Powers*. London: Hutchinson & Co., 1946.

Hanna, Paul A. *British Policy in Palestine*. Washington, D.C.: American Council on Public Affairs, 1942.

Hassan, Hamdi A. *The Iraqi Invasion of Kuwait: Religion, Identity and Otherness in the Analysis of War and Conflict*. Sterling, Va.: Pluto Press, 1999.

Hassouna, Hussein A. *The League of Arab States and Regional Disputes*. Dobbs Ferry, N.Y.: Oceana Publications, 1975.

Heikal, Mohamed H. *Nasser: The Cairo Documents*. London: New English Library, 1972.

———. *The Sphinx and the Commissar: The Rise and Fall of Soviet Influence in the Middle East*. New York: Harper & Row, 1978.

———. *Cutting the Lion's Tail: Suez through Egyptian Eyes*. London: Andre Deutsch, 1986.

Herzog, Chaim. *The War of Atonement: October, 1973*. Boston: Little, Brown, 1973.

Hillman, William, ed. *Mr. President: The First Publication from the Personal Diaries, Private Letters, Papers and Revealing Interviews by Harry Truman*. New York: Farrar, Strauss & Young, 1952.

Hiro, Dilip. *The Longest War: The Iran-Iraq Military Conflict*. New York: Routledge, 1991.

Hirschfeld, Yair. "Moscow and Khomeini: Soviet-Iranian Relations in Historical Perspective." *Orbis*, Summer 1980.

Hitti, Philip K. *A Short History of Lebanon*. New York: St. Martin's Press, 1965.

Hofstadter, Don, ed. *Egypt & Nasser, Volume 2, 1957–66*. New York: Facts on File, 1973.

Hourani, Albert H. *Syria and Lebanon: A Political Essay*. London: Oxford University Press, 1946.

Howard, Harry N. *The Partition of Turkey: A Diplomatic History 1913–1923*. Norman: University of Oklahoma Press, 1931.

Hull, Cordell. *The Memoirs of Cordell Hull*, vol. 2. New York: Macmillan, 1948.

Hurewitz, J.C. *The Struggle for Palestine*. New York: W.W. Norton, 1950.

———. *Diplomacy in the Near and Middle East: A Documentary Record: 1914–1956*, vol. 2. Princeton, N.J.: Van Nostrand, 1956.

Husri, Abu Khaldun Sati al-. *The Day of Maysalun*. Washington, D.C.: Middle East Institute, 1966.

Hussein, King of Jordan. *My War with Israel*. As told to and with additional material by Vick Vance and Walter B. Michaels. New York: Morrow, 1969.

Inbar, Efraim. "The Eastern Mediterranean—The New Western Frontier." *Jerusalem Post Internet Edition*, October 11, 1999.

Ireland, Philip W. *Iraq: A Study in Political Development*. New York: Macmillan, 1938.

"Israel's Security and Her International Position before and after the Sinai Campaign." *Israel Government Yearbook* 5720 (1959/60).

Jabotinsky, Vladimir. *The Story of the Jewish Legion*, Translated by Samuel Katz. New York: Bernard Ackerman, 1945.

Jackson, William. *Britain's Triumph and Decline in the Middle East: Military Campaigns 1919 to the Present Day*. London: Brassey's, 1996.

Johnson, Lyndon B. *The Vantage Point: Perspectives of the Presidency*. New York: Holt, Rinehart and Winston, 1972.

Joyner, Christopher C., ed. *The Persian Gulf War: Lessons for Strategy, Law and Diplomacy*. Westport, Conn.: Greenwood Press, 1990.

Kazemzadeh, Firuz. *The Struggle for Transcaucasia (1917–1921)*. New York: Philosophical Library, 1951.

Kedourie, Elie. "Cairo and Khartoum on the Arab Question," *The Historical Journal* 7(2), 1964.

———. *Chatham House Version and other Middle Eastern Studies*. New York: Praeger Publishers, 1970.

———. *In the Anglo-Arab Labyrinth*. New York: Cambridge University Press, 1976.

———. *England and the Middle East: The Destruction of the Ottoman Empire 1914–1921*. London: Mansell Publishing, 1987.

Kent, Marian. *Moguls and Mandarins: Oil, Imperialism and the Middle East in British Foreign Policy 1900–1940*. London: Frank Cass, 1993.

Kerr, Malcolm. *The Arab Cold War*. London: Oxford University Press, 1971.

Khadduri, Majid. "Towards an Arab Union." *American Political Science Review* XL, February 1946.

Kilic, Altemur. *Turkey and the World*. Washington, D.C.: Public Affairs Press, 1959.

Kimche, David and Dan Bawly. *The Sandstorm: The Arab-Israel War of June 1967*. New York: Stein and Day, 1968.

Kimche, Jon. *The Unromantics: The Great Powers and the Balfour Declaration*. London: Weidenfeld & Nicolson, 1968.

———. *The Second Arab Awakening*. New York: Holt, Rinehart and Winston, 1970.

———. *There Could Have Been Peace*. New York: Dial Press, 1973.

Kimche, Jon and David Kimche. *A Clash of Destinies*. New York: Frederick A. Praeger, 1960.

Kirk, George. *The Middle East in the War*. London: Oxford University Press, 1953.

Kirkbride, Alec. *From the Wings: Amman Memoirs, 1947–1951*. London: Frank Cass, 1976.

Kisch, Frederick H. *Palestine Diary*. London: V. Gollancz, 1938.

Klieman, Aaron S. *Foundations of British Policy in the Arab World: The Cairo Conference of 1921*. Baltimore, Md.: Johns Hopkins University, 1970.

Kohn, Hans. *Nationalism and Imperialism in the Hither East*. New York: Howard Fertig, 1969.

Kuniholm, Bruce R. *The Origins of the Cold War in the Near East*. Princeton, N.J.: Princeton University Press, 1980.

Kurzman, Dan. *Genesis 1948: The First Arab-Israeli War*. New York: New American Library, 1970.

Laqueur, Walter. *The Road to Jerusalem*. New York: Macmillan, 1968.

———. *Confrontation: The Middle East and the West*. New York: Quandrangle, 1974.

Lawrence, Thomas E. *Seven Pillars of Wisdom*. Garden City, N.Y.: Doubleday, Doran, 1935.

———. *Secret Dispatches from Arabia*. London: Golden Cockerel Press, 1939.

Lederer, Ivo J. and Wayne S. Vucinich, eds. *The Soviet Union and the Middle East: The Post World War II Era*. Stanford, Calif.: Hoover Institution Press, 1974.

Lenczowski, George. *Russia and the West in Iran, 1918–1948: A Study in Big-Power Rivalry*. Ithaca: Cornell University Press, 1949.

———. *The Middle East in World Affairs*, fourth ed. Ithaca, N.Y.: Cornell University Press, 1980.

Lenin, V.I. and Joseph Stalin. *The Russian Revolution*. New York: International Publishers, 1938.

Liddell Hart, B.H. *"T.E. Lawrence"—In Arabia and After*. London: Jonathan Cape, 1936.

Lloyd, George. *Egypt Since Cromer*, 2 vols. London: Macmillan, 1933–34.

Lloyd, Selwyn. *Suez 1956: A Personal Account*. New York: Mayflower Books, 1978.

Lloyd George, David. *The Truth About the Peace Treaties*. London: Victor Gollancz, 1938.

———. *Memoirs of the Peace Conference*. New Haven, Conn.: Yale University Press, 1939.

Loder, J. de V. *The Truth About Mesopotamia, Palestine & Syria*. London: George Allen & Unwin, 1923.

Longrigg, S.H. *Four Centuries of Modern Iraq*. Oxford: Clarendon Press, 1925.

Louis, Wm. Roger. *The British Empire in the Middle East, 1945–1951*. Oxford: Oxford University Press, 1984.

Louis, Wm. Roger and Robert W. Stookey. *The End of the Palestine Mandate*. Austin: University of Texas, 1986.

Love, Kenneth. *Suez: The Twice-Fought War*. New York: McGraw-Hill, 1969.

Ludendorff, Erich von. *Ludendorff's Own Story*, 2 vols. New York: Harper & Brothers, 1920.

McKay, Vernon. "The Arab League in World Politics." *Foreign Policy Reports* XXII, November 15, 1946.

McLoughlin, Leslie. *Ibn Saud: Founder of a Kingdom*. New York: St. Martin's Press, 1993.

Maine, Ernest. *Iraq: From Mandate to Independence*. London: George Allen & Unwin, 1935.

Mansfield, Peter. *The British in Egypt*. New York: Holt, Rinehart and Winston, 1972.

Al-Marayati, Abid A. *A Diplomatic History of Modern Iraq*. New York: Robert Speller & Sons, 1961.

Ma'oz, Moshe. *Syria and Israel: From War to Peacemaking*. Oxford: Clarendon Press, 1995.

Ma'oz, Moshe and Avner Yaniv, eds. *Syria under Assad: Domestic Constraints and Regional Risks*. New York: St. Martin's Press, 1986.

Marlowe, John. *The Seat of Pilate: An Account of the Palestine Mandate*. London: Cresset Press, 1959.

————. *A History of Modern Egypt and Anglo-Egyptian Relations 1800–1956*, second ed. Hamden, Conn.: Archon Books, 1965.

————. *Perfidious Albion: The Origins of Anglo-French Rivalry in the Levant*. London: Elek Books, 1971.

Meinertzhagen, Richard. *Middle East Diary 1917–1956*. New York: Yoseloff, 1960.

Meir, Golda. *My Life*. New York: G.P. Putnam's Sons, 1975.

Monroe, Elizabeth. *Britain's Moment in the Middle East, 1914–1956*. Baltimore, Md.: Johns Hopkins University Press, 1963.

Moore, John N., ed. *The Arab-Israeli Conflict*, vol. 3, *Documents*. Princeton, N.J.: Princeton University Press, 1974.

Morris, James. *The Hashemite Kings*. New York: Pantheon Books, 1959.

Mosley, Leonard. *Power Play: Oil in the Middle East*. Baltimore, Md.: Penguin Books, 1974.

Mutawi, Samir A. *Jordan in the 1967 War*. Cambridge: Cambridge University Press, 1987.

Neff, Donald. *Warriors at Suez: Eisenhower Takes America into the Middle East*. New York: Linden Press, 1981.

————. *Warriors for Jerusalem: The Six Days That Changed the Middle East*. New York: Linden Press, 1984.

Nicolson, Harold. *Curzon: The Last Phase, a Study in Post-War Diplomacy*. London: Constable & Co., 1934.

Nutting, Anthony. *Nasser*. London: Constable, 1972.

Official Record of the Second Session of the General Assembly. New York: United Nations, 1947.

Palestine: A Study of Jewish, Arab, and British Policies. New Haven, Conn.: Yale University Press, 1947.

Palestine Royal Commission. *Report*. London: 1937.

Pelletierre, Stephen C. *The Iran-Iraq War: Chaos in a Vacuum*. Westport, Conn.: Praeger, 1992.

Penrose, Edith and Ernest F. *Iraq: International Relations and National Development*. London: Ernest Benn, 1978.

Philby, Henry St. John B. *Arabia*. London: Benn, 1930.

————. *Arabian Days*. London: Robert Hale, 1948.

Pipes, Richard. *Formation of the Soviet Union*, revised ed. New York: Atheneum, 1974.

Postal, Bernard and Henry W. Levy. *And the Hills Shouted for Joy: The Day Israel was Born*. New York: D. McKay, 1973.

Prittie, Terence. *Eshkol: The Man and the Nation*. New York: Pitman, 1969.

Quandt, William B. *Camp David: Peacemaking and Politics*. Washington, D.C.: Brookings Institution, 1986.

Qubain, Fahim I. *Crisis in Lebanon*. Washington, D.C.: Middle East Institute, 1961.

Quraishi, Zaheer Masood. *Liberal Nationalism in Egypt: Rise and Fall of the Wafd Party.* Allahabad, India: Kitab Mahal, 1967.

Rabin, Yitzhak. *The Rabin Memoirs.* Boston: Little, Brown, 1979.

Rafael, Gideon. "U.N. Resolution 242: A Common Denominator." *New Middle East,* June 1973.

———. *Destination Peace: Three Decades of Israeli Foreign Policy.* New York: Stein and Day, 1981.

Ramazani, Rouhollah K. *The Foreign Policy of Iran, 1500–1941.* Charlottesville: University of Virginia Press, 1966.

Reich, Bernard. *Quest for Peace: United States-Israel Relations and the Arab-Israeli Conflict.* New Brunswick, N.J.: Transaction Books, 1977.

Rikhye, Indar Jit. *The Sinai Blunder.* London: Frank Cass, 1980.

Robertson, Terence. *Crisis: The Inside Story of the Suez Conspiracy.* New York: Atheneum, 1965.

Rossow, Robert Jr. "The Battle of Azerbaijan 1946." *Middle East Journal,* winter 1956.

Royal Institute of International Affairs. *Great Britain and Palestine 1915–1945.* London: Royal Institute of International Affairs, 1946.

Rubinstein, Alvin Z., ed. *The Foreign Policy of the Soviet Union.* New York: Random House, 1966.

Sachar, Howard M. *The Emergence of the Middle East: 1914–1924.* New York: Alfred A. Knopf, 1969.

———. *Europe Leaves the Middle East, 1936–1954.* New York: Alfred A. Knopf, 1972.

———. *Egypt and Israel.* New York: Richard Marek Publishers, 1981.

Sadat, Anwar. *The Public Diary of President Sadat,* 3 vols. Edited by Raphael Israeli. Leiden, Neth.: Brill, 1978–1979.

Safran, Nadiv. *Saudi Arabia: The Ceaseless Quest for Security.* Cambridge, Mass.: Harvard University Press, 1985.

Salinger, Pierre with Eric Laurent. *Secret Dossier: The Hidden Agenda Behind the Gulf War.* London: Penguin, 1991.

Sam'o, Elias, ed. *The June 1967 Arab-Israeli War: Miscalculation or Conspiracy?* Wilmette, Ill.: Medina University Press International, 1971.

Seale, Patrick. *The Struggle for Syria: A Study of Post-War Arab Politics, 1945–1958.* New Haven, Conn.: Yale University Press, 1987.

Shwadran, Benjamin. *Jordan a State of Tension.* New York: Council for Middle Eastern Affairs Press, 1959.

———. *The Power Struggle in Iraq.* New York: Council for Middle Eastern Affairs Press, 1960.

Sicker, Martin. *The Bear and the Lion: Soviet Imperialism and Iran.* New York: Praeger, 1988.

———. *The Strategy of Soviet Imperialism: Expansion in Eurasia.* New York: Praeger, 1988.

———. *Between Hashemites and Zionists: The Struggle for Palestine 1908–1988.* New York: Holmes & Meier, 1989.

———. *Israel's Quest for Security.* New York: Praeger, 1989.

———. *Reshaping Palestine: From Muhammad Ali to the British Mandate, 1831–1922.* Westport, Conn.: Praeger, 1999.

————. *Pangs of the Messiah: The Troubled Birth of the Jewish State*. Westport, Conn.: Praeger, 2000.

Smith, Walter B. *Moscow Mission, 1946–1949*. London: W. Heinemann, 1950.

Spector, Ivar. *The Soviet Union and the Muslim World 1917–1958*. Seattle: University of Washington Press, 1959.

Stein, Leonard. *The Balfour Declaration*. New York: Simon and Schuster, 1961.

Stock, Ernest. *Israel on the Road to Sinai, 1949–1956*. Ithaca, N.Y.: Cornell University Press, 1967.

Storrs, Ronald. *Orientations*. London: Nicholson & Watson, 1943.

Tauber, Eliezer. *The Formation of Modern Syria and Iraq*. Ilford, U.K.: Frank Cass, 1995.

Thomas, Hugh. *Suez*. New York: Harper & Row, 1967.

Tibawi, A.L. *A Modern History of Syria*. New York: St. Martin's Press, 1969.

————. *Anglo-Arab Relations and the Question of Palestine 1914–1921*. London: Luzac, 1977.

Towards a Safe Israel and a Free Lebanon. Jerusalem: Israel Information Centre, September, 1982.

Toynbee, Arnold J. *Survey of International Affairs, 1925*, vol. 1. London: Oxford University Press, 1927.

Truman, Harry S. *Memoirs*, vol. 2, *Years of Hope and Trial, 1946–1952*. Garden City, N.Y.: Doubleday, 1956.

Ullman, Richard H. *Anglo-Soviet Relations, 1917–1921*, 3 vols. Princeton, N.J.: Princeton University Press, 1961–1972.

United Nations. *Official Record of the Second Session of the General Assembly*. Lake Success, N.Y.: United Nations, 1947.

U.S. Department of State. *Foreign Relations of the United States 1919*. Vol. 2. Washington, D.C.: U.S. Government Printing Office, 1920.

United States Policy in the Middle East, September 1956–June 1957. Washington, D.C.: Department of State, 1957.

Vatikiotis, P.J. *The History of Egypt: From Muhammad Ali to Sadat*, second ed. Baltimore, Md.: Johns Hopkins University Press, 1980.

Velie, Lester. *Countdown in the Holy Land*. New York: Funk and Wagnalls, 1969.

Weizman, Ezer. *The Battle for Peace*. New York: Bantam Books, 1981.

Wheelock, Keith. *Nasser's New Egypt: A Critical Analysis*. New York: Frederick A. Praeger, 1960.

Whetten, Lawrence L. *The Canal War: Four Power Conflict in the Middle East*. Cambridge: Massachusetts Institute of Technology Press, 1974.

Whiteman, Marjorie M. *Digest of International Law*, 15 vols. Washington, D.C.: U.S. Government Printing Office, 1963–73.

Wilson, Arnold T. *Mesopotamia, 1917–1920: A Clash of Loyalties*. London: Oxford University Press, 1931.

Wilson, Harold. *The Chariot of Israel*. New York: W.W. Norton, 1981.

Wingate, Ronald. *Wingate of the Sudan*. London: John Murray, 1955.

Wint, Guy and Peter Calvocoressi. *Middle East Crisis*. Baltimore, Md.: Penguin Books, 1957.

Yapp, Malcolm E. *The Making of the Modern Near East, 1792–1923*. London: Longman, 1987.

Young, George. *Egypt*. London: Benn, 1927.

Zangwill, Israel. "Nordau." *The Jewish Standard*. January 28, 1994.
Zayid, Mahmud Y. *Egypt's Struggle for Independence*. Beirut: Khayats, 1965.
Ziff, William B. *The Rape of Palestine*. New York: Longmans, Green, 1938.

Index

Abbas II, 101
Abd al-Aziz ibn Saud (King), 9, 14, 47, 51–52, 79, 89–99, 150–51, 154–55, 189
Abd al-Hamid, 6, 9–10
Abd al-Rahman, 79
Abdul Ilah (Prince), 83
Abdul Kader, 84
Abdullah al-Sabah, 209
Abdullah ibn Hussein (King), 7–11, 51–53, 62–65, 68, 78–80, 90, 92–93, 96–97, 150–51, 170, 175, 178, 181–87, 207, 219, 224, 229
Abul Huda, Tawfiq, 176–77, 186
Acheson, Dean, 167
Adli Yeghen, 105, 108
Afghanistan, 2, 5, 117, 135–36
Aflak, Michel, 205
Ahmad bin Yahya (Imam), 206, 211, 213
Ahmad Shah, 132, 135
Ahmed Nami Bey, 71
Ala, Hossein, 164
Aleppo, 11–12, 21, 60, 68–71, 141–42, 204, 212
Alexandretta, 11, 27, 70, 122, 136, 139, 194
Ali ibn Hussein, 62, 93, 96, 98–99

Allen, George V., 167
Allenby, Edmund, 18–20, 41–43, 104, 106–8
Allied Powers, 139–41, 143–47, 159, 163, 165
Alwan, Jasm, 212
Amer, Abd al-Hakim, 200, 211
Amman, 18–19, 51, 62–66, 94, 97, 178, 182, 184, 188, 198, 207, 222, 247–48
Arabia(n), 1, 5, 7–8, 10, 14–16, 71, 79, 89–90, 92–93, 95–97, 99, 150, 155, 188, 273
Arab-Israel conflict, 177, 179, 188, 232, 234–36, 272–73
Arab League, 151–52, 170, 173, 177–78, 181, 183–87, 194, 197, 205–6, 209–10, 267
Arab Legion, 176–78, 181–83, 197–98
Arab(s), 2, 7–20, 26–28, 37–38, 41–56, 59–63, 69, 77–80, 91, 96–97, 136, 139–42, 149–52, 155, 171–79, 181–82, 185–87, 194–98, 200, 203–6, 209–11, 217–18, 220, 223–25, 229–32, 234–42, 244, 248–50, 256, 261, 264, 271–72; nationalists and nationalism, 10–11, 16–17, 25–26, 37, 45, 47–49, 52, 62, 67, 149, 188, 195, 205–6, 211, 231, 244; revolt, 12,

14–18, 89–90, 97; state(s), 171,
173–75, 177–78, 181–86, 188, 192,
194, 199, 203, 206–7, 219, 221,
224–25, 229–32, 236–37, 241, 243,
268, 272

Arafat, Yasser, 248–49, 255

Ardahan, 114–15, 117–18, 123

Arif, Abd as-Salam, 207–8, 210, 212

Armenia(n), 28, 71, 113–23, 148, 271,
273

Assad, Hafez al-, 218, 249–50, 252,
256, 263

Ata al-Ayyubi, 73

Atakchiev, Salim, 162

Atassi, Hashim al-, 72

Atassi, Louai al-, 212

Atassi, Nur ad-Din al-, 219, 222

Atrashi, Salim Pasha al-, 70

Atrashi, Sultan Pasha al-, 70–71

Attlee, Clement, 171, 174

Auda Abu Tayeh, 18

Austin, Warren, 176

Axis Powers, 139–40, 142, 146, 148–50

Azerbaijan(i), 113, 115–21, 123–24,
126, 128–29, 132, 134–35, 146,
148–49, 156, 160–67, 273

Azm, Khaled al-, 212

Azmah, Bashir al-, 212

Azzam Pasha, Abd al-Rahman, 150

Baath(ists), 205–7, 212, 218, 242,
260–62, 266

Badr Khan, 84

Baghdad, 51, 64, 78–80, 82–83, 91, 97,
117, 141–42, 153, 194, 208, 212,
260–65, 267–69

Baghdad Pact, 194, 198, 203, 206–7,
210

Baghirov, Jafar, 162

Baha-ad-din Bey, 24

Bakr, Ahmed Hassan al-, 212

Bakr as-Sadr, Muhammad, 261

Baku, 117–19, 124, 128–30, 135, 148,
156, 162, 164, 169

Balfour Declaration, 2, 35–38, 41–44,
46–47, 49, 55–56, 59, 171

Balfour, John, 181

Balfour, Lord, 32, 34–35, 37–38, 42, 47,
104, 127

Barzanji, Sheikh Ahmed, 86

Barzanji, Sheikh Mahmud, 85–86

Basra, 77, 83, 91, 136, 142, 166, 207,
209, 259, 262

Batum, 114–16, 118, 120, 169

Bayat, Morteza Qoli, 158

Bedouin, 15, 17, 60–61, 63, 188

Begin, Menahem, 240–44, 251, 255–56

Beirut, 12–13, 15, 25, 51, 54, 69–70, 72,
74, 142–44, 210, 250, 252–56, 265

Bekr Sidki, 82–83

Ben-Gurion, David, 56, 178, 186, 196,
199–201, 222

Bentwich, Norman, 44

Bernadotte, Folke, 183

Bevin, Ernest, 170, 172–74, 176–78

Bizri, Afif, 204

Bonar Law, 128

Bourguiba, Habib, 231

Britain, 2, 4–14, 16, 19–20, 26–32, 36,
41–44, 46, 49, 52, 55–56, 59–60, 62,
64–65, 68, 80–86, 91, 96–97, 103–7,
109–10, 125, 128, 131–33, 136,
140–43, 145–47, 149–52, 154, 156,
159, 166, 170–72, 174, 181, 183, 186,
188–89, 191, 193–94, 197–99, 204–5,
210, 225, 229, 259, 270

British, 3–13, 15–20, 25–26, 28–29,
31–32, 34–38, 41, 43–46, 48–50,
54–55, 59–69, 71, 77–85, 89–99,
101–10, 117–22, 126, 128–33,
135–36, 139–58, 160, 166, 169–71,
173–77, 179, 181–83, 186, 188–89,
191–95, 198–200, 206–9, 213–14,
223–24, 259–60; administration,
37–38, 41, 44, 46, 48, 50–54, 77,
79–80, 85; authorities, 25, 41, 46,
49–50, 103; control, 2–3, 10, 20–21,
30–31, 49, 53, 63, 104, 110, 140, 159,
188; empire, 6, 30, 95, 102, 106, 170,
191; forces, 6, 18–20, 29, 37, 43,
45–46, 51–52, 54, 63, 68, 77, 79, 81,
86, 93, 95, 101, 103, 106, 109–10,
118, 127, 132, 134–35, 140, 142, 145,
147, 153, 159, 169–72, 174, 177, 191,
207, 260; government, 7–8, 19,

29–34, 36–38, 42, 45–47, 49–50, 53, 55–56, 59–60, 63–65, 77–82, 85, 91, 98, 104, 106–8, 127–28, 141, 150, 154–55, 172, 175, 270; high commissioner, 43–46, 48–50, 54, 59–61, 64, 66, 79, 81–82, 95, 103–4, 110; India Office, 8, 12, 16, 89–90; interests, 8, 12, 27, 37, 78, 81, 89, 92, 125, 132–33, 140, 152, 155, 172, 176, 191; policy, 5, 30–31, 38, 42, 47, 50–51, 55–56, 59, 63, 78, 80, 89, 97, 102, 106, 152, 170–71; White Paper, 53, 55–56, 140

Bull, Odd, 224

Bush, George, 266–69

Bussche-Haddenhausen, Axel von dem, 36

Byrnes, James F., 163

Cadogan, Alexander, 174, 181

Cairo, 7, 9, 13, 17, 19, 26, 38, 41–42, 44–45, 47, 71, 80, 103, 108, 110, 140, 170, 175, 177, 185, 187, 192, 198, 204, 211–14, 219–20, 222–23, 225, 232, 237–40, 242, 248–49, 268

Carter, Jimmy, 241–44

Catroux, Georges, 143

Cecil, Robert, 33

Challe, Maurice, 199

Chamberlain, Austin, 13

Chamoun, Camille, 210

Chancellor, Sir John, 45

Cheney, Richard, 267

Chicherin, Georgi V., 128–29, 131

Chkenkeli, Akakii, 116

Churchill, Winston, 44, 56, 63–64, 80, 121, 144–47, 153, 158, 163

Chuvakin, Dmitri, 219

Cilicia, 21, 26–27, 68, 122

Clayton, Gilbert, 12–14, 37–38, 95

Clemenceau, Georges, 20, 67–68

Clinton, Bill, 270

Committee of Union and Progress, 14, 29

Copeland, Senator, 50–51

Cornwallis, Kinnahan, 38, 80

Cox, Percy, 77–81, 91, 94–95

Creech-Jones, Arthur, 174

Crewe, Lord, 28

Cripps, Stafford, 148

Cromer, Lord, 102

Curzon, George, 30, 35, 60, 68, 78, 80, 92–93, 104–6, 127–28, 132, 135

Damascus, 9–11, 14–15, 19–21, 44, 51, 54, 60–62, 64, 67–72, 78, 92, 97, 139, 143, 177, 206, 211–12, 220, 222, 226, 248–50, 252–53, 255, 257

D'Arcy, William Knox, 153

Dayan, Moshe, 186, 196, 198–99, 224, 236–37, 241–43

De Gaulle, Charles, 141, 143–44, 223

De Jouvenal, Henri, 71–73

Debbas, Charles, 74

Delbos, Yves, 73

Denikin, Anton I., 120–23, 128

Dentz, Henri-Fernand, 142

Djemal Pasha, 14–15, 19, 24–25, 92

Dobbs, Henry, 81

Dobrynin, Anatoly, 234

Druse, 70–71, 73, 210, 218

Dunsterville, Lionel C., 117–18

Eban, Abba, 223, 229, 234

Edde, Emile, 143

Eden, Anthony, 148–50, 155, 159, 196–97

Egypt(ian), 6, 11–12, 25–26, 28–30, 35, 45, 63, 73, 92, 97, 101–10, 126, 140, 142, 150–52, 170–72, 181–86, 188–89, 191–201, 203, 205–9, 211–12, 215, 217, 219–25, 229–40, 242–44, 247–48, 254, 264; forces, 6, 108–9, 197, 214, 218, 226, 240, 256, 267

Eisenhower, Dwight D., 200, 204, 210

Ekhsanulla Khan, 129, 131

Entente (Allied) Powers, 9–10, 25–26, 28–31, 34, 42–43, 78, 84, 91–92, 103, 119–23

Enzeli, 117, 127–29, 131, 134

Eshkol, Levi, 219–20, 223–24, 231, 233

Farouk (King), 110, 140, 150, 175, 181, 185, 192

Faruqi, Muhammad al-, 13

Fawzi al-Mulqi, 176
Fawzi, Muhammad, 220–21, 223
Feisal ad-Duwish, 90
Feisal ibn Abd al-Aziz (King), 215, 222
Feisal ibn Ghazi (King), 83, 206–7
Feisal ibn Hussein (King), 7, 9–10,
    15–21, 44, 60–64, 67–69, 72, 78–82,
    93–96, 136
Firuz, Muzaffar, 166
France, 2, 9, 12–14, 16, 20, 25–32, 62,
    67–73, 78, 85, 91, 102, 119, 125, 139,
    141, 143–44, 197–98, 205, 210
Franjieh, Suleiman, 249
French, 2, 10–11, 13, 19–21, 25–29,
    31–32, 35, 37, 44, 47, 60–64, 67–75,
    79–80, 139, 141, 143–45, 148, 151,
    154, 197, 199–200, 223, 240; forces,
    20, 31, 68, 70–71, 141, 143–44; high
    commissioner, 69–74, 139, 142; in-
    terests, 13, 144; protectorate, 27, 69
Fuad, Ahmad, 192
Fuad (King), 103, 106, 109–10

Galilee, 27, 32–33, 54, 173, 177, 182
Gaza, 18, 53, 177, 182, 184, 186, 195,
    199–201, 217, 220, 222, 231, 241–42,
    244
Gemayel, Bashir, 251–52, 254–56
Georgia(n), 113–21, 123–24, 134
German(y), 2, 5–9, 11, 15, 24–25,
    29–30, 35–37, 73, 83, 90, 101, 104,
    114, 116–19, 125, 140–48, 153, 157,
    159, 163, 169
Ghazi ibn Feisal (King), 51–52, 82–83,
    259
Gilan, 126, 128–35, 146, 156, 160
Glubb, John Bagot, 176–78, 182, 198
Golan Heights, 219–20, 226, 230, 239,
    241, 248, 255
Goldberg, Arthur, 224
Gourard, Maurice, 69
Graham, Sir Ronald, 33–36
Grey, Edward, 11, 28
Gromyko, Andrei, 173, 204

Haddad, Saad, 250, 256
Haifa, 25, 44, 48, 54, 154, 156, 177, 193,
    239, 251

Haig, Alexander, 254
Hall, William R., 26
Hama, 11, 21, 60, 71, 212
Hammad ibn Zaid, 92
Hammarskjold, Dag, 221–22
Hananu, Ibrahim, 72
Hankey, R.M.A., 151–52
Harbord, James G., 122
Hashemite(s), 8–9, 14–17, 19, 47, 60,
    62, 65, 67–68, 91–94, 96–99, 150,
    175, 184, 186, 188, 198, 205–6
Hashimi, Yasin al-, 82
Hassan (King), 241, 243
Hassan bin Yahya, 213
Hatem, Abd al-Kader, 211
Heikal, Mohamed, 233, 235
Hejaz, 6–10, 14–19, 21, 61–62, 64–65,
    89–91, 93–94, 96–99; railway, 5–6,
    25, 27, 60, 63
Henderson, Arthur, 109
Hilali, Nagib, 192
Hilmi Pasha, Ahmad, 184
Hirtzel, Arthur, 12
Hogarth, D.G., 92
Homs, 11, 21, 60, 71, 212
Howe, Robert, 172
Hull, Cordell, 147–48, 155
Humphrys, Francis H., 82
Husam ad-Din, Sheikh, 44
Hussein ibn Ali (King), 6–20, 26–27,
    30, 37, 59–62, 64, 89–93, 95–98, 182
Hussein ibn Talal (King), 188, 198,
    206–7, 219–20, 223–25, 238, 247–49,
    267
Hussein Kamil, 102–3
Hussein Rushdi Pasha, 103
Husseini, Haj Amin al-, 43–44, 46–48,
    50, 54, 142, 184
Husseini, Jamal, 54
Husseini, Kamal al-, 43
Husseini, Musa Kazim al-, 43, 47–48

Ibrahim Hakki Pasha, 93
Ickes, Harold, 155
Idrisi, Hassan al-, 99
India, 2, 5–6, 8, 28, 30, 66, 77, 82–83,
    85, 97–98, 104, 109, 117, 125–26,

135, 145, 153, 166, 172, 273; government, 12–13, 90

Iran(ians), 2, 83–84, 86, 125–36, 144–49, 153, 156–70, 194, 203, 259–67, 269, 272–73

Iraq(i), 2–4, 10–11, 15, 20–21, 27, 51, 53–54, 63–66, 68, 71, 77–86, 93–96, 98–99, 136, 141–43, 145–46, 149–51, 156, 161–62, 170–71, 175, 181, 194–95, 198–200, 203, 205–9, 212, 222, 230, 239, 259–73

Ironside, Edmund, 132

Ismail, Ahmad, 238

Israel(i), 179, 181–83, 185–87, 194–201, 203, 206, 215, 217–20, 222–26, 229–44, 247–57, 260, 264, 268, 272–74

Istanbul, 6–7, 9, 14, 29, 84, 101, 122

Italian(s), 10, 31, 35, 49, 83, 110, 120, 140–42

Italy, 14, 32, 49, 84–85, 91, 140–41, 143, 264

Jadid, Salah, 218, 219, 249

Jaffa, 24–25, 32, 44, 48, 50, 53, 174, 177, 182

Javid, Salamollah, 160

Jeddah, 9, 92, 96, 98–99, 213, 215

Jernegan, John D., 149

Jerusalem, 26–28, 32, 42–48, 50, 53, 64, 173, 177–78, 182–85, 188, 224, 238, 242–44

Jewish, 23–28, 32–35, 37, 41, 43, 45–46, 48, 52, 54–56, 59–60, 140, 150, 171, 173, 177–78, 271; immigration, 44, 50–51, 55, 140, 171, 222; nationalism, 23, 25, 32–33, 52–53; people, 23, 47, 173; settlement(s), 28, 32, 36, 46, 54, 61, 172, 177; state, 23–24, 27, 36, 46, 52–53, 55–56, 174–75, 177–78, 181, 183

Jews, 2, 12, 23–29, 32, 34–36, 41–46, 48–52, 54–56, 59–60, 140, 171–72, 174–78, 188

Johnson, Lyndon B., 223

Jordania, Noi, 119

Jordan(ian), 187–88, 197–200, 205–7, 209–11, 213, 219, 222–24, 226, 229,

231, 234, 238–39, 242, 247–49, 252, 267

Kamal ad-Din, 103

Katani, Ismat, 265

Kemal Ataturk, Mustafa, 47, 68, 97, 122–23, 201

Kennedy, John F., 214

Karakhan, Leon, 131, 134

Kars, 114–18, 120, 122–23

Kavtaradze, Sergei I., 156–58

Kelly, John, 267

Kerensky, Alexander, 113, 126

Khaddam, Abd al-Halim, 256

Khalid ibn Luwai, 92

Khammash, Amer, 223

Khayrallah, Adnan, 262

Khibiani, Muhammad, 134

Khoda Verdi Khan, 134

Khoiski, F.Kh., 119

Khomeini, Ruhollah (Ayatollah), 261–63

Khorasan, 117, 128, 134–35, 146, 148, 157

Khrushchev, Nikita, 203–4

Khuri, Bishara al-, 143

Kirk, Alexander, 155

Kirkbride, Alan, 62

Kirkbride, Alec, 62–63, 186

Kisch, Frederick H., 45

Kissinger, Henry, 240, 242, 248–49

Kitchener, Lord, 7–12

Kosygin, Alexei, 225

Kuchik Khan, Mirza, 129–30, 132, 134, 135

Kurd(ish), 4, 77, 81, 84–86, 149, 161–63, 167, 207, 209, 260–61, 266, 269–70

Kurdistan, 4, 81, 85–86, 127, 148–49, 161–64, 167, 269

Kuwait, 3, 90, 93–96, 154, 209, 259–60, 264–65, 267–69

Kuzbari, Mahmoun al-, 211

Lahad, Antoine, 256

Lansing, Robert, 128

Lawrence, Thomas E., 17–19, 64, 93, 96

League of Nations, 2–3, 20, 42–43, 50,
    56, 59–60, 65, 73, 78, 81–82, 84, 86,
    110, 120, 122, 129, 136, 171, 259
Lebanese, 73–74, 143–44, 150–51, 210,
    249–50, 252–57
Lebanon, 2, 21, 27, 31, 33, 54, 60,
    68–71, 73–75, 142–44, 150–51, 154,
    156, 173, 181, 209–11, 249–57,
    263–64
Lenin, V.I., 126, 129, 131, 134
Lloyd, George, 108–9
Lloyd George, David, 20, 29–30, 36,
    42, 47, 104, 106, 128, 135
Lloyd, Selwyn, 199
London, 7, 16, 20, 32, 37, 42, 45, 49, 56,
    59, 61–62, 77, 92, 98, 103, 105, 109,
    117, 131, 152, 154–55, 170, 173, 176,
    196
Loraine, Percy, 109
Lossow, General von, 116
Lovett, Robert, 181
Ludendorff, E. von, 118

MacDonald, Malcolm, 54
MacDonald, Ramsey, 46–47, 107
McMahon, Henry, 11–14, 16, 20,
    26–27, 30, 36, 65
MacMichael, Harold, 54
Mafdai, Jamil al-, 82
Mahabad, 161–63, 165, 167
Mahdawi, Fadil Abbas al-, 208
Maher, Ali, 140, 192
Maher Pasha, Ahmed, 140
Mahmoud, Muhammad Sidki, 220
Majali, Hazza, 207
Malik, Jacob, 230
Mansur, Ali, 146
Martel, D. de, 73
Maxwell, John, 101
Mazanderan, 128–29, 131–32, 146, 148,
    157
Mecca, 6–8, 10, 13–15, 17, 25, 47, 61,
    89–91, 93, 97–99, 155, 214
Medina, 6, 8–9, 15–18, 25, 62, 93
Meinertzhagen, Richard, 65
Meir, Golda, 197, 217, 233, 235, 239
Mesopotamia, 4, 12, 14, 16, 27, 30, 42,
    61, 68, 77–79, 83, 90–91

Milner, Lord, 19, 104–5
Mokhtar, Eiz ad-Din, 220–21
Molotov, V.M, 159, 169, 204
Moltke, Count von, 6
Montagu, Edwin, 34–35
Montgomery, Bernard, 171
Moscow, 124, 129, 131–32, 134, 147–48,
    156, 158, 160–61, 163, 167–69, 173,
    203–4, 225–26, 230, 234, 238, 253,
    264–66, 268, 272
Mossadeq, Muhammad, 158
Mosul, 2, 4, 20–21, 27, 81–85, 142, 149,
    153–54, 194, 207–8, 262
Moyne, Lord, 150, 155
Mubarak, Hosni, 264, 267
Mufti of Jerusalem, 43–44, 46–48, 50,
    54, 142, 175–76, 184
Muhammad Ali al-Jabari, 185
Muhammad bin Ahmad al-Badr, 213
Muhammad ibn Talal, 94
Muhammad Mahmud Pasha, 109–10
Muhammad Reza Shah, 146
Mushavir al- Mamalek, 127, 132
Mushir al-Dawleh (Hassan Pirnia),
    130–31

Nahas Pasha, 140, 150
Naqqash, Alfred, 143
Nashishibi, Ragheb, 43
Nasir ad-Din al-Nashishibi, 182
Nasser, Gamal Abd al-, 192–98, 201,
    205–15, 217, 219–26, 230, 232–34,
    236, 249
Negev, 27, 33, 173–74, 177, 183, 222,
    244
Neguib, Muhammad, 192–93
Nejd, 9, 47, 65, 79, 89–96, 99
Nicolas, Grand Duke, 113
Nitti, Francesco, 120
Nixon, Richard, 249
Nuri as-Said Pasha, 51, 82, 141–42,
    150, 194, 207–9

Obaidullah, Sheikh, 84
O'Beirne, Hugh, 29
Ormsby-Gore, Captain, 38
Ottoman(s), 8–10, 14, 20, 23–26, 29, 36,
    43, 47, 70, 84, 90, 97, 102, 114, 116,

125, 153, 209; empire, 1–2, 5–7,
9–10, 17, 23–26, 43, 96, 102, 114,
116, 118, 123, 125, 259; forces, 8–9,
89; government (Sublime Porte),
6–7, 9–10, 14–15, 23–24; rule, 7, 9,
11, 101; state, 5, 15; territories, 13,
20, 25, 72

Palestine, 1–2, 12, 14–16, 18, 20–21,
23–38, 41–46, 48–56, 59–66, 68, 78,
96, 139–43, 150–51, 154, 171–78,
181–85, 187–88, 192, 195–97,
218–19, 224–25, 231–32, 239–41,
252, 268, 271, 273; Mandate, 41, 43,
45–47, 49, 51–53, 55–56, 59–60,
63–66, 68, 171, 173–75, 177
Palestine Liberation Organization
(PLO), 223, 248–51, 253–56
Palestinian Arabs, 44–45, 47, 171–74,
176–79, 182–85, 188, 195–96, 217,
223, 232, 236, 241–42, 244, 247–52,
255, 257, 268
Paris, 67–68, 71–73, 199
Paris Peace Conference, 20, 62, 85,
103–4, 119–22, 127
Passfield (Sidney Webb), Lord, 46
Persia(n), 116–17, 119, 122, 126–33,
135, 145–46, 159, 164, 262
Philby, Henry St. John, 92
Picot, George, 26
Pishevari, Jaafar, 130, 160–61, 166
Plumer, Lord, 45
Ponsot, Henri, 72
Puaux, Gabriel, 139, 141

Qadi, Anwar, 214
Qasem, Abd al-Karim, 207–10, 260
Qavam es-Saltaneh, Ahmad, 164–68
Qawkaji, Fawzi ad-Din al-, 51–52, 177
Qazi Muhammad, 162–63, 167
Quwatli, Shukri al-, 143, 175, 206

Rabin, Yitzhak, 248–50
Radek, Karl, 135
Rashid Ali al-Gailani, 82, 141–42, 145
Rashidi(s), 91–94
Rashti, Sepahdar-i, 125
Raskolnikov, F.F., 128, 130, 135

Reagan, Ronald, 253, 264–65
Reza Shah, 132–33, 135–36, 144–46,
160
Riad, Mahmoud, 222
Rikhye, Indar Jit, 220–21
Roosevelt, Franklin D., 147, 155, 158
Rothschild, Lord, 35
Rothstein, Theodore A., 134
Russia(n), 2–3, 9–10, 12, 14, 26–28, 32,
83, 91, 113–29, 131–34, 147–49, 159,
165, 172, 199, 273; forces, 113–14,
117, 125–27, 129, 134, 144–45

Saad ibn Saud, 90
Sadat, Anwar, 236–44, 264
Sadchikov, Ivan V., 165
Saddam Hussein, 261–63, 266–70, 273
Saed, Muhammad, 157–58
Salal, Abdullah, 213–14
Samir Pasha ar-Rifai, 186
Samuel, Herbert, 35, 43–46, 61–66
San Remo Conference, 38, 42, 68
Sarwat Pasha, 109
Saud ibn Abd al-Aziz (King), 211
Saudi(s), 90–94, 96–99, 150, 155, 188,
203, 209, 213–14, 222
Saudi Arabia, 99, 150–51, 154–56, 174,
189, 197, 200, 213–14, 222, 240,
264–65, 267–68, 272–73
Sazanov, S.D., 28, 31, 121
Shafiq al-Wazzan, 256
Shakespear, W.I., 90
Sharm al-Sheikh, 195, 200–201,
217–18, 221–22, 226, 229, 237
Shaw, Walter, 46
Shawkat Ali, 47
Sherif Pasha, 85
Shuckburgh, John, 55
Shukairy, Ahmed, 223
Shumiatsky, Boris, 135
Sidki Pasha, Ismail, 109, 170–71
Sieff, Israel, 27
Sinai, 18, 28–29, 31, 200, 220–22, 225,
231–33, 236–37, 239–41, 254
Sisco, Joseph, 234
Smith, Walter B., 164
Smuts, Jan, 2, 30
Sokolow, M., 34

Soviet Union, 1, 3, 84, 118, 121,
    123–24, 126–35, 139, 144–49,
    156–64, 168–70, 172–74, 176,
    191–92, 194, 196–97, 203–5, 208,
    213, 219–20, 222, 225–26, 230–31,
    234–35, 237–40, 242, 248, 252–53,
    255, 264–66, 268, 271–73; forces,
    124, 131, 133, 144–48, 159–61,
    163–64, 204, 234, 237; government,
    126–27, 135, 145–46, 161
Stack, Lee, 108
Stalin, Joseph, 118, 126, 131, 146–47,
    158–60, 163–65
Starosselski, Colonel, 131–32
Storrs, Ronald, 7–8, 11
Subhi Bey, 76
Sudan, 104–10, 171, 193, 230
Suez Canal, 2, 5–6, 15, 25, 28–30, 89,
    103–4, 106, 109–10, 126, 189,
    194–95, 197–200, 206, 208, 210, 215,
    217, 220, 226, 229, 231–32, 234–37,
    239–40, 247; zone, 110, 170–71, 183,
    191–93
Suleiman, Hikmat, 82
Sulh, Riyadh as-, 143
Sykes, Mark, 26–27, 31–32
Sykes, Percy, 125
Sykes-Picot agreement, 2, 13, 20,
    26–31, 33, 37
Syria(ns), 2, 10–11, 13–16, 18–21,
    24–27, 29–31, 33, 38, 42, 44, 47, 51,
    54, 60–65, 67–74, 77–80, 93–94, 139,
    141–45, 150–51, 175, 177, 181, 184,
    188, 194, 200, 203–9, 211–12, 218,
    220, 222, 225–26, 229–31, 238–42,
    247–56, 263–64, 272–73

Tabriz, 117, 125, 135, 148–49, 160–62,
    166–67
Taha al-Hashimi, 142
Tahsin Pasha, 98
Taj ad-Din al-Hasani, 143
Talaat Pasha, 36
Talal ibn Abdullah (King), 188
Tariq Aziz, 261, 265
Tedder, Lord, 171
Tehran, 77, 127, 129–36, 145–46, 148,
    156–61, 164–67, 259–65

Templer, Gerald, 198
Thomson, William M., 119–20
Toynbee, Arnold J., 14, 90
Transcaucasia(n), 1, 83, 113–24, 149,
    274
Trans-Jordan, 33, 60–66, 80
Transjordan, 17, 19, 27, 53, 65–66, 71,
    94–96, 98, 142–43, 150–51, 170,
    175–76, 181–87
Treaty of Ankara, 84
Treaty of Brest-Litovsk, 114–16, 118,
    126
Treaty of Muhammara, 94–95
Treaty of Sevres, 85, 122–23
Trotsky, Leon, 126
Troyanovsky, Konstantin, 126
Truman, Harry, 159–60, 163–65, 169
Tuhami, Hassan, 241–43
Turkey, 1, 6–9, 24, 29–30, 36–37, 83–86,
    90, 97, 101, 114–18, 122–23, 125,
    136, 139, 142, 144, 149, 161, 169,
    194–95, 201, 203–5, 211, 269, 273–74
Turkish (Turks), 2, 5, 7–8, 10, 14–20,
    24–25, 28–30, 34–37, 41, 68–70, 77,
    81, 83–86, 89–93, 97, 104, 113–20,
    122, 125–27, 136, 139, 141, 148–49,
    263, 269, 272; forces, 6, 14–15, 18,
    20, 29, 89, 115, 139; straits, 136, 144,
    169
Twitchell, Karl S., 154

United Arab Republic (UAR), 206–8,
    210–15, 218, 220–21, 236
United Nations, 3, 140, 143, 173–76,
    178, 181, 183, 185, 188, 201, 204–5,
    209, 214, 217–18, 220–24, 230, 232,
    237, 240, 244, 251, 255, 264, 268,
    270; General Assembly, 173–76,
    183–84, 200, 204, 217, 221–22; Secu-
    rity Council, 163–64, 181, 195, 200,
    210, 219, 222, 224–26, 232, 235,
    239–40, 251, 266, 268
United States (American), 3, 28–29, 32,
    37, 119, 122–23, 128, 148, 154–57,
    159–60, 164–68, 172, 174, 176, 181,
    194, 197, 200, 204–5, 210, 213–14,
    217, 223–25, 229, 231, 234–35, 237,

239–41, 243–44, 248, 253, 255,
260–61, 264–73
U Thant, 214, 220–22

Vance, Cyrus, 243
Vehib Pasha, Ferik, 114–15
Vishinsky, Andrei, 163
Vossuq al-Dawleh, 128, 130

Wafd, 103–4, 108–11, 140, 191–92
Wasfi al-Tal, 224
Washington, 155, 161, 167–68, 196,
204, 210, 213, 235, 238–41, 244, 248,
250, 253–55, 264–72
Wauchope, Sir Arthur, 48, 52, 54
Wedgwood, Josiah, 46
Weizmann, Chaim, 26–27, 33–34, 37,
54–55, 63
Weygand, General, 70
Wilson, Arnold, 77–79

Wilson, Harold, 223
Wilson, Henry Maitland, 143
Wilson, Woodrow, 2, 35, 42, 103–4,
122–23
Wingate, Reginald, 12, 102–4

Yahya, Imam, 99
Yemen, 15, 99, 151, 206, 211–15

Zaghlul, Saad, 103–9
Zahr-e-din, 218
Zia ed-Din Tabatabai, Sayyid, 132–33,
135
Zionism, 23–24, 35, 37, 42, 60, 172–73,
195
Zionist(s), 23–28, 30–38, 41–42, 45, 48,
53, 56, 59, 63, 66, 150, 174, 176, 178,
192, 219, 232, 273
Ziwar Pasha, 108, 110

About the Author

MARTIN SICKER is a private consultant and lecturer who has served as a senior executive in the U.S. government and has taught political science at the American University and George Washington University. Dr. Sicker has written extensively in the field of political science and international affairs. He is the author of fourteen previous books, including the companion volumes, *The Pre-Islamic Middle East*, *The Islamic World in Ascendancy: From the Arab Conquests to the Siege of Vienna*, and *The Islamic World in Decline: From the Treaty of Karlowitz to the Disintegration of the Ottoman Empire* (Praeger, 2000).